Guerrilla P.R.
2.0

Also by Michael Levine

The Address Book—How to Reach Anyone Who's Anyone

Guerrilla P.R.

Lessons at the Halfway Point

Take It from Me

7 Life Lessons from Noah's Ark

How to Survive a Flood in Your Own Life

Guerrilla P.R. Wired

Guerrilla P.R.
2.0

Wage an Effective Publicity Campaign
without Going Broke

Michael Levine

Collins
An Imprint of HarperCollinsPublishers

Guerrilla P.R. was originally published in 1993 by HarperBusiness, a division of HarperCollins Publishers.

GUERRILLA P.R. 2.0. Copyright © 1993, 2008 by Michael Levine. All rights reserved. Printed in the United States of America. No part of this book may be used or reproduced in any manner whatsoever without written permission except in the case of brief quotations embodied in critical articles and reviews. For information, address HarperCollins Publishers, 10 East 53rd Street, New York, NY 10022.

HarperCollins books may be purchased for educational, business, or sales promotional use. For information, please write: Special Markets Department, HarperCollins Publishers, 10 East 53rd Street, New York, NY 10022.

DESIGNED BY JOY O'MEARA

Library of Congress Cataloging-in-Publication Data

Levine, Michael, 1954–
    Guerrilla P.R. 2.0: wage an effective publicity campaign without going broke/
      Michael Levine.
      p. cm.
    Rev. ed. of: Guerrilla P.R. / Michael Levine.
    Includes index.
    ISBN 978-0-06-143852-3
    1. Small business—Public relations. 2. Industrial publicity. I. Levine,
Michael, 1954–Guerrilla P.R. II. Title. III. Title: Guerrilla PR 2.0. IV. Title:
Guerrilla public relations 2.0.

HD59.L48 2008
659.2—dc22   2007051297

10 11 12 OV/RRD 10 9 8 7 6 5

May I confess that I am not easy to impress?
Having operated at the highest levels of the entertainment industry
for over two decades, I have worked alongside brilliance rarely.

With that in mind, I dedicate this book to the president of my company LCO,
Dawn Miller, for her tireless commitment to a continued legacy of greatness.

Contents

Preface

In the fifteen years since its publication, *Guerrilla P.R.* has become a phenomenon.

Included in the Library of Congress, read by presidents, taught in all the most prestigious business schools in the country (and the world), this book—which I thought was too revolutionary to become so widely accepted—has indeed grown into "the most widely used introduction to P.R. in the world." That's not an exaggeration.

So given all that success, the questions must be asked: Why change it? If it ain't broke, don't fix it; right? What's the point of adding to something that has proved to be extremely successful as it stood? What was wrong with the book the way it was?

Well, at the risk of sounding egomaniacal, I have to start by saying that *nothing* was wrong with the book the way it was—in 1993. And even today, the information that I tried to supply in *Guerrilla P.R.* remains usable and relevant. This edition is not meant to recount anything that was published in the original version. It was all true, and the basics remain true to this day. No need to take a word of it back.

But no one could possibly say that little has changed in public relations since 1993. Indeed, the world is a completely different place now than it was then, and since the point of P.R. is to make your name in the world, changes all over will certainly have an impact on the techniques and principles used to draw attention to a person or business.

Technology has had the widest, deepest, and most profound effect on P.R., as it has on almost every other aspect of American life. In 1993, a cell phone was at least twice the size of the one you're carrying today. Yes, the Internet was an interesting diversion, but nothing was ever going to replace newspapers, TV news, travel agents, bookstores, encyclopedias, and handwritten letters. The average American, asked about a plasma TV, would have wondered what blood had to do with making a television set work better. You wouldn't have wanted a Bluetooth; it would have meant a potentially painful trip to the dentist. A BlackBerry? Well, it was something to put in a pie.

The same condition is true for the editors, publishers, and producers of the world (not about being put in a pie—about the changes in the world). Their technology—the very tool you're trying to access as a P.R. Guerrilla—has changed a thousand times over in the past decade and a half. Things happen faster. News is disseminated in seconds rather than hours. It took weeks for some Americans to learn about the assassination of Abraham Lincoln (and keep in mind—the country did not stretch to the West Coast in those days). It took people in Singapore a few minutes to learn of the death of Anna Nicole Smith, if they were interested, and that was only because the reporting took some time to complete. Technology would have the information to the public in a second or less.

You might as well get used to it now: I'm going to say over and over again in this book that there are two speeds in today's media world—*fast* and *dead*. That's not just a clever catchphrase;

it's an absolute truth. There is no excuse for slowness, and no remedy for its effects. If you don't keep up with the increased metabolism of information flow in today's world, your business will not succeed. Period.

But with increased demand has come a huge jump in the number of hungry media outlets to which you can supply sustenance. In 1993, there was no Fox News Channel. There was no Food Network. There was no XM Satellite Radio. CNN was just getting itself going. MTV was still a music video channel. The words "reality-based show" had never been uttered in Hollywood. *American Idol* referred to someone like Clint Eastwood.

Then, there were the deplorable 9/11 attacks, and everything changed, especially in the United States. Guerrilla P.R. had to change as well. Now, the country's mood was different: first anxious, then angry, then a spectrum of other emotions. It wouldn't be possible to conduct business—*any* business— the same way again. Publicizing those businesses would also undergo fundamental alterations, shifts in the very foundations of the Guerrilla P.R. method.

The world of P.R. had to change. The basic principles of Guerrilla P.R. have remained sound; the philosophy has not changed.

But some of the techniques involved definitely have. They've gotten faster, trickier, and more complicated. In some ways, they've gotten easier, more direct, and yes, faster. Everything, no matter what, is faster.

Since the book's initial publication, there have been some amazing successes in Guerrilla P.R. Consider the unbelievably profitable film *The Blair Witch Project*, which used Internet viral messaging to spread its message and reaped rewards its creators couldn't have imagined in their most fevered dreams. Consider the fact that presidential campaigns have been announced on YouTube.

By the same token, there have been some tremendous Guerrilla P.R. disasters. The February 2007 attempt by some Cartoon Network employees to publicize a new program with suspicious-looking packages in Boston was an attempt at Guerrilla P.R. that didn't take into account the nation's climate post-9/11, and it went in a direction that can't be characterized as anything but wrong.

The rise of the Web log (blog) has also created a basic difference in the P.R. world of today. Now, anyone with a computer, a microscopic budget, and the will to type can create a media outlet of his or her own. Deliver your message—unfiltered, uncensored, and unopposed—to the consumers you want to reach. Do it on a daily—an *hourly*—basis, if you like. Make yourself a star without having to go through the gatekeepers who have held the power for so long.

So why revise a book that has been an unqualified success? Because those who stand still are doomed to extinction in today's media world. If I am to practice as I preach, it is essential that I bring *Guerrilla P.R.* into the twenty-first century not simply intact but improved. This is the book that teaches about the down-and-dirty world of public relations on a low, or no, budget. This is the book that launched many thousand press releases. This is the book that put forth the crazy notion that P.R. need not cost more than the operating budget of most small companies.

In today's world, that means it has to be the book that moves at the speed of technology and shows you how to do the same. It must adjust, as the Guerrilla is required to adjust, to the conditions of the present day. The twenty-first-century Guerrillas, and the book that created them, have to be fast, because the alternative is dead.

And there's still plenty of life left in this Guerrilla.

——Michael Levine
Los Angeles, California

Introduction

There are conditions of survival in a guerrilla force:
they include constant mobility and constant vigilance.

–Che Guevara

Opportunity Knocks

In the middle of the worst drought in California history, a sudden downpour deluged Los Angeles in March 1991. Though the city was grateful for the moisture, the rain caused problems. Under a two-block section of Ventura Boulevard in the San Fernando Valley, a water main burst, causing the street to split apart.

Torrents of water cascaded over the sidewalk. Traffic and business came to a standstill. As workmen toiled to repair the damage along the thoroughfare, no customers could reach any shops. One such hapless establishment was Mel's Diner, a kitschy fifties-style eatery located right in the middle of the affected area. The situation looked bleak as Mel's lunch business dried up amid the floodwaters.

So what did Mel do? He gave away free hamburgers to the

street maintenance crew, and he invited local TV news outlets to witness this noble act of charity. For the cost of a couple of dozen beef patties and a few phone calls, Mel's Diner was all over the airwaves that night, and ever since, business has been better than ever.

Mel showed himself a master of Guerrilla P.R.

In 1970, an ambitious young businessman named Michael Viner sought a way to enter the music industry, though he had little money to invest, and no recording artists lined up. With no other resources than his native creativity, Viner pressed several thousand copies of an album titled *The Best of Marcel Marceau*. It was thirty-five minutes of silence, punctuated by applause. He sent copies not to record distributors but to newspaper writers like Vernon Scott of UPI, who ran an amusing story on the prank record, which was picked up by every paper in America. Other stories ran in major outlets like *Newsweek*.

The record even hit *Billboard*'s Album Chart. Orders began pouring in, and Michael Viner built up a financial war chest with which he then entered the record business in earnest, releasing albums like *Candyman* by Sammy Davis, Jr.

Michael Viner is a master of Guerrilla P.R.

The examples of Mel's Diner and Michael Viner illustrate the central premise of this book: the world is overflowing with opportunities. Opportunities in work, in love, for spiritual growth and emotional fulfillment. It's your mission to remain constantly vigilant so that opportunities do not pass you by.

That's how I view the world. As founder of one of the nation's largest independent public relations companies, I've constantly sought new and more effective ways to heighten the profiles of my clients, and I have scoured every resource available to me in order to find them.

This approach has worked, at least according to my clients, who have included Charlton Heston, Mickey Rooney, Jon Voight, Vanna White, Michael J. Fox, Linda Evans, Fleetwood Mac, and hundreds more. They chose our firm in part because of our attitude, stemming from my ceaseless quest for opportunity.

When I read the morning paper, I don't just keep up with the headlines. I'm scanning for possibilities: letters to the editor or guest editorials for my clients, trends that may end up as surveys, predictions, or other kinds of press releases. When I watch television, I'm not zonking out with a bowl of popcorn by my side. I'm looking for talk shows that might book my clients as guests. I'm looking at news programs to get a feel for the angles of the day. In everything I do, I stress an outlook different from that of most people: I'm looking for opportunity.

As I suggested, this view can be applied to any field of endeavor, work-related or otherwise. As it relates to P.R., anyone—pro and non-pro—can benefit from it. But if you wish to tackle a publicity campaign on your own, this opportunity-driven perspective is key. Adopt it and you'll have joined the ranks of the Guerrilla P.R. army.

What the Pros Can and Cannot Do

The difficult we do right now; the impossible will take a little longer.

—SEABEES' motto

Today, most colleges and universities offer degrees in communications and public relations. Professional P.R. trade associations and think tanks abound. If a teen tells his parents, "I want to go into public relations," he or she will likely get almost the same approving hugs from Mom and Dad as if the kid were to choose medicine or law.

That's because P.R. is a respectable calling. The money's good, the status is high, the demand for services is strong. My company has seen a steady stream of clients who want what we've got, and every year the business grows exponentially.

What do professional publicists do for clients that they cannot do for themselves? For one, we give them the hard-driving personality of that unique human subspecies, the Professional Publicist. The venerated *Dartnell Public Relations Handbook,* considered by some the bible of the business, says: "The P.R. careerist with great potential always exhibits a lively interest in people, events, action. He has an insatiable curiosity and a high energy quotient that lead him to a number of activities not necessarily related to his school courses or working life." Sounds like a good prescription for anyone; but it's a positive I.D. on any capable publicist.

I can tell you that, in general, publicists and P.R. careerists are among the most upbeat, lively, curious, well-spoken, and enthusiastic people you'll ever meet. Their attraction to media is a direct outgrowth of an inner desire to know what's going on in the world, to make sense of the world, and to leave a mark on the world. They merely took that driving passion and channeled it into a logical career direction.

In addition to energy and curiosity, the pro has contacts. More than anything, we offer clients *entree* to the media. We know the reporters, editors, hosts, and producers of every newspaper, magazine, radio station, TV news program, Internet search engine, influential blog, and morning show in America.

We also know the subtle art of pitching a client. Every day we do the journalists' work for them, coming up with ideas, devising angles, showing them why they should do stories on our clients. We tell them what's news, and we get them to agree. (I can't count the number of times I have spoken with intelligent media people who have expected me, the publicist, to concoct their entire story. They tell us, "We just report the news; we don't manufacture it." Personally, I don't buy that. Seventy-five percent of potential news items that reach the average news desk every day never reach the public. The veto power of newspeople decides what's news.

Journalists are among the most dedicated people I know, but the natural laws of inertia come into play, and they customarily expect us to connect their dots. Top professional publicists are good writers, too. We dash off press releases as easily as grocery lists. We conceptualize attractive press kits, photo opportunities, clever press releases, information-packed biographies, and eye-catching events to reshape media perception (and therefore public perception) of our clients. That ability to use language persuasively, whether orally or on paper, is arguably the single most important attribute of the top-notch professional publicist.

With major clients, such as governments, Fortune 500 companies, and other powerful institutions, the role of the P.R. professional takes on even greater dimensions. Clients of this nature aren't merely looking for good press. They expect public relations counselors to foster a widespread and permanent positive perception, an inexorable bending of the public mind toward the "correct" point of view: theirs.

I can cite a classic example. The multinational oil companies have led the entire Western world to believe that life as we know it would cease if society were to deviate in any way from reliance on their products. Forget that fossil fuels cause greenhouse gases that are raising the temperature of the atmosphere and steadily choking the planet to death; forget that plenty of viable energy alternatives are available. Thanks to skillful management of public relations, the oil companies—though largely perceived as avaricious—are nevertheless generally accepted as our best hope for an energy-rich future. It may or may not be true—but we believe it. And you have their hired P.R. geniuses to thank. Or not.

Essentially, the pros see things from two points of view: the media's and the client's. They tailor a client's image and the client's message to meet the needs of the press. At the same time they challenge the media to perceive the client *as we wish them to.* The pros don't always know what's best, but often they're called upon to make critical image decisions for clients, based on experience with what goes over well in print and on the air. It's a formidable assignment; when it works, it's extraordinarily gratifying.

Still, there are some things the pros cannot do. No matter how hard we try to muster a genuine sense of enthusiasm about a client, the bottom line is this: the pros are just doing a job. We are paid to pitch. If the client stops paying, we stop pitching. So concern, caring, and devotion can be turned on and off with the bounce of a check. *Nobody will care about the client and his goals as much as the client himself.*

Similarly, because the pros are in business, there may be certain kinds of assignments we may be unable or unwilling to take on.

Some potential clients, such as a small business in a secondary market, are too narrowly focused. Others may be unable to afford the cost of professional P.R., which can be considerable (up to $5,000 a month, and more). Still others may present image problems. After a change in senior management in 1993, top Washington P.R. firm H&K severed its relationship with several controversial clients, including the scandal-ridden BCCI bank. Said H&K CEO Tom Edison at the time, "We have no business representing sleaze." I have also broken ties to clients when I felt they had crossed the line. My relationship with Charlton Heston, for example, ended after his famous "out of my cold, dead hands" speech in 2000, not because I oppose the right to bear arms (I don't) but because I felt Mr. Heston had fallen under the spell of a radical branch of the National Rifle Association and was tarnishing his legacy by looking foolish.

So you can see there are as many doors closed to the professional as are closed to prospective clients. Add it up, and there may be countless businesspeople, civic leaders, inventors, performers, scholars, directors of charitable groups, and others who could greatly benefit from the services of a professional P.R. firm, yet are unable to connect.

To them I say there is a way out that bypasses the pros, that avoids the high costs, and that proves as effective in securing publicity as the efforts of most professional P.R. companies, if not more effective. It's a method that incorporates everything the pros have—energy, contacts, written and oral skills, and broad perspective—by teaching a new approach. I call it Guerrilla P.R.

The Jungle Fighter

A guerrilla is a jungle fighter, a lightning-quick devotee of the sneak attack. A guerrilla knows his terrain better than his opponents, believes passionately in his cause, and is nearly impossible to defeat. A Guerrilla publicist works in much the same fashion—but without the deadly weapons. Agile, confident, dynamic, making do with far less than his desk-bound professional counterpart, the Guerrilla is a model of compact efficiency.

Resourcefulness is next to godliness. That's the cornerstone of my technique. What a Guerrilla lacks in funds, he or she makes up in moxie. Every press campaign, even the most expensive and sophisticated, is ultimately a grassroots crusade. The goal of any publicist, professional or Guerrilla, is to reach individuals. The pros, as paid pitchmen, can't help but take a less credible posture in representing a client. By taking a close-to-the-ground, one-on-one approach, and wearing his passion on his sleeve, the Guerrilla P.R. trooper cuts to the chase.

In other words, because you are the owner of your business, or the manager of the business, you have more credibility as an *expert* in that business than a professional P.R. agent would have. You can promote not only your business but your *knowledge* of the business, and therefore yourself, by drawing attention to it. You start off with more gravitas before you pitch your story. It's an advantage—use it.

Today, technology permits millions to launch cottage industries at home. Everyone has access to the prime tools: phone, fax, computer, modem, and mailbox. On the road, you have a cell phone with Bluetooth technology, and a BlackBerry that can access your e-mail and send responses, keep your schedule, and hold your address book, among many other uses. But these tools mean nothing to the Guerrilla publicist without the attitude I've described. I'm talking about the attitude that says, "My project is the most important thing in the world, and I'll stop at nothing to tell the world about it!"

So who are the Guerrillas?

- The owners of a Utah ski resort who noticed their guests developing runny noses standing in long lines at frigid ski lifts. Management installed tissue dispensers and made sure the local media knew about it. That year, business climbed, and it's still referred to as the "Kleenex resort."

- The creators of "Lonelygirl15," which began as a video blog on YouTube and became a phenomenon known worldwide——and was always meant to help its creators land movie deals.

- The director, writers, and producers of *The Blair Witch Project*, made for a minuscule amount of money and promoted via viral video on the Web and through a Web site to become unquestionably the most profitable film ever made.

- The Miami florist who ran a campaign in his shop dubbed "Who Would You Most Like to Send Flowers to?" Entry blanks were available to all customers, who enjoyed filling them out. The florist issued a press release announcing the winners (Tom Cruise and Cybill Shepherd). The flower shop gained a good deal of notoriety, and business increased sharply.

- Candy Lightner, who formed Mothers Against Drunk Driving (MADD) in response to the death of her daughter at the hands of a drunk driver. At her first press conference, she and her surviving daughter wept openly while describing their ordeal. An electrifying photo of the two women flashed around the country, and MADD was off and running. Though her emotion was genuine, Candy knew that touching hearts would reach minds.

- The heavy metal band Immaculate Mary, which sought to distinguish itself from the hundreds of competing bands in L.A. At every show, the lead singer threw foil-wrapped condoms into the crowd. Weird, yes, but different and eye-catching.

- The owners of the Improvisation Comedy Club, who wanted to increase the club's visibility. They launched a petition drive to demand a Best Comedy Oscar. Thousands signed the petitions, which were delivered by the boxload to the Motion Picture Academy. Press releases announcing the campaign, the tally, and the delivery were sent, and they even wrote a guest editorial in the *Los Angeles Times*. (There remains, however, no category devoted specifically to comedy.)

- The out-of-work accountant in Los Angeles, tired of discouraging headhunters and go-nowhere want ads, who strapped a sandwich board over his body and hit the streets of Beverly Hills. Emblazoned on his homemade billboard were the words "Unemployee of the Month." He got a good job a few days later.

The Guerrillas are those who take responsibility for their own success or failure. They reject the smug conventions of our specialized society. They say "no" to the advisers, the naysayers, and the consultants, and they bring to their projects the kind of spunky cleverness that typified the old Hollywood. People say movies were better back then.

They say cars were built better back then. They're right. It's because in those days individuals cared more, complained less, and took pride in the whole, the final product, no matter how little may have been the piece of the puzzle they claimed as their own.

Who Needs It?

The 1990s were dubbed the Age of the Entrepreneur. It seemed in those days that *everyone* was starting a business, and it's still true: every year more and more people jump into the marketplace, seeking to turn products, projects, and concepts into successful and lucrative ventures. What kinds of individuals need Guerrilla P.R.?

1. A fledgling manager of a local rock band, hoping to be spotted by major download sites and eventually by recording companies and concert promoters.
2. A director of a free clinic or shelter for the homeless, seeking to increase public support.
3. The designer of a bold new look in apparel, ready to excite the tastemakers in the fashion world.
4. An actor or actress appearing in a small production, hoping to be "discovered" by top casting agents.
5. A shopkeeper in a competitive mall, trying to focus attention on his store.
6. The inventor of an environmentally safe automobile engine, attempting to attract the interest of Detroit or Tokyo.
7. A crusader against drug abuse, needing increased community involvement and financial support.
8. A restaurateur, seeking loyal clientele for her newly opened café.
9. A medical practitioner, hoping to expand his practice.
10. Professors from the rarefied halls of academia, who have lost touch with the real world of business.
11. The franchisee, seeking to distinguish his own store from the scores of copycats in the neighborhood.

12. The author, in search of the widest possible audience for his new book.

13. And even the journalist or other media professional who would like a deeper understanding of the people vying for his or her attention.

You may already have in place an ongoing marketing, advertising, and merchandising campaign on behalf of your business or project. If so, great! Assuming your campaign is working, there's no need to stop. Guerrilla P.R. can simply serve as an ancillary marketing tool. But if you don't have any such campaign, and/or you cannot afford one, then listen up. This book was expressly written for you.

Why a Manifesto?

This is by no means the first book on the subject of P.R., and it wasn't even that in 1993, by any stretch of the imagination. I make no claim of originality on that score. However, thumbing through previously published volumes on the subject, I noticed a major defect running through many of them. Although each explained what to do (some more lucidly than others), none showed the reader how to *think* like a publicist.

Consider the difference between learning a few phrases in a "Traveler's Guide to Spanish" and really learning the syntax of the language. Once you've mastered "Where can I get my pants pressed?" you're no better off than before. You have to learn to conjugate. You have to learn sentence structure. You have to feel the music of the language. This book teaches the grammar of directing public perception.

If you can't think like a publicist, you won't know what to do if something unexpected happens. You won't pitch the talent coordinator at your local morning show in a persuasive way. You won't know whom to call or what to write when an innovative campaign idea occurs to you. In fact, you might not even conjure up those ideas in the first place.

Guerrilla P.R. is as much manifesto as textbook. I show you not only what to do but why to do it. Throughout, I offer my own partisan philosophy of public relations. Granted, it may not be shared by all my colleagues in the profession, but it has worked very effectively for me, especially early in my career before I had a large and well-connected company, and I know it can work for anyone who applies Guerrilla P.R. techniques.

This book is designed to change the way you see the world, insofar as the media are concerned. If you apply my principles, you will emerge a media-savvy urban Guerrilla, fighting and winning the battle for public attention.

But that's not all. I truly believe that many of the philosophical principles of Guerrilla P.R. offer a prescription for living, a manner of interacting with others. It's not a new idea. From Aristotle to Sigmund Freud, the premier minds of their times have pondered the intangibles of human relations. The ideology undergirding my plan for gaining media attention works just as well in getting ahead in your office, or in making friends or customers, as it does in getting your name in the paper.

Just as hard work and initiative in one area of your life have a beneficial spillover effect in other areas, so can your Guerrilla P.R. efforts make you a better—and better-liked—person. I've seen it happen many times.

How to Use This Book

Guerrilla P.R. is a tool for empowerment. But it works only if you use it. In each chapter, I'll outline several principles, give examples, describe methods for practical application, and frequently offer Tips & Traps. In some sections I suggest exercises. Do them. Practice is the key to thinking like a Guerrilla.

Throughout the book, I give real-life examples of creative ideas that have kicked selected P.R. efforts into overdrive. I also cite individuals—I call them Guerrilla P.R. Commandos—who best exemplify the Guerrilla P.R. spirit. Some of them are well known; some are not. All have successfully engineered their own P.R. campaigns. You can learn from them. I certainly have.

Most importantly, I've designed this to be an action manual. That means you should utilize the principles as you devise and initiate your campaign. Refer often to the book. Use it the way a jungle fighter would use a map. Check back frequently to see if you're on track. Don't worry—I'm right behind you.

Dream On

We can't all be Beethoven, but we can all make music. If you own a hamburger stand, don't be consumed with a desire to become the next McDonald's, because you probably won't. But that doesn't mean the game is over. Perhaps you can turn your place into the best burger stand in the city. For that you can strive.

I'm not telling you to avoid dreaming big. If you're not dreaming big, I would question why you're in business in the first place. But dreams occur while we're sleeping. I focus on the waking hours, when steel-eyed practicality goes a long way in making dreams come true.

What you can achieve is limited only by internal factors. Fear and laziness are tougher obstacles than irascible reporters and distracted talk-show producers. Basically, all it costs to make it in the Fame Factory is the price of a few stamps (or better, the non-cost of a few e-mails) and a telephone. What cannot be appraised is the value of imagination.

If you can make a mental picture of yourself benefiting from media exposure; if you feel you have enough creative energy to devote to planning and engineering an original, self-directed P.R. campaign; if you're up to acquiring new skills that will help you comprehend the world of the mass media; if you are prepared to look at media and society in a new and positive way, then consider yourself a recruit in the Guerrilla P.R. forces.

It would be a mistake to promise you too much. In the beginning you may find the going difficult. Not every newspaper or radio station is going to be interested in what you have to offer, and you may feel discouraged at times. But don't be afraid of failure. Teddy Roosevelt said, "He who has never made a mistake is one who never does anything." If you follow my system, not only will you pull off a first-rate public relations campaign but you'll gain a new sense of yourself.

The seeds are within you right now. Forward, march!

1

A Brief History of *Time* . . . and *Newsweek* and *USA Today*

> Three hostile newspapers are more
> to be feared than a thousand bayonets.
>
> —Napoleon Bonaparte

The Nature of Media

More than four decades ago, Marshall McLuhan, the father of modern communications, wrote these immortal words: "The medium is the message."

Today I would amend that to "The medium is the media." Our civilization is utterly dominated by the force of media. After our own families, no influence holds greater sway in shaping the text of our being than do the media that cloak us like an electronic membrane.

We all think of ourselves as unique, unlike any person past or present. Indeed, what gives human life its divine spark is the distinct quality of every individual. Yet, in many ways we are all the same. The task of market analysts, pollsters, and demographers is to identify those characteristics we share and to group us accordingly. If you are in your early fifties, male, Caucasian, a father of two, earn $100,000 or more, and listen to a Top 40 radio station, there are total strangers out there who know an awful lot about you. That's because they understand a lot about your upbringing.

They know you watched *The Mickey Mouse Club* in the fifties, *The Man From U.N.C.L.E.* in the sixties, and *Saturday Night Live* in the seventies; became environmentally conscious in the eighties; and were probably sorry ABC canceled *Thirtysomething* in the nineties. They've got your number because they understand the role the media have played in your life from the moment you Boomed as a Baby. Today, in America, we tune in to over 9,000 commercial radio stations, 1,100 television stations, 11,000 periodicals, and over 11,000 newspapers with a combined circulation of nearly seventy million. This doesn't even take into account online radio stations, blogs, podcasts, video feeds, iTunes, and pay-per-view events.

These are the sources of our opinions on everything from nuclear disarmament to Madonna's recent adoption. Nobody likes to be told what to think, but all of us, every single day, are told precisely what to think about.

As Anthony Pratkanis and Elliot Aronson show in their insightful book *Age of Propaganda,* the mass media are most effective in terms of persuading the public for two primary reasons: First, they teach new behavior; second, they let us know that certain behaviors are legitimate and appropriate. So if the media are encouraging certain buying patterns, fashion trends, and modes of thinking, the unstated message we receive is "It's okay for me to like that, do that, feel that."

In this way our culture evolves, is accelerated, and is disseminated. Like the transcontinental railroad of the nineteenth century, the media link every city, gully, farmhouse, and mountaintop in North America.

Regionalism is fading. The American accent is more uniform; our penchant for migration and blending in is like the smoothing out of a great national blanket. We are fast becoming one.

A common grammatical error occurs when people say "The media *is*" rather than "The media *are*" ("media" being the plural of "medium"). Yet, I sense people who say "the media is" are on to something. They perceive the many arms of the media—TV, newspapers, radio, etc.—as part of one monstrously monolithic creature. The media are "one," too.

Consider "Baby Jessica" McClure, for whom my firm donated public relations services. Jessica was the toddler from Midland, Texas, who fell down a narrow pipe in her backyard in 1987. For thirty-six hours, America was mesmerized by press coverage of her rescue.

Acting as a concerned neighbor, the media conveyed Jessica's plight to the nation. The private agony of the McClure family became the anguish of all America. Think of it: the temporary suffering of one "insignificant" little girl stopped the world's most powerful country dead in its tracks.

(Then, to canonize the experience, the TV movie version of Jessica's story made it to the small screen within a year. You may draw your own conclusions.)

Without those cameras there to catch it, and those TV stations to broadcast it, Baby Jessica's ordeal would have made absolutely no impact on anyone other than her family and those who saved her. Because of the media, all of America for two days became part of Jessica's family.

Contraction and Expansion

Journalists and talk-show hosts like to claim they're in the information business or the news business. But you know and I know they're in the money business just like everyone else. Because practically all media are privately held profit-making ventures, they behave much like any other enterprise, looking for ways to increase the bottom line.

To do that they must expand their consumer base—that is, their audience. They must give the customer what he or she wants. So if your local news station runs a few too many five-part specials on the illicit sex lives of nuns during sweeps month, remember they're only trying to please the viewers.

Creating a successful product means citizens may not always get the information they need. A Harvard researcher found the average network sound bite from presidential campaigns dropped from 42.5 seconds per broadcast in 1968 to just under 10 seconds in 1988, where it appeared to stabilize; the number stayed the same through 1996. That translates into roughly sixteen words a night with which to make up our minds on who should run the country. We absorb more information, yet understand less than ever before.

This is a logical consequence of big media. Their existence depends on keeping the audience tuned in. If TV station "A" covers candidate "B" droning on about farm subsidies, most of the audience will probably switch to station "C" running a story about the stray cat raised by an affectionate pig. Station "A" would be wise to ditch candidate "B" and send a crew out to film Porky and Tabby.

Along with this contraction of information is a parallel expansion of media. Because social scientists have us so precisely categorized, outlets targeted to specific groups flourish. *O: The Oprah Magazine* caters to mature, high-income women. *Men's Health* appeals to middle-income, fast-tracker men. *Essence* aims for black women.

Peter Yarrow, of Peter, Paul, and Mary, tells a great story in his stage show to illustrate how narrowly focused we've become as a society. In the 1940s and 1950s we had the all-encompassing *Life* magazine. Then we cropped our vision down to *People* magazine in the seventies (all of Life wasn't good enough anymore). Things tightened up even more with *Us*. Now we have *Self*. Somewhere, there's just gotta be a magazine just for you. I can just imagine it: on sale now, *Fred Morgenstern Monthly*.

Not only do we see more media outlets, but the flow of information has likewise increased dramatically during the past few years. Fax machines, cell phones, high-speed modems, fiber-optic cable, low-power TV, satellite downlinks—all have reshaped the way we get our information, when we get it, and what we do with it. And the Internet has changed things even more. (See Chapter 4.)

During China's "Goddess of Democracy" protests in 1989, the students kept in touch with the outside world via fax. Instantly, China seemed to leap forward from feudal empire to modern nation. Vietnam was the first "we'll be right back after these messages" war. As napalm rained down on the jungle we saw the war live as it happened. We had no time to process information or analyze events as we were barraged by them. Because of improved communications, the Gulf War had the same effect, only with infinitely more drama. The media may have accelerated the process of dissemination, but as we found out in the days of the first supersonic jets, breaking the sound barrier did not, as some scientists feared, cause planes to disintegrate.

Likewise, instant news did not cause us to psychologically disintegrate.

With the Iraq War and its "embedded" reporters, access was quick but limited. We got the information immediately, but not all the information—at least, not at first. Technology had improved to the point that reporters could report on any event anywhere in the world at any time and it would be seen *immediately*, not after the tape (or earlier, film) had been sent and processed and edited. Vietnam may have started the trend, but by Iraq, technology had really changed the entire process forever.

There's no way to assess what this means to society. To be carpet-bombed by information must have far-reaching consequences to our civilization, but that's for future observers to sort out. Today, we face an intimidating media-driven culture. Anyone looking to succeed in business must first master the fundamentals of navigating the media. To reach customers, donors, or investors—to reach the public—one must rely on the media as the prime intermediary. The methodology to achieve this is known as public relations.

The Nature of Public Relations

Half the world is composed of people who have something to say
and can't, and the other half who have nothing to say
and keep on saying it.

—Robert Frost

I'm often asked whether public relations is a science or an art. That's a valid question. In science, two plus two equals four.

It will always equal four whether added by a Republican from Iowa, a shaman from New Guinea, or an alien from Planet X. However, in public relations, two plus two may equal four. It may equal five. It may equal zero today and fifty tomorrow.

Public relations is an art.

As in any art, there are rules of form, proven techniques, and standards of excellence. But overall, it's a mercurial enterprise, where instinct is as legitimate as convention. Public relations was once defined as the ability to provide the answers before the public knows enough to ask the questions. Another P.R. pundit once stated, "We don't persuade people. We simply offer them reasons to persuade themselves."

Consider it more than simply a way to attract attention or influence people toward buying your product. Public relations is an art that creates an image (hopefully, an accurate one, but certainly a polished one) of you and your business, and presents it in a controlled, planned fashion that will convey *exactly* what you want to say without having to be obvious about it.

It becomes a question of *credibility*. If your neighbor tells you that the Dow Jones average for today has dropped 100 points, you would have no reason to disbelieve him, but you wouldn't necessarily take his information as unquestionably reliable. Maybe your friend got the information wrong, or received it from an unreliable source. He could have just found out at the bar after his third drink, or from a former stockbroker who's bitter about being fired from his job. He has, if not low, then at least questionable credibility on that subject.

But if *The News Hour with Jim Lehrer* tells you that stocks dropped 100 points, you will probably not even consider questioning that statement. To be fair, you'd have little reason to question it. Serving as a respected news outlet for decades, *The*

News Hour delivers stock reports every day from reliable sources and has very high credibility. Even if the show makes a mistake, you are more likely to believe it than your neighbor's true information.

I define what I do as gift-wrapping. If you package a bracelet in a Tiffany box, it will have a higher perceived value than if presented in a Kmart box. Same bracelet, different perception.

Consider the case of one Jean-Claude Baker, the adopted son of Josephine Baker, who owns a restaurant in Manhattan he named after his "*maman*": Chez Josephine. In the spring of 2007, Baker, as is his custom, decided to send postcards with images of *Maman* to 15,000 of his closest friends. A P.R. standard: the targeted mailing.

Because the image he had chosen for the 2007 year's postcard was, at least technically, a bit risqué (Ms. Baker was depicted topless), Jean-Claude decided to make sure his mailing would be in compliance with the postal code. No sense spending a lot of money on postcards and postage if the cards won't make it through the mail.

He set out to his local post office in Manhattan, showed the clerk behind a window the postcard, and asked if there would be any problem with the mailing. The clerk took a look and, without consulting a superior, said the image was pornographic and could not be sent uncensored through the mail.

Jean-Claude felt the ruling was a little prudish, but he didn't want to violate the law. He had the image on the postcards altered so that the word "CENSORED" appeared over *Maman*'s mammary glands. But no, he was told once again that a tiny amount of breast was visible, and the postcards were not suitable for the U.S. Mails.

Mr. Baker, who does not lack for Guerrilla instincts, had a

third version of the image (which had always been an illustration, not a photograph) made, covering any part the Post Office might find offensive. That incarnation was allowed through.

Still, it ate at him (and at his desire for publicity). Jean-Claude contacted civil liberties attorneys and postal attorneys, as well as officials of the U.S. Postal Service itself. In the end, it was agreed that the original illustration, unaltered, would always have been acceptable for mailing.

Some business owners might have been put out by such a rigmarole, while others might simply have accepted the original ruling and moved on with the censored mailing. Not Jean-Claude Baker.

He got on the phone to the press.

On May 9, 2007, an article chronicling the case of *Chez Josephine v. U.S. Postal Service* appeared in the "About New York" section of the *New York Times*. It noted, among other things, that Jean-Claude, whom it said had been running his restaurant "unburdened by excess modesty for 21 years," decided to send out the original postcards, image unsullied, to his 15,000 patrons. He even got an apology from the Post Office.

And he set a press conference for the day of the mailing—one day after postal rates increased by two cents. It was expected to be well attended.

What strikes some people as tasteless self-promotion can be a brilliant Guerrilla P.R. maneuver. Here, while admittedly Jean-Claude was stuck with the bill for 15,000 postcards and had to pay an extra $300 (the two-cent postage increase, which wouldn't have been necessary if the first postcards had been approved) to send them, he also came away with a charming story in the most visible newspaper in the country—and certainly in the city in which his business is run—for the cost of a phone call.

It's even a funny story. But where another business owner might have seen an embarrassment (Baker said the postal clerk had said, loudly, in a crowded Post Office, that he was trying to send "pornographic advertising"), Jean-Claude saw an opportunity. And for one day, at least, his restaurant on West Forty-second Street was featured in hundreds of thousands of newspapers in his hometown.

And now, he's gotten me to write about it in this book. Bravo, Jean-Claude!

Perception Is Reality

Don Burr, former CEO of a popular low-cost 1980s airline, once said, "In the airline industry, if passengers see coffee stains on the food tray, they assume the engine maintenance isn't done right." That may seem irrational, but in this game, perception, not the objective truth, matters most.

It's a matter of *broken windows*, as defined by a study of crime areas by two sociologists in the 1980s. In James Q. Wilson and George L. Kelling's "Broken Windows," published by the *Atlantic Monthly* in 1982, it was put forth that when a tiny crime—a broken window in a remote warehouse—was left unrepaired, it encouraged the perception that the area was not well policed, that the owner of the building either was not present or didn't care, and that larger crimes would be tolerated as well. Wilson and Kelling argued that if the smaller crimes were dealt with quickly and efficiently, the message would be broadcast that this area was not safe for those who wished to disturb the peace. They had best move on.

I believe this theory applies to business, as well. So maybe

Burr was right: if there's a coffee ring on the snack table, people will *imagine* that the engine maintenance is equally slapdash. Taking care of the little things will lead to the perception that the big things are also being handled. It really comes down to what people will assume on the basis of what they see.

How one comprehends given information is all-important in public relations. For decades, baby harp seals were bludgeoned to death by fur hunters, but until the public saw the cute little critters up close and personal and perceived the hunt as unacceptable, the problem didn't exist. Before that, it was a matter of trappers preserving their hardy way of life. The seals ultimately hired the better publicist.

This also works in negative ways. The congressional check-bouncing scandal in the mid- to late 1980s was a case in which individual congressmen's visibility skyrocketed while their credibility plummeted. The Phillip Morris Company, a manufacturer of cigarettes, spends time and money claiming that cigarettes are okay. Nothing they do or say will ever make that true, but they may go a long way in changing public perception of their product. In the early 1990s they sponsored a national tour of the original Bill of Rights document, implying subliminally that no-smoking regulations infringe on our basic liberties.

How's that for a P.R. stretch?

Of course, when terminally ill smokers and their families began enormous class-action suits against the tobacco companies, the public's perception began to turn. But even in 2007, the Motion Picture Association of America decided to add smoking to its list of questionable behaviors that can bump a movie's rating from PG to PG-13 because the image of attractive actors in sympathetic or "cool" roles who were smoking was considered dangerous. You can tell children they shouldn't smoke because they could become ill and die, but when they see someone they think is "cool" smoking, they're going to want to emulate that behavior.

Ultimately, the goal of any public relations campaign is to either reorient or solidify the perception of a product, client, policy, or event. From there, nature takes its course. If the public perceives the product as good, the movie star as sexy, the pet rock as indispensable, then the public will fork over its money. As the brilliant business author Dr. Judith Bardwick has explained, "To be perceived as visible increasingly means one is perceived as successful."

Some may charge that stressing perception as reality is tantamount to sanctioning falsehood. I disagree. The great historian Max Dimont has argued that it doesn't matter whether or not Moses really did have a chat with the Lord up on Mount Sinai. What matters is that the Jewish people believed it and carved their unique place in world civilization because of it. Perception became reality.

Likewise, on a more mundane scale, one will succeed in a P.R. campaign only if the perception fostered truly resonates with the public. I do not believe people are generally stupid or easily duped. You may try everything in your bag of tricks to get the public to see things your way. But it won't work if you don't do things right, or if the public really doesn't want to believe what you're telling them.

You'll pull it off only if the perception you seek to convey fits the reality of the public, the reality of the times. As Pratkanis and Aronson argue, credibility today is manufactured, not earned.

Consider the case of "New Coke." In 1985, the Coca-Cola

company decided it would remove its trademark cola—probably one of the most successful consumer products in the history of civilization—from the shelves because market research had convinced it that the formula used by its closest rival, Pepsi-Cola, was preferred by consumers. Sweetening the mix (making Coke taste more like Pepsi) was considered the way to "relaunch" the product and ensure that the brand would be an elite, worldwide phenomenon into the twenty-first century—and who knows how long after that.

The problem was, the public hadn't been adequately convinced that it really didn't like what it thought it liked. Coca-Cola drinkers positively revolted at the prospect of losing their favorite soft drink. They staged protests, hoarded bottles of "old Coke" before they could be pulled from shelves, and in short made the lives of Coca-Cola executives miserable at the very suggestion of removing the original formula.

But that wasn't the worst of it. When "New Coke" was introduced, *nobody* liked it. It did not attract Pepsi drinkers to cross sides in the cola wars. It alienated Coke loyalists who believed the company had simply lost its mind and was not in touch with the desires of its consumers. Try to find a can of "New Coke" today. Exactly.

If you try to tell the public what it wants, you'd better be sure the public will want that when you give it to them.

P.R. or Publicity?

Often, the terms "public relations" and "publicity" are used interchangeably. They shouldn't be. Publicity is only one manifestation of P.R.—specifically, achieving notoriety through accumulated press exposure. A publicist knows newspapers, magazines, Web outlets, and radio and TV talk shows. Public relations is much more than that. The public relations expert is as well versed in human nature as in editorial deadlines and sound bites.

P.R. can be as macro as a campaign to persuade foreign governments to buy U.S. soybeans, or as micro as a warm handshake. The notion that P.R. is simply a matter of mailing press releases is nuttier than a squirrel's breakfast. As producer, manager, and publicist Jay Bernstein says, "P.R. is getting a front table at the right restaurant, getting you invited to the right party, and getting into first class with a tourist ticket."

A man who has greatly affected my thinking, the esteemed business author and lecturer Tom Peters, tells the story of a visit to a neighborhood convenience store. "American Express was being a little user-unfriendly," Tom recalls, "and it took a good three minutes for my AMEX card to clear. When it finally did, the cashier bagged my purchase, and as I turned to go, he reached into a jar of two-cent foil-wrapped mints. He pulled one out, dropped it in my bag, and said, 'The delay you experienced was inexcusable. I apologize and hope it doesn't happen again. Come back soon.' For two cents, he bought my loyalty for life."

This story is about one small business owner and only one customer, but it's a perfect example of good P.R. But what about bad P.R.? I doubt there's anyone on the scene who has mastered that dubious craft better than sometime billionaire Donald Trump. This is a man who has lost control of his own gilded ship. His lurid infidelities, his profligate spending, his precipitous fall from fortune, and, worst of all, his attempt to exploit the Mike Tyson rape tragedy to promote a prize fight collectively paint a portrait of a thoroughly vulgar mind.

Once he began an infamous feud with Rosie O'Donnell (then on *The View*) over whose looks were worse, things had gotten as bad as they could look. Or so we thought, until the distinguished Mr. Trump appeared on a wrestling pay-per-view event, shaving the hair off the wrestling promoter because he had won a "grudge match" in which the Donald's own bizarre do was at risk.

Was it possible for there to be a worse image in America? To Trump, it appears not to matter. An image is all that counts: good, bad, or really really bad.

The Donald doesn't care what you say about him, as long as you spell his name right. True, whenever he opens his mouth or makes a move, the press is all over him. But his massive celebrity has made him only a famous fool. You are not likely to achieve the degree of fame that Mr. Trump has, but, given his shameful image, I would congratulate you on that.

P.R. vs. Marketing

With Guerrilla P.R. (and P.R. in general), you do not tell the public that your new digital fish cleaner is the greatest invention since the dawn of time. You could easily do that in an ad. Your goal is to lead people to draw that same conclusion for themselves. Otherwise, you're engaging in good old-fashioned—or is it new-fashioned?—marketing strategy.

Companies often relegate public relations to their marketing departments. That might make sense from a corporate point of view, but there's a distinct difference between P.R. and marketing. Going back to the "science vs. art" analogy, whereas P.R. is the art, marketing is the science.

Bob Serling, president of the Stratford Marketing Group, an L.A.-based marketing firm, has written, "Marketing is everything you do to make sure your customers find out about, and buy, your products and services." That's a tall order, and to go about filling it, marketing executives lug around a hefty bag of tricks. To a large degree, they rely on surveys, demographic analyses, and established sales and advertising procedures to accomplish their goals.

But in public relations, intangibles play a far greater role. How do you measure a feeling? It's not easy, but in P.R. we trade in the realm of feelings every day. We may use the media as the vehicle, but the landscape we traverse is contoured by human emotion.

Marketing often goes hand in hand with advertising. The undeniable advantage with advertising is that the advertiser retains full control. He knows exactly what his message will say and precisely when it will be seen. But remember this little fact of life: Most top ad agencies consider a response rate of 1 to 2 percent a triumph. That's all it takes to make them happy. And, like it or not, most people don't take ads as seriously as advertisers would like. Everybody knows they're bought and paid for. These days, they are mostly TiVo-ed and skipped in the watching.

I prefer the odds with major media exposure. True, you do lose a large measure of control, and you never know for sure when or how your message will be conveyed. But the public is far likelier to accept what it gleans from the news media than what it sees in commercials. If Brian Williams says a new sports shoe is a daring innovation, people will give that more credence than if company spokesman Derek Jeter says it. The news—indeed, the truth—is what Brian Williams says it is.

So who tells Brian Williams what's news? The media like

to boast that they rely on ace news-gathering staffs, but in fact they also depend a great deal on public relations people. (That doesn't mean the journalists of America are saps. They're just looking for good stories.) A hungry reporter and a smart publicist constitute a match made in heaven, and it's been that way since the dawn of the Communication Age.

FROM THE GUERRILLA P.R. FILE

In Amarillo, Texas, you'll find the Big Texan Steak Ranch, where the owner issues the following challenge: If you can eat a seventy-two-ounce steak in an hour, you get it free (the cholesterol test is on your own dime). News of the deal traveled far and wide, even to the skies, where I first read about it in an airline magazine.

Glory Days: The Founding of the P.R. Industry

The public relations industry flourished with the growth of twentieth-century mass media, although sensitivity to public opinion on the part of public figures is nothing new. Even Abraham Lincoln got into the act, declaring once, "What kills a skunk is the publicity it gives itself." The fathers of modern P.R. knew the value of simple images to convey powerful messages.

Edward Bernays, a founder of modern P.R., defined his mission as the engineering of consent. He was a nephew of Sigmund Freud, and he strikes me as having been just as perceptive about human nature as was his esteemed uncle. Bernays displayed a genius for concocting indelible images, something good P.R. campaigns require. In one early triumph, he arranged for young debutantes to smoke Lucky Strikes while strolling in New York's 1929 Easter Parade. What Bernays sold to the press as a bold political statement on women's rights was no more than a gimmick to sell cigarettes.

Pioneers like publicist and film producer A. C. Lyles set the pace for generations of publicists to follow. Another innovator, Ivy Hill, is often credited with inventing the press release. Hill believed telling the "truth" in journalistic fashion would help shape public opinion. He sensed editors would not dismiss press releases as ads but rather would perceive their real news value. He was right.

The publicist's ability to appeal to newspapers proved invaluable to captains of industry seeking to shore up their images. Back in the 1920s, Hill masterminded industrialist John D. Rockefeller's much-ridiculed habit of handing out dimes to every child he met. Ridiculous—but effective in its time. (Imagine Bill Gates trying that today—even with dollar bills.)

Occasionally, clients got less than they bargained for. In the late 1950s, the Ford Motor Company hired P.R. trailblazer Ben Sonnenberg to help overcome the negative fallout from the Edsel fiasco. He charged Ford $50,000 for a foolproof P.R. plan, and after three days he submitted it in person. Sonnenberg looked the breathless executives in the eye and intoned, "Do nothing." With that, the dapper publicist pocketed his check and walked out, much to the slack-jawed shock of the Ford brain trust.

Even nations sometimes need help. During the 1970s, Argentina developed a little P.R. problem when its government kidnapped and murdered thousands of its own citizens. Buenos Aires hired the high-powered U.S. firm of Burson-Marsteller to tidy things up. For a cool $1,000,000, the firm launched an extensive campaign involving opinion makers from around the world. A stream of press releases stressed, among other things, the Argentine regime's record in fighting terrorism. Sometimes the truth can be stretched until it tears itself in half.

I don't wish to give the impression that P.R. is strictly a polite version of lying. That's not the case. As I said, P.R. is gift-wrapping. Whether delivered in fancy or plain paper, truth is truth, and the public ultimately comprehends it. The trick is to package the truth on your own terms.

How often have you read about a big movie star storming off the set of a film because of "creative differences" with the director? We all know the two egomaniacs probably hated each other's guts. But if the papers printed that, we'd perceive the situation very differently. By our soft-pedaling the row with words like "creative differences," the movie star's reputation remains intact, even though intuition tells us the star is "difficult."

More Than One Public

Thus far, when referring to the public, I've generalized to mean the population at large: We the People. The sophisticated modern art of P.R. encompasses many more "publics" than that. In fact, selective targeting is a primary tactic in sound P.R. strategies. As you will see, bigger is not always better.

Depending on the goals, a publicist could target any one of various business, consumer, or governmental communities. An inventor who seeks financial backing aims for the financial press and relevant trade publications. A rock musician zeroes in on the local music rags and well-regarded music blogs. A lobbyist might need nothing more than a friendly article in the *Washington Post,* a retailer only the residents in his immediate neighborhood.

Though I've found a few clients easily dazzled by quantity, in P.R. quality is what really counts. A seven-inch stack of press clippings means nothing unless the objectives of the campaign have been met. The scrapbook makes a great Mother's Day gift, but I'd rather see my clients' careers advanced in the right direction.

Figuring out which public to reach is one of the most critical decisions a publicist makes. My orientation—and, I hope, yours—is geared toward the most significant audience vis-à-vis your objectives, not necessarily the widest. You may want to target the people you buy from, the people you sell to, the people you hope to buy from, the people you hope to sell to, the people you work for, the people who work for you, and so on. It's a big world full of little worlds when you look closely.

In most cases I spell out precisely who and what I'm going after, and then proceed aggressively. Don't go for the moon all at once. Set a goal, achieve it, then build on that base. Any good planner knows the advantages of thinking three steps ahead while proceeding one step at a time.

FROM THE GUERRILLA P.R. FILE

The history-making August 1991 revolution in the former Soviet Union began when then-president Mikhail Gorbachev left Moscow for a vacation on the Crimean Sea. Because the whole affair had a happy ending, everybody laughed when, only a few days later, the president of an outdoor billboard company in Detroit ran a series of large ads all over town reading "Welcome Back, Gorby! Next Time Vacation in Michigan."

2

Basic Training

I don't care what they call me, as long as they spell my name right.

—George M. Cohan

Ideas and Innovation

The challenge before me was formidable. I realized my client, Oscar-winning actor Charlton Heston, couldn't possibly be made any more famous than he'd already been for the previous four decades. But as his public relations counselor I was responsible for enhancing his distinguished image and career.

Because of his legendary status, due in no small part to the epic nature of the characters he's portrayed on screen, one area in which I felt Mr. Heston could benefit was showing the public that he was a regular human being, just like the rest of us. I also knew him to be among the wittiest gentlemen I'd ever met (this was before we parted ways over his radical gun control tirades and before Mr. Heston, tragically, began suffering from

Alzheimer's disease). Suddenly, one of those lightbulbs went off. Why not have Mr. Heston guest-host *Saturday Night Live*?

It was perfect. Though selling the concept to both the show and my client took some doing, in the end Mr. Heston did host the show. He was a big hit, and many critics at the time called his appearance a P.R. masterpiece. It all began with a simple brainstorm.

There's a theme running through the examples used in this book. All are based on ideas, not skills. The tricks of the trade are simple to acquire, and easily adapted to a tight budget. The mechanics are not what count. What must be emphasized above all else is the idea itself. From there, all things are possible. H. G. Wells said, "Human history is in essence a history of ideas."

So often I've heard people lament that they don't know how to come up with ideas. As my friend psychologist Dr. Joyce Brothers explained to me, "Our most creative thoughts do not come when we try to force them. They come as a by-product, while lying in the bathtub or when we're busy with the kids." She's right. Robert Louis Stevenson based *Dr. Jekyll and Mr. Hyde* on a dream. Igor Stravinsky composed in his mind the entire ballet *The Rite of Spring* while asleep.

Our best ideas derive from the unconscious, and that's a realm to which we have no practical access.

Yet, the challenge to you is to base your Guerrilla P.R. campaign on ideas. But perhaps you're unsure of your ability to generate them. Take it from me—you possess all you need to conjure up clever and effective ideas. Over the years, I've found that the best ideas are based on four fundamental principles:

Utility. Juxtaposition. Humor. Image.

The four are not interchangeable, and not all four work equally well for any given project. But if you look closely, within one of these principles lies the pathway to your own sensational ideas—ideas that will fuel your campaign.

Utility means usefulness. Most ideas, inventions, and innovations are based on this simple principle. The question to ask yourself is, "What do people need or want that they haven't thought of before?"

One large bank offered customers $10 for every bank error they discovered in their checking accounts. Not only did this help the bank cut down on internal audit procedures, it also brought in 15,000 new accounts and $65,000,000 in deposits within two months. What better form of utility can anyone in business imagine than fostering good customer relations?

Successful Dallas obstetrician Walter Evans sends his new mothers and their babies home from the hospital in a chauffeured limousine. International cosmetics and beauty products giant Estée Lauder originated the idea of giving away a free gift with every purchase. Today, of course, the company is worth billions, and everybody else in that industry similarly gives away gifts.

Los Angeles radio station KTWV, known as the Wave, scored points by dotting Southern California beaches with "Wave" trash cans, encouraging beachgoers to put their litter in the proper place. It was useful, it was effective, and it made the Wave a much better known radio station than before.

Don't worry if the usefulness of your ideas isn't immediately apparent to others. Federal Express founder Fred Smith first cooked up his idea for overnight courier service while still a student at Yale. In fact, a paper he wrote about the idea was returned with a C grade and a scoffing note from his professor. It took six more years before Smith launched FedEx. Today, I imagine his ex-professor is coaching high school badminton, or should be.

The utility principle works not only in business but in shaping a P.R. campaign as well. When a mother-and-daughter country music duo first began to get their career off the ground years ago, instead of performing in circus-like mob showcases at well-known clubs, they performed short sets in intimate hotel rooms for a select audience of media people. It didn't take long for the press to conclude that the Judds were without a doubt one of country music's best artists—a sentiment just about everyone else agrees with today, years after the act stopped performing together regularly.

Utility equals innovation in design and execution. If you own a health food store, how about giving away a fat-and-cholesterol-counter guide? Do you run a sporting goods store? Hand out baseball or football schedules with your logo printed on the back. Do you manage an Italian restaurant? How about an attractive description of the various kinds of pastas printed up on giveaway cards? Then, all you have to do is let the media know about it. Apply the precept of utility, and you will make headway fast.

The second fundamental principle is **juxtaposition**. Woody Allen once said that this is the secret to comedy. I also think it's one of the secrets to many great ideas. Throwing together two disparate personalities, notions, styles, or concepts makes people see things in an entirely different light.

For my client *Entertainment Tonight* host Mary Hart, I helped come up with the idea to have her gorgeous legs insured with Lloyds of London for $2 million. One of the brightest women I've ever met, Mary quickly realized the potential of such a plan. I brought together one of Mary's most attractive assets with the notion of insurability.

Two disparate themes, one wild P.R. idea.

The female hard-core rap music trio BWP sought to bring
attention to itself in a crowded field of sound-alike look-alike
rap groups, and hit upon the idea of incorporating into their
latest music video the notorious home video depicting the beating of Rodney King at the hands of a few L.A.P.D. officers.
They brought together two distinct entities into one, and reaped
enormous media coverage from it.

People are used to seeing Sir Paul McCartney treated like,
well, a knight. But they were not prepared, during the World
Series of 2001, to see him directing traffic outside Yankee Sta-
dium in the South Bronx. Sir Paul was attending the game as a
reaction to the devastating 9/11 attacks, had become a big Yankees fan, and was just trying to help, much as he did when he
composed and sang "Freedom" at a superstar concert he organized in Madison Square Garden. McCartney didn't need extra
publicity, but he did want to get a message out: they're not going
to stop us.

To demonstrate the severity of hunger in the world, a noted
charity staged an elegant black-tie sit-down dinner, but the only
thing served on the fine china was a tiny portion of rice and
beans, representing the typical day's diet for most poor Third
World residents. Again, the juxtaposition of upper-crust dining
manners and starvation food rations made for a powerful P.R.
message.

You too can devise two or more concepts and link them together, forming a similarly impressive synthesis. The alchemy
you create by juxtaposing themes can work wonders for your
business or your Guerrilla P.R. campaign, and you will find that
your creativity will be recognized and rewarded.

Be careful, though. Juxtaposition can look disconnected and
badly staged when not done well. Make sure the two concepts

you're joining are *compatible* and that the point being made is clear. It's the message you're trying to communicate through the image you're creating, not the other way around.

If done right, the third principle, **humor**, rarely fails. Ideas grounded in humor succeed because, frankly, they make us feel good. If you recall your favorite TV commercials (and even discussing the idea of a "favorite commercial" is a little humorous), I'll bet at least half are of the comedic variety. Maybe the fast-talking Federal Express man tickled your fancy, or it was the Bud Light "Tastes Great–Less Filling" debates, or perhaps the turbocharged Friskies kitten. Maybe the Geico Cavemen (who got their own sitcom out of the deal!) made you laugh, or the AFLAC duck voiced by comedian Gilbert Gottfried. Clearly, the use of humor is the most disarming method for hooking others.

Dave Schwartz catapulted his used car business into the stratosphere by renaming it Rent-A-Wreck, a moniker that delighted everyone who came across it. The name alone brought Dave literally millions in media exposure and business dollars.

Personal fitness trainer Bill Calkins got his name in every paper in the country with his annual "Worst Shapes Hall of Fame." Patterned after Mr. Blackwell's "Worst-Dressed List," Bill's list teased those celebrities most in need of diet and exercise. Sample entries saluted such notables as Chicago Bears lineman William "The Refrigerator" Perry ("The Refrigerator is overstocked"), movie critic Roger Ebert ("Should spend more time 'At the Movies' and less time 'At the Snack Bar'"), and rocker Ozzy Osbourne ("The only man to find a rat in his fried chicken and eat it").

Art's Deli, an enormously popular L.A. eatery, has printed on its menus a Yiddish lexicon with hilarious translations, i.e.,

"A Farshlepteh Krenk," which actually means "a drawn-out disease" but, according to Art, means "filling out your own tax return."

When actors Rick Moranis and Dave Thomas sought press attention for their comedy album *Great White North*, based on their lunkhead Canadian characters Bob and Doug McKenzie, they staged a press conference, appearing as Bob and Doug. They even re-created the very set made popular on the original *SCTV* episodes. The press conference was a smash hit, attended by more than a hundred media people, and it brought them widespread coverage.

The chief danger in the use of humor, of course, is that humor is subjective. What's funny to you may not be funny to others. I can't tell you how to be funny, but I do know that all people appreciate wit. My best suggestion is to determine precisely what makes you laugh, and see if it makes others laugh as well.

Finally, you may conjure up an idea based on **image**. This may be the most powerful kind of idea you create, because nothing is quite as searing as a well-constructed image. Consider some of the indelible images we've experienced in the past few years. The Abu Ghraib photographs; the Mel Gibson mug shot; Hurricane Katrina victims stranded in the Superdome and on rooftops, begging for help; thousands of former Enron employees stunned and out of work juxtaposed with the images of their former employers attending a birthday party at which an ice statue of Michelangelo's David urinated vodka; those two smoldering towers collapsing in horrifying images of dust, smoke, and debris. All these images say far more on their own than any possible accompanying commentary.

We're all accustomed to advertisers using images, symbols, logos, and other graphics to convey messages. Months before the movie *Batman* opened in 1989, we were teased with the stark black image of—the Batman logo. The now-famous Infiniti luxury car TV campaign depicted tranquil scenes of riverbanks and cherry groves, never once showing the car. More recently, we've seen green, happy images animated in a commercial to indicate British Petroleum's commitment to making less polluting gasoline, and a calm, soothing beach with gorgeous people on it, alone, saying nothing, doing nothing but enjoying a cold Corona beer. Apparently, the emotional impact of the image is worth more than any intellectual appeal. Guerrilla P.R. practitioners would do well to harness the power of the image when creating ideas.

In one of her campaigns, MADD founder Candy Lightner graphically illustrated the problem of teen drinking by displaying scores of beer cans at a press conference; every can of beer had been purchased by her underage daughter with an illegal I.D. The message was brought home in a stark manner.

Anti-abortion activists sometimes bring the bodies of aborted fetuses (or at least pictures of them) to their press conferences and rallies. Pro-choice proponents carry coat hangers to symbolize the old back-alley abortions. These symbols for the opposite points of view are equally potent.

To draw on the image principle for your ideas, reconstitute your thinking into a wordless language. You might even want to use your own dreams as a guide, as did Stevenson and Stravinsky. Dreams employ symbolic language, and often the emotional impact of dream images is as powerful as any real-life experience.

How do you determine if your ideas are worthwhile? Steve Fiffer, in his book *So You've Got a Great Idea*, makes two salient points.

Though he primarily addresses inventors, his precepts apply equally well to Guerrilla P.R. Fiffer says the key pieces of information in evaluating an idea are these:

1. Determine need. Is your idea beneficial to others? Does it serve a purpose? In terms of P.R., will it help you achieve your objectives by helping to link you and your project together with the media?
2. Is it original? Does it excite? Is it different? The media are always hungry for something new; does your idea fill the bill?

Pondering the answers to these questions will help you steer your ideas into either the development stage or the trash can. It's up to you to make that determination.

Now, what do you do with your ideas? They can serve many purposes, as you will see. Your creativity will ensure intriguing and well-written press releases, can't-miss magnet events (i.e., publicity stunts), effective marketing tools, and articulate verbal pitches to media representatives. Your ideas will serve you in business, in your Guerrilla P.R. efforts, and elsewhere in your life as your springboard for action.

In later chapters, I will go into greater detail on formulating ideas for specific areas, such as writing bios or concocting a magnet event. But part and parcel of the notion of Guerrilla P.R. is the understanding that creativity—not money, power, or influence—is the driving force behind any such campaign. It has been said, "The unexamined life isn't worth living." I would add, "The uncreative life isn't worth living, either."

Looking vs. Seeing

I want you to try something: Take a pen and paper, and open to-day's newspaper. Select articles from the news, entertainment, or business sections. Read carefully and note how often the reporter seems to adopt a particular slant on the article's subject. See if you can detect when the influence of a publicist may have entered into the proceedings.

Watch for these features:

- Quotes from "spokespersons"
- Detailed statistics and interpretation
- Polls and surveys
- Information about place and time of an upcoming event
- Links to outside occurrences, such as a movie premiere, a sporting event, or a theme (like, say, Fire Prevention Week)
- Politicians speaking out about innocuous subjects ("crime is bad")
- Op-Ed articles by guest writers from show business, sports, and politics who normally do not write for the media
- Anything at all to do with entertainment

Any of these should trigger a flashing sign in your mind: PUBLICIST AT WORK. Most of us read the paper or watch the news without giving a second thought to the sources. Yes, reporters regularly dig up their own information, but they often rely heavily on spokespersons and publicists for help, and you should begin noticing that influence. You can no longer simply look at the story; you have to see what's behind it.

Let's make a dry run with a hypothetical illustration. Read the following fictitious newspaper article and mark every sentence, phrase, or fact you sense may have originated with a publicist. Then check the next page to see if you hit them all.

City Council to Rule on Oak Tree Preserve Near Hillside Park

(City Hall): City Council President Ron Preston announced yesterday that the Council will meet next week to determine the future of a centuries-old grove of oak trees outside Hillside Park where developers seek to build a shopping mall. It is also the location of the annual Spring Bazaar, which brings crafts merchants from across the country to the area.

"I've always sought a balance between protecting the environment and the need to create jobs," said Preston. "In this case, the Council has to make a tough call."

Dora Hutchins, director of Save the Oaks, urged the City Council to rule in favor of the trees. "The area around Hillside has been ravaged by developers for decades now. It's time for the city to take a stand and just say no to developers."

Equally vocal has been Jack Larsen, president of the Halo Corporation, which last year acquired leases to the disputed property.

"Our environmental impact study showed Halo's proposal will not adversely affect the area," said Larsen.

"The Oakdale Galleria will revitalize the economy, creating 700 jobs while preserving the natural beauty of Hillside."

Councilwoman Jane Rogers, an outspoken slow-growth advocate, refuted Larsen's claims. Said Rogers, "He knows perfectly well his development will increase traffic, crime, and pollution in Hillside by 65 percent, as well as destroy forever one of the park's crown jewels, the ancient stand of oaks."

The matter was further complicated this week when several bulldozers arrived at the site to remove the trees. A dozen protesters from Save the Oaks handcuffed themselves to the machinery, and were arrested only after hours of tedious sawing of the handcuffs.

Said Hutchins, "We felt we had a right to commit civil disobedience."

Al Rojas of the Spring Bazaar issued his own comment on the controversy. "We hope to stage the Bazaar next May at Hillside, but if not, we will find a new location."

Said Buck Nelson, 14, a regular hiker at Hillside, "I like the trees, but a mall would be radical too. Either way, it's okay with me."

The matter will be resolved once and for all at next week's Council meeting, which is expected to be extremely contentious.

Now let's look at the story more closely. Both politicians have their own press secretaries, who keep their bosses' competing

career interests uppermost on their agendas. Both the developer and the environmentalist employ publicists to issue press
releases, gather statistics, solicit stories from the media, and
cook up ideas like handcuffing protesters to bulldozers. Even
the Spring Bazaar sought to keep itself in the public eye with a
spokesman of its own. The only entity in the story who wasn't
looking for publicity was the fourteen-year-old kid, and maybe
he ought to consider it.

Now scan a few real articles and see what you come up with.
Try it again with your local TV news. You'll see the same forces
at work. There's a lot of time and/or space to fill; something or
someone's got to fill it. It might as well be you!

Tips & Traps

- *The media assume the public is easily bored.* By the time of the
  last *Apollo* lunar mission, the astronauts had to play a game
  of moon-golf to keep earthbound TV audiences tuned in.
  The media's primary goal is to elicit attention. Clue into
  that.
- In Guerrilla P.R., strategies are built on expediency and
  efficacy. *Making an immediate impact is paramount.* Remember: there are two speeds in modern P.R.——fast, and
  dead.
- *Keep up with the news.* Following current events is the responsibility of every aware citizen. Additionally, in Guerrilla P.R. you need to keep pace with the shifting winds of
  culture. Knowing what's hip, happening, and trendy gives
  you more credibility when you design your campaign.
  Sounding like last week's news is the best way to make no
  impact whatsoever.

- *Money does not talk when it comes to P.R.* What matters is the idea and the presentation, neither of which need cost much.
- *A Guerrilla publicist is not intimidated by media.* You must apply a certain amount of pressure on the media, or you will not be heard.
- *You don't have to be great.* It's sad but true: we live a mediocre world, where good is great, and competent is terrific. Be a little better than good, and the world will open its arms to you!

Taking Inventory

In order to be irreplaceable, one must always be different.

—Coco Chanel

I'm surprised how often people believe themselves to be unimportant. Perhaps it's a consequence of our mass society that individuals downplay their own ability to affect the world. To those who wonder whether they make a difference, here's a helpful parable: According to an M.I.T. meteorologist, mathematical models suggest that the beating of a butterfly's wings in Brazil could eventually exert enough influence on natural forces to cause a tornado in Texas. You may think of yourself as a tiny butterfly, but remember, you matter.

What you do has profound repercussions on those around you. This holds true in every area of life, personal and professional. To succeed at Guerrilla P.R., you must *retain a healthy and positive sense of self-importance.* Whether what you do is "important" or not, you will never convince others it is unless you yourself believe it. If you own a balloon store, you'd better believe you not only sell the best balloons in town, but that without them, life as we know it would cease.

I once heard a story about a mattress manufacturer who sought help from a respected P.R. man. At their first meeting, the publicist asked, "What do you sell?" The bedmaker replied, "Why, I sell mattresses, of course." Shaking his head, the other retorted, "No, you don't. You sell sweet dreams and good sex."

It's all about accentuating the positive, showing people the *benefit to them* of what you're offering. You don't sell beds; you sell sweet dreams and good sex. Everybody wants those things. You don't sell life insurance—*nobody* wants that. You sell security for one's family. You don't sell a new car; you sell the freedom to roam the highways and explore the nation.

The Guerrilla publicist always sees his mission in a wider context.

There's a popular bumper sticker that reads "Think globally, act locally." That's the attitude behind Guerrilla P.R.

I've made my position clear on the concept of perception as reality, but that does not excuse you from delivering substance. Ultimately, face value has no value unless it's backed by something real. The first step toward image expansion, toward real depth, begins with self-inventory. You must assess your strengths and weaknesses, your skills, and, most important, your uniqueness.

Uniqueness. Singularity. Distinction. These words must form your Guerrilla P.R. mantra. Nothing I ask of you will be as challenging as defining yourself and your product in wholly exclusive—and beneficial—terms. What's special about your upcoming church carnival? What's different about your nightclub act? Why should I buy your doughnuts and not the guy's down the street? What are you offering that people want? To put it bluntly, who the hell do you think you are?

This is not meant to antagonize. Self-examination should invigorate. But let's go about it in an orderly fashion. Start by answering the following questions (I use the word "product" generically to include every possible project one might seek to publicize). Write down your answers, and then compare them with my subsequent analysis.

A G.P.R. Top-Ten Self-Inventory Questionnaire

1. What attributes of your product are distinct from those of your competitors? In other words, what do you have that people want?
2. Why should potential customers choose your product?
3. Precisely who constitutes your targeted market?
4. What makes you personally qualified to launch this product?
5. List five reasons why your product *cannot* fail.
6. List five reasons why, despite your best efforts, your product probably will fail. (See it from the other guy's viewpoint.)
7. What three traits do other people find most attractive about your personality?
8. What three personality flaws most often hamper your success with others?
9. Complete the following sentence: "I am at my best when I _____."
10. On a 1–10 scale, rate your abilities on the phone, on paper, and face-to-face (1 equals "Complete Dweeb," 5

equals "Not So Bad," and 10 equals "I Should Have My Own Talk Show").

Self-Inventory Analysis

Question #1: As is commonly believed, the media are indeed hungry for stories—but not just any stories. *To be newsworthy, a subject must have some distinctive quality.* Journalists sniff out what's different, not what's the same. Your aim is to dovetail with that thinking.

Ask yourself what separates your product from others. Is there something special about you or about the people who work with you? Anything unusual about your background? Does your product offer features not seen before? Do you provide novel services to your customers? Direct your energies toward originality and creativity.

Those strains of uniqueness ultimately become the melody of your Guerrilla P.R. campaign.

Question #2: This may sound like a marketing question, but it bears directly on your P.R. efforts. You need to crawl into the collective mind of the people you target and see things as they do. If you own a gardening service, what would your customers appreciate? How about a free health checkup on the backyard trees? Now you have something creative and desirable for customers that separates you from other gardeners. Potential customers would choose you because you offer more than just a manicured lawn. And that's something you can publicize.

Question #3: If you know whom you want to reach, it's easy to select your media targets. But first you must decide whom you're going after. If you've just opened an All-You-Can-Eat Wine &

Tapas restaurant, then your customers likely will be young, afflu-
ent, and educated. From there, it's a matter of cross-referencing
the media outlets that appeal to such demographics.

Question #4: Why YOU? This is important because the media will ask you the same thing. As a Guerrilla you are your
product, and if you look bad, so does your product. There's no
hiding behind a corporate apron. Qualifications go hand in hand
with an attractive media-ready personality. If that doesn't sound
like you, don't worry. We'll fix it later. There's nothing about
you that isn't fixable with Guerrilla P.R. (See how I'm pointing
out a benefit to you through using my system?)

Question #5: I ask this because you need to get psyched up.
If you present an original idea to the media, they will look for
a hundred ways to shoot you down. It's vital you have a pre-
planned strategy to quell their native skepticism. Determine
here, in realistic but positive terms, why yours is the product
to beat.

Question #6: This question isn't meant to depress you. It's
just a means of anticipating the slings and arrows of outrageous
media. I assume you've already pondered the potential pitfalls
you face in launching your product. Return to that subject and
explore the likelihood of failure. By doing so you'll be thinking
just like an inquiring journalist. Turn the tables by formulating
counter-arguments. You'll be like Perry Mason: you can't lose!

Question #7: If you have a warm and inviting charm about
you, then much of your battle is won. If you're less than warm
and charming, but have a sharp sense of humor, that's a viable
strong point. Perhaps you aren't the most articulate individual
but you have a doggedly determined personality. List that. High-
light your strengths, because your Guerrilla P.R. campaign will
be molded around them.

Question #8: Similarly, it's critical to take an objective look at your weaknesses so that they can be either turned into strengths or shoved so deep in the closet that they won't have any impact. Of course, it's preferable to transform weaknesses into solid personality assets. Not only does it make you a healthier, happier person, but it adds more ammo to your Guerrilla P.R. arsenal.

Question #9: Close your eyes before you answer this question. Picture yourself operating on all eight cylinders, where nothing and nobody can stop you. You know that feeling of peak performance? That's the state of mind you want while implementing your Guerrilla P.R. campaign. Describe the conditions when you're functioning with optimum effectiveness. Once you spell it out, you can take steps to create that climate every day.

Question #10: This is a question of simple self-examination. It's like Mr. Universe eyeing his reflection in a floor-length mirror and saying to himself, "My biceps need a little more mass here, my deltoids a little more there." It's essential to maximize the basic skills of writing and speaking, so you can do the job right. Without a certain ability on both fronts, pulling off a successful P.R. effort will be difficult. Answer this question honestly, and then we'll work on ways to improve on both.

Now, take a look at your answers and see if a picture emerges. Do you see patterns of enthusiasm and inventiveness? Are the obstacles before you as formidable as you feared earlier? Have you gotten the sense that a P.R. campaign is more feasible than you once thought? I suspect that after completing this survey you're feeling surprisingly good about your chances.

Only You

Let's focus a little longer on the uniqueness factor. It's impossible to overstress its importance. Human beings are not worker ants. Our individuality is what makes each of us irreplaceable. The Talmud says, "If a person saves one life, it is as if he has saved the whole world." We would do well to develop a similar point of view in our business lives. It's certainly part of Guerrilla P.R. doctrine.

I encourage you to look long and hard at yourself and your project. Elevate those elements distinguishing you from all others. Don't hesitate to create some after the fact. When Shari Seligman started an L.A. mobile pet-grooming service, she became just one of many similar entrepreneurs. But how many of her competitors thought to place a gigantic wagging dog's tail on the rear of their vans? Because of her inventive spirit, Ms. Seligman and her van became the stars of a national soft drink commercial. Uniqueness, uniqueness, uniqueness!

What We Have Here Is a Failure to Communicate

There's an old story about the farmer who returns home after listening to a politician on the stump in town. His wife asks him, "Who spoke?" The farmer replies, "The mayor." Wife: "What did he talk about?" Farmer: "He didn't say."

Of the many failings of our national education system, one in particular strikes me as especially puzzling. A young person can ramble along from kindergarten through high school without learning a thing on the subject of communications. Yet, communications is the No. 1 key to success in business.

Most of us learn this lesson too late, struggling for years playing endless catch-up. Some are blessed with an innate gift of communicating, while others study it in college or some other formal setting. Whether or not you have been trained, as a Guerrilla P.R. trooper you're going to have to get in shape as a communicator; otherwise you'll be forced to pay a heavy price.

I've personally known many people who—while they had a measure of talent and a willingness to work hard—have never been able to rise as high in their professions as they would like. I feel certain the one overriding reason was their inability to communicate effectively with coworkers and superiors.

Studies show that TV news anchors rank at or near the top of America's most admired professionals. Most are little more than teleprompter readers, yet they earn sky-high salaries because they are master communicators. I'm not suggesting your ideal role model should be the TV journalist, but you could benefit from adopting many of their tried-and-true techniques, even if you never go before a camera in your life.

The warm steady gaze, the apparent intelligence, the modulated voice, the sturdy posture and self-confidence—these are the components that make anchors so valued in society. Few of these traits come naturally to anyone, especially when they are staring into the lifeless eye of a TV camera. They must be learned, which means anyone can learn them, including you. Incorporating qualities such as these will make you more attractive when you initiate your Guerrilla P.R. campaign. The mysterious qualities that make one person charismatic and likeable, and another less so, have been contemplated by philosophers and businesspeople through the years. Dr. Lillian Glass, in her best-selling book *Say It Right,* identifies Seven Secrets of Great Business Communicators. Here are those secrets:

1. They were confident and unafraid to ask for what they wanted.
2. They appreciated those who helped them.
3. They consistently nurtured relationships.
4. They were tenacious in going around obstacles.
5. They were excellent listeners.
6. They rebounded quickly and completely from rejection.
7. They were friendly and approachable.

These qualities, like all the positive traits I describe, are beneficial not only to the fledgling Guerrilla P.R. master but also to anyone in any walk of life. On the other side of the coin, Dr. Glass describes Five Toxic Communication Personality Styles, all of which you should avoid like the plague:

1. **The Instigator.** One who communicates by trying to make trouble for others, verbally stirring up waters. In P.R., this manifests itself in making subtly destabilizing remarks, and berating those who don't see things your way.
2. **The Accuser.** Hostile and intolerant, this style of practitioner reflects insecurity and self-hatred. One who ravages the competition or makes threatening remarks will get nowhere in P.R.
3. **The Meddler.** An advice giver, often someone in no position to do so. You must approach media people with a measure of deference. Keep your confidence, but remember, they've been around the block a million times. Don't tell them what's best for them.
4. **The Cut-You-Downer.** One who, as Dr. Glass puts it, "will find a cloud in every silver lining." I doubt that anyone

who wants to sell his own project via Guerrilla P.R. would stoop this low, but it's worth noting that chronic gainsaying is about the biggest downer I know of.

5. **The Back-Stabber.** This is communication by sabotage. Obviously, if you stick it to someone, they're going to try to stick you right back. Common sense dictates common courtesy.

Another highly regarded theorist, speech expert Bert Decker, in his book *You've Got to Be Believed to Be Heard,* describes "first-brained communicators" and "new-brained" communicators. The former are those who appeal to the more primal emotion-centered part of our psyches. This is good. Examples of first-brain communicators are Jane Pauley, Oprah Winfrey, and Ronald Reagan. New-brained communicators, such as Michael Dukakis and Walter Mondale, appeal largely to the logic-making and decision-making centers. These two men were among history's biggest losers. We can all learn from their mistakes.

Guerrilla P.R. Exercise

To practice your written and oral communications skills, take a moment to do the following exercises:

1. Recite a passage from a book, newspaper, or magazine into a tape recorder. Then speak extemporaneously on any subject for two minutes. Listen to the cadence of your voice. Is it singsongy, flat, monotone? Be objective in your assessment. Try it again, this time with your own modifications.

2. Tape a few of your telephone conversations. How do you interact with others? Do you interrupt, step on people's words, finish sentences for them? Do you utter nervous

phrases like "ummm" or "you know"? Does your mind wander? Take careful note of your observations. Your telephone persona is of maximum importance.

3. Tape or film a conversation between you and a friend. Are you stiff or fidgety? Do your eyes dart around the room? Do you smile too much? Not enough? Ask your friend for honest feedback on your ability to communicate effectively. Don't rely solely on your own impressions. (We're too hard on ourselves anyway.)

4. Write an essay on your project, thinking of it as your one shot to persuade others of your project's virtues. That's how important the written word is. Much of your campaign will be on paper; and if you free-fall there, your backup chute may not open either. Think in terms of simple construction: a short opening paragraph with a punchy first line, subsequent paragraphs detailing your project's attributes, and a closing summary paragraph that leaves readers curious and excited. Show your essay to as many people as you like, and listen to their criticisms. Rewrite it a few times until you've captured the essence of your endeavor.

Target Practice

Earlier I mentioned the importance of determining precisely who your target audience is. Basically, there are two kinds of "audiences" you may pursue: active and passive. Appealing to each requires slightly different strategies.

An active audience wants to hear what you have to say. Subscribers to political or single-focus publications (e.g., the *Sierra* magazine and the *American Rifleman*), sports magazines (such as *Ski* and *Muscle & Fitness*), and trade publications like *Variety* and *Adweek* constitute an active audience.

They're predisposed to your message because they have a working knowledge of the subject and *have already incorporated aspects of your project into their lives.* If you've designed the world's most comfortable briefs, the readers of *Underwear World* certainly want to know about it.

Conversely, a passive audience isn't looking for anything. John Q. Grump, sipping his morning coffee while flipping through the sports section, isn't necessarily ripe for your message. When he flops in front of the TV, clicker in hand, he isn't necessarily predisposed to hear what you have to say. Yet, he and millions like him are your target. The passive audience is tougher to reach, though hundreds of times larger than the active audience.

In Guerrilla P.R. thinking, *there is no such thing as a mass audience*. Ultimately, you must reach individuals one at a time, which is why this method is effective on both the large and small scales. Keep that in mind: any appeal to your target audience, passive or active, must embody the characteristics used to persuade individuals. *What works for one most likely works for many.*

Use yourself as a barometer. When was the last time someone convinced you of something? What kind of rationale was used? Did it play to your heart or your head? Your emotions or your intellect? Think how often we hear about typhoons in distant lands that kill thousands, yet we usually feel nothing more than a momentary pang of horror. Compare that with well-orchestrated sympathy ploys, played out in the media, such as the frequent stories about the leukemia victim who needs a bone marrow transplant. Our hearts go out to such persons dramatically more than to the nameless victims of the natural disaster. Human nature dictates that we feel for other people one at a time.

Once you dissect your own responses, you'll see quite clearly the tactics used to persuade.

With a passive audience: *Lean toward a personal, more human approach.* When Dr. Jonas Salk invented the polio vaccine, his solicitation to the medical community was geared toward the vaccine's epidemiological applications. When it was sold to the public, all we saw were doe-eyed children and iron lung machines. You too must remember that most people appreciate being addressed on their own level. *Be broad and simple.* Assume that readers or viewers of any particular mass media outlet are far less informed than those of an active audience outlet. Stress rudimentary points and wider connections, rather than microtechnical specifics.

Restrict your use of technical terminology not easily understood by passive consumers. It's not only confusing to throw in a lot of five-dollar words, it also alienates you from your audience, which is obviously dangerous for your project.

With an active audience: *Emphasize the technical.* Active audiences derive pleasure from their possession of particular knowledge. Exploit that by underscoring the more exacting details of your project.

Try a harder sell. Because an active audience is, by definition, more inclined to hear your message, you may present a stronger, more emphatic case. Because you and your target audience are on the same level of understanding, you probably won't be perceived as a flimflammer.

Narrow your focus. Unlike a passive audience, the active audience doesn't require ancillary themes to develop an interest in your project. Astronomers may enjoy reading about newly discovered binary star systems, but down here we just want to know if anyone saw the ghost of Elvis up there cavorting with aliens.

Once you choose between the passive and active audience, you'll be able to tailor your Guerrilla P.R. campaign accordingly.

But remember, you don't communicate with the audience directly. Your message is filtered through the media. The newspaper editor and the radio talk-show producer are your conduits to the audience. Next, we shift our focus toward them, toward the media for whom you will soon be setting traps.

Guerrilla P.R. Marketing Plan Outline

Objective(s):
What do you want to achieve?

Audience(s):
Who can best help you reach that goal?

Definition of product or service:

Message:
Why your audience should want or could benefit from your product or service?
Why are you better than the competition?
What else do you want your audience to know?

Media:
What vehicles should you use to get the message to your audience?

Summary/Results:
How does the delivery of the above message to the targeted audiences via these media achieve your objectives?

Guerrilla P.R. Exercise

1. Consider whether you are targeting a passive or an active audience. Which media outlets serve that audience?
2. Just for fun, ponder switching from active to passive (or vice versa). How would you retool your media outlets? Which would work for you in this new setting? Why would or why wouldn't this plan work?
3. The accompanying Marketing Plan Outline is the standard one we use at my company. Although it takes a slightly different tack, examine it and fill it out.

Target Practice Too

You need not only to target your consumer, but likewise to target your media. But just who are these media folks, anyway? A study I read recently reported that 95 percent of key media personnel are white, 79 percent are male, 46 percent earn over $50,000 a year, 54 percent call themselves liberal, and 50 percent claim no religious affiliation. It certainly sounds like an ivory tower to me.

Actually, I've found reporters, editors, and producers to be an engaging lot overall, naturally curious, and ever on the prowl for good stories. They consider their career a profession, but it most assuredly is not. Professions—that is, medicine, law, and accounting—are challenging fields of discipline and difficult to learn, all requiring state licensing. Ongoing education and recertification are also required just to keep the shingle up.

None of that is true for journalism. Any glib wordsmith with a little luck and persistence can make it on staff or as a freelancer somewhere. Some college experience helps, but even that isn't vital.

Carl Bernstein, of the famous team that broke the Watergate story, joined the *Washington Post* as a cub reporter while still in high school. I'm not denigrating his skills as a reporter. However, I never met a surgeon who got his first job hanging out in front of the operating room looking for an opening in the scrub room.

Although, to be sure, there are some unsavory exceptions, I've found media people to be very much like the rest of us. They have likes and dislikes, as we do, and you can interact with them without worrying about offending their inflated sense of social standing.

Believe me, they don't bite.

However, journalists do possess one useful human quality in abundance: intense skepticism. That old movie stereotype of the cynical, hard-bitten reporter has a basis in fact that lives on today.

Journalists are born doubters. They presume guilt until innocence is proven, and even then . . .

Distrust is vital to their role. Journalists (at least the good ones) are trained to suspect official pronouncements from government officials and other spokespersons. Nobody scoffs like a journalist. They go to great lengths to look beyond the facade of the news and dig up a truer, albeit messier, reality.

That's why they're exceptionally suspicious of publicists. Even though I believe they need us as much as we need them, because we publicists are hired guns, reporters don't often put much stock in our pleas and arguments—at least, not at first. I was told by one entertainment reporter from a large metropolitan paper, "Publicists don't believe in what they're selling. They're just paid pitchmen."

With Guerrilla P.R., that concern doesn't exist. You represent yourself. You believe in your project far more than any "paid pitchman" ever could. What you lack in seasoning, you more than make up for in sincerity.

And that pays off with journalists. They root for underdogs. They listen to "real" people, as opposed to us "unreal" professional publicists. Your very handicap of being unconnected may end up as your biggest asset, because the press will believe in your sincerity more than in mine. And I'm the most sincere person I know.

Above all, remember my Golden Tip regarding members of the media: *They want good stories.* They aren't paid to say "no." They're paid to say "yes" to the right stories. The principal aim of this book is to get them to say "yes" to you.

FROM THE GUERRILLA P.R. FILE

In Woodland Hills, California, one enterprising businessman opened the area's first combination chess club and exercise gym, so patrons might exercise both their bodies and their minds. Though the gym struggled financially for several months, the novelty of its appeal gained widespread attention, including a major spread in the *Los Angeles Times.* Not a bad way to checkmate the competition.

Making a List, Checking It Twice

Your first task as a Guerrilla P.R. recruit is to begin compiling a priceless possession without which you cannot function. It's the heart, the soul, the cosmic center of your P.R. universe. It's your mailing list.

A mailing list is far more than a mere collection of names and addresses. It's your media homing device, your lifeline to the people who can give you the boost your business needs. Having determined your target audience, you must amass a comprehensive list of key names from media and other areas that allows you to mold your campaign.

Don't narrow your names solely to your specific target of the moment. The bigger your list, the greater your options. That doesn't mean you contact everyone on your list each time you send out a press release. You pick and choose who gets what, and block out long-term strategy as you go.

Your list should include not only media but also potentially helpful organization types like chamber of commerce members, colleagues in your industry, government officials, friends and family, and anyone who might be of some help to you. However, in this section I want to concentrate on ways to put together your media list, since the assembly itself may prove to be the most daunting aspect.

Start by dividing your media list into three broad categories—national, local, and specialty—then further break these down by medium: newspapers, magazines, Web sites, blogs, e-mail lists, radio programs, TV shows, etc.

Examples of what sort of outlets should make your list:

National. These include network news organizations like CBS, ABC, CNN, Fox News, and their morning shows; national magazines like *Time, Newsweek, Vanity Fair,* and *People;* national newspapers like *USA Today, Wall Street Journal,* the *Christian Science Monitor,* and the *New York Times;* wire services like AP and Reuters; key syndicated TV shows like *Ellen, Oprah Winfrey, Entertainment Tonight.*

Local. Includes daily newspapers; local TV news and

talk shows; local all-news or talk-radio programs; weekly entertainment guides; local bureaus of the wire services; public access and other local cable TV stations; city magazines, business newsletters, ethnic publications.

Specialty. Magazines, trade publications, and other outlets that relate specifically to your field of interest. If you're a musician, *Billboard, Rolling Stone,* and *Spin* top your list; if you're a chef or restaurateur, then *Gourmet, Bon Appetit,* and the food section of your local paper top yours. Anything that appeals to that narrower active audience you seek would come under this heading.

Compiling the list is like climbing a mountain. It starts out easily enough, but it may soon wear you out. Like most people, journalists don't want to be bothered by unwelcome strangers, so finding comprehensive listings of media outlets isn't simple, although they are available in one fashion or another for a price.

When the first edition of *Guerrilla P.R.* was published, most sources could be found in the local library. On paper. (Books—remember them?) Many compilations, such as *Bacon's Publicity Checker* and *Editor and Publisher Yearly,* are still available in many libraries, perhaps including one near you. If you cannot find them there, you might obtain older outdated editions free of charge from established P.R. firms in your area. Most professionals subscribe and don't need last year's copy once the updated edition arrives, even though most of the info in the old volumes is current.

But today, compared with all other sources of information, the Internet is far more accessible, faster, and in most cases cheaper. Just Googling keywords that might be pertinent to

your business and adding "publications" might get you more titles than you can handle the first day. But other online sources,
like LexisNexis, can be expensive, if somewhat more comprehensive.

Check around. Of course, you could shell out the hefty asking price and buy subscriptions to online versions of the printed
reference materials. It ain't cheap, but it sure does provide every
possible outlet you could possibly want to contact.

If you aren't able to find or afford these directories, roll up
your sleeves and get to work. Your first stop: the local newsstand. Peruse carefully, pen and paper in hand. Write down
the names of every publication you think may be useful to you.
Open the magazines and newspapers, turn to the masthead (the
page that lists the staff), and jot down all key names, titles, snail
mail and e-mail addresses, phone and fax numbers.

Next, head back to the library. Go through the *Readers' Guide*
and other resources that list names of newspapers and periodicals. If you can't locate them, ask the librarian. Start collecting
as many names as you can, and begin shaping your master list.

Assemble your list in a way that's comfortable for you. I
used to use a large alphabetized wheel Rolodex, but now I admit I rely mostly on the address books on my computer and my
BlackBerry. One of my friends puts his information on 3 × 5
inch cards stored in a shoebox. Others keep three-ring note-
books with multiple listings on a page. The operative phrase is
"whatever works." As time goes on, you'll want to update your
list, so it's a good idea to write in pencil.

Remember, your list is a living organism. Don't write down
merely the name, address, and phone number. If you list a TV
station, make sure you include the names of pertinent news
shows and segments, when they air, who hosts them, deadlines,

area of coverage, and any other information that could help you comprehend the nature of the show.

Here's a sample listing:

Bill Gonzo
Anytown News
4444 Main St.
Anytown, CA 90022
213–555–0000

Home improvement columnist
Column runs in Tempo section on Mondays
Deadline for information prior Tuesday
Prefers personal anecdotes from readers

For your list to work, you must find out which newspaper writers gravitate toward what subjects, since many tend to specialize. You do this simply by reading the publications. As I said above, you pick and choose whom to add to your list. Note that there aren't many general field reporters left; most are assigned a beat (e.g., city desk [metro news], business, entertainment, medical, sports, science). If you know who are the reporters for each beat at the outlets you care about, you can then direct your information accordingly, thus saving time and money. That kind of research pays big dividends down the line.

Forewarned is forearmed.

Finally, be sure to keep your list as current as possible. This is the mobile society, remember? Nobody seems to stay put in any one place for long. You'll save a lot of money, time, and paper if you weed out the defunct listings as you go. Your list is like a garden; tend it well.

Michael Levine's Ten Commandments for Dealing with Media

1. Never be boring. Never!
2. Know your subject thoroughly.
3. Know the media you contact. Read the paper; watch the newscast.
4. Cover your bases.
5. Don't just take "yes" for an answer. Follow up; follow through.
6. Never feel satisfied.
7. Always maintain your composure.
8. Think several moves ahead.
9. Be persistent, but move on when you're convinced you're getting nowhere.
10. Remember, this isn't brain surgery. Don't take yourself too seriously (like too many publicists I know). Have fun.

The Art of the Pitch

Before you take on the media, you have to know something about The Pitch. The way you pitch your project can have more bearing on your long-term success or failure with the media than the project's merit itself.

How many times have you gotten in an argument with someone in which you said in a huff, "It's not what you said; it's the way you said it." The same principle applies when you are contemplating your pitch. With the right pitch, you'll get no argument. This is where salesmanship comes in. The term is derived from the old "sales pitch" notion. It requires of you a substantial degree of self-confidence to pull off, but your belief in your own project will help you muster that. It also requires that you become the pursuer.

Remember, as I said, nobody else will care as much as you care. It's your job to aggressively wake people up to the virtues of your project. That's what the pitch is all about.

The information about your project is objective, but your presentation is subjective. When your own subjectivity collides with that of the media, there's plenty of room for confusion, misinterpretation, and disinterest. That's why you must know precisely how to pitch before you make that first phone call or mail a press release.

The Pitch is your *selective oral mechanism for persuasion* (by oral, I mean the words you use and the way you use them). Persuasion *is* the goal: you're trying to convince someone of something, and they might initially be resistant. This isn't a nice casual conversation; it's the Guerrilla P.R. version of a first strike. And there are no second chances with The Pitch. You get it right the first time, or you don't get it at all.

There are several styles of pitching, but all have two principles in common: they appeal *personally* to the individual being contacted, even if he or she is a stranger, and they rely on *logic* to make a case. How you pitch depends on what you're pitching and whom you're pitching to. Time and practice will teach you which style to use.

"Personally" doesn't mean overly familiar or folksy. An overly ingratiating manner gets you nowhere fast. I don't mean you can't exhibit any personality or that you should be unfriendly. I'm saying that the slap-on-the-back, glad-handing "press agent" type of the past doesn't work in today's world. I'm talking about an undertone of humanity in your approach. As my friend Jane

Kaplan, a former staff producer on *Good Morning America,* has told me, "It's a big turnoff to encounter people who sound phony, or too cheery and bright. It's like they've dropped out of Publicity 101."

No matter how impersonal the media seem, they're staffed by real people. Though they sift through hundreds of calls and pieces of mail every day, they invariably respond to what touches their emotions. Reach the *person* in the media, and bingo! you've reached the media.

It's not as if "the media" is just one thing, anyway. Just as there are personality traits that differentiate one person from another and make each one a separate being, each member of the media is a human being. Each one will respond differently to a pitch, based on their needs, their readership, their budget, and their personality. And given the wide range of electronic and print media available—newspapers, magazines, blogs, e-mail alerts, TV, radio, cable outlets, Web sites, and things we haven't thought of yet—each *outlet* has to be considered a separate personality, and each *person* working in the outlet must be catered to separately, as well.

The word "logic" has a cold and calculating connotation to it (blame Mr. Spock), but don't let that prevent you from employing logic when you pitch. Media people need to understand the sense behind anything they're asked to cover, so you have to be sensible. There must be reason along with your rhyme.

Say you own a video rental store (a beleaguered business in these days of Netflix and pay-per-view), and you're cooking up a promotional campaign. Why is that worth a reporter's time? Because surveys show that consumers prefer to rent movies rather than stand in line for them at theaters. And because "cocooning" is the social phenomenon *du jour* (meaning that people are paying attention to gas prices, movie prices, and, well, you name the price, and staying home for their entertainment), your store is the only one responding with free popcorn on Friday and Saturday nights. Something like that will likely cause a journalist to prick up his ears. There must always be a method to your madness. Your pitch simply spells it out.

In all cases, one central overarching guideline in pitching the media (or dealing with anyone in business) is to employ the five F's—to be *fast, fair, factual, frank,* and *friendly.* These concepts speak for themselves, and they go a long way in gaining credibility for your project and in establishing a positive image for yourself as spokesperson.

Fast? I'll remind you: fast, or dead.

Fair? You can't expect journalists, editors, producers, or Web masters to be interested in your story all the time. You have to be able to see their point of view. If six other stores in the area are all offering free popcorn on Friday and Saturday nights, your story isn't unique anymore, and you can't expect even the local weekly to care. Be fair.

Factual? Lying is really, really a bad idea, mostly because they'll find you out. And then you'll never get another item in that outlet for as long as they remember you, which will be forever.

"Frank" goes along with "factual." Reporters know when a story is all hype and no substance. Be honest with them. "My business is really in trouble, and this is what I'm trying to do to save it." It might not work in the short term, but it'll earn you points that will pay off in the future.

Friendly? Sure. But not so friendly that it's creepy. You're representing yourself and your business every time you contact a member of the media. It's best that they think of you in positive terms.

This ties in to an idea I have that we are all ambassadors: when we talk, write, e-mail or in any way contact another person, particularly one with whom we are unacquainted, we are ambassadors. We represent various segments of the population: by gender, by race, or by appearance, in any number of ways. When you contact the media as a representative of your business or project, you are the *face* of that project; the only one the reporter or producer can use to identify it. If you consider yourself an ambassador, someone whose job description includes the idea of making a good impression so as to better represent the larger entity, you will be taking a very big step toward being a star of Guerrilla P.R.

Now, try your pitch with the ambassador concept in mind, and appeal to sentiment. Keep uppermost in your mind the *underlying emotional component* to give your pitch sharpness and direction. Equally essential, you must steer your appeal toward one central message and remain consistent, at least in your first volley of pitching. If you say too much, or mix in multiple pitches, you diffuse your goal. You must give the media a pitch they can hit. Otherwise, everybody strikes out.

You do not have to use the same pitch to all media. One size does *not* fit all. When contacting a consumer magazine, put a consumer-oriented spin on your pitch. If it's a trade magazine, shape your appeal in a more technical fashion. But most important, always put yourself in the shoes of the person you're pitching to. Ask yourself what she's looking for, what he needs or wants. Generous empathy will take you far in Guerrilla P.R.

Some of the most common pitch styles are these:

- **Fastball.** Direct, straight, factual. This is best used when you really have a unique and interesting story to tell, and can tell it with little embellishment (the Guerrilla P.R.

idea of heaven). The fastball is most effective with national media. They're usually so busy they have little time to sift through ancillary material. Remain polite and informative, but keep your focus on the basics of your message and the rationale for media coverage. Don't offer extraneous details unless the person asks for them. What follows is a sample transcript. Don't start out a cold call like this—I'm only trying to impart a general approach. The same "feeling" can be imparted in a letter as well.

"Hello, is this the news editor of the Daily Star*? Hello, Mr. Smith, my name is John Jones. I hope you aren't on deadline. Do you have a moment? Great, thank you. I'm calling regarding the upcoming carnival for the Mid-Valley Youth Center. Perhaps you saw the press release I sent a few days ago. I wanted to see if the* Star *would be interested in running a story on the carnival in advance of the event. Why should the paper do a story? Because our community's youth would easily fall prey to the scourges of society were it not for places like the Center. Because we have top stars from the sports and entertainment worlds coming down to lend a hand. The* Star *is known for its supportive coverage of community events. As you know, the Center could be shut down if we don't meet our financial goals. Perhaps you'd like to talk with some of our kids and learn firsthand how beneficial the center has been . . ."*

- **Curveball.** This approach appeals to the media's innate curiosity. Whereas a fastball stresses logic over emotion, the curveball stresses emotion over logic. This works especially well when you know something about the journalist contacted and the kind of stories he or she tends to do. You tie in other elements and paint a broader picture with the curveball. A sample fictitious transcript:

"Jenny James of the Weekly*? Hi, Jenny, this is John Jones, and I wanted
to talk to you about the Mid-Valley Youth Center carnival next month. You
know, I think it would make a sensational story if the* Weekly *ran a story
on the carnival the week of the event. That piece you did on unwed mothers
last week was very powerful, and our Center is geared directly at kids just
like those you wrote about. Most of our kids come from tough backgrounds,
broken homes, drugs. We've been able to give them a sense of purpose and
direction. The Center has been a positive influence in the community, and
I'd love to have the participation of you and the* Weekly *..."*

- **Screwball.** Humor can often be effective, and with this
  style, it's emphasized. Appeal to the journalist's height-
  ened sense of the unusual. Stunts, sideshows, ancillary
  themes are put to work here.

  A sample transcript:

*"Is this Mr. Williams at Channel 6? Hi, I'm John Jones, and I'm calling
regarding the upcoming Mid-Valley Youth Center carnival. Did you realize that we now have three bands set to perform, each one made up of
former gang members, kids who have straightened out since they joined
the center? Also, I just learned two members of the City Council will
attend, dressed as clowns. I don't want to say which ones. We have a lot
more surprises in store, and I'm wondering whether Channel 6 would
like to do a story on the carnival . . . ?"*

- **Split-fingered Knuckle Curve.** Naaah, I'm not going to take
  this baseball analogy any further.

As you can see, there are myriad ways one can approach the
same basic information. In Guerrilla P.R., you need to be prepared to attempt any one of them as the need arises.

Tips & Traps

- No matter how you pitch the media, please remember the five F's: always be *fast, fair, factual, frank*, and *friendly*.
- Don't be intimidated as you design your pitch. The fact is that nobody will come to you at first. You must be the aggressor, or you will not be heard.
- If you are unduly nervous, turn it around: make your vulnerability an asset. There's no rule that says you must come across as a slick, polished professional. Openness, honesty, and a down-to-earth approach *will* work for you.
- Whether writing or speaking, your objective is to be understood. It's of little use to try to impress others of your great intellect if they can't comprehend what you're saying. As I've said, avoid technical jargon unless you're certain the other person is qualified to understand it. Use vocabulary people are comfortable with. The smartest people I know speak simply and plainly.
- Another excellent piece of advice from Dr. Lillian Glass: Good communication is a give-and-take proposition. Don't think of your pitch as a short speech, after which you get a thumbs-up or a thumbs-down.

When you contact media people, or anyone in business, expect dialogue, negotiation, questions, and answers. Recapture the spirit of conversation. Remember, "con" is the Latin word for "with."

Guerrilla P.R. Exercise

Complete the following to gain practice in thinking logically and personally:

1. You're the director of a local youth center, and have decided to stage a carnival to raise money for new equipment. Briefly list three distinct reasons why this event is necessary—not good, not beneficial, but *necessary*. For each of those three, spin off three other contributing factors, and so on. Carry it as far as you can, so that your final sheet resembles a pyramid-shaped organizational chart. You will see that every point has three substantiating bases, and each of those has three other bases. Of course, when you pitch the media on your own project, you won't inundate them with hundreds of "reasons," but you will have developed an unshakable foundation for your argument.

2. Let's keep the same example of the youth center carnival. As I mentioned, when you make a personal appeal, you tug on human emotions. Take the following sentiments—excitement, sympathy, and joy—then write a brief paragraph making a case for the carnival centering on each of those emotions. For example, if the emotion is, say, fear, the paragraph might read like this:

Without the Mid-Valley Youth Center, hundreds of teens would have nowhere to go after school. Many would turn to drugs and gangs without the positive influence of the center and its staff, and our streets would become more dangerous than ever. Next month's carnival will go a long way in raising desperately needed funds for new equipment.

A successful carnival means our kids won't have to turn to the streets.

Tracking

Before firing up your Guerrilla P.R. campaign, you have one last bit of essential paperwork to take care of: a tracking system.

Every publicist has his or her own method for assessing the headway of a campaign, and a tracking sheet is designed to do just that.

Though there is no set format, most publicists generally follow a grid pattern, with one axis listing names of publications and TV and radio stations, and the other a series of columns with answers to questions like "date contacted," "materials sent," "comments," and "results."

Maintain your tracking system religiously over the course of your campaign. You use it to see not only where you are but also where you've been and where you're going. No other document will better assist you in strategic planning. A Guerrilla P.R. tracking sheet is the only way to get a tangible picture of your progress. It's really like an X-ray of your campaign, and with it you can diagnose what's going wrong (if it is) without relying strictly on abstract feelings or opinions.

Let's say you've prepared a press release. On your tracking sheet list the media outlets you've sent it to, and when. A few days later you call the newspapers and TV stations to gauge their reaction. You should note the name of the person you spoke with. Distill his or her comments into a brief sentence or two on your tracking sheet. If the media contact wants additional material, ship it out, noting on the sheet what you sent, and when.

You can see that by maintaining a thorough log like this, you will always know exactly where you stand with any media target. You can refresh their memories, and remain a step ahead. On the following page, I offer a sample of a tracking sheet I've used, but by all means feel free to devise one that works for you. As long as you have a tracking sheet form in place before you make that first call or lick that first stamp, you'll be in good shape.

Guerrilla P.R. Tracking Sheet				
Date of Contact	Publication/Outlet	Contact/Phone #	Materials Sent/Date	Comments

GUERRILLA P.R. COMMANDO: Candy Lightner

When her thirteen-year-old daughter, Cari, was killed by a drunk driver, Candy Lightner felt devastated, broken, and angry. But she channeled her fury into forming a revolutionary organization that had an impact on America as few others have. Today we're all familiar with the work Mothers Against Drunk Driving (MADD) has done, but not everyone knows the story of Candy's struggle to get her message heard. She did it through sheer grit and determination; she did it with Guerrilla P.R.

Back in 1980, when Candy first launched MADD, she knew nothing about public relations. But one sympathetic reporter helped Candy organize a press conference to introduce MADD to the public. Though it was not well attended, Candy and her surviving daughter explained the harrowing consequences of drunk driving to the assembled media. A photo of the tearful mother and daughter flashed around the world, and suddenly the agony of death from a D.U.I. had a face and a name: Candy Lightner.

Over the years, Candy has undertaken many successful media crusades to spread her message of fighting drugs, alcohol, depression, and grief. She did it all without ever having to hire a slick P.R. firm. "I visited reporters personally, sat down, and talked with them," she recalls. This dynamic woman used the sheer strength of her character to forge a movement.

Along the way, she also picked up a few useful tricks regarding the media. "I'm convinced if we had hired outside P.R. in the beginning, we wouldn't be where we are today," says Candy. "We worked on gut instinct, not by training, as a P.R. firm would." At that first press conference, seeing the reaction to the photo, Candy comprehended how the media hone in on visuals.

"We hadn't planned scenes of crying," says Candy. "But instinctively we knew the media need something dramatic." In a recent campaign to pass a California bill requiring a five-cent tax on alcohol, Candy sent her daughter to purchase a six-pack with a fake I.D. She then held a press conference—with her daughter sitting behind a small mountain of beer cans she'd bought—illustrating just how easy it had been and how enormous the problem actually was.

"You have to tell a story that will supersede other news," she notes, "because you're in constant competition with other issues."

Despite her flair for the dramatic, Candy also learned when to pull in the reins. "You can't beat an issue to death. You don't call them every time there's a drunk-driving death or every time there's a court case you're unhappy with. Make sure when you do contact the media, it's with something very important. Never cry wolf, or they won't come back."

It's hard to imagine Candy Lightner having enemies, but as with any celebrity, some media people feel they haven't done their job unless they take an axe to society's high and mighty. In Candy's case, one reporter said to her, "Nobody's done a bad story on you, and I think it's time." Candy has since learned to avoid such traps.

"I don't think the media are objective at all," Candy asserts. "They're in this for the money, like everyone else. The press tell me it's a matter of being honest with the public. But I've seen a lot of people get hurt by inaccuracies."

Her criticisms notwithstanding, Candy still credits the media for much of MADD's success. "For whatever reason, they took us on as the cause of the eighties," she says. "Thank God they did, because otherwise most of the auto accidents in this country would still be caused by drunk drivers. It was thanks to the media that public awareness was raised."

Her advice to prospective Guerrilla P.R. Commandos: "First, know your issue, your client, or your business thoroughly. Then, do as much research as possible so you speak intelligently. Next, find an angle that will appeal to the public, because that's what the media will want. Finally, use your gut instinct. You're a person first. What would you like to know? What would catch your eye? Answer that, and you're home free."

A modern heroine who has truly changed the world, Candy Lightner, despite the tragedy in her life, is truly home free.

3

First Maneuvers

In human relations kindness and lies are worth a thousand truths.

—Graham Greene, British author

Who You Gonna Call?

By now, you've pulled together a workable media mailing list. You have a phone, stamps, Internet access, and an overflow of good ideas to promote your project. But hold on! You're not *quite* ready to launch your Guerrilla P.R. campaign. Before you take that first step, I want to divulge one of the secret weapons of your entire effort. It's not a wholly novel concept. Much has been written and said about it before, but not often in terms of public relations. I'm talking about networking, or the making and using of contacts.

It's an ancient custom in Australia that when two aborigines meet on the trail, they must stop and talk. In the course of their conversation, they're required to discover a common relative. If they can do so, that must mean they're friends. If they cannot, it automatically means they are enemies and must fight each other. In several documented cases, the search went on for days. That's primitive networking at its finest. Statisticians have theorized that any one of us is no more than six contact links away from anyone else in the world. However, it's getting those first three that counts. In the course of my career, I've met thousands of people from various walks of life. Some turned out to be little more than sources of small talk at a party, but others have become valuable business contacts, clients, and friends. As you know, my philosophy is grounded in an expectation of opportunity. I find it not only in the media I absorb but also—and most especially—in the people I meet.

Think of the popular (and now officially sanctioned, for charity) game "Six Degrees of Kevin Bacon." Through it, virtually any celebrity in the world of entertainment (and beyond) can be traced to the talented character actor. Come up with a name, trace it to a film credit, and the theory goes that within six plays, you'll find a connection to Kevin Bacon.

Networking is like that. A teacher of mine once said, "Nobody is more than three phone calls away." By that, she meant that if you need advice or information, if it's desperately important for you to contact any person on this planet (with the obvious exceptions of the president of the United States, the pope, and various other extremely well-insulated world leaders), it is possible to do so. So the more people you meet and on whom you make an impression, the easier it will be to access those connections as your business or project progresses.

Gerald Michaelson, writing in *Sales & Marketing Management* magazine, says, "If you desire high quality in your business, you must have a high-quantity network." Seventy percent of top management executives accept new jobs at pay levels higher than their previous posts, largely because of their large networks of highly placed contacts. Networking will aid you not only in your own business but in your Guerrilla P.R. plan as well.

A Guerrilla publicist is a provocateur. She engages people, draws reactions from them, makes them think. The more people within your sphere, the more powerful your message becomes. This is true in all realms of life. Even Jesus's message didn't take on transcendent power until hundreds, then thousands, and finally hundreds of millions of people heard it. Throughout the ages, there have been other enlightened individuals with compelling ideas, but none of them had Saint Paul, the greatest Guerrilla P.R. master in history, to get the word out.

Your story may not be of biblical proportions, but you do need to take it to the people, however large or small your target audience may be. So here are a few suggestions regarding networking, how to increase your own circle of contacts, and how to enhance your presence in the process.

First, you don't have to "join" a network. You already belong to one. I'm referring, of course, to your family, friends, and existing business associates. To increase your network, consider the following:

- Seminars
- School and college acquaintances
- Alumni organizations
- Church, mosque, or synagogue
- Business groups like the Better Business Bureau, Rotary, Chamber of Commerce
- Political parties and organizations
- Hobby clubs

- Family
- Recovery groups

All these may bear fruit, but you should be on the lookout at all times. I've made contacts while camping in the mountains, at concerts, standing in line at the bank and in the grocery store, on airplanes, and even once while paying a parking ticket. I happen to be a fairly gregarious person, and I find meeting new people fun. However, not everyone has such an easy time of it. If that sounds like you, listen up.

To expand your base, above all else you have to be likable. As with any other muscle in your body, your personality also needs to be exercised regularly to stay fit. It would be impossible to calculate how important this is. When getting in the P.R. boxing ring, you fight two battles. One is to sell your product or project; the other is to sell yourself. This isn't news to anyone who has ever read a business magazine or self-help book in the past. But it amazes me how often such simple lessons can be lost on people. So let's take a refresher course.

A friend of mine recently bought a copy of Dale Carnegie's all-time best-selling classic *How to Win Friends and Influence People.* She reported that a few colleagues chuckled when they saw her reading it. "A relic from the past," they called it. "Outdated and meaningless," they said. Those people don't know how wrong they are.

Carnegie's "Six Principles to Make People Like You" resonate as convincingly today as when he published them in 1936. They may seem obvious on the surface; but we all know how infrequently they're put into practice. In brief, they are as follows:

1. "Be genuinely interested in other people."
2. "Smile."
3. "Remember that a person's name is to that person the sweetest and most important sound in any language."
4. "Be a good listener. Encourage others to talk about themselves."
5. "Talk in terms of the other person's interests."
6. "Make the other person feel important—and do it sincerely."

These are the fundamentals that make for good human relations on every scale and in every setting. But of them all, I find the fourth principle to be far and away the single most important. Ralph Waldo Emerson said, "Every man I meet is in some way my superior, and I can learn of him." The best way to be a better person is to be a better listener. Listening is integral to our personal and professional progress. The owner of one small supermarket overheard a customer saying she would like fresh fish. He set up a fish bar on beds of ice, and his seafood sales skyrocketed.

In this era of "time famine," people need to be listened to in a non-distracted manner. God gave us two ears and one mouth— as the expression goes—so He must have wanted us to do twice as much listening as speaking. I encourage you to develop the lost art of Shutting Up.

Other skills breed goodwill for those who practice them. Empathy, the ability to deeply feel where another person is coming from, is indispensable. Once you can see things from another's perspective, not only do you develop compassion and tolerance, but also you will be a better persuader of your own point of view.

Don't forget, optimism is also a big turn-on. The world is so filled with whiners, handwringers, and complainers that if you show even a modest level of enthusiasm you're bound to stand out. Equally important is a sense of humor, not only to your Guerrilla P.R. and business endeavors, but to your life as a whole. Am I mistaken, or are people a lot more serious today than they used to be? When I attend meetings these days, I see too many strained faces.

There's a difference between taking your work seriously and taking yourself seriously. If you lighten up, your network will grow, because others will be attracted by the light.

> What you are . . . thunders so that I cannot hear
> what you say to the contrary.
>
> —Ralph Waldo Emerson

There's one big difference between professional and Guerrilla P.R.: whereas the pro drives around all day in someone else's car, the Guerrilla drives his own. There would be no campaign if not for you, and to leave yourself out of the picture would be to sabotage your efforts. I said in the first pages of this book I wanted you to think like a publicist, and I hope you've begun to do that. Now I want you to start acting like your own client.

You are the best media point person for your project. Nobody else can speak with as much passion, knowledge, and insight. You cannot function merely as a funnel for press releases or act as ticket taker for your own carnival. You must become the focus for the media's attention on your project. You must become their resident expert on whatever it is you do.

That means that anytime, anywhere, when asked to speak

to the media—you're on call. Assume a pocket pager has been surgically attached to your body. That's how accessible you must be. So before I get to the chapters that relate specifically to individual media, let's spend some time preparing to become—to paraphrase Tom Wolfe in *Bonfire of the Vanities*—a Master of the Media Universe.

Does the name Roger Ailes ring a bell? He's the astute media consultant who played a major role in Ronald Reagan's 1984 reelection campaign, now runs Fox News, and is nothing less than a modern-day Dale Carnegie.

Nobody on earth understands media better than Roger. He's taught me a lot, and I'd like to share with you a few of his ideas. Earlier in the book I discussed ways to be a better communicator. But Ailes goes one step further by spelling out the keys to effective communicating with media. As Roger states in his book *You Are the Message,* the four essential components of good media communication are these: be prepared, be comfortable, be committed, and be interesting.

That may sound simplistic, but great ideas are often very simple. Mastering these four is no easy trick. They all take practice. Preparation is obvious. You must be thoroughly knowledgeable about your subject when you engage the media. But, as Ailes puts it, others must feel that you know more about your subject than they do. Facts, figures, and philosophy should come as naturally to you as breathing. Proper preparation requires ongoing study, whatever your field of expertise. Even the violin virtuoso Itzhak Perlman still practices his scales. Granted, he does so while watching the Yankees on TV, but he keeps his edge via continuous preparation.

It's important not only that you feel comfortable yourself but that others feel comfortable with you too. Relaxation is the key.

This isn't a book on stress reduction, but I suggest you acquire skills that promote relaxation. TV, radio, and newspaper interviews can make anyone nervous; yet nervousness is the most counterproductive emotion you can show. It smacks of uncertainty, the kiss of death. Watch the "experts" on TV. They always *seem* to know what they're talking about, even when they don't. So stretch, breathe deeply, roll your head, close your eyes, astrally project to Tibet. Slow yourself down in order to pump yourself up for the media. Making others comfortable with you requires a sparkle, a gentleness, a light touch. This doesn't mean you have to totally rearrange your personality, but try to bring out those aspects of yourself that inspire confidence and familiarity. Humor, listening, and noticing will bond you quickly to your media counterparts.

Noticing is no small point. Paying attention is an enormous part of being successful at publicity. Before you pitch a story to a magazine or newspaper, *read* it. More than once. Before you offer a suggestion to a television program, *watch* it. Several times. Before you try to place an item on a blog or on a Web site, *visit* and *read* it. Editors, producers, and other media gatekeepers make the point over and over again to the edge of monotony: the successful pitches are those that come from people who *understand* the outlet to which they are pitching. Be one of them.

Ailes's third essential is commitment. That's just another word for caring. As a Guerrilla, you already care. It's a matter of putting that caring into action and demonstrating it to the media. Every one of the Commandos profiled in this book exemplifies total commitment. You should model that kind of zeal. Maybe we envy it in others because so few people these days feel passionately about anything. The media never fail to pick up on this.

To be interesting is tricky. On one level, we're all interesting in our own way. But once you go toe-to-toe with the media, we're talking about a performance. I've told you how easily bored the media get! They're like a two-year-old child with a short attention span. You have to keep flashing new toys to get them to keep their eyes on you. Your ability to keep them focused makes the difference between being seen on the front page or being shown the front door. One way to do that is to become conversant in the *zeitgeist,* a German term meaning "spirit of the times." Guerrilla P.R. masters collect phrases, anecdotes, punch lines, quotable quotes, and other *bon mots* to keep the focus on themselves and their message. Remember what I said about gift-wrapping? This is another form of it. Read tastemaker publications like *Vanity Fair, Rolling Stone*, and *GQ.* Watch *Entourage* or *Lost* once in a while. Check out the latest Scorsese film. I don't want you to become sickeningly hip overnight, but there's nothing wrong with clueing in to our culture. In addition, put yourself on a mind-improvement program. Commit to reading several classics of literature each year—and I don't mean the latest Stephen King thriller. Cultivate your aesthetic self. It'll make you more interesting.

America is becoming the land of the TV zombie: illiterate, uneducated, unaware. The trend can be reversed only one person at a time, and I say let it begin with you. Read a novel by Dickens, or plough your way through Plato. Have you ever discovered the joys of Mark Twain or Shakespeare, Steinbeck or Flaubert? Have you been enraptured by the late string quartets of Beethoven, Wagner's *Ring* cycle, or early Billie Holiday? Even if, God forbid, your project never takes off, the benefits of acquainting yourself with the great achievements in culture will stay with you always.

Personal P.R. Power

Now, let's put the pieces together. I've already defined public
relations in both macro and micro terms. Establishing good relations with, say, your coworkers is just as noble a P.R. target as
being profiled by *Time* magazine, if it accomplishes your goals.
I've spent time in this chapter exploring ways to make yourself more P.R. ready, and if you practice and refine these skills,
that's exactly what you'll be, no matter what your aim.

Let's say your initial goal is to rise to the top of the corporate
ladder in your place of work. To do that, you may not necessarily need to pursue the media or widespread public attention.
Your target audience may be no further than your colleagues
down the hall, or your customers who walk through your door.
Before I get into the meat-and-potatoes about press releases,
talent coordinators, and city desk editors, let's explore how to
harness your personal P.R. power to influence just those in your
immediate space.

Personal P.R. invokes the same philosophy as engaging in a
full-blown media campaign: you ultimately appeal to "the public" one person at a time. As writer Sara Nelson wrote in an
article in *Glamour* magazine, "No matter what, people will judge
[others]——so why shouldn't [we] harness and direct that judgment?"

Sara is right on the money. Personal P.R. is a matter of con-
trolling to the greatest extent possible the impression you make
on others immediately around you. More than any other form of
"marketing," this is the one we each have the greatest ability to
steer. Over the years, I've acquired a few skills that have helped
me in this regard, and I believe they can help you as well.

Mark Twain once said, "I could live two weeks on a good

compliment." I abide by this statement. It's in keeping with the Golden Rule and all the other priceless precepts by which civilization has prospered over the years. As I've alluded, personal P.R. success depends on being liked and being perceived as a charismatic, powerful person. If you read the advice of mentors like Dale Carnegie and Roger Ailes, you will have the knowledge necessary to pull this off. But as with any endeavor, theory and practice are often very different.

Let's look at the hypothetical example of the junior executive who wants to move up. The greatest lesson I've learned in business is that the most profitable thing you can do is to be altruistic. Giving begets getting, pure and simple. So beyond the smiles and attentiveness, our junior executive needs to take action. He should accept high-visibility assignments others may not wish to take on, and plunge into his work as though the CEO were personally looking over his shoulder.

The Japanese have put down the American worker as under-motivated, and perhaps in some cases this is true. But, by and large, I don't buy it. I think we do know how to work hard, and while some may feel work can be its own reward, I know it also pays off down the line. Our junior exec should ask peers and coworkers for advice, trade favors with them, or even do favors "on the house," cultivating an image as a team player, not a glory hog.

I have seen many cases where someone in business attempts to become popular at work and ends up coming off like a sycophant, or, in common parlance, a bootlicker. This invariably stems from insincerity. While you engage in self-motivated altruism, you must prove to yourself that you mean what you say and say what you mean. Otherwise you come off like an insincere politician kissing babies.

You develop sincerity by establishing a link between what
you do and say today with what you hope to achieve tomorrow.
Why? Because I believe self-interest is the guiding force of the
human universe, even in cases of extreme compassion, caring,
and giving. Before you accuse me of being selfish and conniv-
ing, think it through. Ultimately, everything we do originates
in self-interest. Even an anonymous donation to charity, with
no apparent ulterior motive, results in a good feeling for the
donor, whose self-interest lies in the satisfaction of doing good.
So, if you recognize that zeal, enthusiasm, and devotion, with
no trace of cynicism and disdain, can help you, can boost you,
can actually redeem you in your career, then you should have no
problem working up a good attitude.

Here's a real-life illustration. A good friend of mine happens
to be a major entertainment business attorney. He's represented
many top stars, brokered scores of million-dollar deals, and established himself as one of the premier litigators in Hollywood.
But he didn't start out that way.

For his first few years out of law school, he bounced around
from job to job, working in a D.A.'s office for a while, and looking for a toehold at a few leading law firms. He knew he was
smart; he knew he was ambitious; yet he couldn't understand
why he was pushing thirty and still hadn't found his niche. Although he had always possessed a fine legal mind, his career
didn't begin to take off until he made a few fundamental changes
in his own personality and outlook.

First, he took the sound advice of legendary football coach
Paul "Bear" Bryant, who once told an interviewer, "I've learned
how to hold a team together until they've finally got one heartbeat. There's just three things I'd ever say: If anything goes bad,
I did it; if anything goes semi-good, then we did it; if anything
goes real good, then you did it."

By deliberately relegating his own seemingly selfish needs to secondary importance, my friend found that his colleagues were more and more frequently coming to him for advice and collaboration. He never came on like a wild tiger bucking for senior partner. He made others around him feel as if *they* ought to be senior partner. In this way he cultivated trust, respect, and affection. His personal public relations benefited immeasurably.

This attitude he applied equally with his clients. Like any good lawyer, he rigorously pursued their legal interests, but he went one step further. His newly developed taste for empathy helped him step into his clients' shoes. He believed he was championing what was right. He accepted only those cases he truly believed in, and thus he became more than mere legal representation for clients: he became their friend in the truest sense. Of course he benefited financially as his career mushroomed, but he could look anyone in the eye and say he prospered while doing what he sincerely believed in.

Now, was self-interest his primary motivator? I'd say so. He wanted material comfort, professional status, the power and ability to bring his dreams to life. But none of this would have happened had he not consciously adopted that unique form of active selflessness that engenders personal P.R. power.

Most of this book teaches you how to work with media. But if your objectives are more narrowly focused, if you simply want to make inroads with those around you, then the principles I've outlined in this chapter are your main link to success.

Tips & Traps

- Show interest in other people and subjects beyond your area of expertise.

- If you're a stranger at a function, go with an acquaintance who knows the people there. He or she can introduce you.
- When you meet people, tell them what you do, find out what they do, and get their phone numbers and addresses.
- Make friends when you don't need them.
- Trying too hard can backfire. Center yourself.
- Keep your temper in check.
- Emulate the Japanese: have business cards made, and give them out like candy on Halloween. People do keep them.
- Don't hype your product too much while meeting people in social settings. You're there to make new contacts.
- When you meet people, ask questions about them rather than hog the conversation. Later on, call or write a brief note to let them know you were pleased to meet them.
- As you increase your network, remember that follow-up is the key.
- Remember to keep in touch: make thank-you notes, announcements, holiday greeting cards, and other notices a regular part of your mailings to your list.
- Always, always, always keep your promises.

GUERRILLA P.R. COMMANDOS:
Bob Columbe and Peter Crescent

In a world where phenomena like movies based on theme-park rides and Paris Hilton (for whatever reason) captivate the media, clearly crazy ideas sometimes turn out wildly successful. Take RALPH (the Royal Association for the Longevity and Preservation of *The Honeymooners*). What began as a simple desire on the part of two college administrators to see their favorite TV show back on the air eventually evolved into a national movement with thousands of members, annual conventions, and enough media attention to make Madonna jealous.

RALPH co-founder Bob Columbe recalls his organization's origins in 1983: *"The Honeymooners* had been off the air in New York for two years, and we figured we'd lobby to bring it back." They wrote and called a local TV station for months, but got no response. "We came up with the name of RALPH to make us sound more official," says Columbe. "But there was no initial plan to take it any further than getting the show on the air."

But it did go a lot further. Once they succeeded in getting *The Honeymooners* back on the air, the news media took note. "Everyone we talked to in the media was a fan of the show," notes Columbe. "They looked for reasons to cover us." The pair would send out press releases via the office fax at C.W. Post College, where they worked. Since *The Honeymooners* had national appeal, their releases were picked up all across the country.

RALPH's biggest break came when Peter and Bob appeared on the *Joe Franklin Show* after they had lobbied for months to get on. In their brief guest shot they reached millions. The membership ranks swelled to many thousands. RALPH grew so big that the founders incorporated. Annual conventions were packed events, and the media flocked to cover anything staged by RALPH.

"We did everything ourselves," says Bob. "We learned to capsulize everything of interest into two or three minutes." Bob also caught on to the benefits of visuals. Both he and Peter wore their official Raccoon uniforms whenever they appeared in public. The two developed a keen sense of what the media liked. When Jackie Gleason donated his original Ralph Kramden bus driver uniform to RALPH, Peter and Bob invited the media to attend the arrival of the package via Federal Express. That morning, Peter and Bob's front lawn was jammed elbow-to-elbow with TV cameras, reporters, photographers, and even satellite dishes.

After five great years, the pair folded the organization because they had accomplished everything they'd set out to do. Jackie Gleason, Art Carney, Audrey Meadows, and Jane Randolph became close friends of theirs, but with Gleason's death, they felt it was time for RALPH to hang it up too.

Throughout the experience, Peter and Bob became wise in the ways of media. "You need to know your market," says Bob. "You also need to be available to media, even when it's inconvenient. Whenever any of them needed something on *The Honeymooners*, they called us." Bob also cites his personal passion as a key. "You can't be enthusiastic about something unless you love it. If someone wanted us to promote *The Brady Bunch*, we'd know what to do, but we wouldn't have the enthusiasm. We were successful because we truly loved the product. We sold our enthusiasm as much as we sold *The Honeymooners*."

Though the dizzying world of media fame has faded for Peter and Bob, they have no regrets, only fond memories. "I have three books of press clips seven inches thick," says Bob. "And I wouldn't trade the experience for anything." To the moon!

4

Plugging In:
Guerrilla P.R. in a Wired World

You can't say civilization don't advance, however,
for in every war they kill you in a new way.

—Will Rogers

It's not the world that's got so much worse,
but the news coverage that's got so much better.

—G. K. Chesterton

The Digital Information Age came just after *Guerrilla P.R.* was published, and it changed everything. No, really.

In the world of public relations, speed was always imperative: you had to get your message out to the world before the world either got the wrong message or (worse) lost interest. So speed was never a secondary concern.

But once Internet access became commonplace, once people became comfortable with e-mail and the instantaneous transmission of information, the world of public relations exploded into zillions of pieces, and there was a publicist flying in every direction. Speed was no longer simply important; it was now a necessity. Without it, there was no point in trying to attract attention to your project at all.

But that's not all that has complicated the process in the past fifteen years. Consider this: when *Guerrilla P.R.* was first published, nobody had ever heard of Fox News, not even the people at Fox. The channel launched in 1996.

In 1993, Ellen DeGeneres was a stand-up comedian about to get her own network sitcom. Movies were being rented on VHS tapes in local video stores. Dan Rather, Tom Brokaw, and Peter Jennings were the anchors of the network newscasts. Johnny Carson had been retired for less than a year.

Things haven't just changed; they've changed at light speed.

In order to get your message to a thousand media outlets in 1993, you'd have had to compile lists on paper, print out (on your dot matrix printer) a thousand mailing labels (or address a thousand envelopes by hand), print out a thousand letters, stuff a thousand envelopes, and use a thousand postage stamps (at 29 cents each) and cart them off to the Post Office, then wait several days, if not weeks, for about ten or fifteen positive responses.

Today, you'll have to amass a thousand names on a list in your online address book, write a killer e-mail, and push a button. Not counting the time it takes to compile the list and write the e-mail, you're looking at roughly a thousandth of a second there. So you can see that things have accelerated a bit.

I've made it a mantra in this book: the two speeds of Guerrilla P.R. are fast, and dead. But sometimes, fast isn't fast enough. You have to be amazingly fast, and that means you need to have a strong technological edge in your planning.

No, that doesn't mean you need to buy the best, most expensive state-of-the-art equipment and hire an entire squad of information technology specialists to run your P.R. plan for you. It *does* mean that you need to be thinking ahead, strategizing as to your e-mail blasts, Web site introduction, and information gathering in order to make a true twenty-first-century Guerrilla P.R. campaign work.

In 1993, it would have been impossible for me to contact 229,000 people (and climbing) every day with up-to-the-minute news updates. I'd have had to buy my own television network, or at least a local station, to reach that many people on such short notice. Today, it's almost too easy. And I don't reach 229,000 random names; they're handpicked, high-powered decision makers in business, politics, and entertainment whom I might not have been able to reach at all before, given the gatekeepers in place fifteen years ago. Now, e-mail addresses aren't always incredibly easy to get, but they are available to those who want to do a little digging.

I have a friend who writes mystery novels and wanted to get a "blurb" (one of those quotes on the back of the book from a famous person who says the book is wonderful) from the well-respected television journalist and producer Linda Ellerbee. He did a little online searching, found her e-mail address, and sent a very well-written e-mail asking Ms. Ellerbee to read his book and decide if she'd like to say something positive about it. Within an hour, he had his response: she would read the book. Weeks later, the blurb arrived (she'd loved the book), and it appeared prominently featured on the cover of the book when it was published.

For Guerrilla P.R. purposes, the Internet is a dream come true. Access to the media has never been more available, and communication with reporters, producers, and influencers couldn't possibly be faster, even if they were in the same room with you. With all that advantage, what could possibly go wrong?

Everything. Those who take technology for granted are doomed to misuse it. If you send too many e-mails in your sincere enthusiasm for your project, you will be thought of as a pest—or worse, a spammer. If you overreach and send e-mails to the wrong people, you'll be discarded as irrelevant and forgotten. If you write a bad letter, you can be thought of as an amateur or a fool.

E-mail is a wonderful tool. But like any tool, it needs to be used properly to be effective. An *e-mail blast* is a good way to make an initial announcement to get people familiar with your product, service, or project. It's a concentrated e-mail sent to a large list of potential clients, but not to the media. An e-mail blast is meant to be more a marketing tool than a P.R. tool. That doesn't mean an enterprising Guerrilla can't use it to advantage.

Compile a mailing list of local and national media persons who might be interested in your announcement. Then, send off the cleanest, most persuasive message you can write (or ask someone else to write one, if your literary skills are a little lacking). Make sure the message is to the point, clear, and compelling. And don't put in a heading that makes it sound too commercial: terms like "buy now" or "product" could very well land you in the spam filter of most of your targeted recipients, and that will do you no good at all.

After the initial announcement, though, an e-mail *newsletter* will be a strong way to keep developments current and your name in the minds of the media you're targeting. But it's extremely important to allow recipients to unsubscribe to your updates at any time, and to be scrupulous about removing a name from the list when it is requested. You don't want to develop a reputation as a pest.

At this point, it probably goes without saying that it's essential for a business or a person seeking attention to have a Web site, and it should be a professionally designed one. Doing it yourself, unless you are a Web whiz, is a very risky proposition, as your site is the first face a reporter will connect with your name. If it looks shabby, cheap, or amateurish, you might not get the phone call you would have gotten otherwise.

Your Web site is the place almost everyone—clients, reporters, producers, and consumers—will look first to get an idea of what you're about. If you are promoting a product or service, those who might have a need for that product or service will look at your Web site before calling you for more information. If a reporter finds your initial e-mail even slightly interesting, the Web site will be the first place the reporter will look before deciding whether or not to invest more time in your story.

A Web site should be easy to navigate, contain clear and understandable information, and be interesting. There's nothing deadlier than a bland, uninteresting Web site. Why even bother to post one if you aren't going to put in the effort to keep your guests engaged?

Have some fun with the site, but don't make it so frivolous that guests won't understand it's about your business or project. Make sure the message—the information you're trying to get across—is imparted. If not, you're inviting people in for a party but forgetting to remind them whose birthday you're celebrating.

GUERRILLA P.R. COMMANDOS:
Daniel Myrick and Eduardo Sanchez

When done extraordinarily well, a Web site can become a story in its own right. When the makers of the ultra-low-budget film *The Blair Witch Project* established their Web site, they made a bold choice—the film was never actually mentioned, at least not in the form it actually took.

The idea was that Daniel Myrick and Eduardo Sanchez would make a horror film for the absurdly low budget of about $35,000—most of which was raised by friends and on the film-makers' credit cards—and then create a mythology around the film that would attract enough of an audience that maybe—just maybe—the filmmakers could expect it to be released on home video.

In 1999, when *The Blair Witch Project* was completed and making the rounds at festivals, Myrick and Sanchez put together a Web site that tied in with the movie and enticed people into finding out more about it.

The film was supposed to be what had been left behind after a group of young film students went into the Maryland woods to investigate the myth of the Blair Witch, a sorceress who sup-posedly didn't take kindly to people encroaching on "her" woods. The film, in documentary style, chronicles the trip and leads to the inevitable not-so-happy ending for the young protagonists, who were supposedly never heard from again.

Myrick and Sanchez, the *real* filmmakers, knew that their film, free of special effects and on-screen gore, would benefit from the audience's belief in the story they told. So their Web site did exactly that: it told the story of the Blair Witch, mentioned the recently "recovered" film of the young students who ventured too far into the woods, and *never pointed out that the whole thing was fictional and the subject of a horror movie soon to be seen at a theater near you.* In fact, when the site was posted, the filmmakers didn't even know whether the film would be available to anyone or not.

When people stumbled onto the Web site, without the knowledge that they were looking at fictional footage shot for an upcoming film, they accepted the information at face value: they *believed* in the Blair Witch. Even when the film was purchased for distribution by a studio, and released with every disclosure that it was in fact a fictional story, some fans continued to believe in the mythology the site was presenting.

By the time the $35,000 film had grossed over $135 million and had become by default the most profitable film ever made, it didn't matter whether you believed in the Blair Witch or not—you certainly *knew* about the film.

With an initial investment that was extremely low (luckily Sanchez had some experience with Web design) and an operating expense of about $40 a month (which would be lower now), the publicity generated by the Guerrilla effort online was without question an unprecedented success.

More *Is* More

Online Guerrilla P.R. is only one aspect of the technological advances that are available to enterprising Commandos. With the advances in satellite technology and the introduction of fiber-optic cable in most areas of the country and the world, it became possible for television consumers to have hundreds more channels—and therefore more media outlets—available to them during the 1990s and 2000s.

That means there are hundreds, if not thousands, more opportunities for enterprising Guerrillas. Television has become at once infinitely more vast, but also infinitely more specific. There weren't always the Travel Channel, the Food Network, Discovery Kids, and a separate network just for reruns of shows baby boomers grew up watching. It wasn't always possible for every town to have its own cable access station that looks slick and professional and probably has a news hole to fill.

In short, Guerrillas didn't always have the choices they

have now. They didn't have the chance to promote a product, service, or project on television or radio *no matter where they lived*.

Scour your area. If you don't have access to every cable station available there, find someone who does. Look over the lineup. See which outlets you can approach with your message. Then add those to your media list, and begin the hunt!

Podcasts and Blogs

It's already being said that blogs are on their way out. When *Guerrilla P.R.* was first published, they had barely been invented, and almost no one had heard of them, let alone started one. That's how fast things are moving these days.

For the time being, though, blogs (Web logs) are still a cheap, effective way to publicize. You can either set one up for yourself or try to get mentioned on blogs run by other people; the more credibility in your industry, the better. Either way, the success of a blog placement will fall somewhere between nothing at all and a mention on *Good Morning America*. It's not a huge home run, but it's a solid single.

What's the power of a blog? Consider this: TMZ.com, a celebrity gossip site that posts short items (i.e., a blog) about entertainers and the famous, broke the famous Mel Gibson drunk-driving episode first, and the story *immediately* became a worldwide topic of conversation. In previous generations, the story would have been reported on television, on radio, in newspapers, or in magazines, but now we're looking to the Web more and more often for news and information than to anywhere else.

As a Guerrilla you can take advantage of that idea. Target your message to appeal to Web users: those who start their day with a look at their favorite blogs and Web sites. Make your message short and to the point, easy to digest and dramatic. Make sure that it's told in as little time as possible, to make it more likely your press release (when it's written) might be quoted verbatim on interested blogs. Then, compile your list of bloggers who are influential in your business or with your clientele.

Start by thinking about the blogs *you* read first. What attracts your attention? Which ones won't you ever miss, and why? Which ones are talked about when colleagues discuss the business? Which ones are most likely to be talked about among your clients?

It's pretty easy to contact a blogger--the vast majority of them have "contact" links on their sites—but some of the bigger, more influential ones are a little less open to the public. It's still not hard to get e-mail addresses on most; just Google (or use any other search engine) them, find links to the site elsewhere, and work your way backward through the chain of command. You'll see: you should have a pretty comprehensive list in very little time.

At that point, you can make contact the same way you would with a newspaper or TV station. Simply e-mail the appropriate person with a pitch. But a pitch for a blog should probably be shorter than a one-page letter (single-spaced) would be; it should be a couple of paragraphs, tops. That way, the blogger in question, trying to decide what to write about today, can see clearly if your news will fit into the format he or she has established. Is this a good fit? If so, you might find your words duplicated exactly on the screen.

The success rate with blogs and Web sites is somewhat higher than with more traditional media, mostly because there are so many more online outlets that more are looking for news to report. So don't hesitate. Make your list and get pitching!

Another avenue is to establish your own blog. This has the obvious advantage of being a non-competitive medium. You can *always* feature news about your project if you wish. It also eliminates the step of pitching the blog and trying to convince the blogger that your message is worthy of mention. It's like owning your own newspaper, radio station, or TV network—but on a somewhat smaller scale, of course.

In this case, the trickier part of the task is attracting readers to your blog. You've already gotten the medium to accept your message—you *are* the medium. Now, you have to ensure that people will read the message and, more than that, make certain that the people you need for your business will make it a *habit* to read your information every day.

One of the ways I've skirted this particular issue with my business is to establish the Levine Breaking News (LBN) e-lert, which I'll discuss shortly. This is an attempt (and I think a pretty successful one) to reach the people I'm trying to reach online, but in a targeted fashion. Sending the news as an e-mail means the people I'm reaching get the message *whether they look for it or not*, because I cut out their responsibility to look for it by delivering it directly. It's fast and efficient, but it also runs the risk of being seen as an annoying e-mail that gets trashed on first sight if I don't deliver the goods. It keeps me on my toes every day, finding news items that my subscribers will find interesting and relevant.

You might try that tactic, or you might be more interested in placing your information with an existing blog. But if you want to start your own blog, it's simple enough: just follow the instructions at Blogspot.com or Typepad.com or one of the many other blog sites, pay the annual fee (which varies), and you can be up and running in no time.

This is advisable for an ongoing business concern or a person who is going to be seeking public attention on a regular basis, like an actor, author, business owner, or candidate for office. But for those who are using Guerrilla P.R. for a onetime event, a finite project and only that, it is not advisable to start a blog of your own. By the time you've established a readership that could help you, your reason for blogging will be past, and you will probably shut down the site. It's counterproductive.

If you are an ongoing concern and decide to start a blog, try it out for a while before you "go live" to the Web. See if you have enough news on a regular (preferably daily) basis to keep the site refreshed and the information current. Once readers start visiting a blog, they want to see something new on a frequent basis, or they'll conclude you've moved on, or aren't a very astute reporter to begin with.

See how you like it. If finding something to write about every day is difficult, think about inviting others to blog with you. Split the responsibility with one or more people who might have interesting things to say that won't negate your message. You don't want to ask someone with whom you violently disagree to share your blog—unless that's the point/counterpoint.

Then, you have to publicize the blog in addition to your business or project. It won't do you any good if you report news daily and nobody is reading it. Join listservs that have interest in your business or area. Mention your blog (but join the discussion as well—nothing annoys list members more than people who are there only to promote themselves) and what is being discussed there. *Include the Web address, so people can find it with one click.*

Also, send out e-mails to your regular list announcing the launch of the blog and explaining what you plan to discuss. Again, include the URL. In fact, make it part of the standard signature you use for *all* e-mails, so anyone who's interested can find your blog very, very easily.

Keep your blog current. Update it as often as you can (as often as you have something new to say). Don't always make it about you; add newsy items that have something to do with your field in general—things that people who read your blog would find enlightening or amusing. And then, there's the concept of links.

If you're blogging about something in your field, you can bet the farm that someone else—a *lot* of someone elses—must be doing the same. You already know about the ones who have made a special mark on the area, the blogs that are must-reads for anyone with an interest similar to yours. You can gain some notoriety and perhaps some credibility by linking your blog to theirs.

There's an etiquette involved here. The first thing to do is to contact the owner of the blog to which you'd like to link (and let's define a *link* here in Internet terms—it would be a line on your blog, probably in the margins—that when clicked would immediately open the other blog or site to which you have established a link). Ask, usually via e-mail, if it would be possible to link to their site, and if the other blogger would be interested in linking to yours.

This helps you in two ways: on your site, it will now be demonstrated that you have a connection to a blog that everyone in your universe knows and respects. That lends you extra credibility in the field.

But perhaps more important is the link that will appear on the other blogger's site. That one, on a page that is well established in your area, not only advertises your connection to this respected blogger but will also increase your traffic on the blog site, meaning you'll get more people to read your blog and perhaps establish a pattern that could become an everyday habit, if your content is good enough.

A *podcast* is audio content that is sent directly to someone's computer, iPod, or Web-equipped cell phone. The purpose is to give those people who desire it information about a particular topic.

It's not a typical Guerrilla P.R. tactic to podcast, but for some businesses and individuals, podcasting can be an effective tool. Consider it if your message meets the following criteria:

1. It can be communicated best through audio, that is, someone *telling* the listener about the project, rather than the consumer *reading* about it.
2. You have access to podcasting software, which is not terribly hard to acquire or use.
3. Your information is something that can be *narrowcasted*, or sent strictly to people who have a special interest in your industry or project.
4. You're a natural performer who can communicate through a microphone, not a stiff who'll sound as if a gun is being held to his head and someone is forcing him to read the copy.
5. Your typical target consumer (the person you're most

interested in reaching) is technologically savvy and will have the proper equipment to receive a podcast, not to mention the interest in receiving the information.

6. You have new information often enough to justify a regularly scheduled podcast.

Perhaps more practical is the idea of getting your message onto an already existing podcast, one that people with an interest in your message already receive. This, obviously, would eliminate the need to set up your own podcast, and the technology that would be required. It would also mean that you could tailor your message to a specific audience and deliver it just once for maximum impact.

If you're Web savvy and enjoy this sort of thing, research the podcasts related to your project. Get to know them well—as with any media outlet, a podcast is best pitched by those who are most familiar with its content—and then e-mail the originator of the podcast. Mention your interest in what they do (say you're a fan), and suggest how your message relates to the topic they cover and how it would help *them* to include a mention at the earliest possible convenience.

Such an e-mail, to a podcaster we'll call Bill Smith, might say something like this:

Dear Bill:

I've been director of the Mid-Valley Youth Center for six years, and as such, I've been extremely impressed with your podcast, "Youth at a Crossroads." I never miss a cast, and admire the way you convey a real sense of

concern without sounding preachy. Your recent
edition, "Midnight B-Ball," was especially
significant to us at the Center, as we've had
such a program in place for two years, and
you nailed it perfectly, our entire staff
agrees. :-)

Here at the Center, we're dealing with
many of the issues you've addressed lately.
We're trying desperately to stay afloat amid
budget cuts while trying to increase, not cut,
services to our local teens, who as you well
know, are very much at risk. We provide a safe
haven, some counseling, and programs that the
kids find a healthy alternative to the cancer
of gangs and drugs on the streets. We're
hosting a carnival very soon to try to offset
some of our costs, but that won't be enough.
You know how difficult it is to get people
interested in a problem when they have so
much on their minds already.

Frankly, I need your help. We're trying to
make up for the budget cuts by raising money
privately through donations, and you reach an
audience that would be especially open to our
message, particularly in our local area. If
you could mention the Center—or the carnival—
in an upcoming podcast, or if you'd like to
interview me on air, it could provide an
enormous lift to our efforts. I know you
must receive a good number of requests, as
yours is probably the most respected cast on

the subject, but our dilemma is real, and
I know the good we do is something we can
demonstrate to your audience.

Thanks for your attention. My e-mail
address is below. Please don't hesitate to
use it, and thanks again for the good work
you do. I want you to know that we in the
field appreciate it.

Sincerely,
John Jones, director
Mid-Valley Youth Center

The e-mail isn't all that different from the kind of pitch letter we'll be examining in Chapter 5. But its directness and less formal tone is more appropriate to this lightning-fast technology. Within seconds of your hitting the "send" button, the podcaster you have targeted will be receiving your request.

I've also made it a point to let the podcaster know that I'm a dedicated fan of the cast. I praise the podcast several times, citing specifics. And I go out of my way to treat the podcaster as someone with great respect in the field, always tempering my information with phrases like "as you know" to emphasize that I'm aware Mr. Smith is up on the issues.

My plea for help is based on the assumption that Mr. Smith will respond to the Center's dilemma as a colleague would—that he already knows about the problems I'm facing, and doesn't need to have them explained. I'm also careful to treat podcasting as a legitimate, accepted medium, and not speak to him any differently than I would a television producer or newspaper editor.

Podcasting, whether you do it yourself or deal with those who do, can be a valuable and effective medium for disseminating your message. Don't overlook it when you're planning your Guerrilla campaign.

Start with the Basics

First, consider your objective: getting people to know about your project and to see it in a positive light. How will you achieve that goal? Will you start by sending every news outlet in the country an e-mail announcing your intentions? Will you put up a killer Web site that will attract attention on its own? Will you contact owners of other influential Web sites in your field to ask for a link to your site or, better yet, a mention on theirs?

One of the tools I use in my business is the Levine Breaking News (LBN) e-lert, an e-mail news update sent daily to 229,000 decision makers and influencers in politics, business, entertainment, and many other fields. Obviously, I began this effort after 1993, when *Guerrilla P.R.* was first published, but I believe it to be one of the most effective strategies my company has ever employed.

The e-lert is delivered via e-mail every morning and contains capsule versions of news stories, some specific business-related content, and the odd commentary, all very brief and all made to be easily understood and digested. Its primary focus is on anything *but* my public relations business; it stays dedicated to the news of the world and the country, not which client I might have signed recently. In fact, Levine Communications Office (LCO) is rarely mentioned by name in the e-lert. It's understood that the company is behind the e-mail, but it is decidedly *not* a "publicity sheet" about the office; instead, the e-lert is a product *of* the office that leads by example.

Maybe you can do something similar. It's probably unlikely that you'd like to compile news stories and condense them for an e-mail tip sheet, but perhaps you could do something that's more industry driven—something that would concentrate on your own industry rather than the world as a whole. But let me warn you now: putting together a daily briefing on *anything* is a great deal of work, and you might find yourself growing weary of the grind after a short while. Consider trying out the process for a few days (or preferably weeks) before you start sending it out to your mailing list, to see if you can fill a decent-sized newsletter daily (or weekly, if that's what you decide to do). Or think about having a member of your staff compile it, and see if the items included really do interest you as a reader. If so, you might have an excellent free source of insider publicity on your hands.

Again, though: It's *essential* that you remove from your e-mail list anyone who requests to be left off. Spammers aren't simply ignored—they're *hated*. Don't come within a mile of being considered one.

Tips & Traps

- Don't design a Web site from a template offered by the Web host. It'll look like everyone else's Web site, and you'll lose any advantage you had.
- Blogs are places where opinions are expressed. If you ex-

press a controversial opinion on your blog, expect there to be some people who disagree.

- Update your Web site frequently. Visitors like to check back to see new information, and you should provide it as soon as possible.
- E-mail is a wonderful thing, quick and easy. Don't let it seduce you into thinking you should overuse it. Think about how you feel when you receive too many e-mails from someone in the course of a week.
- Your Web site shouldn't just be informative—it should be *fun*. Think about contests, questions, and entertainment content that would offset your direct message. People won't keep coming back if they're bored.
- Podcasts are very good for reaching a selected, interested audience. Tailor your message to those "in the know" on your subject, and you can't go wrong with this emerging medium.
- Use two e-mail addresses: one for your personal messages and the other for your business or project. It'll help you differentiate between messages and keep your private communications private.
- Never, in any medium, approach an outlet with which you're not very familiar. If you pitch a podcast, listen to at least three casts before sending an e-mail.
- Most pitching is done by e-mail in these accelerated times. Keep a *current* e-mail list of contacts, and update it immediately when a name or position changes.
- Writing e-mails is certainly less formal than writing business letters, but don't fall into the trap of sounding too familiar with someone you're approaching for the first time. Keep your use of emoticons to a minimum. You can use

less formal language, but never forget this is a business arena. You're not immediately a pal here.

- It's desperately important to be fast, but if anything, it's more important to be accurate. Don't toss off a quick e-mail before you check your facts and make sure you're right.

5

Fanning Out:
Expanding Your Guerrilla P.R. Tools

Writing is easy. All you have to do is cross out the wrong words.

—Mark Twain

Letter Perfect

It's very likely the first shot fired in your Guerrilla P.R. campaign will be via the U.S. mail or, in today's world, e-mail. In either format, before you send out a press release, you may wish to contact some media by letter (and we'll use the word "letter" to mean either a physical note on paper, sent through the U.S. Postal Service, or an e-mail, just for the sake of simplicity). By writing directly to an individual, you are far more likely to hear back from him or her or to get the person on the phone with a follow-up call. Letters are a form of direct one-to-one communication and demand a direct one-to-one response.

In addition, a letter is a great way to introduce yourself and your project. Guerrilla P.R. is a personal system, and a letter personalizes your project in a non-threatening way. Cold phone calls can be intimidating to both parties on the line. Press releases usually get mailed en masse. Letters are much warmer because they ideally go to one particular person. Still, as with everything else, there's a right way and a wrong way to go about letter writing.

If you're one of those people for whom the word "write" causes unutterable distress, here's some advice. The best way to write is just to start writing. Let the words flow like water; get your thoughts on paper without editing yourself. Later you'll switch to a stingier mode, thinking of press releases or letters as Western Union telegrams (remember those?) with each word costing a buck. But for now, pour it on. Believe me, it's easier to edit out then add in, so don't hold back on your first draft.

If you need a more savory analogy, think of writing as making a stew. Start with a full pot, and cook down to richer more concentrated fare. The stew won't be as tasty if you keep your batch small and if you add too many seasonings after you've cooked it, and neither will your writing. So, bearing all that in mind, put on your chef's hat and let's return to your letter.

First, begin by writing to *someone,* not to Dear Sir, Madam, or Editor. If your list is worth more than the paper it's typed on or the kilobytes it takes up on a hard drive, it will contain individual names and job titles. Use them. Second, don't write long letters. Nothing over a page. If you do, you'll lose the attention of the person you're writing to faster than an Olympic sprinter on steroids. Shakespeare said, "Brevity is the soul of wit," and at this point in my life I am unwilling to argue with him.

In any written or printed material you send out, appearance

is important. Use high-quality bond paper here—letterhead if you have it—and *always* type. This book is designed to save you money, but if you don't have a computer at all, it's time to join the rest of the world. Spend the money and get one. You flat-out will *not* be taken seriously by anyone if you handwrite. Here's a sample query letter, followed by analysis:

Mr. Bob Smith
City Editor
The Daily Life
Anytown, CA 90099

Dear Bob:

As director of the Mid-Valley Youth Center, I've seen firsthand the perils kids face today. Drugs, gangs, broken homes, illiteracy, and other social ills threaten the nation's future. Yet, many of these problems can be overcome. I know because I have seen the way out.

At the Center, we help teens who might otherwise be lost to the streets. Our success stories include many now-productive members of society who credit the Center with giving their lives direction.

But we're in trouble. A budget crunch may soon spell the end of the Center. With no government funding, our only hope is public support. I can think of several good news angles: How can a facility doing so much good work be forced to close? How did a middle-class white man like me end up working with inner-city black and Hispanic teens? With our remarkable success rate in getting teens off the streets, what are we doing right that nobody else has yet picked up on?

I hope you'll consider running a piece on the Center. Our upcoming carnival will provide a new infusion of money, but it will take even more

to get the job done. I'd like to tell you more about the carnival, and
I hope you'll take a moment to read the enclosed material about the
Center.

   Looking forward to speaking with you soon.

                                        Regards,

                                        John Jones

As you can see, I wrote "Dear Bob" and not "Dear Mr. Smith."
I tend to address journalists on a first-name basis. It's safer to be
familiar in a letter than in person or on the phone, especially if
you have never contacted the person before. Don't be afraid to
create a climate of friendliness. However, the same caveat is in
order. Not every media person appreciates excessive familiarity
at first. So keep your interpersonal antennae up.

   In the first two paragraphs, I give a thumbnail sketch of my
project and injected a brief description of my role as well. In the
third paragraph, I introduce the conflict, the angle, the central
reason for contacting the media. Remember, they're looking for
a story, so you have to give them one. But don't blatantly tell the
person that you "need publicity." Journalists are not in the publicity business; they're in the news business. So your objective
is to provide news.

   Take it a step further: think from the reporter's point of view.
He or she is given a beat to cover—an area either physical (a
section of the city) or conceptual (youth and/or crime)—and is
charged with the responsibility to find what's news in that area
and report on it. Every day.

   That means there's a lot of legwork to be done, and a lot of
time spent getting to know the people who live or work in that

area. Good reporters aren't in their newsrooms that much—
they're out talking to people about the news. They don't have
time to spend sifting through every piece of mail that comes
across their desk or screen. If you don't grab them in the first
paragraph or two, they'll probably round-file your letter and
move on to the next.

It's not that reporters are mean or callous; it's that they have
a job to do. That's to report the news. If you're not coming to
them with *news*, and not a plea for publicity because you're such
a nice person, they're not going to respond. At all. Ever.

So think about what's the most *newsworthy* aspect of your
story. What will interest the reporter's readers, his or her ultimate constituency? How can you play up that aspect of your
story? Once you've determined that, you'll know what information to feature in the top part of your letter.

In closing, I mention my news item—in this case, the carnival—but I don't overemphasize it. My intention is not to sell
per se but to increase awareness, to prime the media for a press
release later. The letter is a teaser to increase the likelihood the
journalist will respond to my appeal down the line. I also mention "enclosed material." It's a good idea to attach brochures,
previous clips, or some other supporting materials. It gives extra weight to your claims. For a nice personal touch, I often add
in a handwritten postscript. Try it!

Don't go crazy with the enclosed material, however. A large
heavy envelope will set off an alarm in a reporter's head: This
isn't news; this is someone with a product they're trying to sell.
So include some backup material, but not so much that the reporter sees your letter and becomes defensive before opening it.

When e-mailing, don't add attachments to your initial e-mail;
this will often land you in a spam filter. Any smart reporter

won't open an attachment from an unknown person, any more than you would. Computer viruses are even more damaging in a work environment than at home, and a virus in a newsroom could be devastating. So don't expect a reporter to open an attachment; accommodate that preference by not sending one.

With letters, as with nearly everything you send to the media, don't count on everything being read word for word. Most people are too busy to carefully scrutinize all of your written materials. They're looking for the basics, which you have to impart succinctly. If you can crystallize your message, you will have not only grateful media people to deal with but, very possibly, receptive media people as well.

Tips & Traps

- Think in terms of summary. Be brief and to the point, always keeping in mind what a story on your project can do for the media outlet, not what the story can do for you.
- Although you need to be concise, emphasize a few interesting details. After all, the story will come alive via details.
- You need to walk a fine line between offering helpful news angles and writing the story for the reporter or editor, Professional pride comes into play, and editors do not appreciate being instructed on how the story should be written. I suggest you err on the side of brevity and allusion.
- E-mail is tricky: it's easy to become much too informal. Don't make the letter sound like a stiff missive from a boarding school headmaster, but don't get so chummy that the reporter will wonder exactly when it was you two went out drinking together.

- This is a lesson that took me a long time to learn: the best kind of writing, especially in letter form, is to write it as you would say it. Gaudy phrases like "as per your request . . ." or "This serves to inform you . . ." are examples of dark-ages writing, and they do nothing but clutter the page. What I do (and I did it writing this book) is imagine I'm actually speaking to someone when I write.

- Ask yourself as you type, "Is this how I would put it if I were talking to someone?" That's not to say you can't attempt to write well, but if you follow this suggestion, what you write will always be within another's grasp.

FROM THE GUERRILLA P.R. FILE

To show its solidarity with Americans reeling from the recession, Domino's Pizza launched an unusual marketing campaign in 1992. The "Eat Your Rejection Letter" project idea was simple: just bring your employment rejection letter to your nearest Domino's, and get $1 off the price of a pizza. Layoff notices worked too, and you could even show the notice to the delivery man for your credit. Is this a great country, or what?

The Press Release

A *Wall Street Journal* report that explained the paper's editorial philosophy and practices noted that 90 percent of its coverage originates with companies *making their own announcements*. Most of the time, those announcements begin with a press release. As I've said, no matter how we perceive the world, news is—and will always be—what somebody else says it is. If you feel your project is newsworthy, and if you are able to persuade the media to go along with you, then your project *is* news. Period! The press release is the basic vehicle of news, and with it a Guerrilla publicist taps into enormous power.

Many books attempt to teach press release writing, but there is no single absolute approach. I've marveled at elegantly crafted releases from amateur do-it-yourselfers, and I've held my nose reading releases from top corporations, written so poorly as to defy belief. Though there are as many styles of press release as writers, some characteristics are shared by all good releases. The basic format for a physical release (as opposed to one delivered by e-mail) is as follows:

Type your release double-spaced on 8½ × 11 inch paper, preferably white, with 1-inch margins on all sides. Be sure to use only one side of the paper (although two-sided would be more ecologically sound, most editors, unfortunately, don't like this practice).

Some publicists I know use eye-catching colored paper, and a few journalists tell me colored paper can be effective. I find it both hard to read and silly, but you should go with your own taste. If you have a letterhead, use it. In the upper right-hand corner, type FOR IMMEDIATE RELEASE, or, if you prefer to have your release held until a certain date, type, for example, FOR RELEASE SEPTEMBER 15.

Always date your release, either in the upper right-hand corner or below the words FOR IMMEDIATE RELEASE. Some place it at the end of the release in shorthand: 091808 for September 18, 2008. It doesn't matter which style you choose, but it's important to note when material is sent out.

Be sure to include a contact name, a phone number (daytime *and* nighttime; cell phone is not at all a bad idea), and an address. Place it under the date, or turn it into a final one-sentence paragraph at the end. It's best to keep the length to one page, but this isn't always possible. If you have a large amount of information, subdivide it into several shorter pieces, such as a biography of you and/or other principals, a one-page news release, or a history of the project (I'll address this later). The key is to break up your information so it's easier to read and so the media won't feel inundated. If your release ends up being more than one page, do *not* staple the sheets. (In the interests of saving trees, you may want to type your release on 8½ × 14 inch paper, if you have a bit more than a page of material.)

An e-mail version of the release, which is becoming more common every day, would have roughly the same format but would include e-mail addresses and Web sites as contact information along with the snail mail address, phone, cell phone, and contact name. It's hard to gauge exactly how long a page will be in e-mail, so it might not be a bad idea to write the release in a word processing program and then cut and paste it into the e-mail—but make sure your margins are set in a way that will make the e-mail easy to read. People don't like to have to keep changing the margins on an e-mail to read it, and reporters, with very few exceptions, are people.

Keep the message simple and the paragraphs as short as possible: no more than two or three sentences. Try to begin your paragraphs with action-oriented verbs. If you're sending your release to TV and/or radio, phonetically spell out difficult names for easy pronunciation.

If you go longer than a page, use a "slug" or identifying word or phrase at the upper left corner (e.g., MID-VALLEY YOUTH CENTER). Don't hyphenate or carry over a paragraph to the following page.

Errors of fact, spelling, and grammar are *totally unacceptable*.

When I spot these in other releases, fairly or not I tend to write off the entire content. I'm sure that's true for journalists as well. Get it right. *All* of it. If you're not good at finding such errors— and spell check is *not* enough—find someone in your office who is good at it, and let that person proofread everything you send out before you send it out. I can't emphasize enough how off-putting and amateurish typos and spelling and grammatical errors can be.

Where applicable, use bullet points or asterisks, and leave as much white space on your release as possible. An uncluttered page indicates an uncluttered mind. It's easier to read and will make a better impression on reporters.

Finally, at the bottom, type three hash marks— # # # —to signify the end of your release. Don't write "30"—it will counter-productively date you.

Once you are secure with the format, you're then faced with the task of writing coherently and effectively, which is far more important but not as hard as you may think. Remember, your release is designed to entice while at the same time convey a news sense. It's a delicate balance. So observe the following guidelines related to content:

The single most important advice I can give you about press releases, and anything you write, do, or say when it comes to media, is this: Be honest. Do not fabricate information, do not blatantly stretch the truth, do not omit pivotal details. If you do any of the above, you will be caught; you will be vilified and written off by the media. Beware. They know where you live.

You're ostensibly presenting "news," so make sure you include in the first paragraph the Five W's of journalism: who, what, when, where, and why. Nothing else is more vital. Because your release is supposed to be akin to objective news, save the editorializing for your quoted material. That's when you have a chance to voice pointed opinions. Your message should be structured in descending order of importance, i.e., most critical information at or near the top, and the lesser points following.

This concept, known in journalism schools as the Inverted Pyramid, imagines exactly that: a pyramid set on its point, with the wide base now on the top. The theory is that the important juicy information goes at the top of the news item—in your case, the release—and then slightly less important information, then a little less important, and so on, until you eventually run out of news and stop writing. Newspapers are written in this fashion because when the story is placed on the page, if it runs too long, the editor will know to cut the information from the bottom of the story because it is less vital. That's how you should write your release, because it is, for all intents and purposes, a news article.

Use strong action-oriented language and clear sentence structure. Never overestimate an editor's understanding. That doesn't mean you should talk down to people or patronizingly spell out basic information. But make sure your message about the nature of your project is understandable to anyone at any level of education. Someone writing about jetliners should write in language comprehensible to someone unfamiliar with aviation.

Keep in mind that not everyone knows all about your business or your project. Not everyone is familiar with the jargon that is inherent to *every* industry and group. You don't have to explain every word, as you would to a three-year-old, but you shouldn't write to a reporter using the same kind of insider language you would use with a veteran colleague. Reporters who don't understand what you're saying will not be inclined to use your item.

Be careful about hype. We all have a tendency to trumpet

our wares, but the media are cynical and do not warm up to overkill.

Don't claim that your greasy spoon diner has the best burgers in the world. That's best left to the world's burger eaters to decide.

While I'm on the subject of hype, beware of overhype in terms of presentation. My friend Trisha Daniels, at one time a talent booker for *The Maury Povich Show*, told me about a publicist who sent a one-sheet press release in a box the size of a microwave oven; and another who sent his release enclosed with a carton of grapefruit. Both ploys caught her attention, but neither worked. One was a pointless gimmick; the other was a flat-out bribe. Trisha didn't hesitate for a second to send the grapefruit back.

Here's an example of a press release I wrote not too long ago for my own firm. Analysis follows:

FOR IMMEDIATE RELEASE

LCO-Levine Communications Office Wins Bulldog Award
Leading PR Firm Recognized for
Campaign on Behalf of Hollywood Stuntmen

LOS ANGELES, SEPTEMBER 18, 2006—PR firm LCO-Levine Communications Office, Inc., has received the Bronze Award for Arts and Entertainment in the 2006 Bulldog Awards for Excellence in Media Relations and Publicity. LCO's campaign increased Hollywood's awareness of stunt coordinators' important contributions to film and television, a potentially integral step in the stunt community's 15-year battle for the Academy of Motion Picture Arts and Sciences to introduce an Oscar category for stunt coordinators.

The Bulldog Awards are the only PR awards judged solely by journalists, and recognition is a true testament to the expanse of a firm's flair for media relations and publicity. The awards recognize results-driven strategic media campaigns, and award recipients must possess a high level of "creativity, tenacity, and media prowess."

LCO's campaign, which was headed up by LCO president Dawn Miller and vice president Liam Collopy, certainly hit all those notes. Prior to the 2005 Oscar season, their client Stunts Unlimited raised the issue of the Academy's neglect to recognize stunt coordinators as Oscar-worthy. LCO decided to initiate a comprehensive targeted campaign, mobilizing the collective support and endorsement of other stunt organizations. LCO used an aggressive grassroots approach, incorporating an online petition, a joint press release, a *New York Times* exclusive, and an education-building campaign with the media, providing research and supplementary information on the enormous skill and talent required to be a stunt coordinator.

The campaign resulted in 93 million impressions. Some highlights are print coverage in *Variety,* the *Hollywood Reporter,* and the *Los Angeles Times,* and broadcast coverage on the *Today Show, Nightline,* and *BBC News.* LCO also secured endorsements from California governor Arnold Schwarzenegger and Screen Actors Guild president Melissa Gilbert, among others.

About LCO-Levine Communications Office

LCO is a proven entertainment PR firm with more than 23 years of experience delivering outstanding campaigns and results. The firm has three specialty divisions—Entertainment, Literary, and Lifestyle—and is committed to providing Passionate, Focused Results. Visit LCO on the Web at www.LCOonline.com

This release, while mostly about my company, also places one of our clients firmly in the spotlight. As you can see, the headline is short and clipped. I often see headlines with three or more clauses, but that's poor form. Faced with a choice of simplicity or complexity, always choose the former. Headlines should be no more than one clause, leading off with the protagonist. If you're pushing the church chili cook-off, write "First Community Church to Stage Chili Cook-off," or something like that, keeping it short by deleting articles like "the," "a," "an."

Even though the chances of your own headline being used verbatim by the press are virtually nil, your headline has two purposes: to summarize the gist of your story, and to grab the attention of the reader. Notice in the above example I led with the name of my firm. That's important in establishing the protagonist of the release. In describing the content, I cut right to the chase: "wins Bulldog Award." It tells the editor what the release is about and doesn't add unnecessary detail. If they want to know more, they'll read farther down.

The first paragraph paints in broad strokes the essence of the release; the second, third, and fourth paragraphs provide support, with the illustration of the campaign for which we won the award, which is important to the story and helps reiterate the client's cause. The only quotes are from the award, not from anyone in my company. I could have used quotes if I'd chosen to, but in this case, when noting an award the company has won, it's best to keep it simple: just the facts. Quotes aren't always required but can be very effective, both in personalizing the release and for sneaking in subjective commentary that would otherwise be inappropriate in a journalistic setting. Let me hammer this home once again: press releases mimic actual newspaper stories, so you must appear to put forth a modicum of objectivity if you want to gain the interest and respect of journalists. That's why we note that the company won an award, and then discuss the campaign instead of talking about how wonderful we are.

For your opener, distill up to three key points into two or three sentences. Be simple and direct, and present your information like a news story. If you like, use language that captures the flavor of your project, e.g.: "The city's hottest chili chefs battle appetite burnout at First Community Church's Annual Chili Cook-off." This opening paragraph should contain answers to the five W's: who, what, when, where, and why.

In your next paragraphs, introduce supporting information. One way to do this is to pull out strains introduced in the lead, and expand on them. No more than two "strains" per paragraph. "Strains" in my example above are references to the campaign to recognize stunt coordinators at the Oscars, which isn't what the press release is about, but adds a lot of interest and lets us note the success we achieved with it.

If you are the main person involved, quote yourself. Make your quotes cogent, concise, and snappy. Break them up into two sections by pausing at the end of the first clause, as in: "It's a perfect way to make our point," he said. "The Chili Cook-off brings in people who might not know about us so we can help introduce them to our service."

Everything publicists do requires a *framework of veracity*. I couldn't just say "There ought to be a Stunt Coordinator Oscar" without explaining why. Everything you write has to have a reason. You must beware not only dangling modifiers but also dangling contentions.

But what do you have to write about? Are you announcing the

opening of a store? A sensational new kitchen tool? Whatever it is, your main hook is your focus. Ideas for subjects are all around you. If you're not sure you have a real news hook, how about a survey? Concoct a question like that florist who asked his customers whom they'd most like to send a bouquet to. Tally the results and turn them into a release. You can do releases on business predictions. Although prophecy is a dubious activity, the media eat it up.

If you're a retailer of some kind, cook up some poll or series of questions you can ask your customers. Take as large a sample as you can and write a press release on it. It's unscientific, but that would never stop the papers from reporting it. Let your imagination run wild with these surveys.

One of my former clients ran a traffic school. I suggested he conduct a survey on whom his students would most like to bump into on a crowded freeway. His release ran in two local papers. It was an utterly meaningless fluff story, but the press had fun with it, and my client reaped enormous exposure for his school.

How's this for an idea? I often arrange for the mayor's office to declare "So-and-So Day" in L.A. for one of my clients. It's a minor favor the city provides almost any citizen for almost any reason (once we woke up to "Freddy Day" for the latest *Nightmare on Elm Street* movie, honoring a fictional serial killer). You get both the certificate and a good excuse to send out a release.

Once you feel comfortable writing, you can begin to stretch out. No single release may be right for every media outlet. In Guerrilla P.R., flexibility is your strength. If you need to tailor a release for one or more particular targets, by all means do so. Keep the following additional concepts in mind:

Tailor to Audience. Ultimately, you must consider the reader, listener, or viewer of the media outlet you're contacting. Feel free to alter your wording to best suit the targeted audience.

Tailor to Outlet. The needs of TV and print journalism are different (much more on this later). For TV, think visually. Your release should entice TV to videotape. For print, that's not as critical. Some publications are more irreverent than others. Some more newsy. Point your release in the appropriate direction.

Tailor to Location. Geography plays a role, too. If your Guerrilla P.R. plan includes a wider area than your immediate vicinity, shape your words to reflect the interests of the region you're contacting. For example, I don't pitch the media in Birmingham, Alabama, the same way I pitch San Francisco. You need to be sensitive to various community mores.

Guerrilla P.R. Exercise

Okay, I've given you a lot of information. Take a moment to digest it all. Now, it's your turn. Write a press release announcing your project or describing your service. Remember to lead with your most important information, and unveil the rest in *descending* order of importance. (In a newspaper, for example, space may become tight, and they'll need to lop off the last couple of paragraphs of your story.)

Once you're done with your first draft, take a good look at your release. Read it aloud. How does it sound? Does it have a conversational ring? If not, have another go at it. In editing, follow the other Golden Rule: When in doubt, cut it out. There is no piece of writing in existence that couldn't have benefited from the blue pencil. Be merciless. Cut until you can't cut any more. Then cut again. Don't worry. English is the most versatile language on earth. Have fun with it!

Keep in mind the well-known advice to writers: "Murder your darlings." If you've kept something in because you're in love with your own turn of phrase, or because you have a little "in-joke" that you're cleverly including for coworkers or friends, cut them now. Before now. This is a business document, and it must be taken seriously. It will be seen by professionals who have better things to do than admire your amazing writing talent. A press release is about *getting out the information*, not about your creative writing skills.

Tips & Traps

- Timing is important when sending releases. If you are announcing an event, obviously you have to send your release some time in advance. If you are looking only for a mention, ten days should suffice for a daily newspaper, three weeks in advance for a weekly tabloid. Magazines, of course, require longer leads, but they rarely run press releases.

- Since speed is the most important factor in modern communication, get e-mail addresses for as many of your target media as you possibly can. E-mail is fast, it's efficient, and best of all it's free. Use it as much as you can without being obnoxious about it. Nobody will call back if they're so tired of seeing your e-mails that they delete your messages before opening them.

- Try sending releases to arrive on slow news days, like the day after a major holiday, or the odd fifth week of the month (many competing companies send releases regularly on the first, second, third, or fourth week of the month).

- If you're announcing an event, you may provide a summary at the end of your release, i.e., WHO: Mid-Valley Youth Center; WHAT: Annual Carnival; WHERE: Reynolds Park; WHEN: August 3, 12:00 Noon.
- Follow-up is key. Wait one day after you feel the press release has arrived, then make your call (more on phone skills later).
- If your release is picked up, send a thank-you note to the reporter or editor responsible. Build bridges wherever you can.

On the next few pages, I've reproduced several more real press releases that were serviced by my firm on behalf of clients. Each illustrates a different objective, but you will notice that all adhere to the basic rules I outlined.

This first is an example of a straight announcement, with the five W's clearly detailed in the opening paragraph.

FOR IMMEDIATE RELEASE

December 2, 1990
Contact: Michael Levine

LCO–Levine Communications Office Announces Dawn Miller as President & COO
After more than 22 years at the helm, publicist Michael Levine hands over the ropes to trusted partner

LOS ANGELES, NOVEMBER 4, 2005—After more than 22 years at the helm of the company he founded, LCO-Levine Communications

Office, Michael Levine has announced Dawn Miller as the new president & COO of the well-known entertainment P.R. firm.

Miller joined the agency more than three years ago when she relocated from England. Joining as the P.R. director, she quickly transitioned into vice president and executive VP positions and led the company through a successful rebranding initiative that sees the company using the acronym LCO. Other initiatives Miller has already overseen include the launch of a Film division, a TV division, and a Literary department as well as leading the company through one of the fastest growth periods in its history, having more than doubled the number of clients with monthly retainers.

Speaking about the appointment, Levine said: "Over the last three years, I have been extremely impressed with the disciplined, focused management style of Dawn Miller and believe this well-earned promotion has LCO poised for its best years ever."

Of her new position, Miller said: "I am thrilled to be assuming this position and feel proud to be leading LCO. This first three years have been a phenomenal experience, and I look forward with anticipation to even greater years ahead."

Aside from her corporate responsibilities, Miller also personally works with clients who include Peter Guber, Robert Evans, and Jonathan Krane, among others, as well as spearheaded the much covered "Stunt Men Petition the Academy for Oscar Recognition" awareness campaign this past award season.

Utilizing her previous experience in the corporate world, where she worked with Sharp Electronics and Manchester United F.C. Miller has also expanded the company's practice into the corporate and business arena, bringing in corporate communications projects for Tylenol, Promo Only, Louise's Trattoria, Irell & Manella LLP, and Carmichael Training Systems, among others.

Miller's new title of president & COO will be effective immediately. Michael Levine will move into the position of founder, and will be focusing on his publishing projects, which include the much anticipated launch of his seventeenth book "Broken Windows: Broken Business" due out next month with Warner Books (www.brokenwindows.com).

Next is a release designed to affix an impression on the media and public regarding a client. There's no real "news" here, but because it centers on a controversial topic and a well-known figure, this story was readily picked up by the press.

FOR IMMEDIATE RELEASE

MICKEY ROONEY CONDEMNS "CANCER" OF DISCRIMINATION ON U.S. GOLF COURSES, VOWS TO PRESSURE SEGREGATED CLUBS

An avid golfer for over 62 years, legendary entertainer Mickey Rooney has spoken out forcefully against country clubs and golf courses that bar blacks from membership. The issue recently came to light with the controversy surrounding a PGA tournament held at Shoal Creek Country Club in Birmingham, Alabama, a facility that never before admitted blacks.

"Of all the major sports, golf is the test of sportsmanship," said Rooney, who has played on every major course in the world. He added, "There's no place in sports for discrimination. Racism is the cancer of America."

Most major sponsors of the Shoal Creek tournament, e.g., Delta

Airlines, IBM, and Toyota, pulled out of the event. Rooney applauded the move. "The best way to strike back is to hit them where it hurts: in the pocketbook," said the actor. "We have to mount continuous nationwide public pressure to guarantee that this sort of travesty never occurs again." Thanks to the loud public, commercial, and media outcry, Shoal Creek finally changed its policy, and recently admitted its first black member.

As for his personal involvement, Rooney stated, "I will refuse to play on any course that discriminates against minorities. Golf should not be a game just for the privileged few, but should be open to anyone. It's good that this issue has finally come to light so that the sport of golf, and the nation as a whole, can address it properly, and wipe it out."

Here's a tongue-in-cheek release concocted over lunch when my client, comedian Robert Schimmel and I were feeling a little silly. This release is complete fiction, and the media knew it. But they love a good chuckle as much as anyone, and the release got tremendous coverage.

FOR IMMEDIATE RELEASE

ROBERT SCHIMMEL PROVIDES VITAL
NEW INFORMATION FOR U.S. CENSUS

(LOS ANGELES): They advertised on TV and radio, they sent information through the mail, they tried everything, but the U.S. Census Bureau still failed to get nearly a quarter of Americans to respond to this year's Census questionnaire. So, as a public service, comedian

Robert Schimmel has been surveying his audiences recently with census questions of his own. The results are quite surprising:

Eighty-four percent of Schimmel's audience respondents expressed that they would be willing to have oral sex with Mike Tyson for a million dollars. Conversely, the same 84 percent claimed they would pay a million dollars not to have oral sex with former British Prime Minister Margaret Thatcher.

An astonishing 97 percent admitted having erotic fantasies about Robert Schimmel. Only 1 percent of respondents claim to have ever been unfaithful to their spouses.

Ninety-nine percent admit to being pathological liars. Schimmel's audience is split down the middle, 50–50 percent, on whether peace will ever be achieved in the Middle East. Virtually all (100 percent), however, believe the Mideast peace process would move forward if Shamir and Arafat could get together at the Hefner mansion, drink a few mai-tais, and party with Miss May, June, and July in the Grotto.

The most-often reported sex fantasy for women involved rubber sheets, Brian Williams, and reduced calorie Miracle Whip.

The most-often reported sex fantasy for men involved a ménage à trois with Mrs. Fields and Jenny Craig.

Not a single respondent (0 percent) can recall having engaged in sexual intercourse with any member of the Brady Bunch within the past five years.

Bucking conventional wisdom, most people surveyed (87 percent) claimed their favorite musical artists to listen to during lovemaking were not Johnny Mathis or Frank Sinatra, but rather Grand Funk Railroad, Weird Al Yankovic, and Menudo.

Eighty-five percent feel pornography to be a blatant form of sexual exploitation and a severe blight on society, and all felt so strongly against it, they would henceforth restrict their personal use of pornography to absolutely no more than three times a week at the most (not counting holidays).

Sixty-three percent have had affairs with coworkers, employees, and clients, not so much for the romantic thrill but for the tax benefits.

Seventy-five percent believe sex is overrated.

Seventy-five percent believe themselves to be underraters.

Schimmel will present his findings to the U.S. Census Bureau, the National Institutes of Health, the U.N. World Health Organization, and *Penthouse* Forum. He hopes his survey will both foster better understanding between the sexes, and result in a few inexpensive dates.

This next release was fashioned to serve two purposes: it was meant to draw attention to a new service my company was beginning to offer, and also to shine some light on one of our clients, both for the client's benefit and for our own. It's a straight information release, but it has a good number of goals to achieve.

FOR IMMEDIATE RELEASE

LCO–Levine Communications Office Launches Digital Entertainment Division, Announces Online Video Network GoFish as New Client

LOS ANGELES, JUNE 27, 2007—Prominent entertainment PR agency LCO-Levine Communications Office (www.LCOonline. com) has today announced the formation of a specialty Digital Entertainment division that will focus on providing PR services and consultancy to companies who are entering, currently active in, or about to be affected by the emerging new media entertainment world. Signing on to the new division is GoFish (OTCBB: GOFH), one of the Web's leading online video networks and a key online destination for both made-for-Internet original programming and user-generated content. The announcement was made today by LCO's president and COO Dawn Miller.

LCO's Digital Entertainment division will provide clients with an understanding of and connectivity within the entertainment world, building relationships with both industry contacts and the media to pave the way for project development and brand growth. In addition, the company will provide publicity to launch clients' online ventures, handle news announcements for deals, and provide a strategic plan and guidance on how to build the brand within the advertising and business communities, critical to the success of many online ventures.

"We are very focused on the changes facing the entertainment industry and our clients today, and so we recognize a need to provide these additional services. It's our belief that as technology and the entertainment world continue to collide we can provide some important guidance and assistance to those involved," added Dawn Miller.

LCO will provide corporate communications to www.GoFish.com and simultaneously publicize their original made-for-Internet shows including dating show *Seduce a Celeb*, starring Andrew Firestone, Mirelly Taylor, and Hannah Cornett and produced by Scott Sternberg; celebrity parody *Hidden Celebrity Webcam* from renowned producers Howard Gordan, Rob LaZebnick, and John Collier; and *Mixed Martial Arts Today,* starring UFC champion Bas Rutten and providing never-before-seen footage of the training. The company will shortly announce a slate of new shows set to launch in the fall.

Other digital clients the company has represented in the digital entertainment area include www.MsDewey.com, the revolutionary search engine from MSN LiveSearch; www.NationalLampoon.com, the most trafficked humor site on the Web; www.HomeExchange. com, the online travel company featured in Sony's *The Holiday*; and www.PromoOnlympe.com, the music industry's leading digital delivery system from labels to radio broadcasters.

LCO's Digital Entertainment division will be spearheaded by LCO president Dawn Miller, with additional management and development from Account Manager Alastair Duncan. The new division will join the company's existing structure, which includes strengths in Film, Publishing, Talent, and Corporate Entertainment & Leisure.

Notice in that example how the first paragraph, although about our new service, very clearly highlights the client, and how the fourth and fifth paragraphs are about clients, not about us. It's not because we're so altruistic that we don't want to hog all the publicity—it's that the news hook here is about how we've gotten a big-name Web client to launch our digital division, and we want to gain a little respect and newsworthiness in association with them. It also allows the release to talk about aspects of our new service by illustrating them with the types of clients already being served.

The press release will be the bread and butter of your campaign. Unlike unwanted phone calls, poorly attended press conferences, botched publicity stunts, and other potential nightmares, you can't go wrong with a press release. If it's well composed, contains useful or intriguing information, and passes the media test as a legitimate news piece or feature story, you *will* have success. *A press release can never ruffle anyone's feathers. Either the reporter will be hooked or he won't.*

To prove it, I'll close this section with a story about persistence. An author doing his own P.R. for a book he'd just published ardently desired to get a review in an important regional paper. He sent a press release and a copy of the book to the paper's editor, who thought it presumptuous for the author to promote himself. The editor threw the package away. The next month, an identical package arrived on the editor's desk, which was also tossed.

This went on for eighteen months straight. A press release would arrive, and the overworked editor would trash it. Finally, out of sheer exasperation and admiration for his tenacity, the editor met with the writer and found that he loved the man's ideas. A big story ran in the paper, and the author sold a great number of books. If he can hang in there, so can you.

Snap Decision

You furnish the pictures and I'll furnish the war.

—William Randolph Hearst

When Paul "Pee-Wee Herman" Reubens was arrested inside an adult movie theater in Sarasota, Florida, in the summer of 1991, he may have felt his reputation was damaged beyond repair. Not true. It didn't truly suffer until a few days later, when the indelible image of his mug shot blanketed newspapers and TV screens across the country. Nothing said more about Reubens's misfortune at that time than those searing images of his scruffy, forlorn face.

By contrast, think how quickly the underwear-free video of Britney Spears made it onto YouTube.com: it took minutes,

maybe seconds. Pictures aren't just worth a thousand words—
they'll dog you the rest of your life, and they'll be available to
the public pretty much instantly via the Web. Be careful.

At some point during your Guerrilla P.R. campaign, photographs will likely play a part, but you need to understand a few
things about their use before you send them out. Pictures can
become an expensive and wasteful enterprise, and since I want
you to save money, pay close attention.

You can't control pictures you didn't take (or have taken)
yourself. Video that shows up on the Web isn't always your
own; it can be taken on someone's camera phone and uploaded
in a matter of seconds. For our purposes, however, we'll assume you're not an international celebrity and therefore have
no major paparazzi difficulties. Let's decide that you're interested in generating some publicity for yourself, and the media
isn't knocking your door down. Do pictures help? It can't be
overstated: newspapers, Web sites, blogs, and magazines all *love*
pictures, and there are few circumstances under which a decent
image will hurt your chances to gain more coverage. But your
control of the image and the way you present it will be crucial.
So take the right steps:

First of all, if the pictures don't look good, don't send them.

There's nothing more pathetic than a press release with a
fuzzy Polaroid print, out-of-focus black and white, or a 3 × 5
inch color snapshot attached. The media cannot use these. They
serve only to label the sender a rank amateur and assure him of
either a chilly or a disinterested reception when he contacts the
media with a follow-up call.

Photos can tell a story. The one of the late Boris Yeltsin standing
atop a tank during the abortive Soviet coup said everything about
his courage and the Communist collapse. But most often, photos

do not tell a whole story. Their primary use for P.R. purposes is adjunct illustration. If you send a picture to a magazine, there is no guarantee it will run, even if it's a good shot, and even if the magazine runs a piece on your project. Space requirements and editorial taste loom much larger in the decision-making process.

Photography can jack up your costs. So you have to know what pictures offer you in a Guerrilla P.R. campaign. Your photo can do one of several things:

- Make more concrete a hazy news angle.
- Put a face to a name.
- Persuade one publication to run a story, if the photo is granted as an exclusive—that is, for its use alone.
- Reinforce an image in the public mind that advances your P.R. objectives.
- Further legitimize your project with a more elaborate presentation.
- Provide an emotional counterpoint to the story (as Candy Lightner did with her MADD photo).
- Add drama and urgency to a story.
- Help reporters "sell" their story to an editor or producer.
- Emphasize the part of your story you want to feature. A reporter might not use your copy in exactly your fashion, and might put the weight of his take on another aspect of your story, but if you control the image and the media outlet has no other picture, that aspect of your story will be the one that stands out.

How do you determine if your release merits an accompanying photo? Just answer "yes" to either of the following questions:

- Is there a central photographable "object" in your news angle, such as a new invention or product, or a recognizable building such as a restaurant, mall, or corporate office?
- Is your news story about an individual, such as a significant new hiring or the appearance of a performer at a local venue?

If you can answer "yes," then by all means consider sending a photo. If the answer is "no," save your money and forget the pictures. It's not worth the expense because the chances of your photo running are practically nil.

If you've made the decision to send a photo, keep a few things in mind. For one, don't expect to get the picture back. This is generally not a problem with a digital image sent via e-mail, as there is no physical picture to be sent back, and you can continue to distribute it and make as many copies as you need. But with a physical photograph sent in the mail, most news organizations keep massive files, and that's the likely resting place for any material sent to them. If you send a picture of a person or persons, avoid the standard head shot. It's boring. Flip through your local newspaper and study the pictures. You rarely see static head shots. Put some action in your photo. And don't be afraid to use well-composed pictures with atypical angles. Arty no; interesting yes.

Always attach a caption to the picture, but never write directly on your print, either front or back. I type the caption on a separate piece of paper and tape it to the back. Keep your caption brief, describing what is in the shot and who, left to right. As an example:

FOR IMMEDIATE RELEASE

PHOTO CAPTION

John Jones, Director of the Mid-Valley Youth Center, is pictured above with Mayor Jones at the Center's May 5th Spring Carnival, which raised nearly $5,000 to support anti-drug programs. Pictured above from left to right: John Jones, Michael Levine, Mayor Jones, and President Bush.

Another way to help increase the odds that your photo runs is to offer it as an exclusive to one particular news outlet. If you do this, write "EXCLUSIVE TO THE DAILY TIMES" on the caption, and *make sure the editor is aware of the exclusivity.*

Tips & Traps

- Cheap cameras just won't do. Your picture must be taken with a 35 mm camera or a digital camera with at least 2-megapixel definition (higher is recommended). If you don't own one, borrow one.
- Your photo does not have to be in black and white, even in publications that don't use a lot of color—they can shoot it in monotone themselves. Make a good study of the media outlet you're pitching, and determine what kind of pictures that are most likely to be used, based on the photos you see in the current issues. Digitization of images has made it much easier to take multiple shots, preview them

on your computer, choose the one (or two) you think will best represent your story, and then send them. But as with all e-mail attachments, don't expect editors or other media gatekeepers to open them until they know who you are, and establish your legitimacy. No newsroom wants to be infected with a computer virus, and they are extremely careful about such things. You might want to call ahead and inform the editor that a picture is on its way. Ask what format is best for them, and if they have a special e-mail address where images are sent (this is not uncommon). Then, send away.

- Make sure your exclusive shot is distinct from the others.
- It's best to submit 8 × 10 photos, but any size is possible with digital photography. Ask about pixel sizes before sending, if you speak to the editor ahead of time.
- Don't send in "mob shots," i.e., photos of a big crowd. Identifying everyone is difficult, they're uninteresting pictures, and they won't run.
- If you're pitching to a print medium, why not see if they'll shoot the pictures themselves? It guarantees quality and makes it far more likely the newspaper will run the shots. For one thing, the publication then owns the rights to the picture and will be more inclined to use it, having spent the money and time sending a photographer out on a shoot. It's not a great bet, but you have nothing to lose by suggesting.
- In terms of photo quality, especially for a shot you hope to see reprinted in newspapers, make sure the print is not too dark. Sheldon Small, who owns Multiple Photo, a top photography lab in Los Angeles, told me this is one of the most common blunders. Pictures always reproduce

darker, and if your shot is dark to begin with, you're in trouble. So lighten up!

The Perfect Press Kit

A press kit is a package of materials to assist the media in comprehending a story. Whether it's for a movie star, a chic boutique, or the Jerry Lewis Telethon, a press kit distills the important features of a story and makes them clear to the media. As I said before, you often have to do much of the media's work for them, and the press kit is one of the best ways to do that.

It's a common misconception that better press kits are necessarily expensive. That's not true. Good press kits embody two central elements: they tell a clear story about who or what they represent, and they display some originality in their presentation. And that doesn't necessarily mean bells and whistles. It may mean simply that they're well written. If those elements are missing, it won't matter how much was spent—the press kit will stink. Generically, most press kits contain the following (although no single item is required):

- A biography of the principal individual or individuals involved
- A photo of same
- A history of the person, place, or thing described
- Reprints of newspaper clippings, if available
- A timely press release, if applicable

Some publicists add such materials as a quote sheet (a collection of quotes from critics, colleagues, commentators, etc., extolling the virtues of the project), canned features (self-written "articles" suitable for reprint in newspapers and magazines), logos, promotional audiocassettes, vital statistics sheets, and even sample products, such as the little box of raisins I found in one promo giveaway, or the 3-D glasses I found in another. (The most phenomenal I ever saw was the one a major record company sent out to promote a new band. Each kit contained not only lavish printed materials but a microcassette machine with a personalized message to me à la *Mission Impossible*. It must have cost tens of thousands to produce and distribute.)

In a perfect world, where you're the richest person in town, you could afford large quantities of fancy embossed press-kit covers, with inner pockets to hold lavishly produced materials. But you're not the richest person in town, so our aim is to devise good press kits on a Guerrilla budget. It can be done, but as with everything else in Guerrilla P.R., most of the capital required consists of your own imagination. First, let's define terms by breaking down the main components of the kit.

Bio

To write a good biography, you don't need the skills of a Hemingway. Unlike fiction, bios are quite formulaic in structure. If you follow the formula, you can generally produce a serviceable bio. That doesn't mean it's a piece of cake to write—all good writing requires thought and effort—but it does mean you have at your disposal clear guidelines to steer you through.

In some cases you may only want to write a short-form bio, which would be akin to a somewhat expanded version of those brief biographies on the backs of book jackets. This short-form version may prove useful as a paragraph in an initial press release. But when it comes to press kits, you will want to include a more extensive long-form bio.

Here's the formula: No more than three double-spaced pages in length (try to limit it to one page or a page and a half if possible). Don't begin with "Mr. Smith was born in a log cabin in Manhattan." Instead, your lead should encompass the salient features of the person *as they relate to your project.* Make it catchy, but not cute.

The next paragraphs should remain current. Describe recent achievements of your subject, especially those the media will tie to your project. Then insert a transition sentence to segue into the person's history. The next couple of graphs describe highlights of his or her past, leading up to the present. Recap place of birth, interesting aspects of childhood, and how the person entered his or her particular field, and provide a summary of pertinent career achievements. Tell the story narratively but succinctly.

Wrap it up with a brief but upbeat concluding graph, catchy but not cute. Remember, this bio will be read—or more likely scanned—by media people unimpressed by hype. If you're too adulatory, the media will scoff. How can you impartially claim something is great when it's you you're talking about? Let the facts speak for themselves.

The following are two bios I wrote for clients before the original release of *Guerrilla P.R.,* which give a good illustration of the formula.

Jason Scott Lee

As Avik the Eskimo in Miramax's epic film *Map of the Human Heart,* actor JASON SCOTT LEE portrays a simple man grappling with overwhelming change. Ironically, his performance in the film, shot near the North Pole, may soon have Jason himself grappling with change. For with the release of

Map of the Human Heart, the world will discover a major new star in JASON SCOTT LEE.

Although he's landed several significant roles in the last few years, from *Born in East L.A.* to the acclaimed CBS feature *Vestige of Honor,* in which he played a Vietnamese Montanyard warrior, Jason Scott Lee took on the role of his life in *Map of the Human Heart.* Written and directed by Vincent Ward (*The Vigil, The Navigator*),the film spans thirty years in the life of an Eskimo villager and his lifelong love affair with a Cree Indian. The film also stars John Cusack, Patrick Bergin, and *La Femme Nikita*'s Anne Pariaux.

"My character is about sharing, giving, and following his heart," notes Jason. "It may seem naive from a Western point of view, but coming from the Arctic, it makes sense that he lives so far out on the limb in both love and war." That describes Jason himself to a degree, although as a native Hawaiian, life above the Arctic Circle couldn't have been more strange.

"No one would want to vacation there," he says, "but it's one of the most amazing places I've been to. The land is constantly melting and developing. Shooting was quite difficult at times."

Perhaps most memorable for him was a scene in which Jason stood alone atop a twenty-square-foot chunk of ice that started floating out to sea while the cameras rolled. Eventually, Jason was out in the channel in rough frigid water. With his ice raft breaking apart, he was rescued just in time.

Most challenging of all was aging his character from sixteen to forty-five. "I would get up at 3:00 AM to begin the four-hour makeup process," recalls Jason. "I used that time to bring myself to a slower rhythm and prepare." All in all, the making of *Map of the Human Heart* and playing such a demanding role fit right in with Jason's natural sense of adventure and inner exploration.

Raised in Hawaii, Jason Scott Lee grew up playing sports. He was an excellent surfer and gymnast, and for a while delved deeply into Hula, which he found a powerful form of expression. While in high school, he became interested in drama, but didn't study acting until attending college in Orange County, California. There he met acting coach Sal Romeo, then in the process of launching a new theater in Los Angeles. Jason had shown much promise in acting class, and was invited to join the theater.

Not long after moving to L.A. he connected with an agent. Jason successfully won his very first audition for a small comic role in *Born in East L.A.,* the 1986 hit by Cheech Marin. "I play one of the vatos," says Jason.

Later roles included that of a hoverboarder in *Back to the Future Part II,* and the lead in the moving after-school special *American Eyes,* in which Jason played an adopted Korean youth searching for his roots. When time permitted, he also performed on stage at Sal Romeo's Friends & Artists Theater, which he found enormously gratifying.

"If you seek certain truths in acting, it's a never-ending adventure," says Jason about his profession. "It takes on both a spiritual and technical aspect, and teaches you to be honest." As for his approach to a role, Jason has no absolutes. "There is no 'method.' I use anything and everything within my reach," he says. "All the world's a stage."

As for the future, Jason eagerly looks forward to more film work, as well as returning to the theater when time permits. He is a talented artist, and he sketches whenever possible. Writing and directing are other dreams he also expects to realize one day. As for now, he has his hands full nurturing an acting career. Yet he sees a strong parallel in his work as an actor and his larger role as a human being. "By being honest in your life, you can transfer that onto the screen," he notes.

JASON SCOTT LEE: a star of tomorrow with feet firmly planted in today.

Lynn Montgomery

The most common advice to writers is "Write what you know." That's just what Lynn Montgomery did in creating *The Torkelsons,* a Buena Vista production from Michael Jacobs Productions, which premieres this fall on NBC, airing Saturday nights at 8:30 PM. Unlike most half-hour comedies, *The Torkelsons* draws its humor from real-life situations . . . literally. Millicent Torkelson, the matriarch of the Torkelson family (played by Connie Raye), is actually based on Lynn's grandmother, a proud Oklahoman who raised thirteen children.

"Millicent is a real survivor," notes Lynn. "She's in her late thirties, poor, and yet instills in her five kids a genuine joie de vivre." Reflective of Lynn's Southern-influenced sensibility, *The Torkelsons* is very much a character- and language-driven show. If William Faulkner or Tennessee Williams had ventured into the world of the sitcom, they might have come up with something like *The Torkelsons.*

As creator and writer of *The Torkelsons,* Lynn Montgomery crafted a uniquely personal vision of a quiet Southern world. "The show was born out of the folklore from my mother's early life in Oklahoma," says Lynn. "I grew up in Southern California, but spent every summer in Oklahoma on my grandmother's farm."

Though *The Torkelsons* takes place in the present day, the show's humor and characters are timeless. Millicent's fourteen-year-old daughter, Dorothy Jane (played by Olivia Burnett), struggles for independence and understanding. Millicent, whose husband left the family one day, balances loneliness and the pain of abandonment with love for her children and a powerfully positive outlook.

"So much of TV is mean-spirited," observes Lynn. "I hear over and over from people, 'Why isn't TV written for us?'" With *The Torkelsons,* Lynn Montgomery has sought to remedy the situation, bringing to the television screen a large measure of simple human values and gentle humor.

Lynn Montgomery herself shares many of the same values. Born in the L.A. suburb of Ontario, Lynn recognized at a very early age her own gift for storytelling. She grew up in a close and loving family, which supported her creative endeavors. A graduate of U.C.L.A., Lynn worked as a fashion model in Paris for a year before returning to the United States to launch a writing career. After serving as a writer of syndicated radio specials for Westwood One, she began writing screenplays in the early eighties. She sold *In Sorrow, In Secret* to Columbia, *Oklahoma Christmas* for CBS, and *Crucible* for Jon Voigt, yet none of her scripts were produced. Then in 1984 she wrote and produced *Child Abuse: The Day After,* a documentary on the failings of the child protective custody system. It won a local Emmy for Best Documentary that year.

Lynn continued writing short stories, poetry, plays, and scripts, and finally her persistence began to pay off. In 1988 Disney Studios contracted with her to write and develop TV pilots and films after they read *Queen for a Day,* Lynn's screen-play based on her Oklahoma past. Recalls Lynn, "I never had a doubt, from the moment I first wrote it, that this material would sometime be seen by a large audience." Several incarnations later, a half-hour four-camera version, dubbed *The Torkelsons,* was presented to NBC.

"When Brandon Tartikoff read the script, he said to me, 'Lynn, I read this at a time in my life when I needed something life-affirming, and *The Torkelsons* was it.'"

As writer and creator of the show, it would seem Lynn has her hands full, but she is currently completing several other pilots, a movie for television, and other works in progress. Despite the load, she's not at all a Hollywood fast-tracker. Lynn owned a bed-and-breakfast inn near Big Bear, California, for a time, and also formed a poetry workshop at a shelter for homeless children in Santa Monica. "I'm not just writing," she points out, "I'm living too."

Together with her artist husband, Richard Kriegler, Lynn makes her home in Los Angeles, and looks forward to having a family of her own in the near future. In the meantime, she'll continue creating memorable characters and valuable stories. "I've always been a storyteller," says the soft-spoken writer. As Americans will soon learn watching *The Torkelsons,* she also happens to be one of our best.

As you study these two examples, notice a certain flow. I've written a lot of these, so it comes rather easily to me. But with practice, you can do it too. As an exercise, write your own bio following the suggestions described. Strive for flow. After you've composed a first draft, cut at least 25 percent of what you wrote. Tighten it up as much as you can. It's really not hard to nail it down.

Photos

My previous comments about photos don't apply uniformly to a press kit. If your press kit contains a bio of an individual, you may wish to include a photo, preferably an 8 × 10 black-and-white head shot. Your virtual press kit *must* include a high-resolution digital photo of the individual, but it should also have something a little less formal and predictable, in case the publication wants to add color to the story. If your subject is an event, a product, or a place, a photo can be helpful in making your project more concrete in the minds of media people. But a photo isn't always essential. If you play your cards right, you'll make the media come out and photograph or film you, rather than having to run the expense of printing photos yourself. It's always best to have the media do the photography, since it indicates a definite interest in your story and also will usually result in a better image. And that's what you're always shooting for. Remember, a statement gains more *credibility* when it comes from someone else, and a photograph seems more *official* when the media outlet sends a photographer. It's all a question of perception.

Clips

Obviously, if you've never mounted a press campaign before, you probably haven't amassed a collection of press clippings on your project. But it ain't necessarily so. It's possible there have been stories on your project, or closely related projects, before your arrival on the scene. You might have blogged about your project, or there might have been others who did. Run a Google search on your project, or company, or even your own name, and you'll likely find that there have been mentions in online or print media that even you haven't heard about. Don't despair: that's great! But even if there are no such articles, it's perfectly legit to include reprints of stories that simply pertain to your subject.

For example, say I wanted to include some clips in my press kit for the fictitious Mid-Valley Youth Center. I would include recent hard-hitting articles from the national or local press on gangs or community efforts to help troubled teens. These would add ballast to my pitch. Reprints from other publications tend to legitimize your project by showing journalists that other media felt the subject worthy of coverage.

It doesn't matter that none of those articles mention the Youth Center by name, or even refer to it indirectly. They are acting as a foundation, providing legitimacy and credibility to the issues the Center addresses. Let the reporter become concerned about the problem, and then provide yourself or your project as a possible solution, and you'll see an increase in the number of interested responses you get to your pitch.

If you do include reprints in your press kit, paste them up as precisely as possible and photocopy them on one sheet of paper, two-sided if necessary. With PhotoShop and other software programs, it's easy to make things fit together, but try very hard to keep the print legible. You don't want a reporter to have to pull out a magnifying glass in order to read your clippings. For one thing, the reporter won't do it, and your press kit will end up in the round file. But avoid more than one sheet for any one article, because media people are usually too busy to do any more than glance at what you send them. Use only the most persuasive clips, and don't try to overwhelm your quarry with size. Let quality carry the day.

Canned Feature

A canned feature is a newspaper article you write yourself. Many small papers and magazines lack the staff to report on every subject that interests them. A canned feature can significantly help the media help you. However, they aren't so easy to write. Unlike a bio, which is written by the numbers, a feature doesn't always follow as strict a formula. And if you're already nervous about your writing ability, composing a full-fledged article may spook you.

Not to worry. Though I've never worked as a journalist, I know a few of their tricks. First, keep paragraphs brief. Newspapers are well aware of the short attention span of most readers, so you need to make your piece scannable. Next, pack your article full of quotes. Keep in mind that the quotes don't have to be anything you've actually said out loud. In public relations, if you write a quote, and the client (in this case, you) signs off on it, then it's a legitimate quote. But try to make the quotes sound like something you'd actually *say*. Too many press releases include quotes like this: "With the industry in its current state of flux, it takes the experience and talent of a seasoned professional to slice through the difficult patches and make the system 100 percent workable." *Nobody* talks like that! It would be better to make it more conversational and say, "Things in the industry are tough right now. But because our staff has a lot of experience and knows the territory, we can help clients through the hard times."

Reading the newspaper, you'll notice that most light features contain an abundance of quotes. That's because usually a reporter would rather have the subject tell his own story. This fulfills the journalist's need to remain objective, and it gives the reporter that much less story to write; they love that.

So, for example, if I wanted to write a canned feature about the Youth Center, I would first select a theme: "Financially struggling center helps troubled teens despite adversity." That's not the headline; it's just the theme you've chosen for yourself.

You have to focus on what the message is going to be, and stay with it throughout the feature. With that premise, I'd write a brief headline and lead paragraph, recap the center's history, then let the quotes speak for themselves. Thread quotes together with a narrative to lend continuity, and always end your piece with a quote. Lace in new words to say the same thing, i.e., "He says," "He comments," "He notes." But don't get too fancy: "He expounds," "He pontificates," or "He elaborates" will look pretentious and stick out like a sore thumb. Don't distract with fancy words. Let the story tell itself.

Here's my own attempt at a canned feature:

Youth Center Endures Despite Ongoing Budget Battles

While gang wars claim young lives in the streets, many lives have been reclaimed at the Mid-Valley Youth Center, now in its fifth year of operation. But today, the Center faces its biggest fight yet as it struggles for solid financial footing. It's a fight the Center may not win.

Center Director John Jones has his doubts about the future. "We're really being squeezed right now," says Jones. "Many of our funding sources have dried up, including half of our government monies." The Center had been 50 percent funded by the county until earlier this year, when the Board of Supervisors voted to slash programs like the Center.

"With only private funding, we cannot offer the same kinds of activities for the kids as we used to," notes Jones. Already, a successful Midnight Basketball program has had to be cancelled; arts training offered in the afternoon has been cut back by half. The Center has provided not only sports and recreation facilities but an on-site job counselor who helps teens find summer work. In addition, the Center has sponsored drug rehab and anti-gang programs, encouraging inner-city teens to avoid self-destructive patterns.

"Our success rate has been higher than many other similar centers because our staff came from the neighborhoods and really cares about the kids," commented Jones. "Some of them are volunteers who give their time and energy simply for the reward of knowing they've done something to help keep their community together."

In order to stay afloat, the Mid-Valley Youth Center is preparing to launch long-term fundraising. A carnival, rummage sale, candy drive, and other projects will be scheduled throughout the year. Says Jones, "We need the community to give back to a place that has given so much. These fundraisers could go a long way to keeping us going."

Launched five years ago, the Mid-Valley Youth Center was the first self-contained center of its kind in this part of the city. With gang and drug activity dominating the neighborhoods, the arrival of the Center was met with initial skepticism. But soon, the comprehensive program brought results. According to local police statistics, violent crime in the area was down 23 percent within a year. Despite the success, the Center faced continual budget crises.

But Jones remains confident. "We've stared down guns, crack, murder, and despair, and we've triumphed. I'm sure this budget battle is one we can win too."

Any canned feature you write will echo your own leanings. But such features can be useful in presenting your case in a more impartial setting. And it's always a hoot to see your own self-

congratulatory words gracing the pages of your hard-hitting local newspaper.

That's not to say that a newspaper—or an online media outlet—will print your feature exactly as you present it. You can't
count on any media outlet to simply accept what you've written
and re-create it in newsprint or megabytes. A decent reporter
will rewrite to the newspaper's style; a good reporter will call
with his or her own questions, do a live interview, and write
a piece based on the information you'd provided, but with the
media outlet's angle explored and presented.

Don't for a second consider this an insult. You were trying
to get media coverage, and you've succeeded beyond all realistic
expectations. You've got a legitimate news organization interested in your story. You shouldn't be concerned that you can no
longer control the way in which that story is presented. It's best
to remember that adage about there being no such thing as bad
publicity (there really is, but not in this case). If they're writing
about you and raising your profile, you have accomplished your
goal. Open a bottle of champagne and celebrate!

Vital Statistics and Quote Sheet

In many ways, you have to play midwife to your own media success. Spoon-feeding information to the media and doing their
work for them not only endears you to them but increases the
chances they'll go to bat for you. A quote sheet or vital statistics
sheet typifies the kind of visual aid the media love.

On one sheet of paper, can you list fifteen informative statistics about your project or about your subject in general? If
you don't think so, think again. Go to the library, go to the
computer, go to Google, delve into research. You can quantify
almost anything. If you own a retail store in an exciting growth

industry, find out how many similar stores have opened nation-wide in the past year. If you are a divorce attorney, cite the latest numbers showing the percentage of marriages that end in divorce. Find ten similar facts, and you've got yourself a vital statistics sheet.

Here's a sample fact sheet I received from a local homeless shelter network recently. Notice that it says nothing about the shelter program itself, but by recitation of these stark facts, it reinforces the need for such a program:

Sample Fact Sheet on Homelessness

Los Angeles County has the dubious distinction of being the homeless capital of the nation. In 2006, the Los Angeles Homeless Services Society placed the number of permanently homeless persons in the county on one given night in 2005 at 82,291. Of those, 72,413 were not living in shelters, hospitals, jails, or other facilities.

- Almost 20,000 of those were classified as "families."
- Between 700,000 and two million people are home-less every night, according to the U.S. Conference of Mayors.
- Families with children present the fastest growing sec-tor of the homeless population.
- 28,000 to 32,000 children are homeless in L.A. County.
- Since 1980, budget authority for all federal housing assistance programs has been cut by more than 75 percent. By 2006, funding for HUD programs had declined by $3.3 billion (or 8 percent) in comparison

to 2004, once adjustments for inflation are made. For 2007, the Bush Administration proposed further cutbacks of $1.3 billion.

- Since it is estimated that some homeless people find shelter during the year, the number of those who are homeless for any part of the year 2005 was 221,363.
- More than one in five people in the county will seek food assistance this year.

A quote sheet consists of statements by individuals directly bearing on your project. Don't include epigrams, such as those I've sprinkled throughout this book. Rather, use only those that pertain specifically to your project or field of interest. If you have a collection of reviews of your product, excerpt the best of them.

If you can collect several quotes from well-known people commenting on your area of expertise, use them. For example, if you're an inventor marketing a new skin-care product, perhaps you can find recent quotes from dermatologists, government experts, movie stars, or anyone else talking about skin care. This augments your pitch by expanding the arena beyond yourself and your project.

Here are some examples of quotes appropriate for a quote sheet:

> "The spirit is there in every boy; it has to be discovered and brought to light."—Sir Robert Baden-Powell, founder of the Boy Scouts (England)[1]

---

1. Of course, all the quotes except for that of Sir Robert Baden-Powell are fictitious.

"The Mid-Valley Youth Center's midnight basketball program, which had been ridiculed by this paper when first proposed, is unequivocally a complete success. We were wrong, and we're glad."—Editorial, *The Herald-Star*, June 25

"I visited the Mid-Valley Youth Center to talk to a few kids, and ended up staying for five hours. The energy there is incredible; I wish I had it on the basketball court every night."—Lawrence Timmons, point guard, Los Angeles Lakers

"It would be a terrible shame if the Center had to close down. My son has stayed off drugs, and out of gangs, and I can only credit the Center with giving him a place where he knew he'd be welcome every day after school."—Edna Williamson, local resident

Backgrounder

You may want to include a backgrounder if your business or project is based on highly technical knowledge, requires an understanding of its history, or is in any way tied to complicated subject matter. A backgrounder is simply a document, of any length, that thoroughly explains the background of your business. It is rarely quoted, but it will serve to properly educate the media people as to the nature of your project.

Video Press Kit

In the original edition of this book, I debated whether to include video press kits in this book because of their cost. "Most Guerrilla P.R. budgets cannot encompass a video press kit, but I felt

I should at least give you the information and let you decide for yourself," I said then.

Well, video isn't expensive anymore. *Good* video is another question. Do *not,* under any circumstances, send out a piece of video that was shot on your cell phone. Do *not* ever try to represent your project or your business with amateurish, unedited, cheap digital video shot with your brother's camcorder with no lighting, no script, and no prior planning. It will, I assure you, end up as an embarrassment to you and the very entity you're trying to present in a positive light in the press.

But that doesn't mean you can't include anything but a high-budget Hollywood-style video with your press materials. On the contrary: it's never been easier and it's never been cheaper to produce an impressive-looking package of moving Guerrilla P.R. that anyone with a DVD player can watch seconds after opening the envelope.

A video press kit provides much of the same information as a written press kit, but tells the story visually. It is *not* a *home movie.*

Even if you own a top-flight video camera, think twice before you decide to make a promotional video on your own. If you aren't a filmmaker, you won't have a refined sense of editing, pacing, and cinematic composition. Not everyone can do this. But if you think your project would benefit from video, find out if there's a film school in your town, or a local college that teaches film. You may snag an ambitious film student willing to help you at no cost. He or she may even be able to provide film, camera, editing facilities, and actors. If there's a grade at stake, you'd be surprised how enterprising students can be.

Once you've decided to go ahead with a video press kit, remember a few key precepts:

- Don't make the video too long. Unlike with written material, scanning a video is a chore.
- Combine movement with static shots to lend visual variety.
- Combine voice-over (i.e., offscreen narration) with on-screen presentation of information—think of it as a Power-Point presentation with moving video.
- If you are going to be the chief spokesperson for your project, put yourself in the video. If that makes you nervous, see the section in subsequent chapters about media coaching and appearing on camera.
- Insist on quality. No shaky handheld cameras, no fuzzy sound. Even if it costs you only a few hundred bucks, make it look like a million. It's not hard: digital video equipment is not expensive, and in the hands of a film student who has a spark of inspiration and the first chance in a lifetime to show it off, a micro-budgeted video can look incredibly impressive.
- A script is not simply a sales pitch. Think about the *tone* you want to set for your video. Is humor appropriate? Do you want to dramatize a certain section using actors who will act out a scene (again, students can be found who will probably do the job for nothing)? Think about the *visuals*, or there will be no point in making a video component of your press kit. If it's all about words, you can just write them into a press release and save yourself some time and money.
- The video press kit is meant to inform. In your script (and you *will* need to write a script), make sure the important points are covered. But remember, this tool shouldn't be used in lieu of a written press kit, only as an adjunct.

- Duplication is no longer a tremendous problem. Any computer that can burn DVDs is a duplicator, and the discs themselves are not expensive. It may be time consuming, and it might require some additional prior planning, but you can make enough copies of your DVD to impress the people who'll be watching, and to keep your costs manageable at the same time.

Video press kits can be extremely effective. But don't attempt one if you have no sense of dramatic presentation or a visual idea. There's no point in sending out a bad video press kit, but a well-planned one can have a serious impact on your campaign.

Magnet Events

One afternoon twenty-five years ago, five L.A. businessmen met at a local coffee shop. Though they'd established careers in diverse fields, they were brought together by a common passion: a love of chocolate. These five chocoholics decided to form an organization of like-minded zealots, and the Chocolate Lovers of America was born.

They struggled at first, sending out newsletters and releases, trying to get press attention. But what put them in the national limelight was an appearance in the annual Doo-Dah Parade, Pasadena's loony alternative to the Rose Parade. The perennial briefcase drill team and a squad of cop-slapping Zsa Zsas are typical entrants in this marching madhouse.

The Chocolate Lovers of America entered the Doo-Dah Parade dressed as chefs throwing chocolate kisses to the onlookers lining the street, who literally ate 'em up. After that, the CLA was at last in with the in crowd.

When the Mel Brooks film comedy classic *Blazing Saddles* opened in 1974, the publicist in charge staged a screening of the western spoof at a drive-in. Only horses were allowed in, each tied by its reins to the speakers' stand. "Horse d'oeuvres" were served, and a "horsepitality" suite was available as well. Oh, and of course, the press was invited.

Staging a magnet event like these is one of the best ways to draw attention, and for my money, it's a most appropriate alternative tactic in the Guerrilla P.R. arsenal. We used to call them publicity stunts, but that term has fallen into disfavor. In some ways, I prefer it because it smacks of daring. As with anything you do with the media, there should be some semblance of a news angle, but as you already know, the media cover the ridiculous as often as the sublime.

The key to conceiving magnet events is thinking tangentially. Of all the components of Guerrilla P.R., this one allows the most freedom. Dream up anything you want as long as it ties into your project, somehow, in the end. The Planet Cafe, a faceless little restaurant in Chicago, landed a feature on the NBC *Nightly News* for cooking up Pajama Night: show up Sunday evenings in your sleepwear and get 10 percent off your bill. A little weird? Maybe. Effective? No question.

I've mentioned how Bob Columbe of RALPH made news when he called out the media to witness the arrival of Jackie Gleason's *Honeymooners* bus driver's uniform, which the Great One shipped from Miami to Long Island. It was just a coat in a box, but Columbe's front lawn was so packed with media that the delivery man had trouble making it to the front door. As another example, one business author hired people with sandwich boards strapped to their bodies to promote his book in the financial district.

It was the same with Jean-Claude Baker and his restaurant, Chez Josephine, in New York City. Jean-Claude managed to get the *New York Times* to cover his event, which wasn't an event at all. But he declared his postcard-censorship incident to be an event, held a press conference about it, and voilà! there it was in the Newspaper of Record.

It's simply a question of being *different*, of doing something that everyone else doesn't do. The unexpected, the unusual, and the flagrantly bizarre will always get press coverage, even if it's not all positive. Think about your message, and then try to come up with a way to dramatize it in a new, fresh, innovative fashion. It's a cliché, but I'll say it: Think outside the box.

To devise your own magnet event, ask yourself the following questions:

How willing am I to toy with my image? Magnet events sometimes involve unusual—sometimes absurd—escapades, and this might clash with a more decorous reputation. As an example, I think it unlikely that either a Republican or a Democratic Senate majority leader will ever cruise the D.C. Beltway on a wheat harvester combine in order to push his farm bill (not that it wouldn't be fun to watch). But if the nature of your project allows for some spirited fun, then proceed.

Should I inject some sort of theme into my magnet event? Zany for the sake of zaniness is useless. The media don't have time for that. You must concoct something that tells a story. MADD launched candlelight marches in several cities commemorating the many dead and injured victims of drunk driving. Find a way to symbolize some aspect of your project through the magnet event.

Is my magnet event visually compelling? Whatever you do has to be photographable. When the radical AIDS activist group ACT-UP interrupted Catholic church services and poured blood on the sanctuary steps—offensive though it may have been—it made for indelible images. ACT-UP was on every newscast in America that night. I'm not suggesting that you in any way break the law—in fact, I'll say you shouldn't ever do so—but if you develop an outlaw imagination, you'll grant yourself the freedom to come up with all kinds of ideas.

Once you've selected an event, plan not only the details of the event itself but also the media attention you hope to solicit. Use the same basic tools of phone, e-mail, press release, fax, and network, but, to retain an element of suspense or surprise, couch your wording with a touch of secrecy. Build suspense. Cultivate curiosity. A magnet event is one circumstance where you don't give the whole story.

For example: From 2005 to 2007, billboards appeared in the Philadelphia area with a simple message seemingly scrawled on a blackboard: "I Hate Steven Singer." The only explanation offered was a Web site, ihatestevensinger.com. That was it.

The billboards became the talk of the area, and eventually it was discovered that they referred to Steven Singer Jewelers, based on a story the owner, forty-nine-year-old Steven Singer, told about a man who bought his wife of twenty years a diamond ring at his store, and was rewarded that night with "something more than a thank-you." Nine months later, their third child was born, and the husband, exhausted from late-night feedings and diaper changes, came back to the store to say the catchphrase later emblazoned on the billboards.

By *not* providing any information, Singer had created curiosity about his name, which also happened to be the name of his business. By withholding some information, you might also generate interest in your project before your event.

Entice the media, and they may just go for it.

Tips & Traps

- Remind the media to send a photographer.
- Budget carefully. You don't want to run up a big bill staging a fancy event.
- Magnet events can be time consuming. Make sure you allot enough of your own schedule to planning, organizing, and staging yours.
- Walk through the event on site beforehand. The more you know about the terrain, the fewer surprises await you.
- You may want to invite more than just media. Perhaps the public at large can join in. Youth groups, church groups, or any other organized group might add the right populist touch.
- For something like this, get help from family, friends, or colleagues.

Michael Levine's Top-Ten All-Time P.R. Stunts

1. In 1809, writer Washington Irving staged his own kidnapping to promote his book *Knickerbocker's History of New York*.
2. John Lennon and Yoko Ono's infamous 1969 weeklong

"bed-in" honeymoon at which the Beatle and his wife donned pajamas for peace.

3. A publicist for Frank Sinatra planted a concert audience with bobbysoxers paid to fake hysteria. It caught on!

4. In 1964, the Beatles were about to land in New York City, and while they were hotly anticipated, there wasn't much of a crowd at the airport. Publicists from a local radio station and their American record company organized teenagers to greet the group at the airport, and the British Invasion was launched in full.

5. During the contentious 1968 presidential campaign, the anarchistic Yippie party ran a pig for chief executive. (He lost.)

6. Mel Brooks's comedy classic *Blazing Saddles* was given a P.R. send-off with a horses-only-transportation premiere at a drive-in theater.

7. At the Live Aid concert on July 13, 1985, Phil Collins appeared at the London show—and the Philadelphia show. On the same day. He flew the (now-defunct) SST Concorde from London to New York and played at both shows. Much good publicity was launched, and $70 million was raised for charity.

8. Sir Paul McCartney launched his album *Memory Almost Full* in 2007 with "secret" club concerts in London, New York, and Los Angeles. About three hundred loyal fans were given free admission to the shows in clubs that generally held about seven hundred people. McCartney, never a slouch in terms of promotion, played Beatles tunes as well as new songs, and appeared in an animated commercial for Apple's iTunes and the *Larry King Live* show with Ringo Starr the same week.

9. Hands Across America: in 1987 millions joined hands to raise money for the nation's hungry.

10. The relay of the Olympic torch across America in 1984. Thousands participated, from children to wheelchair-bound athletes, and many more thousands cheered along the path. It set the stage for the most watched and most exciting Olympiad ever.

More Write Stuff

A canned feature is a piece you write to include in a press kit— and to be honest, that's often as far as it gets. But you can generate first-rate clips for your press kit by writing articles for print media as a sideline.

If they run in the paper, you get not only clips but credibility, stature, and a potential audience of thousands or millions. Best of all, with your byline adorning the piece, you establish yourself as an expert in your field, which means the media will come to you for information and analysis from here on.

A letter to the editor of your local paper is one great way to get started. News articles that relate in some way to your project, even obliquely, offer a golden opportunity to write in. Newspapers always need well-composed letters responding to the issues of the day. You may not get much response from such a letter, but, included in your press kit, it shows you have a style that grabs the attention of editors.

Still, the editorial section does get read. Perhaps it's not the most widely read in the paper, but it's the most closely read. Devotees of the Op-Ed pages are often intellectual, highly educated, and influential. Op-Ed pieces ("Op-Ed" stands for "opposite the editorials" or "opinion and editorials") are another excellent way to make you and your opinions known. Although these pages are largely composed of syndicated columns, every newspaper on occasion runs unsolicited essays by local citizens. The general guidelines are these:

- Keep the piece short, no more than four hundred to five hundred words (two to three typed pages, double-spaced).
- Write in the first person. This is the opinion section, after all, so allow your personality to run free.
- Write the piece as if it were a blog entry. Keep it short, keep it to the point, and make sure you back up what you say.
- Even as you strive to make your piece flow, make each paragraph unique. Begin with an overriding theme, presenting that theme in the first two paragraphs, then cite several supporting examples.

Read twenty Op-Ed pieces, and you'll see what I mean. The following is an example of an actual Op-Ed piece I wrote that ran in several publications. Notice how I build on my theme from paragraph to paragraph. Though this piece wasn't directly about me or my business, it served to augment my standing within the P.R. and business communities.

THE CASE FOR INTERNSHIPS

by Michael Levine

America may be the Land of Opportunity, but this is also the Land of the Big Trade-Off. Sure, you can have that nice house, but you're going to have to become a mortgage slave to keep it. You can drive that fancy sports car, but you'll have to fork over an insurance premium as hefty as the GNP of some Third World nations. The Bible says that in life, if you want honey, you get bees with stingers. For anything worth having, there's a price to pay. It's the same with a career. Most professional positions require experience, but in this classic Catch–22, how does a young college student or graduate gain that experience? Well, it's just as Mark Twain said: "Never let school interfere with your education."

I believe the intern programs in place at companies like Coca-Cola, Procter & Gamble, CBS, and my own provide the best chance for young people to enter and grow in many professions. Although the work is demanding, with little or no immediate financial return, interning is a textbook example of a win-win situation.

When a young student comes to my public relations company and tells me he's willing to intern, a distinctly modern social contract is entered into. Though he is not a servant, and I am not a teacher, if he does some unpaid work, we'll do some teaching. The company gets the opportunity to observe eager and smart young people who energize the company. Like a farm team, interns are prospective employees, and we get to watch them in action.

For the intern, the rewards are far greater.

First, most interns are college students, and nearly all receive valuable college credit for their services. Beyond that, interning teaches the neophyte how to function in a complex, real-life, adult business environment. Derek Jeter could have studied the physics of baseball for years in a classroom, but he never would have won World Series or MVP awards if he'd never stepped up to the plate, literally. No classroom can substitute for visceral, palpable learning in an authentic setting.

Problem solving, initiative, creativity, and cooperation are all fostered as the intern struggles to carve a niche for herself. To make it as an intern, one must embody the qualities of any effective worker, and the rewards go far beyond the merely educational. Many interns go on to highly successful careers.

Interning is practical. In an ever-tightening job market, it provides career preparation, and enables a young professional to develop marketable skills and demonstrate potential to a prospective employer.

But beyond the practicalities, there's a bigger picture that needs to be addressed.

For too many, America has become the Land of the Freeloader and the Home of the Lazy. People seem to want it all, right here right now, with a minimum of effort. Dreams of winning this week's Lotto game have supplanted that dream of building a life built on Freud's twin peaks, "Lieben und Arbeiten," love and work.

The old-fashioned work ethic is, if not dead, then surely on the critical list. America says it wants to be No. 1, but many refuse to expend the effort to get there. We can do it, but there's only one way, and that's simply to work for it, and work hard. For centuries, apprenticeship was the equivalent to today's technical college. The spirit of apprenticeship is still alive in interning. If America's workforce whined a little less, and had a little more of the initiative of my highly motivated interns, maybe this country could find a semblance of its former glory. No, they do not get paid. But as my interns have so brilliantly demonstrated, nobody works for free.

Don't just limit yourself to the editorial page. You should strongly consider writing your own articles for trade and consumer publications, too. I've done many, and I don't think anything has proved as beneficial in establishing my personal credibility with the public. My article for *Psychology Today* on the psychology of beauty triggered the most e-mail and snail mail response that any article for that magazine had ever generated. That not only means *Psychology Today* might be interested in another article if I decide to write one, it also means that my story was being talked about, and my name mentioned, much more widely than before the article ran. So: how do you do it for yourself?

If you aren't sure what to write, try a "list article." That would be something like "Ten Things You Can Do to Improve Your Sales Right Now" or "Eight Secrets to Better Lawn Care." Equally feasible is a Q&A-style piece that would address similar concerns. Just pose five to ten of the most commonly asked questions regarding your business or project, and then answer them in the same punchy style described above.

Whatever line you're in, I'm sure you can concoct a list or a series of questions like this. They're easy to write and very easy for readers to grasp. Best of all, editors love them. The key to dreaming up subject matter is to think in terms, not of your own benefit, but of the benefit of the reader. Of course, you're out to promote yourself and your project, product, or service, but editors and readers don't care about that. You must think altruistically if you want to reap rewards.

Op-Ed pieces to newspapers can be freely submitted as unsolicited articles. But before you write any other kind of article—for magazines, for example—you must first write a query letter to the editor, as detailed in the previous chapter. I don't care how wonderful your piece is; most unsolicited manuscripts get thrown away without being read (unless the publication has a published policy of accepting them).

So write a short letter first, introducing yourself and your concept for the piece, and giving maybe a two-paragraph taste of what you plan to write. The letter shows you're professional, respectful of the editor, and, most important, that you can indeed write. If the editor likes your idea, he'll request the full article, and you will have thus established a permanent rapport with an important media player. And don't underestimate the shelf life of these pieces.

Unlike newspapers, which wind up on the recycle stack the next day, magazines may stick around a long time. A friend of mine still gets inquiries for his business based on short pieces published up to five years ago in a trade magazine.

A few suggestions when preparing to write: Take an inventory of all you know about your chosen topic, but also include what you don't know. This will determine what, if any, research you need to do. You can get the ball rolling by coming up with a catchy title or opening line. Check into books and magazines. If you have Internet access, use your modem to link up with the vast information-sharing computer network. Keep track of catchphrases and buzzwords to lend an authoritative tone to your piece; but remember, you don't have to be the ultimate expert. Your goal is to present a crisp, thoughtful article that benefits the reader first of all and, with a little luck, will benefit you too down the line.

One other tip: Editors like to give things away to readers, especially if they're free. If you can include in your piece an address where readers can obtain a no-charge premium—say a newsletter, a product sample, or additional information (with your name or your business name on it)—all the better.

Giving Good Phone

Conversation is the art of never appearing a bore.

—Guy de Maupassant

I wonder sometimes how business was transacted before the invention of the telephone. Of all the technological pillars that hold up our civilization, the phone is the most intrinsic. Without it, the foundation would collapse. I could live without the internal combustion engine, MTV, and the microwave oven. Maybe even without TiVo. But not without the telephone. And now, especially not without the cell phone—that thing has become part of my body, like a third ear.

Neither could any Guerrilla P.R. plan. While professional publicists may travel to Hollywood movie premieres or tag along on cross-country interview junkets, the Guerrilla variety are primarily housebound. Even when you're on your Bluetooth, you are more likely to be making a trip to the supermarket than the Cannes Film Festival; you're much more apt to be found on your phone in the dentist's waiting room than in Steven Spielberg's outer office. Your wings of freedom are found on the telephone lines, so you must use the phone wisely—and often—if you are to succeed.

P.R. people have a reputation for being abrasive, hyper, and cynical on the phone. I keep all those traits in my arsenal, but they are not the sum total of my phone persona. I would venture to say that those tools don't get used more than a fraction of the time—I use them only when necessary—and they certainly shouldn't be your stock-in-trade, either. As is true in all aspects of life, you catch more flies with honey than with vinegar. Civility is the lubricant in the machine of human interaction, and you should always be your most polite when dealing with media. I've mentioned how busy journalists are. Be sensitive to that. I always begin a conversation, even with reporters I know well, with "Do you have a minute to chat?" If they give their okay, I'll press on, but I make sure I obtain their permission first. Then I know they have consented to participate in the conversation.

Let me remind you once again of the importance of listening. Too often, conversations aren't true dialogues as much as a pair of monologues, with one party pondering the next point while the other speaks. Pay attention. Listen to the other person, and trust yourself to think on your feet. People like to be listened to. They like people who listen to them, and the more people like you, the more inclined they'll be to help you out.

Now, as for pitching by phone, I assume some or all of the following have been or will be done:

- You have sent a press release in advance of the call. (Sometimes, cold calls are necessary, but do your best to avoid them.)
- You are *thoroughly* familiar with the media outlet you're contacting, including personnel, style, and audience, and you are reasonably familiar with the work of the reporter you contact.
- You're speaking with the person you intended to reach. Not an assistant, not a colleague, but the real McCoy. (I know this isn't always possible, and you may at times have to deal with underlings.)
- Don't be insistent; go with the flow for a while.
- You are prepared to answer any questions. This is something to take seriously, and you won't know whether

you're ready unless you practice first. Conduct a mock conversation with a friend. Have the friend pepper you with all sorts of questions, even hostile ones. You have to be ready for anything.

- Once in contact on the line, begin by summarizing the central point of your release. Even if the reporter received it, he or she may not clearly remember the content. After your summary, repeat the reason for your call—that is, you're looking for an advance story on your project, coverage of the event, a calendar listing, etc.

- What you say next depends on the reply you get. If the reporter shows some interest, offer a new tidbit of information not included in your release. Give reasons why the publication should want to cover your project, all the while keeping in mind the lessons from before: they need news angles, and they seek to serve their audience.

- Take your cues from the person you speak with. If you detect irritation or impatience, say something like "I won't take any more of your time" or "Give me just a minute more." You can press the journalist somewhat for an answer, but if she says she can't commit just then, accept it and ask when you may call back for a definitive answer.

If you are met with utter indifference, ask leading questions that require a response. For example: "Have you found that the paper has done stories like this in the past?" (it's not a bad idea if *you* can cite an example) or "Would additional news angles help you?" (and then provide them). If the journalist still isn't biting, offer to send more material (if you have it) and say you'll call back in a few days. Gentle persistence erodes stubborn resistance. Of course, record everything on your tracking sheet.

These suggestions are generic to all media. Getting what you want by phone involves careful manipulation of the call. You must feel in command even as you behave deferentially to the person you speak with. As the saying goes, you get no second chance to make a first impression.

Tips & Traps

- Call from a quiet place. Background noise is distracting to both you and the party you're calling.
- Modulate your speaking voice to avoid a monotone.
- Don't come off like a Boy Scout, but do speak with enthusiasm and vigor. If you don't believe in your message, nobody else will.
- Never show anger or frustration with the person you call. Even if they're behaving abominably, you have to keep your cool to keep your connection.
- If the person you're trying to reach isn't in, don't always leave a message when you call. Sometimes media people rely on their voice mail to screen calls. If you leave two dozen messages, you will probably never hear from the reporter. Call with the intention of speaking to someone, but leave only a tiny handful of messages.
- If you still have trouble contacting the person, call his or her editor and explain your circumstances. Surprisingly, editors and managers are oftentimes more easily reached than those they supervise.
- I can't think of anything worse for your business than being unreachable or missing important calls. If you don't have a cell phone, get one now, before you read the next

page. If you don't have an answering machine or your cell phone doesn't have voice mail (virtually unthinkable these days), change companies and get the machine. You can't *ever* be unreachable.

Tech Talk

I have often believed that technology is the enemy of reverence. Now, that doesn't mean I'm a Luddite with a built-in mistrust of all things that plug into an electrical socket. It means that the more we worship the technological and the more we lean on it and demand explanations for every mystery ever considered, then the more we lose our sense of wonder and our drive to accomplish.

Believe me, I have no desire to return to the days before the Internet, before television, before cell phones, fax machines, Bluetooth, BlackBerry, electric lights, radio, printers, computers, software, hardware, telephones, TiVo, air-conditioning, hybrid motors, nuclear energy, e-mail, digital cameras, camcorders, or dishwashers. I don't regret that we discovered how to make fire. I'm not sorry someone rounded the corners off a rock and made a wheel.

But I do think we are a technology-obsessed society, one that has too much regard for the explained and too little for the unexplainable. The more we lean on what we've created, the less incentive there is to transform that which we were given to begin with.

I think the iPhone is a very cool gadget. When it was launched in June 2007, the iPhone—Apple's all-in-one device that combines a cell phone, MP3 player (iPod), and wireless Web browser while adding digital pictures and a gorgeous touch-screen display—was the most coveted gizmo on the planet. People lined up for days outside the Apple Stores in Manhattan, San Francisco, and other cities for the privilege of spending $599 (plus another $59.99 per month for the service) on an iPhone.

But I'm more impressed with the way the iPhone was launched than I am with the device itself. The introduction of a device that nobody needed but everybody wanted was a brilliant stroke of P.R. (albeit not of the Guerrilla variety, since Apple had an enormous budget to play with).

At the same time that the entire consumer electronics industry was gathered in Las Vegas at its annual trade show (the largest of any industry in the world), Apple, in San Francisco, stole the thunder of all the new gadgets, gizmos, and megabytes being shown off at the trade show by throwing a little party for its latest innovation—the iPhone.

Months before it would make its debut in stores, the iPhone was already an object of intense interest. *USA Today* quoted David Yoffie, a professor at the Harvard Business School, as estimating the free publicity's value at $400 million and saying, "No other company has ever received that kind of attention for a product launch. It's unprecedented."

How did Apple do it? First, it helps to have a solid-gold reputation as one of the most innovative and user-friendly companies in the world. Apple has a very small percentage of the computer market in the world (perhaps 4 or 5 percent), but it has a reputation as the groundbreaker, fostered by such products as the iMac and the iPod.

The iPod, indeed, was the product that put Apple in the nation's—and the world's—consciousness as a great consumer company. That little device, described in a book title as *The*

Perfect Thing, became as ubiquitous as the Walkman had once been for Sony. It quickly took on the status of a generic: people would say "iPod" when they meant *any* MP3 player, just as they say "Kleenex" when they mean any tissue. So it didn't hurt that Apple was coming off a product launch that had been monumentally successful.

Also, it had a star: Steve Jobs, the once-estranged founder of the company, had come back to Apple years before the iPod or the iPhone and had reestablished himself as the consumer-friendly Bill Gates. Jobs, in his jeans and running shoes, was the guy we all thought we could take out for a burger. Except that whenever he appears, he turns into the Great and Powerful Oz, and new and exciting products leap from his fingers. It was a major boon to Apple that Jobs was on hand to introduce the iPhone.

Apple insisted on control over its product. It made the iPhone available only to customers of AT&T Wireless (formerly Cingular) because that company would let the iPhone be what Apple wanted it to be without interference.

There was enough press coverage of Jobs's introduction of the iPhone to create a new country. Magazines ran cover stories. Television news led with the iPhone. The Internet? It was nearly impossible to escape the iPhone. All this because a man stood on a stage and showed off a new telephone to a group of journalists.

Technology may very well be the enemy of reverence—I believe it is—but it can be a great deal of fun. And that will always make it possible for a man like Steve Jobs to attract a tremendous amount of publicity. We're just waiting for the Next Big Thing.

People Get Ready

I imagine at times you've been miffed by my commanding you to "be interesting" or "perform" without some instruction as to how. Let's start with some basics I've gleaned over the years. My theory about "perception as reality" holds true on every level. So, in your dealings with media and the public, you want to make a good impression every time. This section is meant to help you prepare for in-person interviews, TV appearances, and glad-handing of all kinds. Research has shown that people form strong opinions about others during the first seven seconds of meeting someone. Non-verbal signals are critical in determining the impressions individuals make on others. Appearance, dress, body language, and attitude all contribute.

Consider the famous Nixon-Kennedy debates in 1960. People watching on TV overwhelmingly felt Kennedy, with his easy manner and good looks, was the hands-down winner. Those listening on radio felt Nixon won, based on the content of his answers. That historic series of debates was a defining moment in establishing the immutable power of the mass media to influence events.

Peggy Klaus, a media readiness consultant and an astute observer of human behavior, assists actors, news anchors, and corporate leaders with what she terms "physicalization," or ways in which the body moves. She emphasizes that our gestures should involve the least amount of stress. One should present oneself with ease and fluidity, seeking and finding a comfort zone.

This holds true not only for the body but for the voice. Former British Prime Minister Margaret Thatcher's voice dropped five tones after her election, some feel because she was trying to sound more "mannish." As a result, she was constantly hoarse.

Later, she reverted to her natural speaking voice. She had found her comfort zone, and so must you.

Clearly, even on your level, the right signals must be sent from the start. So, when you are gearing up to meet with the media, observe the following:

Once again, do your homework. This goes for any contact you make with media reps. Know as much as you can about the newspaper, magazine, radio show, or TV show in question. Know who the anchors are, what section the reporter writes for, when the show is broadcast. If they perceive you as knowledgeable about them, they'll be more likely to treat you with respect.

Be on time or even early for interviews, staging events, or anything else involving media. Punctuality is a sincere form of courtesy; tardiness is a dire form of disrespect. This is especially true with TV. They're on extremely tight schedules, and you could throw a king-size wrench in the works if you waltz in late.

Dress appropriately. Despite the title of this book, you shouldn't dress like a Guerrilla. I don't suggest you rush out and order a closetful of Armani suits, but dignified dress is a sign of self-respect, something you always want to convey. When you are on TV, dress is paramount. Unless your project is tied into the art world or counterculture, make sure your attire is neat, well tailored, and on the conservative side. It will pay off.

Use open body language. In Guerrilla P.R. you're a walking billboard. Everything you do communicates a message, including your body language. Look at yourself in the mirror. Are you expressive with your hands? Do you

shift around? Do your eyes dart? Study yourself as if studying a lab animal, and be just as analytical.

Listen attentively. Listen to the questions asked, and read
beyond the questions. Media people are diggers. Why do
you think they call a hot story a scoop? Because they have
an insatiable desire to get below the surface. You have to
be ready to provide that, but you can only if you pay attention. By listening, you'll be able to steer the conversation
your way.

Until now, you've been assembling all the parts of your Guerrilla P.R. machine. Now it's time to throw the switch and put
your machine in gear. In the next chapter, we reach out to the
various media, making your vision a reality.

GUERRILLA P.R. COMMANDO: Si Frumkin

There was a time when the term "Soviet Jewry" usually made people think of diamonds from
Moscow, but that was before Si Frumkin came on the scene. A Holocaust survivor, the Lithuanian-
born Frumkin arrived in America in 1949 as a young man anxious to start a new life. He built a
successful business, earned an M.A. from the University of California, and started a family, but his
real passion became the Jews he had left behind in the Soviet Union.

In the late 1960s and early 1970s, along with a small band of supporters, Frumkin embarked
on a true Guerrilla campaign to increase awareness of the plight of Soviet Jews. Over the years,
he evolved into a media master, and almost single-handedly he rallied the public around his issue
with his tactics.

Nothing was too dramatic for Si. He spray-painted the words "Save Soviet Jews" on the side
of the first Russian tanker in L.A. harbor. He hired a helicopter to fly over the Super Bowl trailing a
banner reading "Save Soviet Jewry." When Leonid Brezhnev visited Richard Nixon at San Clemente,
Si released five thousand helium balloons with the words "Let My People Go" emblazoned on

them. Wherever and whenever he could, Frumkin and his cohorts appeared at Soviet cultural events dressed in their indigenous Soviet costumes, handing out literature, creating a stir, and making people feel uncomfortable.

His creativity brought constant media attention. He launched a campaign to have Americans send their unused holiday cards to the Soviet embassy in Washington, pleading to release Soviet Jews. He staged a musical at synagogues around Southern California. He even jokingly contemplated a "Martyrs for Soviet Jews" campaign wherein he and his friends would break their legs skiing at Mammoth Mountain.

"We wanted to have bathing beauties stand before City Hall with signs, but we couldn't get enough pretty girls," he says.

Si's prankish wit helped him survive the long days of struggle, but his instinctive understanding of the media made him a natural Guerrilla P.R. genius. "The first thing we wanted was to get the media talking about us," he recalls. "In many cases the publicity we received was because we were confrontational. We never did anything overtly violent, but the media love confrontation. If we annoyed people, too bad."

Si made a distinction between his P.R. goals and those of others. "It was not a question of winning people over," he notes. "Normally the aim in P.R. is to get people to like you because you want them to buy your product. That was not true for us. We wanted to convince the world of our strength and the rightness of our cause. My feeling was that those people hostile to us because we picketed a basketball game would never be sympathetic anyway, and they didn't matter."

Working with next to no budget, Si relied on street smarts. He set up a darkroom to develop his own photos of magnet events and rush them to the papers. And he understood the needs of editors. "The average planning desk at a TV station or newspaper has about three hundred items every morning," says Si. "They have to decide where to send the five or six available crews and reporters. We tried to make things 'sexy.' We poured blood and excrement in front of buildings, burned Soviet flags, whatever was visual."

His activities made him the reigning "expert" on Soviet Jewry, so the media called him whenever comment on the subject was needed. "They didn't call me because I was wonderful, but because I had the information." Today, with so many Jews departing the former USSR, Si feels vindicated and ecstatic. "It's a miracle," he says. "Ten years ago, if I were told a million Jews would be leaving with many more to come, I wouldn't have believed it."

His advice to other Guerrilla publicists: "Believe in what you're doing. Be totally dedicated, and be ready to work eighteen-hour days. Learn enough skills to check up on the professionals who supposedly know better. Chances are they don't know any more than you do."

You can find out more about Si at www.sifrumkin.com.

6

Data Smog

The Media. It sounds like a convention of spiritualists.

—Tom Stoppard

As I've noted, one of the main differences between 1993, when the original edition of this book was published, and now is the geometric proliferation of media sources. In 1993, there were newspapers, magazines, television (with far fewer stations), and radio. That's not the case today.

With blogs, Web sites, podcasts, MP3s, DVD, and so many other media choices, there has developed, in my view, a condition I'll call *data smog*. It's the thing that happens to your brain when too many media outlets bombard you with messages: your eyes glaze over, your mind wanders, and you are no longer a valid consumer of information. You're a zombie.

You don't even *know* it, either. We are assaulted with media messages, it has been estimated, every few seconds these days. Try to remember the last time you walked into a bar that *didn't* have a television on. Think of the last time you watched a newscast that did not have more news crawling across the bottom of the screen like a tiny version of the ribbon in Times Square. Newspapers, even as they condense in number, are offering smaller, quicker, more easily digestible nuggets of information with considerably less depth and analysis. And that doesn't even begin to assess the impact of the Internet.

Whether you're a fan of Matt Drudge or Arianna Huffington, I'm willing to bet you get at least some of your news every day from an Internet source. Yahoo!, Google, Reuters, and countless other Web sites offer looks at the news that you can customize to emphasize your own interests and to exclude that which you don't find interesting. Every major news organization has at least one Web identity, and even if you're not concerned with anything but leisure, you can get sports scores, cartoons, interviews with celebrities, and fashion trends, among millions of other things, just by checking in with bloggers, Web sites, and podcasts or Webcasts.

Add that all up, and you have the top three inches of the iceberg that sunk the *Titanic*. There are so many media outlets now that it's utterly amazing we don't all have our own television shows. Clearly, someone else is using up our fifteen minutes of fame.

Given that, is it any wonder that we don't sometimes overload? It's impossible to walk out of the house (iPod buds in ears; Bluetooth cell phone at the ready with games, video and text messages; car equipped with GPS, DVD, and XM satellite) and drive or commute past video billboards, BlackBerry e-mails, laptop using Wi-Fi on the train—and *not* feel overwhelmed by it all.

Data smog envelops us without our even being aware of its existence. We ignore most of what we see and hear because we simply can't consciously process that much information all at

one time. We don't listen to most of what we're told, and we
don't see much of what we're shown, not because it wouldn't
interest us, but because we can't cut through all the interference
being created by millions of messages coming at us, whether or
not they're intended for us, all at the same time.

We are a civilization with attention deficit disorder, and we
have been brought up to be that way by media sources and corporations desperate for our attention. It's not an evil plot (well,
most of it isn't, anyway); it's simply a question of everyone trying to take advantage of the media avenues open to them in an
attempt to reach a wider audience.

Perhaps Guerrilla P.R. has contributed to data smog. Because
it is no longer prohibitively expensive to communicate with large
numbers of people, more and more companies and individuals
are trying to do so. And they are contributing to the pollution of
information that surrounds us and jams our frequencies.

What does that mean to you as an aspiring Guerrilla? It
means several things:

- You have to work harder—there's way more competition
  than there used to be.
- You need to be careful to tailor your message to a target
  demographic—decide who your audience is, and aim specifically for that group.
- You must be even more creative. Creativity is even more
  important now than it was in 1993; not only do you have
  to find your audience, but also you have to cut through the
  interference of other messages just to get their attention.
- You must have a clear, focused, understandable message
  that can be communicated in seconds. Details will be
  sought out by those who are interested, but that will happen later.

- You must choose your media outlets carefully.
- You probably need to use more than one media outlet.
- You have to entertain as you inform, or you won't be noticed.
- You need to consider *every* medium, from a video loaded onto YouTube to a full-fledged television campaign—it's all up for grabs now.
- You need to carefully consider your message, to make sure it's the one you want to convey. Using the wrong words or focusing on the wrong aspect can be a huge mistake.
- You don't need to have a higher volume level to break through—what you need is a more direct frequency to your audience. Where do you get *your* information?

Danger Ahead

Data smog is a danger not only to the consumer of information, who might miss important news or simply overdose on data if he's not careful, but also to the provider. Guerrillas who make the wrong moves in an ill-advised attempt to cut through the smog might not make the right choices. And in the Guerrilla movement, making the wrong choice can be devastating.

Make no mistake: There have been many Guerrilla P.R. disasters, plans so ill conceived, so poorly designed, or so badly implemented (sometimes all three) that they might have attracted media attention but have also done their originators irreparable harm. Guerrillas aren't firing blanks—we're using real guns and bullets out there, and if you are standing in the wrong place with the wrong plan, you can get shot.

It's easy to understand why some of these catastrophes have occurred. Data smog blocks all messages, good and bad, and can seem impenetrable by conventional weapons. But hauling out a nuke because it will make a loud noise is like using a shotgun to kill a fly; it might not work, and it can do unforeseen damage.

You want an example? In February 2007, some employees of Turner Broadcasting's subsidiary Cartoon Network decided to publicize a segment of the channel's *Adult Swim* programming called *Aqua Teen Hunger Force* by placing battery-powered cartoon advertising signs that resembled suitcases at various points around several cities, including Boston, Massachusetts. A Guerrilla plan to get commuters, especially, to notice the name of the cartoon show and to wonder what it might be—a concept not all that different from the "I Hate Steven Singer" billboards in Philadelphia.

The problem was, these Guerrilla devices looked far too much like potential bombs.

The devices, which included circuit boards, were seen at various places in Boston, and the city, not wanting to make a fatal mistake, closed parts of bridges, subway stations, an Interstate highway, and the Charles River on February 1. It arrested one man and eventually settled with Turner Broadcasting for the cost to the city. Turner ended up paying $2 million to Boston—and no, that wasn't free publicity.

It wasn't the kind of publicity you want, either. Jim Samples, general manager and executive vice president of Cartoon Network, resigned just over a week later. The show's ratings did not spike, and a film based on it tanked at movie theaters when released a few months later.

Turner didn't mean to create that kind of panic—the devices weren't *supposed* to look like bombs—but it was devastated by the incident. Anyone who says "there's no such thing as bad publicity" should look closely at the news reports that ran on February 2, 2007, and see how well Cartoon Network is portrayed. While it didn't cripple the division or the parent company, there was nothing about that tactic that in any way enhanced the image of anyone at Turner.

Say Pepsi, Please

Need another example of a P.R. disaster that could have been caused by data smog? Go no further than the Mother of All Business Disasters, the Edsel of the soft drink industry, New Coke. We've discussed this product and its remarkably bad introduction already, but now let's ignore the enormous marketing blunders that were made and examine the message Coca-Cola was broadcasting.

When it decided to change its formula (based largely on market research that showed people liked the taste of Pepsi better), the Coca-Cola company had several P.R. choices open to it: the new product could be an addition to the existing product line, it could be marketed as something separate without the name "Coke" at all, or it could step in and replace one of the most successful products in history. The company, for reasons known only to its executives, chose the last—the worst—alternative.

That's a marketing decision, and we won't bother to speculate on it. Instead, let's look at how the company might have explained its decision to the consumers, an amazingly loyal bunch of millions who had catapulted the original product to the very top of every conceivable sales chart. This is the constituency, the family. These were the people who had made this globally successful company what it was.

And here's where the company really made the worst possible decision.

In essentially telling its consumers, "Don't worry—trust us. You'll like this better than the product you've been loyal to for decades" and then letting out the information that the new formula *was supposed to taste more like Pepsi*, Coca-Cola was making a statement equivalent to telling Boston Red Sox fans that the team had decided to be more like the New York Yankees, and in keeping with that philosophy, had decided to trade away its marquee players for several Yankees prospects. Blood would no doubt run in the streets of Boston.

It wasn't bad enough that Coke was telling its customers it was making a more Pepsi-like product *for them*. The company then added injury to insult by completely removing the original product—the one consumers had been buying with undying loyalty for their entire lives—from store shelves, presumably never to be seen again. There might have been a way to communicate that action so loyal customers *wouldn't* feel betrayed, but it would have taken a P.R. miracle of untold proportions. Instead, the Coke executives merely stated their decision, yanked the "original formula," substituted the imposter on store shelves, and sat back, presumably waiting for the accolades and increased profits to which they felt entitled.

Needless to say, it didn't work out that way. Instead, there were protests at supermarkets. Boycotts were announced. The reviews of the new product were negative. It was a matter of weeks before one of the world's largest companies was brought to its knees and forced to immediately reverse a policy it had spent years creating and implementing.

With more communication between the customer base and the company, with a sensitive approach to those people who had indeed sustained Coca-Cola for years, it might have been possible to save New Coke—probably not as a replacement product, but certainly as an augmentation to the product line. But either arrogance or immense indifference to the consuming public (or both, a deadly combination) caused the executives to issue edicts rather than explain their position. Today, with blogs and e-mail blasts, it would be even easier to communicate directly with consumers, but for a company as large as Coke, there was no reason to be imperious and uncommunicative, even in 1985.

Keep in touch with the people who keep you going, and do so through carefully orchestrated Guerrilla P.R. assaults. But always keep in mind that communication is a two-way affair. Expect feedback—in fact, *encourage* feedback. Revel in it. It will tell you what you need to know to succeed beyond the level you're reaching today.

Tips & Traps

- Cut through data smog with *originality*, not volume.
- Assume your audience is inundated with information and ask yourself, what's *different* about what I'm saying?
- Remember that reporters and media gatekeepers are just as badly afflicted with data smog infestation as anyone else—maybe more. Keep your message short, focused, and different.
- Stunts can work, but most of the time they make you look silly. The man who created a 30-foot résumé and hung it over the rooftop of a Manhattan office building got plenty of news coverage—and no job.
- In a video-obsessed society, how you look does count.

Michael Moore always wears a baseball cap—it's his signature. If he didn't wear it, nobody would recognize him. What's *your* signature?

- If you do run into a Guerrilla P.R. disaster, own up to it *immediately* and make amends. Turner Broadcasting didn't deny it was behind the botched Boston campaign, and paid for the security measures it had necessitated.

- Focus on your target audience—it doesn't matter what the general public will pay attention to if your consumer doesn't care about that. It doesn't matter if most people wouldn't notice something, as long as the people you're targeting will.

- Statistics can be compelling, but they're overused. They won't cut through data smog unless they're so dramatic they take your breath away. Even then, don't start a press release with a statistic.

- Data smog is caused by information overload. Your job is to get media exposure. Make your message different by saying *less*—just use your one most compelling argument, and forget the rest until you've got their attention.

- Keep this in mind: What would make *you* stop and pay attention?

GUERRiLLA P.R. COMMANDO: Jill Buck

Since *Guerrilla P.R.* was published in 1993, I've been touched and honored by many letters, e-mails, and faxes sent by readers who say the book has helped them. None of these is more gratifying to me than the communication from Jill Buck, founder and executive director of the Go Green Initiative Association (GGI).

Jill started GGI, which is a simple, comprehensive program designed to create a culture of environmental responsibility on school campuses across the nation. Founded in 2002, the Go Green Initiative unites parents, students, teachers, and school administrators in an effort to make real and lasting changes in their campus communities that will protect children and the environment for years to come.

It started simply enough: "I, as a PTA president of my kids' elementary school, wrote the program in May 2002 on my kitchen table, and it has now eclipsed the entire environmental education industry," Jill says. "We operate in thirty-nine states, Europe, Africa, Mexico, and will be taking the program to mainland China by the end of 2007. I am a featured speaker all over the country, and have been covered in many press outlets, large and small. We have an incredible list of partners, including both President Clinton's and President Bush's Federal Environmental Executives."

According to Jill, Guerrilla P.R. was instrumental in starting and growing GGI. "From the genesis of the program, I was thinking globally and acting globally. My vision from the get-go was to create the most successful EE program in the world, which is why nothing has surprised me, overly impressed me, made me take myself too seriously, or made me lose focus on the ultimate goal. Every baby step I took in accordance with [the book's] advice was headed in one, linear direction, though to some on the outside, it looked to be a confusing scheme."

She used the techniques described in this book to network and create alliances, in what Jill calls "the hopscotch approach. One partnership led to another, then another, and ultimately to the big one I really needed. Similarly, one media hit led to another and another, until I was in *Working Mother* magazine. I knew there were key partnerships I needed to form and key publications in which I needed to be featured in order to (a) acquire the necessary funding to operate the program, i.e., appeal to sponsors; and (b) increase the number of schools that signed on . . . which also impressed potential sponsors and media outlets. I had to create such a sharp upward growth curve that no 'similar' program could compete with me, so that I could attract 'green' corporate sponsors."

With a Guerrilla P.R. plan, she adds, "it was easier than I thought because the industry itself didn't take me seriously enough to consider me a threat to their reliable source of corporate sponsorship. It was truly a Guerrilla story."

At the time she wrote the GGI, Jill was neither an environmentalist in the conventional sense nor an educator. "I was a thirty-two-year-old mother of three who passionately wanted to leave her children a clean, healthy planet; teach her kids environmentally responsible behavior; and work with local schools to do likewise. When I wrote the GGI, I gained support from some key figures in the environmental and educational world early on, but it took a lot of nervous phone calls and presentations that made my knees shake. Those partnerships led to others in a 'hopscotch' fashion, and within two years, the GGI was the leader."

Five years after her initial forays into Guerrilla P.R., Jill heads a program that she says finds opportunities for publicity "falling into our lap every week." She continues to contact media outlets and has gotten unsolicited calls from *The View*, *Ebony* magazine, and the game show *Deal or No Deal*. "They knew our reputation, and liked the 'Tiffany wrapping' we recently gave our Web site when we 'threw a grenade in the middle of it' back in early 2007. As Michael says in Chapter 13, 'a guerrilla is never satisfied . . . [must] keep vigilant . . . [knowing that] the enemy is always lurking.' My organization operates based on that advice every single day, and that is how we have stayed out in front of those who have a vested interest in seeing us fail."

Jill believes her Guerrilla P.R. plan began with Step One: identify the target audience. "I had the advantage of actually *being* the target audience . . . a PTA mom."

She notes the comment in this book that one should "try to do something first." Jill did so by aiming her program at an unconventional target audience: PTA parents. "We went one step beyond WIFM . . . I went straight to WIFMK (What's in it for my kids) and found that this was an even stronger motivator than anyone in the EE world could have imagined. Practically overnight, I had people who wouldn't cross the street to save a spotted owl passionately involved in the GGI. Why? Because the crux of my program was simple: protecting children's health through environmental protection. I made a conscious decision that our business was child advocacy, not environmentalism, and that human/child-centric emphasis has made all the difference in differentiating ourselves from our 'competition.' Even our logo sends this message loud and clear. As long as parents love their children, the message of the GGI will resonate."

Guerrilla P.R. is designed to be done on the cheap, and Jill notes that her first Web site for GGI was built on her home computer, with help from her sister-in-law, for a hosting fee of $50. Again, she made sure the message was clear and the target audience was specific: "Every page had pictures of kids and parents. We emphasized diversity of ethnicity, age, and gender to ensure that every visitor to our Web site could see themselves and their children as part of our family of GGI schools."

GGI then began identifying secondary audiences who could help in spreading the word. "The sub-targets were teachers, students, school administrators, municipal officials, public policy makers, and, finally, environmentalists," Jill explains. "I thought of it like Coca-Cola; they sell the same product to every demographic, but their commercials on MTV are not the same as their commercials on HGTV or ESPN. Same product, but presented to different audiences in a way that respects their needs and tastes. I knew that I had to equip my primary target audience to answer those questions in their own communities, so I began speaking at PTA conventions all over the country, and ensuring that they could 'sell' the program to all the sub-target groups. And because a guerrilla leaves nothing to chance, we went a step further. I worked closely with a handful of schools, and developed carefully orchestrated success stories, and then made a promo DVD showing principals, teachers, parents (besides myself), superintendents, and mayors telling their enthusiastic stories and testimonials on the GGI. The DVD went out to PTA leaders in all 50 states. If any parent champions had difficulty selling the GGI to their principal, they popped in the nine-minute DVD and let the principal hear from his own linear counterpart how easy, fun, and rewarding it was to be a GGI school."

Guerrilla P.R. is about finding ways to get your message out without spending money, so Jill took the concept a step further and helped generate publicity for the schools who used her program. "If they could generate publicity for their schools or their communities for GGI accomplishments, it would help them spread the program in their area more quickly. We put out sample press releases for our schools to use, and helped them develop relationships with their local media. And guess what . . . their publicity became OUR publicity. I'll never forget receiving the front page of the newspaper in Agawam, Massachusetts, with our logo taking up one fourth of the page, and a front-page story about the schools all 'going green.' This began to happen all over the country, and before long national magazines and large papers were calling me, and running stories on the GGI."

She found that much of her work was networking, something Jill is especially well equipped to do: she is very charming. "I worked very hard to develop a good rapport with members of the media," she says. "If I traveled, I tried to meet with them when I was in town, take them to lunch, and always begin my conversation with 'I saw the article you wrote on [fill in the recent date], and I thought you might be interested in how my organization is working on the same issue.' I did my homework on individual reporters and made sure that my pitches were never generic. That made the conversations interesting to them AND to their audiences."

Jill made a packet of press clips that began with a first article about GGI in a publication called *U.S. Mayor*, and she eventually spoke at a convention of mayors. "I made a copy of that article and sent it along with a cover letter and packet of information to a hundred mayors across the nation. I cannot tell you how many relationships developed from that mailing," she says. "The same thing happened when the National School Boards Association endorsed the GGI and asked me to write an Op-Ed in their publication. I made copies and sent it out to the state school board associations in every state. Again, many good relationships and new client schools came from that endeavor."

With judicious (and inspired) use of Guerrilla P.R. tactics, Jill Buck has taken a concept from her kitchen table and created an amazing environmental group that unites parents and schools in an effort to, as her slogan says, "prepare the future for our children." It's an admirable goal, created by a woman who knocks me out.

7

First Attack:
The Print Media

Dealing with Newspapers

Picture the newsroom: a hangar-sized warehouse of cramped cubicles, clacking computer keyboards, ringing phones, and human bodies in perpetual motion, racing to meet unforgiving deadlines. Now picture the overworked reporter juggling three or four stories at a time. The phone rings. It's you on the line, pitching your project to this harried, disinterested grouch. If you think taking your call is his idea of a good time, think again. But don't let that stop you.

And that's just the view of a newspaper newsroom. Consider the chaos that television news, even at the local level, entails. The same telephones and computer screens, but a constant deadline and a studio in one corner where all the lights and the cameras live. Bloggers and online reporters work at home, for the large part, although the bigger sites have offices and newsrooms, too. And everybody, at every moment of the day, has e-mail to read.

There's a widespread notion out there, mostly fostered by journalists themselves, that reporters have no need for publicists. Don't believe it. Reporters need sources. If you become a source for a story, then you're what the reporter needs, and that puts you in a position of considerable power. How you exercise that power is what counts.

To score with newspaper reporters and editors, you have to comprehend their requirements. First, news value is central to their thinking. They aren't interested in hype. Fluff is fine, but hype isn't. Everything Paris Hilton generates in the press may strike you as hype, but because it's *her* hype, it's transformed into news. You aren't yet in as fortunate a position.

As for whom to contact, there's a wide array of job titles at a newspaper: executive editor, managing editor, city editor, ad infinitum. You'd be best served by trying to reach those on the front lines, such as section editors, features editors, and general or beat reporters. The higher-ups in management don't have much to do with day-today reporting. Thankfully, newspaper writers and editors are far more accessible than their TV counterparts. If you call the switchboard and ask for someone by name, chances are good the very person you want will pick up the phone.

Bloggers and online reporters are best contacted via e-mail. There's almost always a "contact us" link on the Web site, and indeed, many newspapers now include the reporter's e-mail address in his or her byline or at the bottom of the article.

Newspapers, especially, are feeling the pinch of the digital age and want to foster a close relationship with their readers. Take advantage of it. Newspaper reporters are eager to answer the phone, almost without regard to who's calling.

That's not always true, especially if you're calling writers at major papers. Hurtling the heavily defended lines of voice mail alone is enough to put off many hardy souls. There's no getting around the fact that large daily papers in the top fifteen markets, such as the *Los Angeles Times* or the *New York Times,* run differently than do smaller town papers like the *Des Moines Register.* But it's only a matter of scale. The smaller papers are in many ways more effective. Although not as many people read them, they tend to have more impact in their given communities. Besides, they tend to have nearly as much access to news sources as their big brothers in the big cities.

Rebecca Coudret, a reporter for the *Courier-Press* in Evansville, Indiana, is quick to note that her paper is a link in the Scripps-Howard chain of more than three hundred newspapers across the country. Any story she writes goes out on their wire and has a potential reach of millions. So if you live in a small city and fret that your audience would be limited if you stayed parochial, relax. If your local paper hits your target audience, then that's the paper you want to be in, and it may reach out farther than you guessed.

When you contact a newspaper, keep your news angle uppermost in mind. Most likely you've already sent a press release and/or press kit. So, once you've got a reporter on the phone, *avoid the hard sell.* Saying "You *have* to cover this" just won't work. My reporter friends uniformly claim their disdain for pressure from outsiders. You must be willing to bend, even to the point of losing. Better to miss out this time and keep a friendly contact than to go for broke in an obnoxious manner and lose out permanently.

The same principle is true when applied to TV and radio: local stations will afford you more and easier access than network affiliates and huge cable stations. Local cable access is probably the easiest, because it has the lowest budget (so it can't afford to hire a lot of reporters and relishes any local stories brought in by publicists) and lives and breathes local news, but it has the smallest audience. It is a concentrated audience that lives where you live, works where you work, and shares your interests. Remember that local news wants local stories, so play up that angle as much as you can.

Be friendly, but not gushy. Nobody likes to be sucked up to. Your manner should steer clear of the sickeningly familiar.

Know the reporter's work. I say this over and over. You will genuinely flatter a writer if you indicate that you're acquainted with his or her work. Don't fake it. If you refer to a piece that ran a week ago, you'd better have read it. Aside from garnering goodwill, you can make more sensible suggestions about the nature of the reporter's coverage of your project.

Be sensitive to deadlines. Most newspapers are dailies. That means that every day the Herculean challenge of putting out a newspaper is met by these individuals. Give them credit. Reality for newspaper writers is the deadline. Like an ever-moving wall of molten lava from a Hawaiian volcano, deadlines are unstoppable. So if you're pitching an event, make sure you give the writer plenty of time to work with your request, and don't call when he or she is under the gun. Morning papers have late-afternoon deadlines, so call in the late morning. Conversely, afternoon papers should be contacted in the late afternoon, after they've gone to print.

TV and radio news broadcasts have *constant* deadlines, but you should know the station's schedule. If the news is broadcast at 5 PM, it's a hideously bad idea to call at 4:45. Understand that reporters—even those who might be open to your story—have a job to do and a drop-dead moment when it must be done. You don't want to be a distraction or, worse, an annoyance. It's easy to give in to your impulse for immediacy, but take it from me: you want to wait until the reporter is open to your pitch.

Remember that many journalists have an inflated sense of self-importance. There's a reason why so many people out there distrust the media. Many media people believe they're on a mission from God, and they can be unbearably arrogant at times. You could be the next victim of a cynical writer spoiling for a fight. Counter with a professional attitude, quiet enthusiasm, relentless cordiality, and an ironclad pitch.

When it comes down to negotiating a story idea, there are several options to go after. They include

Feature. A full-length descriptive article on you, your project, or related topics. These tend to be the most beneficial to you because of their length, prominent placement in the paper, frequent use of photo illustration, and prestigious journalistic cachet.

Q&A. A simple question-and-answer interview. These can be reprinted in their entirety or condensed into much shorter pieces. Either way, they make for excellent coverage.

Round-up. When you or your project fit into the scope of a larger piece a writer is working on, a round-up story may be your best bet. Say you own a computer dating service. A writer may be working on a "Love and Speed

Dating" think piece, and your insights may dovetail nicely. Take it if you can get it.

Column item. Some journalists write regular columns for the paper. Perhaps you can interest one of them in devoting one of their columns to you. These articles tend to be more emotional and subjective, which can be a real boon to you and your project. Other columnists report on upcoming community activities and events. You may benefit greatly from such a column mention. Usually local columnists focus on only local issues.

Calendar. This is nothing more than a line item notice in a calendar of events. But you'd be surprised how well read these pages are. At the very least, make sure your event is listed.

It's okay to suggest to the reporter what you feel might be best—it demonstrates that you're a regular reader of the paper, especially if you can cite a recent piece that was similar. He or she may then direct you to another writer or editor. Make sure everyone you talk with has received or will receive press materials. Sometimes, reporters pass them on to editors, and vice versa. Determine that before you send along another e-mail or package.

What if your pitch works and the reporter wants to do an interview or story? Congratulations! But being on the receiving end of an interview requires preparation. The proper handling of interviews can make or break your Guerrilla P.R. campaign, so let's lay some groundwork.

First of all, even though the reporter seems to hold all the cards (after all, he or she will ask the questions and write the story), you do have a considerable role in shaping the tone of the interview. The reporter may frame the questions, but you frame the answers. You'll probably sense right away if the writer is sympathetic, bored, skeptical, or downright hostile.

No matter what, you need to concentrate on positive responses. Do not get defensive or evasive. Keep your language and decorum on a high level, because a reporter will pounce on anything he or she senses might be controversial.

Here's a fictitious interview that shows how to gently deflect tough questioning:

> **Q:** "The Mid-Valley Youth Center seems to be a black hole for public and private funds. Why are you once again turning to the public to pump more money into a losing proposition?" (This question is hostile, full of loaded terminology like "black hole" and "losing proposition." Reporters often goad subjects into giving more info than they intended to reveal, and this is one effective way of doing that. Don't duck the question, but deflect hostility by absorbing it into your own agenda.)
>
> **A:** "I understand why some people may get that impression, but it's more important that people understand how our budget process works. I have for you a complete financial audit conducted by an independent accounting firm, which shows how prudently our funds were used. We're seeking new funding now because the current economy has made it tough to keep existing programs going."

Steering the conversation hinges on telling reporters what *you* want them to hear, not what they hope to hear. To do this, never lose sight of your objective. Of course you should respond to skeptical or tangential questions, but your challenge is to return to your main points without coming off like a snake oil salesman.

In essence, the interview is like a game of tennis, of give and take. What you give depends on what the interviewer serves you, and the same goes for him or her. Anticipating the interviewer's questions, rehearsing (but not memorizing) your answers, and amassing a collection of transition lines ("What you said reminded me of . . ." or "I should also mention that . . .").

Another tip: Unlike TV news, print media find detailed statistics useful. Provide as many as serve your case. But avoid appearing to blow a smokescreen made of numbers. Reporters are trained to question everything, so be sure your case is airtight and your statistics relevant.

If the reporter interviews you at your place of work (assuming your workplace is the location of your project), be open. Show him or her around; offer as much information and access as possible. Reporters will draw their own conclusions no matter what you do, so you may as well expose them to everything germane.

The process doesn't end once the interview is over. If later you think of other points you failed to mention, call the writer immediately. Make sure you get the correct phone number before you part company. Don't pester writers too much as to when the story may run. Most reporters have little control over this, and frequent calls will only alienate the writer.

After a story does run, if it's positive (or even if it's constructively critical), you may wish to call or write the reporter with your thanks. But here again, reporters' pride comes into play. They usually don't feel they did you any favor by running a piece about you, whether positive or negative. Reporters believe in their own objectivity: they think they are writing news, neither positive nor negative, just true. It was a simple matter of news to them; so sometimes thank-yous can be insulting. Use your own judgment.

Remember, there's no scientific definition of news. It's whatever people are talking about. You want to become news, so get them talking!

Guerrilla P.R. Exercise

In a mock interview, have a friend ask you a few general questions, and see if you can navigate the conversation entirely in your own direction.

Tips & Traps

- Although it's common practice, avoid doing interviews in restaurants. They're noisy and distracting, and it's hard to make a good impression with a piece of steak stuck between your teeth. Meet in an office or another work setting.
- To whatever extent possible, see that the reporter tapes your interview to ensure accuracy. I don't need to tell you about the pitfalls of being misquoted.
- Yes, an interview is business, but it's also human conversation, not an interrogation. I find it effective to lock into the other person's humanity. Liveliness, friendliness, openness, all have an impact, no matter what the reporter says about keeping his or her journalistic distance.

- Pause often; reflect on your words. You're on the record now (unless you tell the reporter otherwise, and *before* the comments are made), and you want your words to reflect your truest and best sense of yourself.
- Don't forget to ask the reporter to send you a clip. For one reason or another, you may not always have the opportunity to obtain one.

FROM THE GUERRILLA P.R. FILE

Kraco Enterprises, one of the nation's largest auto-detailing and accessory companies, together with publicist Alex Litrov, cooked up a scheme in 1988 to find America's long-distance commuter champ. Word of the contest spread throughout the media, and finally they found their winner: Rod Conklin of Darien, Connecticut, who commuted a total of 408 miles each day from his home to Boston and back. The story was picked up by CNN, *USA Today*, and UPI as well as by many local newspapers and TV stations. Kraco was mentioned several times, and the whole campaign was a raging success.

Now if only someone would help poor Mr. Conklin find a job closer to home.

Dealing with Wire Services

At every press conference held by every president since Franklin D. Roosevelt, the privilege of asking the first question goes to the reporter from the Associated Press, America's most important wire service. The reason is simple. AP is picked up by every newspaper in the country and most of the world as well. The wires provide eyes and ears to papers too small to cover the world. In fact, despite what ABC says, more people get their news from the wires than from anywhere else.

There are other wire services besides AP. UPI, Reuters, Gannett, and syndicates like King Features, the New York Times Syndicate, and the Los Angeles Times Syndicate are a few of the largest; although some, like the New York Times and the L.A. Times syndicates, send out only those stories that have appeared in their newspapers. The twenty-four-hour cable news networks also syndicate some of their stories to newspapers, as does *USA Today* (through Gannett). But all wires furnish members and subscribers with reams of stories covering everything from the White House to the local five-and-dime. Like other news media, wires hunger for stories and scoops, and they could play a significant role in your Guerrilla P.R. campaign.

Wires differ most markedly from newspapers in that they produce nothing printed. They service subscribers electronically (in the old days it came over a teletype "wire," hence the name). Though the large wires have bureaus in most major cities, their inherent anonymity may make them a little harder to find. However, you generally need look no further than your nearby metropolitan white pages or Google.

Once you locate them, proceed with caution. Unlike your local paper, which serves and is beholden to the community, the wires serve a much larger constituency and can be much less inclined to jump on your story than the daily down the street. The local bureau, however, is usually looking for something it can "sell" to the syndicate overall, and therefore might be open to your pitch if you deliver it well.

Whereas daily papers often assign beats to reporters, such as city desk, entertainment, or sports, most wire service writers are general reporters covering everything under the sun. As busy as newspaper journalists are, wire reporters are unbelievably overworked, usually juggling four or more stories at a time.

Everything I said about sensitivity to the journalist's workload goes double for wire reporters.

Ironically, though, unless they're covering major national stories, most wire reporters are not subject to the crushing deadlines of the dailies. They have more time to labor over detail and give their stories a little more scrutiny. So, pitch them solely on the merits of your story. Wire stories tend to reflect a more universal nature so that they can run in any paper anywhere. A proposal with too local an angle is likely to be turned down. Pitch accordingly. Think broader.

It's the opposite of pitching to the local paper or station: a national (or international) wire service by definition is not interested in something that will have *only* local appeal. It doesn't send its stories to papers only in one area—the very function of a wire service is to send news from places *other than* the local area. Local papers, after all, can afford to send their reporters to nearby stories—it's the far-away ones they need to have covered by the syndicate. So keep that in mind. Give your story a universal spin, something that will appeal not only to your area but to people around the country and around the world.

Our fictional Youth Center, for example, would have to abandon any mention of its upcoming carnival or appearances by local officials; the newspaper in Helena, Montana, probably won't care about that. But if the story were to be suggested as a larger one—something involving the effect of budget cuts on beneficial programs, for example—it might interest a wire service. The Youth Center might become only one component of a larger article that quotes numerous sources, but its plight would reach readers from coast to coast.

And while I'm on the subject of wires, don't forget to consider America's syndicated columnists. I'm sure you read a few

of them regularly. Although it's a long shot that Dave Barry or
Liz Smith will do a story on your project, they shouldn't be ruled
out, and they are by no means the only fish in the sea. There
are dozens and dozens of important columnists in this country,
writing on everything from gardening to politics to child rear-
ing. If you write a well-composed letter to one of them, either
in care of the paper you read or directly to the syndicate, you
just may have a shot.

The key is knowing the writer's work and style. Many tend
to use parables and personal illustrations to make their points.
That's where you might fit in. In your letter, suggest a column
idea or theme to which your project may apply. With a good angle to dangle, there's a chance you'll hear from the columnist.

Tips & Traps

- Never blanket a bureau, i.e., pitch to other reporters in
  the same office if the first one has already said "no." Word
  will get out (believe it or not, reporters do talk to each
  other), and your name will be permanent mud.
- Your story will be best served by the nearest bureau.
  Though it might seem like you're closer to the nerve center if you contact the New York or L.A. office of AP, stay
  close to home. If you live in Pittsburgh, call the Pittsburgh
  bureau.
- Wire reporters tend to work closely with member and
  subscribing papers. They read them carefully and know
  what's going on in the communities. They pick up stories
  from the papers, just as the papers pick up stories from the
  wires.

- If you have had some success with your local paper, even if it's not a member of the syndicate, be sure to mention that to the reporter. News services love to pick up stories that have already been covered locally. It lends an air of legitimacy.
- You should be careful with columnists with respect to time. You may not hear from them or their staffs for quite a long while (imagine the volume of mail they must receive), and you shouldn't put too many eggs in this one basket.

Media Facts

- There are 1,456 daily newspapers in America.
- There are 917 newspapers that have Sunday editions.
- There are approximately 7,000 weekly papers in America.
- There are over 5,000 trade publications in the United States.
- There are 156.3 million U.S. adults who read one or more magazines each month.
- The circulation of U.S. dailies is 52.3 million.
- The *Hartford Courant* in Hartford, Connecticut, is the oldest daily in America, founded in 1764.[2]
- The top ten newspapers in America and their circulation[3] are as follows:
  1. *USA Today* (2.52 million)
  2. *Wall Street Journal* (2.05 million)

2. Source: *Editor & Publisher*, 2004.
3. Source: Audit Bureau of Circulation, 2006.

3. *New York Times* (1.68 million)

4. *L.A. Times* (1.23 million)

5. *Washington Post* (960,000)

6. *Chicago Tribune* (957,000)

7. *New York Daily News* (795,000)

8. *Philadelphia Inquirer* (705,000)

9. *Denver Post / Rocky Mountain News* (704,000)

10. *Houston Chronicle* (692,000)

- The *Reader's Digest* reaches over 80 million people each month.

Dealing with Trade Publications

Whatever line of work you're in, there are trade publications covering it. In my business, *Variety* and the *Hollywood Reporter* fit the bill. In the music industry, it's *Billboard;* in the fashion world, *Women's Wear Daily;* and for Madison Avenue, *AdWeek*. Trades can be micro-specific. Out there right now you can find avid readers of *Footwear News, Banking Software Review, Travel Agent Magazine,* and *Water Waste Digest*. We all enjoy reading about our own business. It makes us feel connected to our own special industry or service.

A study conducted by the Opinion Research Corporation found that 40 percent of business customers rated trade publications as their chief source of information about their particular product or service. That's a significant number. Even though a favorable trade story may seem like preaching to the choir, once your peers think you're hot, soon the public will too.

Trades can be dailies, weeklies, or monthlies, and many of them run special annual or bi-annual editions. They all require different lead times, so be cognizant and act accordingly. Trades function much like consumer publications. They like scoops, exclusives, and breaking stories. But you'll discover right away that trade reporters are true experts in their fields. They possess refined knowledge in order to communicate to a rarefied audience. When you pitch them, address them as absolute equals in terms of comprehension of subject matter.

Keep in mind, too, that trade publications have their own Web sites, they have bloggers on the industry, and, in some cases, they will report news of the industry long before the mainstream press gets to it. Keep all aspects of a trade publication in mind when you're pitching your story idea.

As with some consumer publications, trades are advertiser sensitive. Many times I've seen businesses "buy" stories in the trades by purchasing ad space. This is unethical, and I hope you never find yourself in such a position. If you're ever told bluntly that you must buy an ad to get a feature, walk away. Your dignity isn't for sale. Worse than that, you can assume that people in the industry know which trade publications will sell you editorial space, and your credibility will be damaged along with that of the magazine you pay. It's not a good Guerrilla P.R. move to pay for editorial, anyway.

Some may call this a naive attitude, but I've become successful without having to resort to such a stratagem. You don't have to either. If a trade publication decides to do a story on you, make sure the reporter has *all* the facts. Send her as much additional written material on your project as possible, including information that has nothing directly to do with your Guerrilla P.R. campaign. If a personal interview and/or tour is in order, roll out the red carpet. Remember, this is a person who ostensibly knows as much about your business as you do, so don't even think about trying to embellish the facts. The trade journalist is one reporter who will definitely see through it.

In addition to pitching trades for stories on you and your project, you may offer to submit your own article or guest editorial, just as we discussed for the consumer press. I would say the trades are much more likely to run your piece than a daily paper because you're coming from an insider's position of strength. And there will be an added boost of insider credibility because you're not talking to the general public—now your message is reaching people with an existing knowledge of your industry. Make sure you speak with an editor before you set pen to paper, though. You could set yourself up for disappointment if you go to the trouble of writing a piece and then get no response from the trade publication. Or, they might already have a competitor's piece in type. With anything you write, observe the following guidelines:

- Don't offer the same written work for publication by more than one trade. That violates the honor code of exclusivity.
- Try to keep your piece on the shorter rather than the longer side. You'll make a greater impact and keep the attention of your audience.
- Seize on one or two (at most) simple themes. Marketing expert Bob Serling, in a short article he wrote for a leading marketing journal, made his points using the term "leverage" as a hook. Every paragraph heading used this term to make its points.
- Remember what I said about writing in the previous two chapters. Good writing is good writing, no matter where it ends up, and everything you write should come off as

polished and well thought out. Get people you trust to
read your article before you send it off in an e-mail. Make
sure you've checked (and not just spell-checked) for typos,
mistakes, and poor grammar. Be sure that what you're
sending will represent you well.

Because they're supported almost entirely by advertising
from within the industry they represent, trades are industry's
cheerleaders. Unlike their counterparts in the newspaper world,
trade reporters generally aren't out to get anyone. They prefer
to be viewed as boosters. Thus, if your angle is upbeat and positive, you stand a good chance of making it in the trades. Trade
stories make excellent clips and can really get a Guerrilla P.R.
campaign off and running. So give the trades your best shot.

Dealing with Magazines

I don't know about you, but I have a hard time throwing away
magazines. Whereas the daily paper is hurled on the recycle
stack at the end of every day, year-old copies of *Time, Newsweek,*
and *Rolling Stone* keep popping up in different corners around
the house.

There's something permanent about a magazine. If it's in-
scribed in the pages of *Time,* it lives forever. In my experience,
magazine editors are more selective in what they choose to print.
Perhaps because most magazines are monthlies, editors' jobs are
on the line with every issue. Each story is make or break. Magazines and legitimate tabloids like the *L.A. Weekly* or the *Village
Voice* have longer lead times than newspapers, up to five months,
and more if you're new to them. There's less space in magazines

than in newspapers, so every word counts more. For the news-oriented weeklies, like *Time,* summary and analysis are the watchwords. Their editors assume a high level of astuteness on the part of readers.

Just because you have a Guerrilla P.R. approach doesn't mean you don't belong in *Newsweek.* You simply have to "nationalize" your pitch. If you recall the section on pitching, I urged you to create variations on your pitch to apply to different media. For national magazines, you have to broaden your concept.

To use the Youth Center as an example, instead of pitching the magazines on the reduction of crime in the area, I would stress how America can turn its troubled youth around with the right mix of compassion and dedication and the value of volunteering for the community's good. You get the picture.

Keep in mind that many well-known magazines occasionally run special issues (also called one-shots), such as *Sports Illustrated*'s swimsuit edition and *Entertainment Weekly*'s summer movie issue. Some are far more esoteric or accessible than those. When you speak with editors, find out if any such specials are being planned. You might fit in. Much more than newspapers, magazines are graphics conscious. Editors agonize over who or what goes on the cover, while teams of designers labor over each issue's layout. As we saw with *Vanity Fair*'s celebrated cover of the nude and pregnant Demi Moore, this obsession is understandable. It was estimated that a picture of Princess Diana when she was alive would add $1 million to the value of the issue of any magazine that featured it on its cover. That's power. Keep this in mind when you pitch.

Not that you'll have any impact on layout, but if the writer or editor senses your awareness, you'll gain stature. Don't be afraid to offer suggestions here and there on ways to illustrate your story. They may not accept them, but they'll respect your involvement.

Phoning is not as effective as writing when contacting magazines. Not all writers are on staff. Many are freelancers whom you can't reach by phone anyway, but they can always receive forwarded mail. Fire off some letters to writers you find particularly intriguing. Not every newspaper article has its writer credited, but practically all magazine pieces have an accompanying byline. All writers have editors, and all magazines have mastheads, so it's pretty easy to figure out whom to contact.

Obviously, e-mail is quicker and more efficient, but getting e-mail addresses for specific editors or reporters on a magazine can sometimes be difficult. Try calling the magazine's editorial office, or if you can find a pattern for the way the company handles e-mail addresses (many simply make it first initial last name @ publication.com for every staffer), try sending it out that way.

Also be aware that most magazines now have Web content, and it's not always the same as what's in the traditional paper edition. If you strike out with the magazine itself, try seeing if the related Web site might not be interested in your story.

Weekly tabloids catering to individual communities have slightly different requirements. Though they don't encompass the global scope of *Time*, they often emphasize analysis, investigative reporting, and expanding the range of local stories. So if you want a meaty feature, you have to present to them a bigger picture. Say you own a small business in a revitalized area of your community. Suggest a round-up story idea focusing on the rebirth of the local economy, using your shop as an example.

Magazines can frustrate you. Because of limited space and their paranoia about what goes in, you may find yourself up against a wall much of the time. But keep trying. A good magazine lends credibility to a project. The writers tend to write at a higher level than their newspaper counterparts, primarily because they have more time to turn in their pieces. Besides, most magazines, in order to be profitable, usually enjoy a far wider circulation than almost any metropolitan daily paper. Even if circulation isn't great, magazines get passed around. Statistics show that the average copy of a magazine reaches 4.8 readers. The moral is this: do your best to make magazines a part of your G.P.R. diet.

FROM THE GUERRILLA P.R. FILE

Columbia University research fellow Harold Zullow made the papers across America with his unusual sociological studies. Zullow theorized that the pop charts are good predictors of the overall direction of the national economy. The thesis states that either pessimistic songs or truly awful songs make it to No. 1 just before an economic downturn. His proof: "Escape (The Pina Colada Song)," "Keep On Truckin'," and "The One That You Love," all utter treacle, and each hit the top spot just before a recession. Just goes to show that if you concoct a weird-enough theory, you'll attract the media like a moth to a flame.

Other Print Possibilities

The world of print journalism doesn't end with the daily paper, the trade publication, and the weekly edition of *People*. Entire forests are devoured every year to feed our insatiable appetite for print. As a Guerrilla publicist, your M.O. is to cover every base, especially those the pros tend to downplay.

If you live in a college town, there's probably a college paper on campus. They're usually student-run; and you'll find college kids enthusiastic and open to new ideas (unlike their jaded counterparts at the daily). True, most of the articles are campus oriented, but once in a while they jump on atypical stories. If you can tie in your story to an issue on campus, or if you can relate your business to the college (if you're a "townie"), you might find a friendly ear in the campus newspaper office. They are by nature very accessible, so give your college paper editor a call.

Don't neglect community ethnic newspapers. There are hundreds of important newspapers across America that serve the African-American community, such as the *L.A. Sentinel* and New York's *Amsterdam News*. Obviously, these papers cater to the needs of their readership, but they are almost always open to important stories, interesting sidebars, or announcements. Spanish-language papers, like *El Diario* in New York and *La Opinion* in L.A., all have English-speaking staff reporters who will cover your story if it has merit for their readership. You can reach a vast audience by tapping into these kinds of papers. Organizations and businesses distribute in-house newsletters and are often open to outside stories. Check with large companies in your area to see which have such a program. Also, every pastime has a specialty publication (they're called "buff books") to call its own, e.g., *Car & Driver, Ski, House Beautiful*. Do you fit in with any of them?

Many churches, mosques, Buddhist temples, and synagogues have newsletters, too. If you're a member, perhaps there's a way to contribute a piece to your in-house publication. Write a letter to the editor of the newsletter, or submit a short piece on how your project is helping the congregation. Think political. Your local or state Democratic, Republican, or third-party committee probably has a publication. Once again, you may be able to create a piece that relates your project to your political activities.

Last Word on Print

It's said we're becoming a nation of illiterates. Fewer and fewer people read anymore. Daily papers are dropping like flies; SAT scores are down; kids know more about the latest Pink video than what's happening in the Middle East. The future looks bleak.

But our society remains glued together by the printed word. Our institutions, our economy, and our entire society are welded to the written word. As high-minded as that sounds, it most definitely trickles down to the Guerrilla P.R. level. If you were to get on TV and not in print, you wouldn't last. The account of our civilization ultimately will be told in the written record, not the video, even in the short term.

Think about it: television reaches a huge audience, but it's fleeting. You're on for a five-minute spot on the local news, and then you're gone. Even people using TiVo to record the news are probably not going to save your appearance (with the possible exception of your mom, who will be too proud to delete it). But print will last. It will be archived, probably on the publication's Web site, and findable with very little effort for the foreseeable future. Don't disrespect print because it's "so yesterday." It's also "so tomorrow."

I placed my chapter on print before the one on TV because I believe it to be the most important. Yes, you will be seen by more people if you appear on TV, and perhaps your project will gain a greater lift from a guest shot on *Oprah* than from a piece in the *New York Times*. But perception is reality. If you are canonized by a *New York Times* article you will have achieved a level of legitimacy far greater than any TV stint can deliver. Go for it all, but by all means, go for print.

GUERRiLLA P.R. COMMANDO: Angelyne

She's as much a part of the Los Angeles landscape as the Capitol Records Tower and the Hollywood Sign. For nearly twenty-five years, billboards of the pouty-lipped, platinum blonde Angelyne, perched atop her pink Corvette, dotted the boulevards and byways of the city, creating a pop culture heroine the likes of which we haven't seen before. Most people have wondered who the hell she is, but over time, the ubiquitous billboards of "the girl on the Corvette" have become a true Southern California icon.

The Angelyne mystique arose out of L.A.'s preoccupation with fame and image. For no reason other than her striking appearance on the billboards, Angelyne became a symbol of L.A.'s fast-lane mentality. Her fame has spread throughout the world, though most people aren't quite sure who she is or what she does. Many would guess the doe-eyed vixen to be a first-class bimbo. They should guess again.

Angelyne happens to be a supremely intelligent businesswoman who is wise in the ways of self-promotion and Guerrilla P.R. Without ever hiring a publicist, she turned herself into a permanent part of the city's persona. But how?

"I'm a rebel," she told me, "very much into being original. I detest clichés." The former rock singer claims a lifelong devotion to achieving celebrity. "When I was three I knew I would never feel right until I became famous," she says. "Fame made me feel more normal." To achieve her goal, Angelyne embarked on a campaign to get her image before the public.

"I started with posters," she recalls, "then bus shelters. Next, we put out small billboards, then larger ones. We finally painted my picture on a ten-story wall at Hollywood and Vine. After that, the media were all over me." Angelyne estimates she gained $10 million in free publicity because of the massive media exposure from the billboards. Her posters included her management phone number, which hasn't stopped ringing since Day One.

Thanks to her innovation and perseverance, Angelyne's movie and personal appearance career has taken off, more than paying for the cost of the billboard campaign. Her chief advice to others hoping to entice the media: "I relate to the media the same way I relate to men. Never touch anybody. Tease them until they come to you. I have never had to call anybody for anything. They called me."

As special as she feels herself to be, Angelyne is convinced everybody has within him or her the makings of a star. "We can become free agents unto ourselves," she says. "In the future, I think everyone will be able to make the most of their artistic side."

Angelyne has certainly made the most of her abilities. She won the fame she wanted and paid nary a penny for the media exposure. Today, she's probably having the last laugh. That's life in the big city.

8

Second Salvo:
Electronic Media

Local [TV] news has always been more ukelele than symphony.

—Howard Rosenberg, *L.A. Times*

Television

In the past fifteen years, the "vast wasteland" has gotten a whole lot vaster. The proliferation of digital TV opened up grand new vistas for viewers, with more choices available now than were ever imagined just a few years ago. CNN, Fox, MTV, and HBO have taken their place at the table of mega-profits alongside the shrinking networks, while public access and UHF channels continue to mushroom. Consider how many Emmy Awards have been won by cable stations in the past five years. In 2006, broadcast networks made a comeback in the Primetime Emmy Awards to win more in one evening (all awards considered, including technical ones) than cable networks. The broadcast networks (defined that year as ABC, CBS, Fox, NBC, WB, and PBS) won fifty-two of the awards handed out by the Television Academy that night. Which was more than were won by cable stations; they took home fifty-one.

Answering the old question "What's on tonight?" isn't so simple anymore.

For the Guerrilla P.R. strategist, TV is essential. TV is power; if you get yourself on the tube, power passes to your hands, and success in your efforts is almost guaranteed. Yet, despite the many similarities among the various media, TV is a breed unto itself. For one thing, a newspaper exists in the realm of space, TV in the realm of time. One involves imagination, the other image. Even on talking-head news shows like *Face the Nation,* the image is what counts. The congressman rambling on about third-quarter housing starts may be a womanizing blowhard, but if he looks and sounds good up there, his most important message—"Reelect me!"—comes through loud and convincingly.

Because of TV's time constraints, practically every moment on the tube is scripted down to the millisecond. TV is not so much a marketplace of ideas as it is a big show. Even news programs—local and national—are just shows. To make it on the air, your project must become part of the show, a part people will want to watch. If not, no matter how deserving you may be, the only TV you'll appear on is the one in the department store with the camcorder trained on you. Yes, you can upload a video of yourself to YouTube, but even then, you'll have to promote it to get it seen. Unless you're doing something unbelievably unique (and probably damaging to your image), even YouTube is going to be too large a medium to tackle on your own. You need to be seen on legitimate television to gain credibility.

To be part of the show, you have to know how TV works. For Guerrilla P.R. purposes, let's divide the medium into its constituent parts:

News. This includes everything from Brian Williams to the goofy weatherman on Channel 6. News programming has diversified greatly over the last twenty years. The advent of CNN and Fox News, the expansion of local news, cable, and a plethora of prime-time shows originating with the network news divisions (like *60 Minutes, Dateline,* and *20/20*) have dramatically increased the broadcast hours devoted to news. News is also what happens on the local cable access channel, the local PBS affiliate, and the local station's five o'clock newscast. It is the time when television is, at least on the surface, trying to inform.

Public affairs. Although public affairs programming has decreased since F.C.C. deregulation in the 1980s, it still constitutes an important outlet for varying points of view on issues of public interest. Most network affiliates in major markets have their own Sunday newsmakers shows, which usually cover local political subjects. And again, local stations, cable affiliates, and basically anyone with a digital video camera and a question can be considered a "public affairs" program these days. Never rule out *any* outlet unless you are required to pay for the airtime, or if there's no chance your message will be relevant to the program involved.

Infotainment. These shows, more than any other, have flourished in the past few years. There are two types: the town meeting and the simulated news show. The town meeting variety started with Phil Donahue back in the seventies, featuring a charismatic host and an inquisitive studio audience. Now we've got Oprah, Ellen, and Jerry Springer, to name a few. They cover two basic catch-all themes: real life and Hollywood. You'll tune in to find either Will Smith pushing his new movie or three recovering alcoholic Satan worshippers in love with the same paraplegic transsexual. Like I said: real life. Sim-news shows are among the most reviled and most watched in the country: *A Current Affair, Hard Copy, Inside Edition*, and *Entertainment Tonight* are among the best known. These shows thrive on sensationalism. Sex, scandal, and sin are their stock-in-trade. But once in a while they cover more wholesome subjects . . . like you, perhaps. They're not easy to book, especially if you're not incredibly outrageous, but they're worth a thought.

Morning shows. NBC's *Today* is the granddaddy of morning shows. CBS and ABC have *This Morning* and *Good Morning America*. Nationally syndicated shows like *Live with Regis and Kelly*—as well as the many local outlets such as *Good Day New York, Home,* and *Today in Minneapolis*—provide invaluable exposure opportunities. All stories that run on these types of outlets have some national or universal significance.

TV is a much bigger deal than print. A newspaper reporter need bring along only a pad and a pencil, sometimes a tape recorder, to ensure accuracy. On the other hand, a TV news crew includes a reporter, a sound technician, a camera operator, a producer, and a driver, often of a van equipped to cover anything from a cat up a tree to a foreign invasion. An appearance on the set of a news broadcast or talk show involves dozens of people, from makeup artists to assistant directors to videotape editors. In a word, TV is *complicated.*

TV news, like print, has an inflated sense of journalistic scruples. Though few news stars have come up in the realm of hard-nosed print reporting, TV journalists like to believe they represent the same grand tradition of news coverage as, say, the *Washington Post.* Despite a few isolated instances where that is indeed the case, basically comparing the two is just silly. Television news, particularly on the local level, is a *show*, and print journalism, even in the sleazier daily tabloids, involves reporting more than it does glamour. You'll rarely see a male newspaper reporter wearing makeup.

With the average report lasting somewhere around a minute, local TV news is a sham. It's sports, weather, and the nightly murder and fire report. It's headlines read by ex-beauty queens and pretty boys, and woe to him or her who doesn't look the part. There's little analysis or in-depth reporting; and come sweeps month, we're likely to be deluged with five-part series on lesbian nuns or fifty ways to tell if your wife is cheating on you (ten a day for five days).

Yet, despite its deficiencies, TV news can be more dramatic and memorable than any other shared experience. From the death of a president in 1963 to the 9/11 attacks in 2001; from Watergate to Interngate, the Gulf War to the crumbling of the Soviet Union to the burning of L.A. after the Rodney King verdict to the invasion of Iraq, television news has given shape and meaning to the events of our time. I wouldn't trade it for anything.

Your main task is *knowing whom to contact*. Don't worry about getting yourself on the *CBS Evening News* (though I hope that's part of your long-term game plan). Instead, concentrate on local outlets first. You may have a wealth of choices, especially if you live in one of the top twenty-five U.S. markets.

Most cities have affiliates of all four major networks. Each has its own news division. Many independent stations have their own news programs as well. In L.A., we have the big four (CBS, NBC, ABC, Fox), CNN, the CW, Fox News, three independents, PBS, and several UHF channels with news programming, including two in Spanish and others in Korean, Japanese, Farsi, and Chinese. There are countless local cable outlets for each section of the city and its suburbs.

Most news programs run credits at the end, especially on Fridays. Look for the names of assignment or planning editors. Those are your initial contacts. TiVo the news one night and freeze-frame on the credits (they go by pretty quickly). Write down the names of anyone with the title "producer" or "news editor." Send them your written material. All newsrooms have "future files," and everything sent gets looked at, considered, and put in the file. If the station has full-time medical, business, or consumer reporters, and your project applies, you may contact the reporter directly, but generally it's prudent not to call a reporter. He or she would have to check with the assignment editor anyway, who might be miffed if bypassed.

Be current with the station's format. Know the anchors, the reporters, the weather and sports staffs. Once you make the call, proceed much as you would with a newspaper editor. The assignment editor handles that day's schedule; the planning editor looks ahead to the next few days, so depending on when and what you're pitching, you'll know whom to ask for.

Reiterate the main points of your press release, make your pitch, and remember to keep visuals uppermost in your mind, because that's how TV tells its stories (and, of course, record everything on your tracking sheet). The editor will not promise you anything. Crews are always scarce, and even when editors say they'll be there, all it takes is one apartment fire, and the crew meant for you is off on a new assignment. Because TV news, especially local news, is unable or unwilling to delve into thoughtful analysis, its coverage tends to be shallow. Because it emphasizes image, it tends to cover stories on the basis of their photogenic appeal rather than their intrinsic news value. Given all that, TV news is much more open to the influence of publicists than are newspapers.

Station personnel may ask themselves, "Are we being used?" when contacted by publicists. Sometimes even when the answer is "yes," they'll cover the story anyway. That exclusive videotape of the world's largest pizza is just too good to refuse. They may acknowledge on the air that it's a promotional event they're covering, but cover it they do.

That doesn't absolve you from trying to pitch a genuine news angle, much as you would to a newspaper. If you are the author of a book on, say, work stress, and you need a news peg to hang your pitch on, tie it into a broader subject like increased lawsuits stemming from on-the-job stress. You relieve the station from crassly promoting your book, you've given them a news angle, and you'll be the "expert" they interview on the subject.

I mentioned the overwhelming impact of time on the newscast. It's a real concern. Commercial breaks come when they're supposed to come, and any interview, no matter how compelling, will be dumped in a second if the floor director mimes a knife slicing across his throat. However, in another way, time has opened up dramatically in television. Not many years ago, the TV news day lasted at most ninety minutes, from 5:00 to 6:30 PM. Now, it often starts at 6:00 AM, continues until 9:00, reappears at noon, breaks until 4:00 PM, then continues until 7:00. In L.A., one independent station begins its nightly newscast at 8:00 PM and ends at 11:00 PM. Taking the entire day into account, that's a lot of time to fill.

For twenty-four-hour cable news outlets, there never is a bad time. Those are national stations, however, and harder to crack with a local story. Often they will pick up stories from local affiliates, so start your quest with the locals and hope that the work and the reporter are impressive enough to make your story worthy of a look on a larger level. You never know.

Even though TV news limits the amount of time devoted to one subject (other than on *Nightline* or *News Hour with Jim Lehrer* on PBS), the impact is great. As one news director for a local network news operation told me, "Five minutes of undivided attention is better than a distracted glance at a newspaper."

If TV news decides to cover your event, make sure you have the proper contact names at the station, and get direct phone numbers. Going through a main switchboard is like trying to get through to the pope. Make sure your times are synchronized, and meet the crew at the appointed hour. Get cell phone numbers if you can, because that's how most of these people operate: they're rarely in their own newsroom, but always reachable by cell. After you've made contact, give the reporter *your* cell number, and hope that he responds in kind. If he doesn't, be more forward, and ask.

Escort them where they need to go, but don't be too pushy. These people have done this sort of thing a million times before, and they know what they're doing. Help them get started, then get out of their way.

If you're the one being interviewed, you can finally pat yourself on the back as a full-fledged Guerrilla: you set up your own campaign and made yourself the focal point. But being on camera is an art unto itself, and I address that in detail later in this chapter.

Tips & Traps

- Never call a TV news department in the afternoon. Every-one is getting ready for the broadcast. Always call in the morning. Obviously, this doesn't apply for a twenty-four-hour news channel, but it does for a reporter whose show is on at a specific time each day. Figure out her schedule, and work around it.
- Avoid calling during sweeps months (February, May, and November) unless you have something that either feeds their ratings mentality or is genuinely significant news.
- Stunts, like sending custom coffee mugs or showing up at the station dressed in a silly costume, don't work any-more. News personnel are far too busy to watch the pa-rade go by.
- Here's a tip from a news director: The best times to get on TV news are weekends, holidays, and the day after holi-days. Business and government offices are closed, making these invariably slow news days. Try to arrange your cov-erage on those days.
- Weathercasters often mention upcoming local goings-on in their reports, especially charity-related events. Con-sider that as an option.

The national morning shows are among the crown jewels of desirable publicity outlets. Their audiences number in the many millions, and in some ways the big three—*Today, Good Morning America,* and *The Early Show* on CBS—set the tone for the news day around the world. They, like the national network news pro-grams, are also among the most difficult to get on. But as for-mer *Good Morning America* entertainment producer Jane Kaplan notes, "We have two hours of programming each day that must be filled. We're open to anyone who has a good idea."

Keep in mind, too, that some of the morning shows have special extended versions that include local segments. *Today in New York* is still the *Today Show* but will not broadcast nationally. If you have a local story that will work and has broad appeal, that might be a place to pitch.

Approaching the morning shows is not much different from your appeal to any other outlet. E-mail first, follow up with a call, and get right down to business with the producer you contact. The key here is framing your story with that universal theme anyone can relate to. If you own a retail outlet and you're offering something unusual to draw customers, tell the morning shows that you're demonstrating what one small-business owner can do to combat the recession. If you sell electronic equipment, tell them you're levying your own voluntary symbolic tariff to protest unfair foreign trade practices.

This is your chance to go for something grandiose: What also works for the morning shows—and anyone for that matter—are stories that pack an emotional wallop. Touching medical miracles, odd animal escapades, and gripping scenes of urban violence will always wind up on any news program, morning, noon, or night. If you have some way of pulling on heartstrings to pitch your story, that will help your chances immeasurably. Morning shows—and I'm not being a sexist here, the data will bear me out—are largely watched by women, so stories that will appeal to women will have a better chance with the assignment editors there.

Public affairs is a relatively small segment of TV programming but a significant one. Most licensed television stations devote a percentage of their broadcast time to public affairs.

If your project in any way serves the community at large as a social service or local improvement effort, look into public affairs programs as an outlet. They may not devote an entire show to you alone, but as part of a roundup or overall theme, you can be included on a panel. Check with your local PBS affiliate; they have many public affairs programs and a constant need for experts on specific topics.

Regarding cable and public access, many new shows are popping up all over. If you receive cable or satellite TV, study your online guide for news, infotainment, and public access programs. Watch them and see how and where you might fit in. Small shows are more willing to take chances on lesser-known guests. They aren't always seen by large audiences, but they make for excellent video press kit clips for future use, and they give solid practice for the big time, i.e., the national talk shows. Public access TV is so wide open that you can create your own show and book yourself as sole guest on every segment. Of course, that may be too ambitious for you, but you'd be amazed by how many people watch public access cable.

As for the infotainment and talk shows, these outlets could turn out to be the most important aspect of your TV campaign. And they're not as hard to get on as you might think. I'm told by a friend who worked there that 25 percent of the themes for Sally Jessy Raphael's show came from viewer mail, and I'll bet that statistic holds up for most of the talk shows. You *can* suggest yourself as a guest, and by doing so with artful persistence, you'll be remembered and called on when the theme for the show is right.

One author of a book on men and women wrote to the *Oprah Winfrey Show* with this intriguing hook: "Contrary to popular belief, men do not discriminate. They are equally unethical to both sexes." Soon after, she was kibitzing on the air with Oprah. As with any other media outlet, before you contact a show, study it. TiVo a week's worth. Get a feel for the interests and moods of the host. Read the credits to learn key staff names. Then, contact them in the usual way: send a press release and kit, wait a few days, then make your call. Let me reiterate: Don't call them cold. These people are far too busy to talk to strangers, and you will kill your chances of making it on the show if you call before you write.

Once you have sent the material and you're ready to make that call, ask for the producer, assistant producer, talent coordinator, or talent booker by name. These people put together the show and its guest list. Of course the host has input, but he or she usually comes into the process later on. Your first hurdle will be the producers.

By now you know to vary your pitch depending on the outlet. The talk shows need something spicy. I'm not saying you have to falsely inject sex appeal, but you need to find a theme that works for them. If I were pitching the Youth Center, I'd stress the sensational issue of drug-related gang violence. That's an electrifying subject, one that will spark discussion, and it can be developed into a theme for a show.

A friend of mine once represented an author of a book on movie flubs. He pitched Geraldo at Academy Award time for a show based on Oscar's greatest goofs. The producer loved it, and the author did the show, selling many books as a result. The key was shaping a theme to fit both the show and the project. But keep in mind that these shows are highly competitive. If *Oprah* books you, don't expect to appear on *The View* the next day. That goes for local shows as well.

If you persuade the producer to book you, your next hurdle is the pre-interview. This is akin to a trial to determine whether you'll prove an interesting guest. As Trisha Daniels of the *Maury Povich Show* says, "The entire on-air segment is based on the pre-interview. I've seen segments canceled because of a bad pre-interview."

Remember, the talk shows don't care about your project; they care about producing a watchable show. If they determine you're not watchable, you're not going on. If they decide you fit the bill, and your project gets a plug, so much the better for you, but it's of no consequence to them. So you have to pull out *all* the stops on the pre-interview. Whether by phone or in person, imagine your pre-interview is the real thing. Muster all the charm, charisma, eloquence, and insight you can when talking with the producer. Stay focused on the merits of your project or issue. Use every great line in your repertoire. Show humor, intelligence, and, if possible, controversy. They love controversy.

If you own a restaurant and you're militantly for or against smokers' rights, let them know. If you're an entertainer and you feel strongly about censorship, express yourself. Don't be afraid of your own convictions. They serve you well on talk-show TV.

Image and Essence: A TV Guest Prepares

Self-improvement books overflow with cute little phrases to help readers remember the authors' infinite wisdom. I begin this discussion with a cute little phrase: SOCO, or *single overriding communications objective*. When discussing your project on TV—or anywhere, for that matter—you'll be home free if you boil your message down to its SOCO.

TV is about image, the visual image we see and the intuitive image we sense. Your message should be concise to the point of haiku when you convey it on television. Practice by writing two paragraphs defining your project and its aims. Now, cut that by 50 percent. Cut it again by another 50 percent. Continue cutting until you're left with two sentences. Using correct grammar, combine the two into one. That's your SOCO. Everything you say to an interviewer should emanate from this central theme.

With TV, it's not what you say but how you say it and how you look when you say it. Ninety-five percent of communication on TV is non-verbal. So demeanor and appearance play an enormous role in communicating your message. When Christine Craft was fired from her anchor position at a local TV news outlet simply because of her less-than-glamour-queen looks, many people were outraged by this seemingly crass and sexist move. I, however, was not. Anchors are paid to read news and attract viewers. If they turn viewers off, they have failed. Usually, in this country, that means a pink slip. I don't condone it; I merely recognize it as a matter of immutable fact.

On the other hand, CBS was criticized roundly in 2007 for hiring Katie Couric to be the first solo female anchor of an evening newscast, because it was considered a cosmetic move—one that was more about the way the anchor looked than the performance being delivered, measured by journalistic standards.

I had no problem with Couric. If America wanted a kinder, gentler anchor who happened to look really good, I thought that was fine. But there was a problem: America didn't want Katie Couric on the *CBS Evening News*. The proof was in the ratings. Although Couric started out very strong, her ratings quickly plummeted, and immediately the sharks started to circle. Was it a "colleague" who leaked potentially damaging information about Katie to the *Philadelphia Inquirer*? Did Dan Rather really refer to Katie when he said CBS was "tarting up" the news?

It didn't matter: the ratings were low, and the public wasn't interested. Looks aren't everything.

Not only must the message be compelling, but so must be the messenger: you. Most people's analysis of their own social abilities is much too harsh. They perceive deficiencies within, but go overboard in self-criticism. The trick is not to add unfamiliar traits to your TV personality but to keep at bay those traits that don't work for the camera. We all conjure this perfect person in our heads, trying to look and sound like Diane Sawyer or Jon Stewart. But we never measure up. I implore you to remove the judgments.

Are you shy and funny? Outspoken and contentious? Serious yet insightful? Don't change who you are. Just withhold the negative traits while accentuating your strong points. Observe TV personalities you admire. They share one common quality: they're relaxed. That's because they're comfortable being who they are. They're settled in. I've met many of them, and off camera they're remarkably similar to their on-camera persona. Their image mirrors their essence. All well and good. But how do you then translate that to the experience of being on TV? Keep in mind a few simple rules:

Know your material. How many times will I say it? You should be so prepared—if Regis Philbin woke you in the middle of the night and asked you an obscure question about something remotely connected to your project, you'd immediately be able to answer intelligently! And don't talk in jargon! Speak in plain English.

Seek congruence with the interviewer. The interviewer is the boss, so you have to quickly get a feel for his or her rhythm and direction. Think of the interview as akin to riding a horse. As equestrians adjust their bodies to match the gait of their animal, so should you adjust your attitude to the temperament of the interviewer. If he's rapid-fire, couch your answers in a compatible fashion. If she's probing and antagonistic, appear understanding and forthcoming.

Slow down. If you want to appear edgy and unsure, speak fast. If you want to sound confident and intelligent, speak slowly. I know this is hard to do, because in my early interviews I tended to speak much too rapidly. You have to consciously will yourself to decelerate. If you do, I guarantee you will not only sound more relaxed but also feel more relaxed.

Be succinct. The worst thing you can be on TV is a bore. Long-winded answers to questions send viewers running for their clickers. We live in the world of the sound bite, and any answer you give exceeding thirty seconds hasn't been honed properly. That doesn't mean you can't tell a good story or that you should carry a stopwatch, but do practice brevity. By the same token, one- or two-word responses don't work, either. You have to be articulate and keep to the point.

Emphasize the positive. Whether or not you espouse a controversial view, be upbeat. Find areas of agreement with the interviewer, the panel, and the audience. Don't let them put words in your mouth, and don't oversell your project; but look for ways to stay on the bright side. If asked negative questions, answer the question you would rather the host had asked.

Don't panic. If things become nasty, stay calm. Avoid talking over your host, but if he is really going for the jugular, go ahead and lay it on thick. Talk back, talk over him, give 'em hell. The host knows the audio track will sound hopelessly scrambled if two or more people talk at the same time. I promise you, to avoid viewer tune-out he will eventually shut up, and you can have your say. But if all else fails, and you're being unfairly abused, walk off. Society is built on mutual respect, and if someone refuses to offer that, what are you doing there?

Relate to the audience. Barring white supremacists, adulterers, and murderous babysitters, I find most talk-show guests generally win the sympathy of the audience. Overall, audiences don't have the heart to attack guests as the hosts can, although they will if provoked. Look the audience in the eye, and be forthcoming with answers. You can win them over. Confidence is a must, but a spoonful of humility doesn't hurt either.

Go with the flow. As carefully scripted as these shows are in theory, once the cameras roll, anything can happen. My friend Randi Gelfand, then talent coordinator at the *Joan Rivers Show,* tells the story of a guest appearance by Angela Bowie (ex-wife of rock star David Bowie). Apparently, Angela was less than forthcoming about her wild life in the world of rock and roll. New York shock jock Howard Stern, who was a guest earlier in the hour, spontaneously came back to the set and showered Angela with shocking tabloid-style questions, getting her to open up about her sordid past. Angela was ready for anything, and you should be, too.

A Word on Coaching

Media coaching is a rapidly growing industry. Entertainers, corporate executives, politicians, clergy, and regular folks are lining up to learn how to behave in front of the camera. A friend of mine in this business prefers the term "image consulting" because her advice is applicable in any public situation, not just with the media. Although image consulting can be helpful, it's often beyond the scope of Guerrilla P.R. The cost can run into the thousands, though some consultants offer one- or two-hour makeovers for considerably less. They usually entail a quick diagnosis of the subject's personality and an audition on videotape. If you have the money, one of these sessions could prove valuable. Otherwise, use your own camcorder or even the mirror, and do your own image consulting. I think you can objectively size yourself up and make the necessary adjustments.

Here are a few pointers:

Tips & Traps

- Wear soft dark colors, minimal patterns, and monotone outfits, but never whites, which bleach out skin tones. Avoid shiny accessories or clacking earrings and bracelets. The rule of thumb is to "mirror your audience," meeting the dress standards of the group before whom you appear.
- Acknowledge your nervousness before you go on. If your shoulders are up above your ears, it's time to do some shoulder rolls. A certain amount of nerves is good, because it gets the adrenaline flowing, but you shouldn't focus on your jitters.
- Once on camera, sit straight with hands folded in your lap, but don't be frozen in one position. Small movements are indeed exaggerated on the tube, but withholding movement, hiding, takes an enormous amount of energy. Relaxation is the key.
- Look at the interviewer, *not* the camera.

- Never interrupt unless, as I said before, you're being unfairly dominated or talked over.
- There are no bad questions, only bad answers.
- Shape your answers to sound personal rather than dry and technical. You really don't have to impress anyone with your intellect.
- Nervous before you go on? Try visualization of serene settings or deep breathing. Once you're on, imagine that the set is your own living room and you're just having a conversation with an acquaintance.

Guerrilla P.R. means selling yourself as well as your project. The two are inseparable. TV offers you the best chance of cementing the connection. A successful TV campaign will set the stage for enticing future opportunities, because if you become a show's regular "expert" on a given topic, you will have devised a P.R. annuity that keeps paying dividends for a long time.

Media Facts

- 112.2 million U.S. households have at least one television (that's 99 percent of us).
- 35 million of them have HDTV.
- 65 million American households currently receive cable.
- Sales of DVD players in 2006 totaled 19.7 million units.
- There are 1,527 TV stations in the United States: 691 VHF and 836 UHF. Of those, 314 are public stations and 1,186 are commercial. The typical household tunes in to TV 48.5 hours a week.
- The average cost of a prime-time 30-second TV commercial is $350,000.

- The top cable networks (as of December 2006) are these:
    1. Discovery (92.5 million subscribers)
    2. CNN (92.3 million)
    3. ESPN (92.3 million)
    4. TNT (92.1 million)
    5. USA Network (92.1 million)
    6. Lifetime Television (92.1 million)
    7. Weather Channel (92 million)
    8. Nickelodeon (91.9 million)
    9. History Channel (91.9 million)
    10. ESPN 2 (91.8 million)[4]

Making Radio Waves

All this talk about TV skirted one obvious issue: with television, you almost always have to go to them. The national morning shows can send a crew to interview you if need be, but if you want to hit the major U.S. cities with a TV blitz, you're going to have to buy a fistful of airline tickets to hit each town—a nice way to blow your entire Guerrilla P.R. budget. However, this isn't so with radio.

From the comfort of your own bedroom, you can do forty radio interviews across the country in a couple of days, covering as much as with television, if not more. Radio is clearly the easiest and least expensive method for reaching a maximum number of people. Unlike TV, there are practically no boundaries on radio in terms of taste and subject matter (not that TV talk shows are all that tasteful). I once heard a morning talk radio segment devoted to the issue of Asian immigrants capturing and

4. Source: National Cable and Telecommunications Association.

eating neighborhood dogs. The show was known as the *Breakfast Edition*.

Radio, especially the Guerrilla P.R.–rich target of talk radio, is ever on the lookout for controversy, for something different. If it ties in with the news of the day, great. It was talk radio that a few years ago launched a nationwide campaign to mail teabags to congressmen contemplating a hefty pay raise for themselves. People *are* listening out there.

Most cities have at least one talk radio show. Some are nationally broadcast, like Terry Gross and Rush Limbaugh, who are heard by astronomical numbers of people (up to half a million at any given quarter hour). Getting on radio is easier than getting on TV, although it's never a cakewalk. Many of the same rules apply: know the show you're pitching, send written material first, find out the name of the producer. But you do have more latitude because you're free of the visual component and because so much radio programming is produced at the local level, much more so than in television.

One effective way of reaching talk radio producers is to submit your name and project to *Newsmaker Interviews*, a publication subscribed to by dozens of radio stations across the country. In its simple format, potential guests and their topics are described in detail, with a contact name and number listed at the bottom.

I urge you to send your information to *Newsmaker Interviews*. Otherwise, you'll need to track down the myriad talk radio shows across the country. Some published listings do exist. Try *Radio & Records,* a respected industry trade newspaper based in Los Angeles. They have a comprehensive talk radio section and editor, as well as published specials on the format.

Whether you're shooting for a local, regional, or national talk radio campaign, once you've nailed down your contacts, keep these pointers in mind:

- Most producers get their ideas from the other media like newspapers and TV, not from publicists or direct appeals. It's wise to link your idea with some other current item in the news.
- Like other media producers, talk radio producers are extremely overworked. Because they don't really cover breaking news the way TV and newspaper journalists do, they may not be as accessible. Be persistent. Eventually you'll hear back from them.
- Talk radio producers and hosts really like controversy. Maybe you have a new theory of nutrition that says fat and cholesterol are healthy in the diet. That'll get you on the air very quickly. Talk radio is contemporary America's version of the soapbox in the town square, and anyone can climb on top of it.
- Demonstrate you know the show by mentioning something you heard on the air recently, and perhaps tie that in with your pitch.

As a Guerrilla, you want maximum exposure, so I recommend linking as many radio shows as possible in a given amount of time. Set a goal of, say, five shows, five cities, within two weeks. Not only will it help your P.R. effort, it will vastly improve your skills as an interview subject.

Once you're asked to go on the air, you may do the interview in the studio or by phone at home. If the station is in your area, try to go down there. That way you meet the staff face-to-face, and grease the wheels for possible future appearances. Otherwise, doing the interview by phone is just fine.

Usually, the producer will call you and hook you into a special extension. You'll hear the show over the line, and within a few minutes you'll be introduced. *You don't have to be nervous.* It's just like talking to a friend. Obviously, you want to keep your language clean and diction clear. This is an audio medium, so modulate your speaking tone to give your voice a little more color, and keep your answers concise.

Take your cues from the host or interviewer. He or she calls the shots. Never interrupt the host or step on his or her words. Apply what you've learned about steering the conversation, but keep that deference to the host in mind. Unlike with TV, they can cut you off in a second. One nice thing about radio: because you're "invisible" you can jot down notes to yourself while on the air to remind yourself of other points you want to make. It doesn't hurt that you can do the interview in your pajamas, either.

Media consultant Peggy Klaus urges her clients to "make a fan" of the microphone. "I tell them to imagine someone they love and who loves them is sitting there just dying to get the information," she says. "This helps elevate the enthusiasm in the voice."

As with print, you should collect your radio "clips," i.e., record your appearances and assemble a little cassette of your best sound bites. A digital recorder will help, and they're not expensive. You can use this as part of an audio press kit to help line up future radio appearances.

Even if your talk radio show efforts fizzle this time, don't give up on radio. You can always call in to the talk radio show as a regular citizen. You can cloak your call around some current event, but there's no reason why you can't slip in commentary related to your project. All radio stations have community affairs programming, and even pop music DJs announce up-coming events. Check with local stations to see how and when to submit press releases for announcement. Speaking of DJs, many stations have loony morning and afternoon announcers who throw into their shows every crass and crazy concept they can dream up. If you have the right personality, you just might fit in with your local shock jock.

Every station has a news department, and though they're mi-croscopic compared with TV news departments, don't neglect them. Sending a press release only costs a stamp. A single men-tion on the air may not have a dramatic impact, but taken cumu-latively, radio is a superb outlet. You reach more people in one shot than you do with the average newspaper, and it's easier to obtain than a TV appearance. Radio is America's clearinghouse of ideas, so step up to the mike!

FROM THE GUERRILLA P.R. FILE

In 1990, California celebrated the twentieth anniversary of the personalized license plate. One car company sponsored its own star search for the best vanity plate in the nation. The winners included "O4A4RE (Oh, For a Ferrari)," found on a Penn-sylvania Honda; "OUT5OGZ," seen on the back of a Mercedes-Benz; and the grand prize winner adorning the rear bumper of a frenzied movie executive: "IM2BZ2P."

Computerize Yourself

In 1993, I wrote, "If this book were being written ten years ago, this section would not have been included, but that's how fast personal computers have changed the landscape." Well, to paraphrase Al Jolson, I hadn't seen *nothin'* yet.

Since the original publication of *Guerrilla P.R.*, computers have risen to a dominant position in almost every media outlet. Consider that CNN debates between presidential candidates in 2007 were held in conjunction with YouTube.com, and you'll get an idea of what I'm talking about.

But there are ways to access computer communication and increase your profile that have nothing to do with traditional media outlets. Listservs and BBSs (bulletin board services) are the beginning of the online picture.

Most BBSs aren't free. They require a subscription, and in many cases you must provide credentials of some sort just to be considered.

These BBSs post an amazing array of information, from simple announcements to controversial opinions. It's like a high-tech CB radio on which any subscriber can air his or her feelings or news. Although there are many hundreds of BBSs, if you're serious about this, sign up with one of the commercial online companies. They offer such features as electronic mail, databases, and even online conferencing.

A BBS is often tied to some activity or profession. Listservs are usually groups of people who share an interest and want to discuss it. They can be *very* passionate about their opinions, and unless you want to antagonize some members to make a point, it can be a little dicey at times to post to a list or a BBS.

Keep in mind that there are rules of etiquette on such lists. As with most online communication (e.g., chat rooms), it is rude to write IN ALL CAPITALS. You can find yourself flamed, or badly maligned, if you use inappropriate language (except on lists that don't mind such things). The best thing to do is to lurk, or read posts for a few days before posting, and always *read the rules* when you sign on to a new service. They're almost always posted on a public Web site.

GUERRiLLA P.R. COMMANDO: Luke Dommer

"Having had more guns pointed at me than I can count, I knew I was fighting a cultural value system," recalled the late Luke Dommer, founder of CASH (Committee to Abolish Sport Hunting) and crusader on behalf of American wildlife. By passionately taking on a cherished institution, Luke embarked on a long-term struggle that took him face-to-face with angry hunters, a well-organized gun lobby, and the ire of America's macho faction, all the while fighting a losing battle with the cancer that took his life.

A burly ex-Marine and ace marksman, Dommer made a good living as a graphic artist before recognizing the devastating impact society wreaked on the environment. He chose to devote his life to preserving life on the planet, relying on old training for guidance.

"I looked at this from a military point of view," said Dommer. "First, you reconnoiter the enemy and find the weakest point in his line. I determined hunting was the weakest link in the chain of animal and ecological abuses."

Working on his own, Luke established CASH and filed a series of lawsuits to stop hunting in New York state parks. His actions drew the fury of hunters, whom he credited with his first P.R. successes. "They're the ones that promoted me," said Luke. "I was routinely written about in hunting magazines, and when the lawsuits began, I was naturally the one the media contacted for comment."

Luke also had himself listed in the *Yearbook of Experts, Authorities & Spokespersons*, a bible for talk-show producers. Soon he was appearing on radio and TV, first regionally and later nationally. He wrote articles for Op-Ed pages and magazines, printed in such publications as *USA Today*, the *New York Times*, the *Philadelphia Inquirer*, and animal rights tracts. He was written up in *Omni* magazine and in newspapers in communities where hunting was an issue.

Because he sold himself as a genuine expert, Luke cornered the market in his field. He debated more hunters than anyone else, and appeared on at least four hundred radio and TV programs beginning in 1976. One lesson he learned: Let a belligerent opponent ride roughshod over you. "I had one guy interrupt me, be rude to me on a talk show," Luke recalled in his interview with me in 1991. "He got lots of complaining letters, even from hunters."

Years of experience taught Luke much about the nature of media. "I had to reach beyond the animal rights movement and give the mass media a logical reason to look at sport hunting," he noted. Luke didn't believe Guerrillas should look for too much too soon. "I believe in starting at the first rung of the ladder," he told me. "You gain experience gradually on your way to the top. For example, don't go on a show you can't handle. Eventually, like me, you make it to the top of the ladder."

Luke enjoyed doing his own media campaign. "I reach more people than anyone else in the movement," he said. "It doesn't cost the animals a dime. My opponents spend millions each year on propaganda, but the media I've done came because they called me."

Luke continued his struggle, knowing full well he might not see his dream of the abolition of hunting in his lifetime. "Scientists predict we may lose another million species of plant and animal life in the next ten years," he noted somberly. "There's a continuum of death going on. But whatever I do, when I weigh it against the universe, I know I'm just a speck. But seeing this become a national issue after fourteen years of sacrifice has been my greatest reward."

The world will miss Luke Dommer, one of the best Guerrilla P.R. masters I have ever encountered.

9

Reserve Ammo:
Press Conferences, Parties, and More

If people around you will not hear you, fall down before them
and beg their forgiveness, for in truth you are to blame.

—Fyodor Dostoyevsky

The Press Conference

It's a publicist's dream come true: assembled under one roof,
the cream of the national media—TV, print, radio, wire services—gathered together to hear a special announcement from
you. That night, every station in town runs a piece, and the next
morning, every newspaper carries a story and photo taken at
the conference. It's the ultimate high.

In reality, few press conferences (or news conferences, as
they're sometimes called) are ever as well attended as hoped.
But we keep staging them because they remain one of the
most efficient ways to disseminate information to media.

When they go well, you experience a powerful feeling of accomplishment.

Although press conferences are a staple of the professional publicist, Guerrillas should not devote an inordinate amount of energy to them. For one thing, they are often boring and are way too respectable. Guerrillas stir things up, and unless you plan an audacious event, a press conference may be too tame a tactic.

For another thing, media people resent turning out for any event that imparts information that could just as easily have been mailed in press release form. But, despite the risks, the press conference can be an important weapon in your arsenal. So here's what you need to know:

The central function of a p.c. is to announce and exhibit something specific: Lindsay Lohan is named spokeswoman for Al-Anon; Maroon Five launches national tour; General Motors phases out gasoline-powered cars in favor of non-polluting electric engines (I can dream, can't I?). P.c.'s are often cut-and-dried, and though the media ask questions, the inquiries are usually limited to the subject at hand.

You don't do a press conference to announce how happy you are to be in business, or tell the world your product is simply maaahvelous, or that you're in favor of more money for AIDS research. A p.c. has to scream a headline; otherwise, skip it. If you have something clear-cut and enticing to present to the media en masse, terrific!

In other words, a news conference has to have some news to impart, or it will be badly attended, sully your fledgling reputation, and defeat its intended purpose. Be careful with conferences, and schedule them only when you have something of serious importance to announce—not something that could be summed up in two paragraphs on a press release.

Consider a press conference, but brace yourself. Most likely, media people won't give a darn. Making them care enough to attend is your main task.

Start by sending out a special press release/invitation. Tease them by holding one or two details back while alluding to a surprise. Be dramatic. A touch of theater doesn't hurt, since a p.c. is by definition theatrical. You have a stage, performers, and an active audience. So make your invitations inviting. Here's a sample:

PRESS CONFERENCE
PRESS CONFERENCE
PRESS CONFERENCE

April 17, 2008

Lancel Corporation to Announce
New Pollution-Free Automobile Engine

The goal of creating affordable non-polluting transportation will take a giant leap forward when Lancel Corporation unveils its new Paracel A-1 automobile engine at a press conference to be held May 5 at the Lancel Manufacturing Plant in Norwood. With manufacturing orders from the big automakers already in hand, Lancel predicts the solar-powered Paracel A-1 will revolutionize the automobile industry.

Speaking at the press conference will be Lancel president Mitchell Barlow and chief designer Evita Cheslow, who will demonstrate the engine's capabilities and answer questions.

WHAT: Press conference announcing Paracel A-I solar automobile engine.

WHEN: May 5, 2008, at 9:00 AM.

WHERE: Lancel Corporation, 4567 Geary Ave., Norwood.

PHOTO OPPORTUNITY: Design staff, executive staff, prototypes of engine will be available.

CONTACT: John Jones

213–555–1111

Mail your invitations no later than two weeks beforehand. It's one thing to send a press release and follow up with a call. That's no skin off anyone's back. But to ask a news organization to dispatch a reporter or crew to a p.c. is asking a great deal more, so you have to give them time. Make follow-up calls a few days after you send the invitation and see if you get any nibbles.

In these conversations, build on the excitement. Will there be any special guests? Will there be any kind of unexpected stunt? Will you bring on dancing girls or barking seals? Whatever it may be, make an effort to tease the media, to spark their curiosity. Then, call again two days before the event and one more time early on the day of the event for final confirmations of attendance.

Timing is important. Did you notice I scheduled the conference for early in the morning? That's important, so journalists can attend and still meet any of their regular deadlines. Location and setting are also important. It should be held somewhere that's easy to reach for the media in your area. Indoors at a hotel conference room. Your company parking lot. Your front lawn. If you're demonstrating some kind of cause, say an anti-drug message, how about holding the p.c. in front of a school with a known drug problem? If it's for an upcoming homelessness charity, go to skid row to dramatize the problem.

Think in terms of visuals that may heighten the dramatic effect. Make sure you also provide food and adult drinks. It may sound petty, but the media expect to be fed, so pop for refreshments. Other amenities to consider are easy and free parking, availability of telephones, restrooms, and seating. See that there are electrical outlets for TV lights if your p.c. is held indoors, and place the cameras in the back of the room. And make sure, for photographic purposes, that the background behind the lectern or dais is plain and simple. A curtain or an unadorned wall will do fine.

Once assembled, hand the media any additional materials necessary to put together a full and accurate story, such as an updated press release, press kit, etc. Begin on time, and don't drag it out. You may feel nervous performing before so many people, but if you're prepared you have nothing to worry about (sound familiar?).

Your opening remarks should be concise and to the point, recapping the information in your press release. Visual aids are a plus. PowerPoint is never a bad idea.

These add color and reinforce your message. If other people are due to speak, move them right along. Everyone should make his or her presentation, and then open up the floor to questions.

As in so many aspects of this business, the best-laid plans often get turned on their head. If you can stay loose with it, though, you may come out all right. I recall one incident in which my client Dr. Joyce Brothers was in town to attend a press conference. The night before, she had left her shoes in the hotel hallway to be picked up for shining. The hotel lost her shoes, and because of time constraints she was forced to attend the p.c. in her stocking feet. Turned out she got more coverage because of that than for anything else that day.

The key to answering questions is preparation. Before a presidential news conference, the chief executive runs through a series of mock questions so that he can be ready for any inquiry. You should do the same.

In one-on-one interviews elsewhere, you may turn off the tape and say something off the record, but not at a gathering like a p.c. Everything done and said at a press conference is on the record. So be careful not to mention anything you don't want discussed or reported.

In fact, be careful about what you say, period. You know the expression about the camera never blinking. Microphones are equally vigilant. The way you express yourself can determine whether you have a positive, neutral, or negative impact on the media and the public. Even the president of the United States has to watch what he says. In the 1993 election race, George H. W. Bush was overheard making some rather incomprehensible remarks to voters in New Hampshire while the cameras rolled. I quote them verbatim:

"Somebody said we prayed for you over there. That was not just because I threw up on the prime minister of Japan either. Where was he when I needed him? But *I* said, Let me tell you something. And I say this. I don't know whether any ministers from the Episcopal Church are here. I hope so. But I said to him this. You're on to something here. You cannot be president of the United States if you don't have faith. Remember Lincoln, going to his knees in times of trial in the Civil War and all that stuff? You can't be. And we're blessed."

I include this not out of disrespect for George H. W. Bush

but to show how easy it is, when we speak off the cuff, to fail to convey what we mean. When you're "on" during the p.c., you are on, and everything you say can and will be scrutinized.

Once the conference is over, stick around for any informal follow-up questions the press may have. It's a good idea for you to tape the event to check for media accuracy as well as to study your own performance. If it goes well, ideally this first press conference won't be your last.

FROM THE GUERRILLA P.R. FILE

To make its own kind of statement about fighting the recession (and, not coincidentally, to gain some favorable P.R.) the *Boston Globe,* the Hub city's major daily paper, began offering in March 1993 free situation-wanted ads submitted during a limited time by unemployed individuals. More than five hundred submissions a day flooded the paper, with the *Globe* promising to keep the campaign up until every single ad had run.

Let's Party

People think we Hollywood types spend our days doing lunch and our nights attending parties. Well, they're right. Only we don't have any fun doing it. Actually, parties are one of the best ways to spread goodwill, good cheer, and good P.R. At most parties, few people overtly discuss business, yet a lot seems to get done. That's because in America, everybody wants to feel that he or she has tapped into the Good Life, and a party invitation is the quintessential membership card.

Why throw a party? Perhaps you're celebrating the expansion of a business, the release of a new product, the arrival of an honored guest, or the beginning of a new campaign. Parties get things off to a festive start, and media people, if not the media themselves, love them. Unless there are celebrities in attendance, parties don't often get direct media coverage, but I believe in their efficacy as wheel greasers.

As a Guerrilla you don't want to spend a lot of money. The good news is that it's definitely possible to mount a successful party on the cheap. All you need are the bare necessities: food, drink, music, and people. Start by making your invitation alluring. Make people want to come. Whom to invite? Your network, business associates, some friends, any media people you've become acquainted with, and even some you may not know.

Though you don't want anything like a kiddie party, consider attaching a theme to your affair. Whether it's a color scheme or a consistency in the decor, dress, music, or food, make your party an event by giving it thematic structure. How about a sixties party, with black-light posters and Jimi Hendrix music? How about something Asian, where the guests must first remove their shoes before hitting the sushi table?

Pamper your guests. Washington diplomatist hostess Perle Mesta used to say that the secret to a successful party is in the greetings and good-byes. When each of her guests arrived she would say, "At last you're here," and when they departed, "I'm sorry you have to leave so soon." Keep food lines short, have an ample supply, and make sure guests know where the restrooms are.

As for you, you're a Guerrilla, so mix it up. Work the room, visiting as many people as you can. Concentrate on the individual

you're talking to, listen carefully, and don't let your eyes wander from the other person's. Feel free to move on when the conversation has run its course. Go into it with a burst of energy,
and leave when the energy fades. Try lines like "Excuse me, but
I see someone I haven't seen in ages," or "I think I'll try one of
these hors d'oeuvres." They sure have worked for me.

If you see people you don't recognize, introduce yourself
with a smile. A friendly face will break the ice, and, as I've said,
a handshake can be as important to your public relations as a
packed press conference. Remember the trick of repeating the
person's name when you shake his or her hand; it will help you
remember it later on and for the rest of the evening—a valuable
piece of information.

Above all, remember a party is not the place to conduct serious business. Take numbers, exchange cards, make promises,
but keep the conversation—and the party—on a spirited note.
If it's feasible, grab a microphone, make a toast, thank people
for attending. Mention your project in brief, but don't distract
your guests from their pleasure. If your project was the reason
they came, they'll remember the next day, and the next.

Tips & Traps

- Don't overdo the tables and chairs. People tend to cluster
  at parties and not spread out. With fewer places to sit,
  more partygoers will mingle. It can be risky, but sometimes you end up with a fantastic party that way.
- Have enough help on hand to handle things. Whether you
  hire people or have friends and family helping out, make
  sure they dress appropriately, know what they're doing,

and keep things running smoothly and unobtrusively. You don't want guests to feel burdened or neglected.

- Plan surprises. Midway through the proceedings, stage some kind of novel event involving the project. Don't let it go on too long, but definitely make this a key part of the evening.
- Timing for a party is tricky. If you plan it for midweek, many working people (including media) are too tired to come out. If it's on a weekend, often people prefer to do other things. Consider carefully.
- If you can't remember the name of the person you're greeting, extend your hand and say your name. The other will likely do the same thing.
- Lighten up! Once the party begins, it takes on a life of its own. Just go with it and have a good time.

Monkey-Wrenching

This section is not for everyone. It's not even for me. But being Guerrillas, some of you may have projects that require bold action. If your project involves a political or social cause you believe in strongly, there may be times when you need to go a step beyond the mainstream to bolster your P.R. profile. Sometimes those steps involve walking a line dangerously close to law-breaking, something I do not *in any way* advocate. But I'm not against the concept of tantalizing the media with the potential for controversy or confrontation.

I cherish our right to protest, even when I don't agree with the protesters. Though most Americans give lip service to that right, some get uptight over the sight of angry demonstrators and picket signs. That's understandable. As the L.A. riots in

1992 showed, sometimes the line is crossed from legitimate protest to civil insurrection.

Most of us prefer to go about our lives without having other people's concerns thrust in our faces, especially if we don't agree. But America is a great country precisely because we have the right to protest. As a Guerrilla you may wish to take advantage of that right to engage the media, thus furthering your cause.

Don't be torn because you think you're just "using" the media to draw attention. The media are as jaded as can be, but they know a good story when they smell it. If you mount a demonstration over some scurrilous local abuses, and you get a significant volume of people to join you, let the media know.

A few guidelines: Don't give too much advance warning. Unlike other events, a protest has to seem spontaneous, a convulsive expression of the will of the people. If the media smell friction, they'll be there, you can be sure. I'd say forty-eight hours' notice should suffice.

When you call, let the assignment editor know you're in charge. When the crew arrives at your protest site, introduce yourself, hand the reporter or producer your literature, offer yourself as an interview subject, and help them get situated. Make your protest noisy and passionate. Have colorful signs with cogent slogans carried by your comrades. Most such protests are completely peaceful and tolerant. Occasionally they are not, especially if you draw counter-protesters. A shouting match between opposing sides of an issue always makes great copy, or great video for the evening news.

If, unfortunately, law enforcement is involved, only you can decide how far you want to take things. As we saw with the anti-abortion protests in Wichita during the summer of 1991, sometimes things get out of hand. For true believers, the threat of arrest is no obstacle. That's a decision you have to make on your own. But I don't recommend it. Jail food stinks, and it's tough getting fingerprint ink off your hands.

You also run the risk of being branded a publicity seeker. Personally, I have nothing against that. After all, that's what I do, but you know how people think. Anybody in the public eye, championing a cause, is subject to derision, and usually he or she is blamed for cunning in gaining the media spotlight. There's a price to pay no matter what you do in life; in my opinion, you're better off opting for wider media exposure. That way, your message will get out to the people. Otherwise, you can sit at home with your scruples and shout your slogans at the TV screen.

PSAs and Editorial Replies

Part of your Guerrilla P.R. campaign is the effort to establish yourself as an expert in your field. One way to do that is to take advantage of public service announcements (PSAs) and editorial replies. All television stations that broadcast editorials (and most do) are required to provide airtime to opposing points of view. They are also required to devote a certain portion of their programming to PSAs, which are, in effect, free commercials on matters of public interest. If you see an editorial that in some way relates to your project, consider contacting the station to respond. Editorial replies provide an opportunity to have your face and name broadcast across the city and further solidify your expert standing. To make this happen, contact the news department at the station and ask for the editorial director. Tell him or her that you represent citizens with an opposing view, and you'd like to reply. Send information on yourself and your project, such as your press kit.

If they give you the green light, you'll be informed of the parameters. You'll probably have sixty seconds to make your point. When writing your reply, think in bursts of quick three-sentence paragraphs, with your opening comments being the most potent.

Begin by summarizing the station's view and stating why they're dead wrong. Detail a handful of reasons, again expressed in short easy-to-understand phrases. Close by urging a different direction, chiding the station for taking its position. That's it! You're a politician now!

As for PSAs, both TV and radio stations will make airtime available with a ten- or thirty-second "commercial" for your project if it's a bona fide charity or message of cultural, medical, or safety interest to the community. Contact your local stations' community affairs departments, explain your mission, and inquire whether you can make a PSA. Because you have such an extreme time limitation, you must make your points quickly and effectively. Approach the writing of your PSA as if it were a TV commercial; that is, you must leave a strong impression on the viewers or listeners.

Tips & Traps

- *Start out with a bang.* You must grab your audience from the outset, and the best way to do that is with a punchy and arresting lead sentence or two. Watch and listen for other PSAs, and you'll see what I mean.
- *Stay focused.* With only thirty or sixty seconds, you have time to make only one main point with a couple of illustrations. Don't lose sight of your main point.

- For TV, provide interesting visuals for use as backdrop.
- Most PSAs are read by on-air announcers, whether TV or radio. That being the case, *you must have a well-crafted script.* Be sure to time it before you send it in. Obviously, you must include your name, address, and phone number, just as with a regular press release.

Trade Shows and Conventions

It's a common sight. Bikini-clad coeds reclining on car rooftops or demonstrating some new Japanese techno-toy; famous athletes signing autographs for the mobs crowding the floors of large convention halls; spectacular sets with all kinds of electronic bells and whistles on display. The trade show is a modern-day carnival of commerce, and there's not an industry in America that doesn't stage one of its own.

When the next convention comes to town, the wise Guerrilla should seriously consider a preemptive strike.

Trade shows, such as the annual Consumer Electronics Show in Las Vegas, and conventions, like the National Association of Theatre Owners, a movie business conclave, bring together under one enormous roof virtually everyone who's anyone in a given industry. It's the perfect setting for glad-handing, politicking, protesting, viewing what's new in the industry's products, making a scene, making a friend, or just plain learning.

My friends Sandy and Howard Benjamin, when launching their independent celebrity radio interview business, descended on the National Association of Broadcasters annual get-together, plastered the place with flyers, and remained, as they put it, "in their faces" for the entire three days. It got their fledgling company off to a good start.

If you have the wherewithal to travel to a convention in your line of work, do so. It's worth the registration fee to mingle with your own and to test whether your Guerrilla P.R. plan has merit. Use a touch of showmanship, salesmanship, and marksmanship to score your points. These events are people oriented, not media oriented. They provide you with a perfect opportunity to practice your personal P.R. skills.

When get-togethers are held in hotels, many corporate participants open up their suites to all visitors. Work these rooms. Make friends, expand your network, make an impression. This is P.R. on the micro-scale, rather than the macro-scale, but it is no less important.

Any one of those conventioneers could be the person to turn your business around, open a new door, or offer an unexpected opportunity. There's something about the convivial atmosphere that lends itself to solidifying relationships with colleagues. Take advantage.

Sometimes you can strike gold in other settings. Jerry Porter, president of Metrospace Corporation, a large commercial real estate consulting firm, makes a point of landing new clients by attending shareholders' meetings. If he isn't a stockholder, he simply buys a few shares of stock, entitling him entry to the annual shareholders' shouting match (sometimes). Says Jerry, "While the company puts on its dog-and-pony show and the executives are schmoozing with the people, I'm out there greeting them, shaking hands, and scheduling follow-up meetings." Now, that's clever.

Good Works

I don't care if it sounds crass to you, but being a Good Samaritan is good for business. Individuals and companies that do charity work go a long way toward cementing a positive image within their surrounding communities. I believe it's important for you, too, to weigh your options in this area.

Sometimes this can indeed become crass. I recall the cynical manager of a famous pop musician who called me in a desperate search for a charity outlet for her artist, because he'd recently been mentioned in unfavorable press accounts linking him with drugs and alcohol. She thought a picture of her wigged-out guitar player giving a teddy bear to a terminally ill child would solve her artist's problems.

I'm not talking about that kind of thing.

I'm talking about top sports agent Leigh Steinberg, who, before he negotiates the contract of an NFL or major league rookie, has the athlete set down on paper the extent of his charitable works. If the athlete doesn't commit to extensive charity appearances and donations, Steinberg won't represent him.

I'm talking about the corporate blood drives, where a factory parking lot is turned into a temporary sea of gurneys, with employees rolling up their sleeves to give a unit of blood. I'm talking about sponsoring a fundraiser for Jerry's Kids, or organizing a litter pick-up. I'm talking about the San Diego doughnut shop that regularly gives away thousands of day-old doughnuts to mission rescues and halfway houses.

I believe business is inextricably linked with the well-being of the community, and as a matter of simple justice, it is incumbent upon us to help make this a better world, whether or not we receive much publicity for our efforts. At the same time, I have no problem with making sure the rest of the world knows about it.

If you were to sponsor a similar charitable effort—say a 10-K run for cancer research, or a turkey dinner for the homeless— it's beneficial to all for the media to be informed and to cover the event. You gain better employee and citizen involvement, you spread the word that such activities are worthwhile, and you gain that all-important positive public perception of you and your company or project, even if the P.R. you get from it has a relatively narrow focus.

How about a holiday tie-in? Andy Lipkis of Treepeople sponsored an urban beautification tree planting on Martin Luther King, Jr., Day in Los Angeles. Do you have out-of-date computer equipment in your office? Why sell it when you can reap much greater P.R. benefits by giving it away to your neighborhood elementary school? Is it feasible to have schools visit and tour your operations? Can you provide employment or intern opportunities to area youth? Did you ever consider sponsoring the preservation of a nearby historical landmark?

These kinds of projects are so easy to do. If you're not sure how to proceed, try hooking up with established charities like the Red Cross or the American Cancer Society. With their vast experience, they can help you organize and publicize your event (unless, being the Guerrilla publicist that you are, you opt to do that yourself). The main thing is, you're helping to repair the world just a little bit. And like I said, that's good for business.

Speechmaking

It was one of the highlights of my life. Standing before an assembly of graduate students at the Harvard Business School, I delivered a lecture, stating my observations about the current business climate. As I spoke I thought to myself, "Imagine, me, who never finished college, addressing America's best and brightest."

I concluded my remarks that day with a wonderful quote from author H. G. Wells: "Some ideas are so stupid, only intellectuals believe them." Several hundred future captains of industry leaped to their feet, cheering my words. Clearly, I had struck a nerve.

Giving speeches ties in with our oldest and greatest human legacy: oral communication. All P.R.—indeed all of human communication, technological and otherwise—is simply an extension of it.

In this day and age, too many people have unfortunately mangled the meaning of the word "rhetoric." Politicians and pundits use the term to mean insincere blather, deliberate obfuscation, or, in plain English, caca. Yet, "rhetoric" actually means the fine use of spoken language. It is a lost art; indeed, the very word to describe it is lost.

But I don't want it to get lost on you. Hitting the speakers' trail can be one of the very best adjuncts to your Guerrilla P.R. campaign strategy. Even though your reach per audience is much smaller with speechmaking than it is with media, you shouldn't underestimate the impact. There are drawbacks to conventional press exposure. Someone leafing through a newspaper might spot an article about you and your project, give it a passing glance, or perhaps even read the entire piece, and then, with the turn of a page, move on to the next article.

In a flash, you're yesterday's news.

Not so with public speaking. In such a setting you have the full undivided attention of an audience that is ostensibly there to hear you speak. If you deliver a strong speech, the effect can linger far longer than in many other forms of P.R.

Do you have anything to say? The answer is "yes." If you are the owner of a business, you can address business gatherings on the subject of your specific industry, or on general business topics. If you are in a specialized field, such as medicine, education, law, entertainment, or sports, you can set yourself up as a perceptive insider. What you think matters; you'd be surprised by just how expert in your field you probably are already.

Getting a forum for your public-speaking career isn't as hard as you may think. Schools; churches and synagogues; health-care facilities; business clubs like Rotary, Kiwanis, and the Chamber of Commerce; seminars; conventions; political clubs; and many others—all use and are in constant need of speakers. Speakers' bureaus abound. Find them and offer yourself. You do not need extensive prior experience to sign up with a speakers' bureau, only a willingness to present your ideas.

If your only public-speaking experience is limited to your bar mitzvah or the fifth grade Thanksgiving pageant, fear not. It's not as terrifying as you remember. I don't want to take too much space in this book to teach the art of speechmaking, but a few choice tips are in order.

Tips & Traps

- Before you make that speech, you need to know a few things about the venue and your audience. James Robinson, in his terrific volume *Winning Them Over*, suggests you find out how much time you've been given to speak, when you're expected to arrive, how the evening's program is to be structured, whether a lectern and a P.A. system will be in place, who will introduce you, and whether there will be a Q&A period after the speech. Knowing just what to expect will help you relax.

- Write out your speech completely. Even if you prefer to work without a script and appear spontaneous, you should put down on paper the gist of your remarks. It will help orient you. If you choose to work with a script, transfer the speech to 3 × 5 inch cards in large type. Cards are easy to work with and fit easily into your pocket.

- If given a choice of a short speech or a long one, opt for the short. Unless you're a mesmerizing orator, going on too long is the kiss of death. As a rule of thumb, I'd say twenty minutes maximum.

- Use simple, plain English, full of action and rhythm. Keep the ten-cent words for your college theses. At the same time, don't be afraid to draw on your natural eloquence. You may not be Martin Luther King, Jr., but it's all right to take advantage of our beautiful language.

- This is one bit of advice you probably already know: Lace your speech with humor. Levity loosens up a room and makes you instantly more likeable. Humor sourcebooks for speechmakers and toastmasters abound in the library.

- Making a speech can be nerve-wracking, and often the voice tends to rise. Be aware, and try to keep your voice in the mid-range.

- Join Toastmasters, an organization devoted to making you adept at public speaking. It's a great investment of your time.

GUERRiLLA P.R. COMMANDO: Dick Rutan

December 23, 1986, the day Dick Rutan and Jeana Yeager landed their storm-battered *Voyager* aircraft after nine days of non-stop flight around the globe, was not only a glorious day in aviation history. It also marked a signal achievement in the annals of Guerrilla P.R. The *Voyager* would never have gotten off the ground if not for the nationwide support for the project generated by Rutan's skillful handling of the press. Clearly, he piloted the media as well as his plane.

Flying since the age of sixteen, Rutan is a decorated Air Force lieutenant colonel who, after retiring from the service, settled into a family-owned aircraft company. He developed a sterling international reputation as an ace test pilot; but Dick's dreams encompassed greater achievements. In 1981 he launched the idea of the *Voyager*, a lightweight aircraft that could fly around the world without stopping for refueling

Though Dick was well known within the aviation press, he and Jeana would need massive financial and moral support from the public to make this dream come true. From his Mojave Desert base east of Los Angeles, Dick carefully courted the media to spread the word about *Voyager*.

"We had a couple of philosophies that worked well for us," says Dick. "We always maintained a sense of openness and sincerity. Sometimes people try to use the press for some hidden agenda, but when they came here they found genuine people who would take the time to talk with them."

In preparing his and Jeana's encounter with the media, Dick studied the history books. "I went back to Charles Lindbergh," he notes. "He served as a model for how not to handle the press. If someone wrote a story on him that wasn't 100 percent accurate, he would rant and rave at the reporter. Because he grew more reclusive, writers had little information to write about him. It all snowballed, and the more recalcitrant he became, the more the press hated him."

Dick took this lesson to heart. When articles appeared that were at least 50 percent accurate, he took the time to thank the writer. However, he always insisted that all interviews be taped, which led to 90 percent accuracy in most stories. "We never alienated anybody," says Dick. "They usually stayed on the right subjects: adventure, human spirit, volunteerism." Dick also had another trick up his sleeve. "I'd give the reporters about 90 percent of what they wanted, but I'd always hold something back so they'd return again."

His openness with the press even included the tabloids. When the *National Enquirer* requested an interview, Dick was a little hesitant because of the paper's trashy reputation. But he invited the reporter up, treated him with the customary graciousness, and, believe it or not, ended up with a highly favorable and accurate story in America's favorite scandal sheet.

Working with media, Dick quickly learned the ground rules. "They may talk with you for thirty minutes," notes Dick, "but all they'll end up using is four or five sentences, and you have to be sure to give them those. Make them dramatic and personal."

Today Dick Rutan is one of the most requested speakers on the circuit, inspiring audiences across the country with his message of opportunity and vision. As for advising others on any dealings with the media, Dick cautions against Lindbergh-style criticism.

"You have to be open and friendly with the media," he notes. "Goodwill is very infectious, and you can build strong personal relationships. You should also understand the constraints the press is under, and work with them, not against them."

Dick often closes his speeches with these words, which also express the heart of the Guerrilla P.R. credo: "What you can accomplish is limited only by what you can dream." Amen.

10

May Day, May Day

When I make a mistake, it's a beaut!

—Former New York mayor Fiorello La Guardia

When Things Go Wrong

The man who coined the phrase "When life deals you a lemon, make lemonade" has my sympathy. On more than one occasion, I've found his book—with that title—mired in the cooking section of my neighborhood bookstore.

Early on I said P.R. is an art. For that reason, Guerrilla P.R. doesn't take a by-the-numbers approach. You can't go by the book because there is no book. So even the best-laid plans of Guerrillas and of pros sometimes go awry, just as half-baked schemes occasionally succeed.

My aim has been to reorient your thinking, to alter your habits of imagination, so you devise a strategy that works *for* you. Despite my tips, Guerrilla P.R. is entirely instinctive and self-directed, and thus subject to no immutable laws. So, having implemented your campaign, you may find things haven't exactly gone according to plan. Either you aren't getting the publicity you hoped for, or you're getting the kind you don't need: the negative kind. But relax—there are ways to circumvent such problems.

When fighter pilots lose power in an engine, they don't consult the manual. They respond instinctively. The information in this chapter will help you react in much the same way when things go wrong. How you handle bad news reflects greatly on how your good news will be accepted by the media in the future.

Major Disaster No. 1: No Press

It's a sad sight I've grown accustomed to in every city I visit. Mini-malls, America's immortal contribution to late twentieth-century architecture, stand on nearly every corner, offering shoppers a startling array of choices in nail boutiques, tanning salons, doughnut shops, and one-hour photo labs. The mini-malls stand as mute testament to the power of the American dream of entrepreneurship and captaining one's destiny. They also stand as very eloquent testament to the failure of that elusive dream.

Strip-mall business bankruptcies and space vacancies have skyrocketed in the past few years, surely owing in large part to overall economic conditions, but also, I believe, to the lack of P.R. initiative on the part of new business owners. Every single one of these malls and their stores seems identical. Each needs to stand out from the pack. Each needs some good press. Yet, few ever seem to go for it. Mini-mall businesses are the perfect example of those who need press and usually never get it. But what about you? Whether you own a business or are involved in some other kind of project, perhaps the most devastating response you can get from the media, should you seek their attention, is to get no attention at all.

You've got an impressive mailing list, selected your targets, assembled a press kit, mailed press releases, called papers, TV, and radio. You're pumped, primed, ready to take on the world. But you find your tracking sheets are blank. Nobody gives a damn. What now?

First, let's do a reality check. Reexamine your written materials. Bring trusted friends and family back into the discussion. Look for signs of poor presentation or unimaginative pitches. You should have noted these long ago when you sensed the media were yawning as you pitched them. But these kinds of problems should be remedied now.

If you feel your fundamentals were sound, look to your outlets. Could you have chosen the wrong ones? Reconsider your target audience and media. Perhaps you should expand in another direction? If you were going for the financial press, maybe *Business Week* was a little too far out of reach at this time. How about a smaller business journal in your neck of the woods? Take another long look at your list. Comb through the names you have. Perhaps you should move up to regional and national media? Or ratchet down to local and smaller press? This kind of retooling can often make a miraculous difference.

Although you may think you've exhausted the possibilities, go back to the library, newsstand, or bookstore. Seek out different media guides with expanded listings, and add new names to your master list. Every week, fledgling publications make their debut, and perhaps you can get in on the ground floor with some of them. The key here is to reignite your initial enthusiasm and keep up the search.

Recontact the journalists you've contacted before. Being careful to keep the focus on newsworthiness, inquire again whether they can run something—anything—on your project. If your presentation has been professional, courteous, and energetic, you should arouse a certain degree of sympathy on the part of the reporter or editor. But never ever say anything like "We really need some publicity." Reporters were not put on this earth to give you publicity, and they will invariably take great offense at such a statement. And don't forget, you have at your disposal a variety of Guerrilla techniques: magnet events, press conferences, protests, parties, mailings.

Stir new ingredients into your P.R. stew. Maybe now you should conduct that survey, poll, or trend prediction, and thus generate a new slate of releases? Could this be the time to throw a gala party? Have you called local TV stations to see about an appearance on a public affairs program? Maybe this would be a good time to send that picture to the paper, or write a letter to the editor? Just like a big-league hurler, you want to mix up your pitches to become as effective as possible.

What if you don't have time to waste? What if your charity event is just around the corner? You'll have to work quickly. Select the two or three most important outlets, and concentrate your efforts there. Do as much of the journalistic legwork as you can, present it to the outlets again, and this time stress the urgency of the matter. If you still get no response, at least make sure all local calendar listings are reserviced, make your follow-up calls, and get a mention that way. The main point is this: If you're being ignored, you have to shift your focus to something un-ignorable. Synthesize the key elements of your project, and create something controversial, newsworthy, challenging, funny, or unprecedented. Even if it's tangential to the heart of your project, it will get you coverage, and that's what you want.

Don't beat yourself up if you have to make changes. George Bernard Shaw said, "Progress is impossible without change, and those who cannot change their minds cannot change anything."

Moi?

What if you've followed all these steps and still find the media turning their backs? Publicist, heal thyself. Maybe there's something about you that needs a little work. Don't be hurt or offended by this. I'm talking about a little fine-tuning to make that personality engine of yours hum. Start by taking stock of the basics. Examine your dress, grooming, and interpersonal performance. If they check out, move on.

If you did or said something you shouldn't have (after all, you *are* new at this), keep your composure. The more relaxed you are, the less you will appear to have screwed up. Only a creep would write you off for one gaffe. If you accidentally misled a reporter, offer a sincere apology, make amends, and pick up the pieces. Don't resolutely avoid mention of your mistake; it makes you look sneaky.

People appreciate openness and honesty. Above all, forgive yourself. You don't have to be perfect. That's one of society's most pernicious lies—that we can do it all, have it all, and be it all. You're a human being. You have your own mission on this earth, but that's between you and God, not between you and the daily paper. Carry on with that mission. Return to your Guerrilla P.R. posture. What's the worst that can happen? What's the best?

Major Disaster No. 2: Bad Press

There it was on ABC's *World News Tonight*. An exposé revealed that a new series of history textbooks for high schoolers, published by the top educational publishers in the nation, were riddled with inaccuracies—over five thousand, in fact. Among the mistakes, the books claimed that we dropped the atom bomb on Korea and that both Martin Luther King, Jr., and Robert Kennedy were killed during the Nixon administration (it was, of course, during the Johnson years).

A senior executive of one of the publishers courageously faced the cameras to explain the disaster. He blamed human error and admitted there was no justification. Then, helping to trash his own case, he added, "History is more than dates." I had to avert my eyes. I don't know which is worse, too little good publicity or too much bad publicity. The former is no doubt frustrating, but the latter can be devastating. It can ruin a business; it can ruin lives. I hope you will do everything possible to avoid negative press in the first place, but should you get sideswiped by it, don't freak out. Here's what to do.

If you are faced with a crisis (e.g., the media are all over your tail for some alleged misconduct, impropriety, or misstatement), your first duty is to respond immediately. Do not delay in dealing with the problem. Remember how the Soviets covered up Chernobyl? They couldn't have looked worse. In fact, the fallout from their secrecy and cover-up was arguably more damaging than the reactor explosion itself.

How you handle the bad news will play a large role in how your good news will be met by the media in the future. But to meet a crisis head on, you have to prepare in advance. While designing your Guerrilla P.R. campaign up front, ponder also a few worst-case scenarios.

Make a list of potential problems, then opposite them list all your explanations and courses of action. That way, you'll be ready when a hostile press knocks on your door.

And I do mean hostile. It's a chilling experience to stare into glaring TV lights, to have a steel bouquet of microphones thrust in your face, and to be battered by terse questions from people you don't know. If you're confronted with this, center yourself as best you can, and remain calm. Answer positively, offer facts, and show an upbeat attitude. If you don't know the answer to something, say so.

If worse comes to worst, you can always say "no comment," but those two words have a dreadful ring. It's better to say something like "I'd really prefer not to comment about that at this time." But a "no comment" can't be attacked. It keeps you in balance while the crisis blows over. You don't want the heat of the moment to cause you to say something you'll regret. Remember, today's headline is tomorrow's fish-wrapping.

One of the worst drubbings I ever saw anyone take from the press was that administered to Rob Lowe, following the embarrassing release of his homemade pornographic video in which he engaged in sex with an underage Georgia girl. Some of my friends and colleagues still say his career never recovered, but I think he played it smart. He refused comment for a while, then came back with what I felt was a sincere apology. Later, he was able to joke about his circumstances with an appearance on *Saturday Night Live* in which he made fun of himself. This diffused the discomfort people felt and allowed him to return to the mainstream, tossing off the incident as "youthful indiscretion."

Today, after a successful starring role on *The West Wing*, his career is back on track.

But I'd say the textbook illustration of skillfully handling bad press came with the Tylenol tampering tragedy in 1982.

As you probably recall, some lunatic laced several bottles of the pain medication with lethal doses of cyanide, and before anyone could do anything about it, seven people were dead.

The manufacturer met the crisis head-on. Without delay, all Tylenol products were withdrawn from the shelves. An all-out effort to find the culprits was launched; immediately, new tamper-proof measures were introduced that changed the industry. Most important, the company took the time to let a jittery nation heal. The company was prepared, acted coolly and responsibly, did not duck the tough questions, and, in the end, retained its dominance in the market. The company used the media to show genuine concern and a determination to take the lead in resolving the crisis. It was a message of courage and leadership via public relations.

One of the single most important points to keep in mind when facing a negative situation of your own is to follow the old dictum: The best defense is a good offense. You must never go on the defensive. By anticipating negative questions you can stand ready to counter with positives.

For example, let's say you're a developer who bought a large apartment complex occupied by senior citizens, and you plan to turn it into a luxury hotel. The old folks are due to be turned out. That's the kind of juicy Simon Legree story the media love. But if reporters demand to know why you're putting seniors on the street, don't say, "We're not putting seniors on the street." That's like Nixon saying, "I am not a crook." It merely confirms what you're denying. Instead, you should say something like this: "I'm glad you asked me that because now I have a chance to explain to the public what we are doing. Not only does every resident have six months rent-free to search for alternative housing, but we'll give each one a six-month extension if need be. In addition, we're actively helping the residents find new housing, and we'll pay their moving costs. If anyone in this neighborhood is willing to do more, I'd like to meet him."

Here's another hypothetical scenario: You're launching a new manufacturing center in a small neighborhood worried about increased traffic, air pollution, and noise. Instead of denying, or getting defensive, tell the media (and thus the public) that you're offering staggered work shifts, increasing the local tax base, and increasing property values, and that you're donating a certain percentage of your profits to a local charity. In other words, you take away from the hostile press the very weapons they plan to wield against you.

If I were to boil it down to one word, it would be this: courage. That's what it takes to weather such a storm.

I know these guidelines seem hard, but you *must* follow them, or you'll come across as just another lowlife caught by the vigilant free press. *It's how you come across that matters.* So act your heart out. Be a De Niro or a Streep. Pretend to feel differently than you do. It takes an emotional toll, but in the end it will be worth it.

FROM THE GUERRILLA P.R. FILE

Though we've all experienced a bad meal every once in a while, nothing can compare to the queasy stomachs the directors of a major book publisher (not this one) experienced in February 1993, when it was discovered that one of the recipe ingredients in a recently published cookbook presented a potential health hazard. The cookbook featured a recipe recommending lilies of the valley as an edible flower for cake decoration. Turns out this is a poisonous plant to eat (though not to grow and handle). The publisher immediately sent out a press release, recalled all copies of the book from wholesalers and retailers, and offered a toll-free number for all customers who desired a full refund. A good example of a responsible company acting promptly and correctly.

Major Disaster No. 3: Inaccurate Press

Actually, I don't think of this as much of a disaster, but it could create problems. As I've said, P.R. is a gamble because you don't have authoritative control over what appears in print or on the evening news. Sometimes your message is truncated, misinterpreted, or juxtaposed with issues or symbols that defeat your purpose. Sometimes the media just plain get it wrong.

For example, a couple I know, Richard Epcar and Ellyn Stern, both actors, did a segment for a national TV magazine show. The setup showed them performing a scene for a noted Hollywood casting director. The scene went well, and the casting director raved about the couple's acting. The magazine show's producer asked the casting director, "Isn't there anything you can say that's not quite so positive, just to give it some balance?" The casting director replied, "Well, I suppose the scene did go on a little bit too long."

Wouldn't you know it—the only sound bite that wound up on the show was the director's single negative line. Not one word about what wonderful actors Richard and Ellyn were. Sad to say, there's not much you can do about this sort of thing.

The media are often in a hurry and frequently get facts wrong or cut a piece to fit given space or time limitations. If a newspaper gets something wrong, you can request a retraction or a correction (though the publications don't always comply). The same is sometimes true of TV news. You should make your request firmly but without rancor. If a retraction does run, then you've gotten two mentions for the price of one.

But by and large, you'll have to let this sort of thing go. You just have to take your lumps and look on the bright side. After all, you did get some media coverage, and that means your message got through on some level. Generally, I feel it's better to get skewed press than none at all. If you keep your cool, you can always come back to them later. Handling it psychologically is no mean trick. Just don't take personally anything negative or incorrect the papers write about you. The longer you play this game, the thicker your skin will become. Believe me.

Online inaccuracies can be even more infuriating, as they take on a viral life of their own. If someone writes something untrue about your project in a blog or on a Web site, there can be hundreds of links to the inaccurate information within minutes. It's a major problem, and worse, it can be unbelievably irritating.

But beyond correcting the error in your own blog, or on your own Web site, and then asking friends to link to your correction, you shouldn't try to do too much. Complaining to the online reporter who missed the point or flubbed the fact would be satisfying, certainly, and maybe even helpful if you can convince that person to make a correction, but it can be a death blow to your reputation if you come across as acrimonious and/or petty. You have to take the high road in these cases, or stay silent. Starting a "flame war" is the worst possible solution. You'll just gain a reputation as a thin-skinned blowhard who couldn't take it when someone pointed out an unflattering truth—no matter how false that "truth" might be.

Money Troubles

Guerrilla P.R. is grounded in low-cost techniques. But what if they're not low enough? I speak often of appearance, perception, quality. These things can't be plucked out of thin air. They require an unavoidable minimum outlay of money. So in this section, I offer a few tips that help you save some dough.

Your biggest costs will likely be printing, mailing, and telephone. As for the first, obviously you should shop around for the least expensive copy store; unless you're working on an extremely small scale, a home printer just isn't going to cut the mustard. Many have computer terminals that offer desktop publishing. I don't recommend handwriting envelopes, so if you don't own a computer, it's probably time to think about buying one, or leaning heavily on your friend next door who has one. Frankly, I'm willing to bet you own or have access to a computer and a printer, but there's certainly one at a local college or high school that you might use. Photocopying costs are low, usually no more than a dime a copy, so that shouldn't bust your budget.

Perhaps you can ask local printing firms if they'd be willing to tack your materials on to the end of a big job at a reduced cost. They may be more inclined to do this if your project is of a charitable nature, or if you're likely to become a regular customer who will give them a lot of business. It's a good way for them to use up excess paper that might otherwise go unused or tossed.

Photo duplication is another matter. If you want photos reproduced in bulk, it can be very expensive. One way to minimize costs is to get the photo right the first time. Professional photographers, however, charge an arm and a leg, so you may be better off taking your own. If you do, be sure to use a high-quality 35 mm single-lens reflex camera, or better, a high-quality digital camera that doesn't require film and can reproduce sharp, clear images on your computer that you can then crop or enhance with a program like PhotoShop. Have a photo lab produce a proof sheet, rather than prints of everything on the roll. That way, you select the one or two pictures you want and make copies only of them. Of course, bulk copies bring the unit price down, but that can still be expensive. Work with smaller quantities at first until you need or can afford more photos. Or get yourself a photo-quality printer and some photo paper and do the whole thing yourself. But again, large quantities are going to be impractical to do at home. It's better to send the photo, along with a press kit, via e-mail and let the media outlets reproduce it at no cost to you.

Press kit covers can run you quite a bill, too. Instead of having them printed, run off a quantity of attractive 3 × 5 inch labels with your logo on them. These you can place on blank press kit covers, which you can buy at any stationery store. You can buy blank labels and print them out by the page on your home computer. This will create a final product just about as professional-looking as the real thing. But if you're going to buy ready-made labels, be conservative in your initial quantities. The unit price is high, but it will still be far less than if you were to buy in bulk. You simply may not need large amounts in the early going, especially if your P.R. focus is primarily local.

As for mailing, a stamp is a stamp. You will probably never generate the quantity of mail that may entitle you to a Postal Service discount. But you can still keep your expenses down with a degree of vigilance. Hand-deliver materials if the addressees are close by. Make sure your list doesn't have any duplicate names or titles. For example, both the assignment editor and the planning desk coordinator at Channel 12 may not need to be on your list. And send as much information as you can by e-mail, which is, after all, as close to free as you can get (there is a monthly fee for Internet access, but you were going to pay that anyway).

You should also avoid heavy packaging material like thickly padded envelopes or cardboard inserts to protect photos. Usually, mail is delivered in tip-top shape. These items only serve to drive up your costs (not to mention creating needless waste). Saving on phone costs is easy. For long distance, call before 7:00 AM, especially if you live in the western United States and you're calling east. One trick you may try is to deliberately leave a message, making the other party call you back and pick up the tab, though you risk making the other party very sore unless they want you. But most long distance and local phone companies offer myriad savings plans, and some can prove economical to you. Call your phone company for details, but beware—some plans don't amount to much.

It's also possible—and sometimes preferable—to use your cell phone as your primary phone. You can get a monthly plan with unlimited long distance calling to save money on individual calls, and those people who call you back are much more likely to find you immediately if the phone is clipped to your belt.

If you get a G.P.R. campaign going full steam, people are going to want to talk with you and meet with you. That may mean travel to other cities to meet the media. Although some, especially the national shows, will pay your transportation, most do not. You're on your own. However, you have to weigh the cost of a plane ticket against the potential gain. In the end, the extraordinary exposure you receive on a national TV appearance could more than pay for itself. Overall, as with anything in society, to do a P.R. campaign right involves expenditures. But unlike marketing or advertising, P.R. is dramatically inexpensive, and the return is potentially tremendous. You get most of the benefits of a well-planned ad campaign without the burdensome costs. So even though Guerrilla P.R. isn't free, it's darn close.

The Art of Troubleshooting

Don't you just hate those Pollyanna types who always look on the bright side? Who whistle while they work, with a song in their heart? Who always think the sun'll come up tomorrow? Well, sorry, but I'm one of those types. I am a natural-born optimist, which partly explains my obsession with opportunity. The problems we all face day to day are no less fraught with opportunity than the good things that come our way. It's possible to make something positive out of the tough situations I described above.

Look at losing political candidates. After investing so much of their money, prestige, time, energy, and personal life, they so often walk away with nothing but a massive campaign debt. Yet, so often I see them carrying on and smiling all the way. Sure, they hurt inside, but I suspect by and large they adopt an attitude of "Well, I gave it everything I have, and there's nothing to hang my head about." More likely, they're saying, "I'll get them next time."

I'm not saying you have to enjoy the hard times, but you can develop a new perspective on life's challenges. In terms of Guerrilla P.R., it means seeing your efforts framed by a wider view. Your business, your project, your life and well-being, do not revolve around a guest shot on *The View*. P.R. is something you want, not necessarily something without which you die. It's one of life's great ironies: sometimes, the less you care to have something, the more you're likely to achieve it. Go for everything you want with all your heart, but keep something in reserve just for you. If you win, great. If you lose—hey, it's only a game.

GUERRILLA P.R. COMMANDO: Wayne Perryman

Wayne Perryman, a former gang member, is an author, a labor relations executive, and one of his city's most active community leaders. But his favorite endeavor is helping the disadvantaged African-American youth in his native Seattle. Among his notable achievements: the nationally lauded Role Models Unlimited, a program designed to provide positive adult male role models for kids, and the Harold Reynolds Children's Foundation, run in tandem with the former Mariners second baseman.

In fact, Wayne has so many projects going simultaneously it's a wonder he has any time to breathe, let alone direct his own publicity campaigns. But from the very start of his community service work, Wayne has run his own P.R. show, learning as he went along exactly how to entice the media.

"The media want something newsworthy," he says. "Selling newspapers meant they had to have something unique in terms of public interest. No matter what I was doing, I tried to give it a new twist to make sure, from a journalistic standpoint, there would be some excitement in covering it."

That's precisely what he did by publishing the nation's first anti-drug storybook for young children, *What Mary Found*, as part of the Harold Reynolds Children's Foundation. Wayne knew that Reynolds wanted to do something for kids, but he warned him against doing anything that had been done a hundred times before.

"All it takes is thinking your project through," says Perryman, "and presenting it in such a unique way, it touches the emotions."

That's the key to any Perryman pitch: emotion. "When your project is devoid of emotional appeal, the chances of selling it are almost nil," he notes. "If you reach the heart, you generally will get the response you want."

To get there, however, requires a solid foundation, as Perryman well knows. "Anyone doing their own P.R. should take a community college course in creative writing and/or public speaking," says Wayne. "Monitor news anchors and journalists. Watch *Good Morning America*. Guests on these have only seconds to make their points. The question is, when the lights hit you, can you tell your story? You have only one chance, and you'd better be prepared." Given Wayne Perryman's sterling reputation in the Northwest, he considers his good name a priceless possession. "You use P.R. to build on your credibility," he says. "The collective press you receive over time helps you sell your projects. Even if you sometimes end up with bad press, they can't damage you if you have a good reputation preceding you."

Though his Role Models project has received network attention, Wayne continues to focus his energies on a local basis. That's just fine with him; making a difference in Seattle has always been Wayne Perryman's main mission, and fortunately for him, it's a mission accomplished.

11

Intelligence Gathering: Planning Your Next Step

One man that has a mind and
knows it can beat ten men who haven't and don't.

—George Bernard Shaw

How'm I Doing?

Assessing the success of your Guerrilla P.R. campaign can be simple. If your project is a church carnival, and, come event day, it's packed to the rafters, then you did your job well. But if your project involves longer-range goals that aren't so easy to measure, like increasing community awareness of a public policy issue, or getting a new storefront business off to a good start, then you have to read different tea leaves to know how well you're doing.

One of the truisms of a well-mounted professional public relations campaign is its pervasiveness. When a big star has a new summer movie coming out, or a top author hits the talk-show circuit to push a new book, the cumulative publicity effect hits like a hurricane. You'll see that person's face everywhere you look, on magazine covers and round-the-clock TV interviews, even if the movie's a turkey or the book's a loser.

The well-connected P.R. pros wield enormous clout, and many face a good deal of criticism, some justifiable, with naysayers decrying the outsized demands of a select group of top Hollywood publicists. That certainly isn't the case with Guerrilla P.R. While the pros may brew hurricanes, you're looking to create a stiff breeze. You'll still make the trees bend, but not snap.

To calculate the effectiveness of your Guerrilla P.R. campaign, take stock of the following:

- Are sales up?
- Is attendance increasing?
- Are the phones ringing more?
- Have you had more hits on your Web site? (You can add a counter to your home page for free, if you don't have one already.)
- Have people commented on seeing your project mentioned in the media?
- Do you notice an increase in donations?
- Are calls being returned more than before?
- Are people treating you differently? (You know how awestruck folks get when encountering anyone deified by media celebrity.)

These sorts of things can be explained by forces other than a P.R. campaign, such as ancillary marketing efforts, word of mouth, or seasonal timing. So to pinpoint the impact of your Guerrilla P.R. campaign, you have to conduct some kind of survey. Either by verbal inquiry or written form, poll your customers and find out what drew them to your project. If they read about it in the paper, get specific. Which articles did they read? What impressed them about it? Some small business owners regularly hand out to their customers little cards with specific questions about how they first heard of the store and other similar points of inquiry. I urge you to do the same.

The best and simplest way to honestly assess your progress and performance is to play schoolteacher. You should literally give yourself letter grades in various categories. The categories should include specific P.R. objectives (i.e., the local daily paper, the morning talk radio show), success in reaching target audience, ability to define your own message (as opposed to having the media inaccurately shape the definition), and diversity of media (i.e., did you get no TV or radio? Were you featured in the trade press when you were also going for the consumer press?).

Here's what each grade should mean:

A. All your objectives were met. The coverage you received was extensive, the spin given your project was positive, and response from your target audience met or exceeded expectations. Pat yourself on the back—but only for a moment, because success is a short-term affair unless you keep on top of it.

B. You got most of what you wanted. Response was generally favorable, but perhaps one or two important goals were not met. Perhaps you felt your own performance was not as dynamic as you would have liked. Reexamine your plan, take note of what went right, and emphasize those aspects in the next leg of the campaign.

C. There was some press coverage on your project, though not enough of it was positive or prominent. Perhaps you achieved some of your target media coverage, but it turned out to be the wrong choice, and goals for your project were unmet because of errors in judgment. You need to begin the formulation process again, exploring new angles, new pitches, and new avenues for publicity.

D. Nothing went right. Despite your best efforts, you received little or no press, or bad press, or nobody showed up or cared. It's time to start from scratch, developing your interpersonal skills and rethinking your strategy for media. All is not lost, but you have your work cut out for you.

F. Forget about it. You have to either change careers, hire someone like me, or join a Tibetan religious order.

Take a look at your grades, and see where you flourished and where you floundered. This will give you an instant picture of where you need to improve and where your strengths lie. Also look beyond the grades themselves, and analyze your data in terms of the quantity and quality of coverage. We professionals do this all the time in refining our techniques for the next campaign. Assuming that you too will want to take your P.R. efforts to the next level, assessing your P.R. data is crucial.

As carefully as we may try to select our targets, often we take shots in the dark. P.R. reminds me of the old "linguini on the wall" routine. "How do you know if the linguini is done? Throw it on the wall. If it sticks, it's done." You may try many different Guerrilla P.R. techniques to publicize your project, but whatever sticks is what works, and vice versa. If your data show that more people responded to your appearance on a local radio call-in show than to a guest shot on the local morning show on Channel 6, that tells you where some of your personal strengths lie, as well as which media respond best to your project.

Once you isolate your successful media efforts, retrace your steps. Go over your tracking from the campaign, examining your pitch style, responses, and reactions. Do this not only with your successes but also with your failures, to determine why some aspects of your campaign didn't work. I see nothing wrong with recontacting media people with whom you had success and debriefing them on what it was about you and your campaign that worked for them. You can use this information for future appeals. Next go-around, you may return to the well, appealing again to publications and broadcasts that covered you previously. Or you may wish to retackle those outlets that said "no" early on. Both strategies have merit, but be aware: many media will not touch a story a second time, especially if it's within a year of the first article or segment. But this is not the eleventh commandment, and if you can continually come up with fresh new project hooks, there's no reason why you cannot sustain an ongoing media presence.

In addition, thanks to your successes, when you return to the naysayers to pitch again, you will now have evidence to show just how media-worthy you are. You will have gained newfound credibility that keeps building as you go. That's the beauty of publicity.

You're the same worthwhile and deserving person you always were, but now the media have knighted you thus, which makes it really true.

Time to Trade Up

So—you've surveyed your customers, collected data, pinpointed the media sources of your P.R. success, reexamined your success with those outlets, and sketched a second-tier plan. Most likely you can proceed upward on your own, following essentially the same path you took before. You should be better at writing, phoning, and interviewing than you were the first time; your increased confidence should mushroom into bigger and better results.

Managing an ongoing campaign is different from launching one. You may not always have a splashy announcement or a magnet event to draw attention. But you should maintain regular contact with media to keep your profile high. Once you have your links at the outlets, regularly send them releases. I don't mean every day, and I don't mean to announce that your Doberman had his tonsils out. But if you hire a new employee, begin distributing an interesting product, or move to a new building, then let the media know about it. You may not get coverage, but the constancy of regular mailings keeps you in their faces, and they'll definitely remember you.

If you were lucky enough to cultivate friendships with any media people during your initial campaign, now is the time to cement them. Do lunch, do dinner, take time to fraternize. It doesn't guarantee a story next time you need one, but it does guarantee a fair hearing, which is not something everyone gets from the media.

This is the time to solidify a perception of yourself as an expert in your field. If you own a downtown fish market, you must be the one the local newspaper calls when it's doing a story on fish. How do you do this? Careful cultivation of your prior media success. This is where reprints of clips can be most valuable. You should be sending out mailings to your list, even if you have no immediate news angle. If you keep the editors informed of your standing as an "expert," I promise you they will eventually come to believe it too.

Also, make sure you're listed in the *Yearbook of Experts, Authorities & Spokespersons* (or Expertclick.com), the bible of talent bookers on radio and TV. It may cost a thousand bucks to run your ad, but it will be seen by influential media personnel. And see to it the media are part of any consumer marketing effort you undertake; that is, keep them fully informed. Again, even if they do no reporting this time, they will remember who you are the next time you need them.

What if your reach exceeds your grasp? What if you set your sights on loftier P.R. goals? Can you pull it off on your own, or is it time to trade up? If you're willing to relinquish a measure of control to establish a long-term, high-publicity profile, if you find your ability to make contacts has hit a ceiling, and if you've got the bucks, you may wish to consider hiring a pro.

Don't think a professional will solve all your problems. Pros strike out as often as they get base hits, and home runs are never a sure thing. They will still likely utilize you as the spokesperson, and you may end up expending nearly as much time and energy on their P.R. campaign for you as you would on your own.

Obviously, having written this book, I believe anyone can successfully mount his or her own Guerrilla P.R. campaign. But deciding on going the professional route rests on the following criteria:

- You have the financial resources to afford the $1,000 to $5,000 monthly retainer.
- You are simply too busy reaping the rewards of your first G.P.R. campaign to devote more time to future publicity efforts. Your new targets include cream-of-the-crop outlets like *Newsweek* magazine, the *Wall Street Journal,* or the

CBS Evening News, and you have been unable to make any headway with them.
- You need to maintain an ongoing long-term, very high-level, national P.R. presence that would best be maintained by an independent professional.

Only a fool would do his own dental work. Similarly, someone who wants to become the next Madonna will need help on the P.R. front. Madonna was too busy doing her thing to spend time calling attention to it. Although she is a P.R. genius, she is not the one picking up the phone dialing *Rolling Stone* or faxing press releases to UPI. Her coterie of publicists do that for her. But let me put in a plug for hanging in there on your own. As you have gleaned from the G.P.R. Commandos info, this is indeed something you can do yourself. Relying on her own initiative, Candy Lightner made it to the network news, as did Jill Buck and Dick Rutan. Before they started, none knew much about how media functioned, but they learned as they went along. Their instincts were sharp, but no sharper than yours.

Moreover, you keep control when you do it yourself. Sometimes, pros alter a client's persona to entice the media. That doesn't mean we lie; we just emphasize certain media-genic qualities over others. But that can backfire. You know yourself better than anyone, and you can't help but develop a more honest profile if you handle the P.R. chores yourself.

Besides, it's very rewarding to pull it off yourself. I'm in the P.R. game for a living, in no small part because I enjoy the rush of success. You will experience that with your own successes, too, and the longer you hang in, the greater will be your achievements.

Have I Got a Career for You

Who knows? You may be so good at this that you might want to make a career out of it. Don't laugh. If you have a knack for persuading media to do your bidding, then you possess an extremely marketable skill. Perhaps you can hook up with a local P.R. firm on a part-time basis, or find a mentor who can teach you further techniques or steer clients your way. Maybe you can do pro bono P.R. work for charities or causes you believe in, or work as an intern for an established firm.

In fact, I have an offer you may just want to take me up on. Remember that feature article I wrote on the subject of interning? I was deadly serious about it. If you feel you can benefit from a tour of duty as an intern, I'll take you on at my firm in Los Angeles. Really. No kidding.

Write to me at the address given in the Acknowledgments of this book; tell me about yourself and why you'd like to intern at my company. Of course it's not a paid position, but you will get priceless hands-on experience at a top P.R. firm, learning from the professionals on my staff. There is no real education without experience. This is a golden opportunity to gain that experience. Drop me a line. I do have openings, and I would love to hear from you.

Also, if you like doing P.R. or learning more about it, I suggest you subscribe to the various professional journals, enroll in workshops, join professional associations, or take a college course. These kinds of activities can't help but improve your mind as well as your business.

Can you make it as a pro? First, ask yourself if you're merely interested in the field, or whether you have a burning maniacal rage. There's a big difference. Without the burning maniacal rage to succeed, you'll have trouble making it. For the first five years of my P.R. career, I worked two shifts, first from 9:00 AM to 6:00 PM. Then, after a quick trip home for a shower, I'd return to the office and work from 7:00 PM to midnight. People would ask me how long I'd been a publicist, and I'd say "ten years" because of those two shifts.

It's not for everyone. Even today, about twice a week I hand in my resignation to myself. But whether or not you pursue a career in P.R., you can continue to move up in your own ongoing G.P.R. campaign. You'll find maintenance easier than starting up, because you will have a growing list of media contacts on whom you can rely time and again. In your second- and third-tier campaigns, you can take greater risks and attempt to reach higher targets. Before you know it, the media will be calling you. That doesn't mean you drop the ball. You'll always need to keep yourself visible, but the sledding gets easier when the media want you before you want them.

Strut Your Stuff

I told my staff the other day that you don't have to have goals. You need them only if you want to succeed. This is true in all areas of life, including P.R. Someone once said, "Scratch a publicist and you get a milkman." That is, we milk our ideas for all they're worth. You too must expand your vision in order to do Guerrilla P.R.

As with the simple exercises in the first chapters of this book, you should continue to build a portfolio of ideas. Henceforth, spend fifteen minutes a day jotting down ideas. I mean all kinds of ideas, from new brainstorms to clever witticisms, to incorporate in your next press release.

Do it on a notepad, or talk into a digital recorder. It doesn't matter how, only that you do it. Your ideas may stink at first, but watch how quickly you refine your mind. Soon your manila folder marked IDEAS will begin to bulge. Because ideas can come at any time, keep pads everywhere—at home, in the car, at work, by the bed. Ideas are like slippery fish. If you don't spear them with a pencil right away, they'll be gone. But remember, the good Lord did not issue you a limited supply of creative energy. Once you get one idea, there are plenty more where that came from.

Besides, you will want to begin thinking long-term. Most Guerrilla P.R. efforts are geared to short-term, isolated-event publicity. But you may wish to cultivate a longer-range game plan as well. No matter who you are or what you do, whether you're project oriented or personality oriented, well-managed ongoing media relations are no longer a luxury in business but a stone-cold necessity. By sustaining your contacts with the media, you reserve for yourself a twenty-four-hour hotline to the people. Not only do you create interest in specific events, but you *establish a permanent presence in the consciousness of your target audience and the public at large*. That's the difference between short-term and long-term P.R. goals. One is event oriented, the other consciousness oriented. When people think of hope for the gang problem, they'll think of the Mid-Valley Youth Center. When they think of whatever it is your project entails, they'll think of you.

The operative phrase here is "ongoing." You should maintain a steady stream of press releases or other P.R. efforts to keep the media aware of you and your project. You can't believe how quickly they forget: media people are hardwired for the present. The old adage "Live for today" is the blood credo of the media, so if you're not on their minds today, they'll have forgotten about you by tomorrow.

I'll give you one classic example, although it's more of a marketing and advertising story than a P.R. story. Remember when Nissan used to be called Datsun? The company in Japan knew that changing their name would be a long and difficult adjustment for Americans. But over a ten-year period of gradual but constant reminders in their ads, in their showrooms, and in the media, they managed to remove one name from our consciousness and replace it with another. Now, the term "Datsun" sounds funny; Nissan sounds natural. That happened because the company understood the importance of uninterrupted media manipulation.

As for you, perhaps your project isn't as complicated as an international automobile company, but given your own scale, you will want to keep up an equally compelling long-range media profile. Remember, it hardly costs a thing, and the payback is beyond measure.

GUERRiLLA P.R. COMMANDOS: Andy and Katie Lipkis

TreePeople is known around the world not only for its extraordinary efforts to plant trees but also for planting a love of trees in the hearts and minds of children and adults everywhere.

Founded in the early seventies by Andy Lipkis when he was only fifteen, TreePeople exemplifies the kind of originality of purpose that not only gets good things done but also brings out the best kind of Guerrilla P.R. Today, with his wife, Katie, Andy Lipkis and Treepeople remain the premier organization of its kind.

Considering the fact that TreePeople always worked at a grassroots level, it's not surprising that Andy and Katie took a Guerrilla approach to P.R. From their L.A. headquarters atop Coldwater Canyon, they have directed large-scale urban tree-planting projects, visited schools to give away seedlings and educate young people on the ecological importance of trees, undertaken massive ad campaigns, written a best-selling book (*The Simple Act of Planting a Tree*), and maintained a sprawling tree nursery to fuel their dreams of international reforestation.

To pull this off, Andy knew he had to sell himself as hard as his ideas. As he wrote in his book, "People who cared about the environment were portrayed on television as outcasts, and people who expressed concern over this issue were do-gooders." Andy changed that image to one of lively enthusiasm, backed by a spirit of fun and genuine concern. With Katie's writing skills, the two made a formidable team.

To illustrate just how effective they were at organizing and publicizing, let's take a quick look at their successful three-year campaign in the early eighties, which they called the Million Trees Story. The goal was to plant one million trees in Southern California before the 1984 Los Angeles Olympics. First, TreePeople enlisted the aid of a top ad agency, which donated all its services. The campaign rallied around these slogans: "Turn Over a New Leaf, L.A.—Help Plant the Urban Forest" and "Urban Releaf."

The nobility of the campaign goals led to a PSA starring actor Gregory Peck. Radio's help was enlisted too, with thirty-second and sixty-second taped PSAs and scripts for on-air announcers sent to every station in town. Fresh scripts were sent regularly during the two-year campaign, with each good for use (timely) for about a month. A billboard company donated ad space. The local ABC news affiliate signed on with a five-part series on the campaign. In the end, by securing high-visibility media and pro bono services, and enlisting corporate sponsorship for its cause, TreePeople succeeded in its ambitious Million Trees campaign. Though there were pitfalls, basically the organization emerged all the more savvy.

"We've never had a public relations budget," writes Andy. "In every case, the national media attention we've received has been unsolicited. Why is this? We believe it has something to do with our genuine respect for most of the media folk we've worked with. They're a priceless resource. Don't overuse or try to trick them."

12

Theme and Variations

Innovation has never come through bureaucracy and hierarchy.
It's always come from individuals.

—John Scully, former chairman, Apple Computers

Throughout this book, I have offered my concept of how a Guerrilla P.R. campaign can be mounted. Many of the illustrations came from my own personal experience, and others were drawn from my knowledge of other people's efforts. The Guerrilla P.R. Commandos spotlighted are, in my mind, the cream of the crop, but they certainly aren't the only ones who exemplify the approach I urge.

There are many people in all fields who recognize the critical importance of P.R., and who wage and win publicity battles every day. Most of them had little or no money to invest in a P.R. campaign. Few or none had any formal training in this area. Yet, all had the moxie and the instincts to use the media and their interpersonal P.R. skills to achieve their goals. I'd like to now share with you several examples of real-life people I've known who showed me just how tenacious and inventive the Guerrilla P.R. practitioner can be.

The Actors

Los Angeles is a town where every waiter is a struggling actor, and every shop clerk has a script he's trying to sell. The competition among wanna-bes and almost-theres in the film, theater, and TV communities is unimaginably fierce, with the average member of SAG (Screen Actors Guild) earning only an annual pittance from his or her acting ability.

The only way for actors and actresses to make it—aside from the talent and dumb luck factors—is to work as hard on marketing themselves as they do on remembering their lines. Two young actors who personify that kind of perseverance are Richard Epcar and Ellyn Stern, a married couple who have managed to maintain successful careers in entertainment by relying on their own ingenuity to reach their target audience.

Richard had a big role in the 1993 Chevy Chase film *Memoirs of an Invisible Man*, appeared in many TV shows such as *Cheers* and *Beverly Hills 90210*, and has written and directed scores of children's films and English-language adaptations of foreign film hits like *Cinema Paradiso* and *Women on the Verge of a Nervous Breakdown*. He also does a good deal of work adding his voice to documentary projects and video games. Ellyn has worked in many motion pictures, including *The Man Who Loved Women*, and such TV shows as *St. Elsewhere* and *General Hospital;* provided scripts and voices for Saturday morning cartoons and foreign films like *Babette's Feast;* and written several children's books. The two of them are constantly working while many of their peers wait for the phone to ring. And there's a good explanation.

"Without P.R., we don't work," says Richard, "and we've been doing this for thirty years." What they've been doing is simply applying P.R. techniques to keep their names and faces constantly in front of their target audience: casting directors and producers. They send out a steady barrage of postcards with their pictures on one side and a personalized note on the back. They take advantage of the "Breakdown" service, which furnishes casting directors and production companies with casting information by having their materials included on daily deliveries.

"It's like a mail service, but not many actors know about it," says Ellyn, who notes that names and addresses of casting directors are easily obtained from listings kept by the Casting Society of America. The two also scored a major P.R. coup a few years back when they created their own one-on-one showcase for casting directors. "We and other actors pitched in to rent a small theater. Then we would pay the casting people a small honorarium to get them down," recalls Richard. "We would each do a short five-minute scene, and that way get to know personally these important people."

Later on, the actors' and producers' unions battled over the ethics of paying casting directors to watch actors work. It was a mini-controversy in Hollywood; yet, even in this case, Ellyn's comments about the issue were constantly quoted in *Variety*. The two never failed to make their presence felt in the trades.

Every time either landed a job, they'd send an announcement to the telecastings and filmcastings columns in *Variety* and the *Hollywood Reporter*. By reading the trades and learning their formats, Richard was easily able to write usable copy for those particular columns.

Richard has booked himself on cable TV talk shows, and both made sure they were photographed at the Hollywood parties they occasionally attend. "You have to use all your connections," notes Richard, "and you can't be shy about it." Adds Ellyn, "You also have to have a positive attitude. That's what propels you."

So, by combining initiative to do the P.R. legwork, and never dropping the offensive, Richard Epcar and Ellyn Stern have managed to sustain their careers in the ultimate dog-eat-dog business. Lessons from Richard Epcar and Ellyn Stern: Persistence and relentless efforts are vital if one seeks to impress decision makers who don't remember what they had for breakfast. Find P.R. resources nobody else has thought of yet, and seize the opportunity.

The Realtor

Realtors are the most optimistic people in the world. The market's never bad, sales have never been better, and any house they show is the most perfect dwelling ever constructed. It's enough to make you sick sometimes. But at other times you meet people in the real estate business who sincerely try to do the best possible job for their clients and to make sure they find the right house for the right price.

One realtor who exemplifies this first-rate service attitude is Dale Fay, longtime owner of the Century 21 Oak Tree franchise in California's San Fernando Valley. Dale has been a realtor for many years, working her way through the ranks to become one of the Valley's top salespersons.

She bought her franchise at a time when the real estate market in Southern California was in a true tailspin. Friends called her crazy, but Dale knew what she was doing.

"People in the community need to know you," she says. "I figured it would take two years before anybody would get to know us, and opening then would establish us to be there at the right time when the market picked up."

To ensure that once and future clients will remember her, Dale relies on several strategies. Since referral is the most important source of business, she makes sure her present clients are happy. She's always ready to go the extra mile, clean up the house she's showing if the owners aren't home, and make herself available by phone literally twenty-four hours a day. She carries a few bottles of champagne in the trunk of her car in case she closes a deal on the spot. Her attitude is "Once a client, always a client." Dale mails out forty pieces of literature and information to clients up to five years after the sale of a property. "It keeps our name in front of them."

But she also has to court potential customers. To do that, Dale regularly offers free seminars to likely first-home buyers; sends out cards and mailers offering free home market analysis; and, for good community relations, sponsors food drives and Easter Seals benefits.

"Our P.R. message is 'We're different because we know more and we serve you better,'" says Dale. To impart that message, Dale has simply lived up to it. As for the media, she maintains cordial relationships with the real estate reporters for L.A.'s two daily papers.

"I bombard them with press releases, knowing full well they can't run them all. But if I send them ten, I know they'll run at least two." Dale's principal G.P.R. tactic: "If you show interest in others, they will like you," she says. "I have six kids, so I'm prepared to deal with people in all kinds of situations, and that's all this business is."

Lessons from Dale Fay: Pinpointing a target audience, and finding new ways to reach and keep this public attentive, are essential to long-range growth in P.R. and business.

The Used Car Dealer

"I'm pretty lazy," says Dave Schwartz, founder of the Rent-A-Wreck chain of auto-rental and sales outlets that deals with slightly unsightly but perfectly functional automobiles. "I found making mistakes takes extra time, so by avoiding mistakes, I save a lot of time and aggravation."

That kind of self-effacing approach has taken Dave far, from the unassuming owner of a small L.A. used car lot when he was a teenager, to the multimillion-dollar franchise of Rent-A-Wrecks across the nation.

His original company, Bundy Very Used Cars, drew attention not only for its amusing name but also for its first-rate service. Once he changed the name to Rent-A-Wreck in 1973, he was hardly prepared for the torrent of attention he received.

"The same day I changed the name, CBS was here filming a story," recalls Dave of the power the new name held. Soon—totally unsolicited—Dave was written up in *People,* the *New York Times,* and the *Wall Street Journal,* and he appeared on the *Donahue* and *Tom Snyder* shows. The name drew attention; the attention drew overwhelming business; the business drew more attention. "Our name was our biggest asset," he says. "We just used reverse psychology."

Despite his phenomenal success, Dave still works at his original used car lot every day, greeting customers and perpetuating the good service that made Rent-A-Wreck such a hit. "We never have an argument at the counter," he notes. "If a guy's a few hours late, or the gas tank isn't topped off, we don't worry about it. For us, service is everything. Again, it's because I'm lazy. I don't want anybody uptight, because that takes extra work to sort out."

Because he doesn't in any way fit the tycoon mold, Dave has had fun with his media encounters. He was given a standing ovation at a national used car convention, well covered by the media. For his profile on *Lifestyles of the Rich and Famous,* Dave drove around in one of his old clunkers. But his interpersonal P.R. tools are, for him, the most important. "You have to bring someone down to the comfort zone immediately," he says. "The reason U.S. business is down is because Americans don't take that extra step. A guy who just works for the money is in a bottomless pit."

So, with Dave, starting out with a fantastic business name got his foot in the door. But it took a potent dose of personal P.R. power to sustain his business over twenty years. Lessons from Dave Schwartz: Coming up with an irresistible name for his business, Dave not only generated overwhelming press coverage but launched an empire. In one tongue-in-cheek phrase he defined his company and captured the essence of his easygoing attitude. Yet, he never forgot that service is the key to commercial longevity. His business flourished because he cared about his customers' needs. That, combined with his company's name, attracted media attention.

The Hoaxster

It's likely you've never heard the name Alan Abel, but I'll bet my last dollar that you're familiar with his "work," if that's what it can be called. Alan is much more than a Guerrilla P.R. genius. He's a pure Guerrilla, a true saboteur, a troublemaker of the highest order. The only people he makes trouble for, however, are members of the news media. The rest of us can't help but snicker with glee at his antics.

Alan is the guy who stages monumental media hoaxes. Like the time he faked Ugandan dictator Idi Amin's wedding to a New England debutante; like the time he arranged a photo-op for the Ku Klux Klan symphony, sitting at their music stands, robes and all; like the time he had his own lengthy obituary very prematurely printed in the *New York Times.*

He says he does it to educate and amuse the public while at the same time catching lazy reporters off guard. Time and time again, journalists have run with his phony stories, only to turn around red-faced shortly thereafter. Some pundits praise his wit and skill; others condemn him as a two-bit scoundrel doing harm to the public. I say he's a P.R. genius who has an unmatched eye for what the press goes for.

Other examples of his handiwork include Omar's School for Panhandlers, the International Sex Bowl Olympics, and Princess Di's chocolate pumps, which she supposedly wore and later ate at a royal function. None were true, but the press dutifully reported them all, proving the veracity of those immortal words from the late New York newspaper publisher James G. Bennett, "Many a good story has been ruined by over-verification."

Lessons from Alan Abel: The press will jump overboard for a good hook. After all, the media consist of nothing more than curious individuals. Combine Abel's knack for ideas with your own "true" stories, and you cannot fail to attain coverage.

The Comic

"Life is an improvisation," says funny lady Claire Berger. "You don't have a script." Maybe not, but when it came to piloting her own stand-up career through the competitive waters of the comedy business, Claire must have done something right. Especially when it came to guiding her own publicity, it seems she was blessed with as much P.R. talent as comedic gifts.

In the 1990s, happily married for fifteen years and the mother of two young children, Claire was something of an anomaly as a comedienne. She didn't go out on the road for fifty weeks a year, but rather found a place for herself as a warm-up comedienne for top network sitcoms like *Seinfeld, Murphy Brown,* and *Night Court.* A warm-up keeps the studio audience entertained before filming and in between set changes. But when she migrated to L.A. from Chicago eight years ago, she didn't know a soul.

"I hate people who say, 'It's who you know.' I say, 'It's who you get to know.'" That attitude made her many friends in Chicago, no two-bit town itself. While working for the city library, she hosted her own radio talk show, worked stand-up, and was a member of the ensemble cast of *Second City.* She was always successful, in part because she comprehended the power of media.

In Chicago, the entertainment columnists for the two daily papers are especially powerful. A mention in their columns can mean a major career boost. Claire hounded them until both caught her show, helping to establish her in her hometown. Her last booking in Chicago came when she was seven months pregnant. She dubbed it The Raging Hormones Tour, which caught the eye of the media, and all shows were sellouts.

Once she moved to L.A., she found her niche as a warm-up. When the *New York Times* came out to do a story on the subject of warm-ups, Claire made sure she was interviewed. The piece ended up more like a glowing profile of Claire than anything else, and this she used to get herself more work. Her clip file was so thick with first-rate press that she was actually turned away by a professional publicist, who told her, "What do you need me for?"

Claire was also clever in going after jobs. When the TV series *Chicken Soup* was looking for a warm-up comedian, Claire sent the *New York Times* article wrapped around a pint of chicken soup. Of course she got the job.

Today, Claire does a good deal of comedy for corporate functions and some motivational speaking, particularly at colleges. Her humor continues to pay large dividends for her.

Lessons from Claire Berger: Creativity in pitch will pay off. Finding a unique niche and becoming the best in it helps pave the way to success. Especially in the entertainment field, columnists wield great power. Even a one-line mention in a column can have long-ranging aftereffects. Use every option at your disposal.

The Restaurateur

Sometimes it's impossible to trace the origins of a movement. Innovations in art, language, and pop culture often seem to emerge out of the collective unconscious. But it's not at all difficult to identify the start of the surge in popularity of Thai food in this country. Tommy Tang, a Thai refugee who personifies the classic rags-to-riches tale, is the master chef who introduced Thai food to the trendy L.A. and New York restaurant scene. Today, with his two Tommy Tang's restaurants and a complete

line of retail food products, a video, and a best-selling cookbook, *Modern Thai Cuisine,* he remains the undisputed king of the
Thai food movement.

Much of his success is due to his wife, Sandy, a marketing
analyst by training, who helped launch Tommy's career through
clever use of Guerrilla P.R. and self-directed marketing. "The
first couple of years of the restaurant, I did all the P.R. myself,"
recalls Sandy. "I'm a firm believer in P.R. Once a restaurateur
starts thinking he or she doesn't need it, that's the beginning of
the end."

For starters, back in 1982 Sandy and Tommy threw an opening night party at the restaurant, inviting all their loyal patrons
from the previous restaurant where Tommy had worked. Press
came, celebrities came, and the resulting mystique catapulted
the restaurant to immediate notoriety. Sandy made a point of
personally greeting and mingling with customers every night,
and she maintained constant contact with the local food press.
"There's an element among the population very interested in
what's going on," says Sandy. "They read restaurant reviews and
want to know the hot places to go."

Sandy also made sure Tommy Tang's was involved with charities, such as S.O.S. (Save Our Strength), a hunger-fighting organization, and AIDS research. The restaurant also caters the
famed Comic Relief benefits that combat homelessness.

Other catchy and provocative innovations devised by Sandy
included staging yearly parties on the restaurant's anniversary,
the introduction of a preferred diner's card, and stocking a full
line of retail products, such as Thai seasonings and sauces, cook-
books, and a home video.

Sandy's key advice is to make sure the media are given suf-
ficient information. "If you don't, you won't spark their interest,

and then you can't blame them if you don't get the press you want." Though their operation is now too big for Guerrilla P.R., Sandy never takes it for granted. "Every day," notes Sandy, "I wake up and think, 'What if this was all taken away?' That keeps me on my toes."

Lessons from Sandy Tang: Keep in close personal contact with your customers. They are the ones who ultimately ensure your success. Even though the critics are unable to review a restaurant over and over, the press need to be in your corner, so keeping them up-to-date regularly is a good investment of your time and energy.

And don't sit on your laurels. As quickly as success appears, it can be taken away. As with the Tangs' strategy, it's wise to be ever innovative, looking for new ways to expand.

The Entrepreneur

They say nothing is as powerful as an idea whose time has come, and that was certainly true for Jeffrey Ullman, the man who pioneered the concept of video dating (later a concept that would be taken online as his company grew with the technology). His company, Great Expectations, founded in 1976, spawned an entire industry, born out of our modern-day explosion of alienated singles. A self-described video Guerrilla prior to forming his company, Jeffrey had a good sense of the zeitgeist (German for "spirit of the times"), and his idea of pairing singles who meet each other via extended videotaped interviews took off quickly.

But that doesn't happen without tremendous effort. As a journalism major Jeff had a keen awareness of the central role the media might play in his company's success, and he wasted no time in securing publicity for his fledgling dating service. "When we started," recalls Jeff, "I called up the local papers and asked for their Singles Reporter. They didn't know what I was talking about, so I asked to talk to a reporter who was single."

Trusting the validity of his own entrepreneurial idea, Jeff persuaded reporters to actually experience a video date. "It was a crapshoot," he says, "because they might not have had a good experience, but it turned out they did." After a story would run, and sometimes even before it ran, he'd call up the wire services, ask for an unmarried reporter, and inquire whether he'd seen the article in the paper. Inevitably, he got them curious, and an entirely new wire story would be generated.

At the time, the *Merv Griffin Show* was an important TV outlet. "I booked myself," says Jeff, recalling one of his most audacious moves. "I called up and asked for the executive producer. When the secretary answered, I said, 'Did Jean [the talent coordinator] call you?' When the secretary got flustered, she put her boss on the line, and I pitched him. He liked the idea of booking me, and said he'd check with Jean. I then called Jean and asked, 'Did Murray call you?' It was the presumptive close all the way." Jeff ended up making four appearances on the show over the years. He also was featured on the CBS show *48 Hours* twice, in *Newsweek,* and in other important media outlets.

Having fended off the competition for so long, Jeff has drawn some valuable conclusions about media and P.R. "Print is more powerful in generating ideas," he notes. "When people are exposed to a new concept, such as video singles introduction, they need to mull it over, sort of intellectually kick the tires. That isn't possible with TV. With reading, your mind has to be active."

Jeff's advice to fledgling Guerrilla publicists: "Know what it is you're selling," he says. "Reduce it to as simple a statement or phrase as possible. Imbue it with both facts and emotion so that others will feel about it as you do. And above all, always tell the truth to the media, or else they will bite you back very badly."

Lessons from Jeff Ullman: Don't be afraid to be a little outrageous. Jeff was aggressive with the media, and it paid off for him. Because he was so sure of the validity of his idea, he easily mustered the confidence to assertively pursue press.

The Music Man

Although he has always personally detested the term "New Age," there's no doubt that Windham Hill Records founder Will Ackerman almost single-handedly launched that genre of music in the late seventies. He guided his own fledgling company, operated out of his garage, into a multimillion-dollar enterprise. Windham Hill Records, known for its pristine audio quality, elegant graphics, and tranquil acoustic instrumental music, took the lead in a musical format that has by now swept the world. It's hard to imagine that it all began in 1976 when Will, a house builder at the time, had to borrow $300 to record his debut album of guitar music, *In Search of the Turtle's Navel*.

"I'm flattered by the articles that see me as some marketing genius who saw a niche in the U.S. music scene and understood demographics," he says, "but nothing could be further from the truth." Will only knew he wanted the best, so he tracked down the finest pressing plant in America to make the records, insisted on top-quality album artwork, and, of course, signed only those musicians who moved him. Although he had no money in the beginning, his enthusiasm and naïveté worked for him. "I was utterly genuine," says Will. "That's why everyone went for it. There was no pretense, no hype. This was something done with a great deal of love and quality."

In the sphere of publicity, Will started out as a novice but soon mastered it as well. "My ambitions were modest at first, but once I taste blood I go after something," he notes. "I went for publications like the *Boston Weekly, Village Voice,* making cold calls." The unusual quality of the music attracted attention, while Will's articulate manner and passion for his product helped establish him as a forceful spokesman, not only for Windham Hill but also for the genre of New Age music, though he never enjoyed that label. "It wasn't flattering to me. The press has a desperate need to codify." Windham Hill grew so large that by the early eighties, Will had signed a distribution deal with A&M Records, which shifted the company from a handmade cottage industry to a major player in the international record business. Until that time, however, all marketing functions, including P.R., were performed in-house. The label was featured in articles in virtually every news and music publication in America.

Ackerman attributes the company's success not only to the quality of its music but to the intense pioneering spirit exemplified by him and his staff. "The world is thirsty for anything genuine," says Will. "I believe the audience responds with extraordinary loyalty when they find something they can believe in."

Will also writes music for film and video, runs a recording studio, and had a Grammy-winning recording as recently as 2004. He never stops, and his enthusiasm has never waned for a moment. As he says, "I was once asked, 'Will, when will you compromise?' I replied, 'Where is it indicated in my past that compromise has ever been advantageous to me? I've gotten where I am because I didn't compromise. The lesson I've learned is quite the contrary. The more adamant I am about doing something different from the trends of society, the more likely I am to distinguish myself in what I'm doing, and to find a loyal following.'"

Lessons from Will Ackerman: This brilliant man speaks for himself. That last quote of his says everything one needs to know about initiative, courage, imagination, and the Guerrilla P.R. attitude. Will Ackerman is a model, not just for P.R. but for life. The people profiled in this brief chapter embody the Guerrilla P.R. spirit I've tried to describe in this book. No two are alike, as no two should be alike. Each found distinct prescriptions for pursuing his or her distinct P.R. challenges. You cannot precisely copy what they did, because their circumstances were unique, but you certainly can pattern your demeanor and your outlook after these winners.

It's my great hope that someday, in future editions of this book, I will add your name to this list of champions.

13

Concluding Thoughts:
A Call to Battle

There is only one success—
to be able to spend your life in your own way.

—Christopher Morley

Ethics

Maybe you've heard the old joke, "What do you call five hundred
lawyers at the bottom of the ocean?" Answer: "A start." A little
macabre, perhaps, but funny because, fairly or not, we tend to
perceive lawyers as unethical. Americans don't take kindly to
cheaters, even though so many good citizens play fast and loose
with society's rules.

How many of us are 100 percent honest on our taxes? Who
among us has never rolled through a stop sign, swiped a pen from
the supply cabinet, or called in sick when we really weren't?

Most people look on the P.R. profession as one populated by liars, cheats, and tellers of tall tales. It would be untrue to say we don't have our share of miscreants, but most publicists are honest and principled. That doesn't mean we don't bend the truth when it suits our purposes. We do. Likewise, in your own Guerrilla P.R. efforts, you too may find yourself at times facing moments of choice: do I stretch the truth or do I blow an opportunity?

Here's what the *Dartnell Public Relations Handbook* has to say on the subject: "There is no branch of public relations that can stand up under misleading or tricky tactics without hurting the practitioner." It's vital that we take some time to explore issues of ethics. They apply in every field, from medicine to law to simple commerce. Ethics constitute the unwritten and unenforceable laws that allow us to get along with one another. Without ethics—as we saw in the tragic L.A. riots of 1992—we have a complete breakdown in the moral order of society. The riots were an example of that on a grand scale. You represent only yourself, but within that self-contained universe, you must uphold the highest sense of ethics.

At the outset, I say to you *never deliberately lie*. By that I mean the following:

- Do not make a promise you know you cannot keep.
- Do not fabricate anything about your project that you cannot in some way substantiate.
- Do not mislead the media about any of the central merits and attributes of your project.
- Do any of these, and, as they say in the movies, you'll never work in this town again.

Media are, however, accustomed to embellishment, aggrandizement, and hype. For example, here's my reconstruction of an actual phone call I overheard from a publicist to a newspaper reporter regarding one of her clients:

> *"I'm telling you, [the client] is to die. Her talent is so ... well, let's just say I never heard a singer as gifted, ever. I'm not kidding. She makes Whitney Houston sound like my father does in the shower. Have I sent you a tape? What??? I haven't?? I'm getting one over to you by messenger right this very second. I'm packing it up as we speak. You must hear her. I guarantee you're going to mention her in your column next week. Not because I said so, but because you're gonna want to. I'm telling you, she's to die."*

There is absolutely nothing wrong with this. It is merely thrusting an emotional component into your pitch. If you want to give the media an enthusiastic spiel, they may not buy it, but they would certainly not accuse you of lying. Nevertheless, this is a far cry from intentional fabrication.

Ethics is more than a simple matter of right and wrong. You will truly hurt yourself if you behave unethically. You can't get away with falsehoods, with backstabbing, with intentional and malicious manipulation of people and media outlets. The folks out there are far too smart to be taken in. The only result will be the complete discrediting of you and your project. So if you're one of those people who has no moral problem with unethical behavior, think of such a stance simply as bad for business. You can take the morality right out of the equation, but I hope you can see it as more than just a business decision.

Ethical behavior is important in all aspects of life. I cringe when I see decent people justifying abhorrent business practices simply because "that's the way it's done." There's no excuse for that. Maybe powerful people—including powerful publicists—can get away with it. But you, as a Guerrilla, cannot. So walk the straight and narrow.

Do what you can to aggressively pursue your P.R. objectives, but don't cross the ethical line. You'll sleep better at night.

Excellence

Former secretary of state Henry Kissinger tells the story of a young assistant whom he asked to prepare a lengthy policy analysis. After several days of slaving away, the aide submitted his work to the boss. Kissinger returned it with a note, demanding it be redone. The assistant stayed up all night revising it, but the second draft was returned again. After three drafts, the exasperated aide asked to see Kissinger, telling him, "I've done the best I can do."

Kissinger replied, "In that case, I'll read it now."

What is easy is seldom excellent. Some people believe excellence can be achieved through cunning, that being tricky is a valid substitute for hard work. That's bull, plain and simple. Guerrilla P.R. is like any other effective business strategy in one respect: it works only if you put the proper effort into it. There is no shortcut through the fire walk.

I have presented to you in this book a path and a direction. It is up to you to find your way. To have given nothing but ultra-specific ideas and formulas would have been to dishonor your native gifts of invention, improvisation, and ingenuity. Implicit between the lines is the conviction that each person knows what is best for himself or herself. Only you know how far you can push things; only you know when you haven't pushed hard enough.

With all my emphasis on perception, in truth, perception goes only so far. You can't pretend to lead. If you want to be perceived as a leader, start leading. If you haven't yet become the leader you want to be, then be what you are becoming. That's not psychobabble but sound advice. I've applied it many times in my career. When faced with unfamiliar situations, I try to imagine how I want to perform. Then I work backward and figure out how to do it. It's easier than you think. It just takes a little self-confidence. That, in fact, is one of the fringe benefits of Guerrilla P.R. Anyone with enough money can buy an ad in a newspaper or rent a plane to scrawl a message in smoke in the skies. But to bring about a real article in a newspaper or a segment on the evening news, something that will have an impact on millions of people, and to do it using only one tool—your brain—well, not everybody can do that. I believe you can. As was once said to me, "The only real voyage of discovery consists not in seeking new landscapes but in having new eyes."

While putting together this book I remembered an incident from a noisy Hollywood bash I had attended a few years back. Among all the pretty people mingling, drinking, and attempting to impress one another, I noticed a world-famous director standing by the bar unnoticed, talking quietly with someone.

A woman standing next to me poked my arm and said, "Look who's over there." I acknowledged the great man. The woman said to me, "He certainly made his mark on history, didn't he?" My reply to her: "We can all leave our mark on history."

Go, and make yours.

Appendix

Two Interviews

Not everyone with a Guerrilla P.R. outlook is a Guerrilla publicist. Some are involved in other fields but have developed a keen understanding of the Guerrilla view of things. Two such people, both good friends of mine, are Bart Andrews and Alan Caruba. One is a noted author and literary agent; the other is a professional publicist, albeit an unconventional one.

In researching and preparing this book, I spoke with dozens of people, both Guerrilla P.R. practitioners and media representatives, and all were universally helpful to me. However, Bart and Alan were exceptionally wise in their insights and experience. The interviews I conducted with them proved to be extraordinarily astute. In reviewing them, I felt they should be reproduced here.

As you read them, try to get a feel for both Bart's and Alan's dynamic view of the P.R. process. Neither views P.R. in a strictly linear fashion—that is, Task A precedes Task B which precedes Task C. Rather, they see it as an ongoing multilinear process, interconnected, geodesic in shape. Read on, and glean as much as you can from them.

Bart Andrews

A former TV comedy writer, Bart began researching the life and career of Lucille Ball in 1975 for a book that has now become a best-selling classic, the *I Love Lucy Book*. Bart went on to write many other books, including a companion volume to his first Lucy book, *Loving Lucy*. Bart is at the same time a highly successful literary agent, having represented such authors as Vanna White, Sally Jessy Raphael, Smokey Robinson, and many others. Although his specialty is book publishing, his comments can be applied to any P.R. endeavor:

MICHAEL LEVINE: Bart, do you think authors generally need to hire outside publicists, or should they do their own P.R.?

BART ANDREWS: I discourage hiring out because (A) it's very expensive and (B) it's a big gamble for an author to expect to recoup that money based on royalties. It's simply not money well spent. The question is, do you want your face out there for reasons of ego, or are you doing it for the book?

ML: Does P.R. serve a narrower function in publishing than in other fields?

BA: P.R. success is much more difficult to gauge in realms other than publishing. For an individual to really know if you're getting anything out of personal P.R. is nearly impossible. You can't monitor it the way you can with a book. If you appear on *Good Morning America,* your sales will substantially increase overnight. You can punch up the numbers on a computer. All you can do with an individual or, say, an idea, is head for the nearest street corner and ask someone, "Hey, did you hear about so-and-so?" If they say, "I just read about him in the paper," then you know.

ML: What are some of your general observations about P.R. and media?

BA: There are certain things you do to publicize anything. In my area they usually involve radio, TV, and print. Those are generic. I happen to have a knack for keeping my eyes open when opportunities present themselves. I met Sally Jessy Raphael in 1976 when she was doing a radio talk show in New York. I appeared on her show for the Lucy book, and we became great friends. I never forgot about her after that first interview, and kept in touch with her. Today, I'm able to pick up the phone and book myself or one of the authors I represent on the show.

ML: What do you need to know going in, before you contact the media?

BA: You've got to know whether your pitch fulfills some requirement of the show's audience. If you're selling a cookbook, don't pitch Geraldo. It amazes me how people still do things like that. You've got to watch or listen to the shows, or read the paper or magazine. True, TV and talk radio are hungry for subjects. I hear constantly how viewers send in ideas for Oprah and Sally segments. They're not ivory towers. But you have to give them ideas that will fill up an hour. Once you're on with something people want to hear about, you become a Good Guest. They'll call you from then on. But you have to sustain the relationship. Keep sending them your material.

ML: What is more important, marketing or publicity?

BA: Between the two, I'd take publicity. For each dollar spent you get more out of P.R. I sent a copy of a book by one of my authors to *USA Today*. Total cost was $8 for the book and $3 for postage. The book's theme caught someone's fancy, and the paper ran an entire page on it. How much do you figure a full-page ad in *USA Today* would cost?

ML: I often stress communication skills. What about you?

BA: People in the media are too used to professional quality to put up with crap. I get stuff submitted to me handwritten, with typos. Even if they have the kernel of a good idea, if the presentation is poor, I file-and-forget in the wastebasket.

ML: What advice would you give to people contemplating their own self-directed P.R. campaign?

BA: If you really want to make the effort to get publicity, you can do it. It takes perseverance. People always want the end product, but too often they don't want to do the work to get the end product, or they don't have the ingenuity to figure out how to get it. You've got to be really cold about yourself, and decide if you've got the right stuff. But it's definitely possible.

Alan Caruba

Although he's one of the most in-demand public relations counselors and counts major associations, corporations, and celebrities among his clients, Alan Caruba of Maplewood, New Jersey, possesses the soul of a Guerrilla P.R. master. His resourcefulness, creativity, and almost superhuman energy have allowed him to benefit not only his clients but himself as well. In 1984, for example, he launched The Boring Institute as a lark, and now he sends out his eagerly awaited annual list of the year's Most Boring Celebrities to the international media. His National Anxiety Center has become a resource for insightful commentary on the national stress caused by daily scare headlines. Both these ventures reflect not only his own imagination but his skills in securing media exposure.

In a recent conversation with Alan, we talked about many aspects of P.R. On some things we agreed; on many others we did not, but I reproduce for you the text of our interview to give you a fresh alternative perspective.

MICHAEL LEVINE: HOW do you define P.R.?

ALAN CARUBA: P.R. is a craft. It doesn't lend itself to the committee approach. It's an information-gathering, packaging, and dissemination process.

ML: I suspect many people view P.R. people as hypesters and liars.

AC: That is a mistaken viewpoint, often encouraged by the media, who are almost entirely dependent on P.R. to perform their work. I would say 80 percent of any newspaper or news broadcast is utterly dependent on news stories and ideas from P.R. professionals. Today's journalists are often less newsgatherers than news processors. Most journalists sit at the desk working the phones and complaining bitterly they're getting too much mail, too many news releases going to too many editors. Media people sometimes sound to me like crybabies.

ML: You're not really so bitter about reporters, are you?

AC: On the contrary, I have many friends who work in the media, and, having been a former full-time journalist, I feel a real kinship. I have always viewed everything I do in terms of journalistic standards. When I write a news release I am writing a news story. That's the way every news release should be written, as if it could go in a newspaper or magazine, or be read on TV verbatim. The first question any P.R. person should ask himself is: *Is this newsworthy?* Does this product or service lend itself to what is happening in the news these days? Is this a product or service which will help people lead better lives?

ML: What kinds of obstacles do publicists run into?

AC: Commonly, it's the expectation of a client that he will be on page one of the *Wall Street Journal* or the cover of *Business Week* within a matter of days. Most clients have no idea what P.R. is, or they believe it requires no significant skills or background. It's important that they understand that developing and maintaining a level of recognition and credibility for the product or service, or the company and principals, doesn't happen overnight. In terms of street-smart P.R., you have to figure on three to four months start-up before there's any real response to what you're doing, because it takes the media that long to get familiar with what you're sending them.

ML: What are your thoughts about American journalism?

AC: For the past decade we've had some of the worst journalism imaginable. They ignored the Savings & Loan debacle, totally missed the looting of HUD, and were caught totally off guard by the breakup of the Soviet Union. We've had major problems sneak up on America without a single journalist noticing. We had to have the *Challenger* blow up in front of our eyes before anybody asked whether NASA was doing anything wrong. The media, which love to complain about publicists, should remember that many of us have tried to bring to light significant national problems, trends, and even scandals. I think P.R. people represent the best definition of the First Amendment, because we *do* believe in free speech and freedom of the press. It's essential to our own function of advocacy.

ML: How do you feel about the increase in media outlets in the past ten years?

AC: We've gotten nothing but more of the same. Though we have more cable stations, the news remains largely homogenized at both the national and local levels. There isn't a single local news show that doesn't begin with five minutes of murder, mayhem, and fires. It's a major misrepresentation of the real issues affecting the people watching. Viewers are lucky to get a nine-second sound bite of the governor saying something really important. The rest of the time, what passes for local news is mostly drivel. We have more coverage, but we're often not getting news of much value.

ML: What about your personal responsibilities as a public relations counselor to be attuned to the media?

AC: I read the *New York Times,* the *Wall Street Journal, USA Today,*
and my local daily every day, and easily fifty publications from
various industries and political points of view every month. Anybody in P.R. has to be a bit of a renaissance person in that you
cannot function from a narrow perspective. You always have to
understand *the larger context* in which people make their decisions, including the economy, current political issues, and social
and cultural factors. One does have to read rather widely among
the more serious publications like the *New Republic* and *U.S. News
andWorld Report* to understand what's happening. Moreover, one
must also read trade publications like *MagazineWeek* and *Advertising Age.*

ML: What does a P.R. professional need to know about media
in order to succeed?

AC: First, a handful of news wire services determine what
we read and hear today. Many people don't understand—if your
story is picked up by AP, UPI, Reuters, or Gannett, to name a few,
you reach out instantly with enormous impact. If your story is in
the *New York Times*—I don't care if it's only two paragraphs—the
impact is a smash. There is a relatively small group of print media
that determine to a great extent the national news agenda.

ML: What about TV?

AC: The networks have been steadily losing audience share,
and one network may be close to abandoning the news function
almost entirely, which would be a tragedy. You see news playing
a lesser role on the networks, because they've taken a beating
from one of the most extraordinary enterprises to come along
in years, Cable News Network. We're seeing the news function
reformulated on the networks in shows like *Anderson Cooper 360,
Dateline,* and, of course, the old standby *60 Minutes.* We also get

a lot of news from the talk shows, which desperately try to fill an hour every day. Much of what starts out as chatter on talk shows ends up as major news stories, and vice versa.

ML: Have you observed serious blunders on the part of neo-phyte public relations practitioners?

AC: Many people don't understand that you have to *think in advance*. Whom among the media will I approach? What kind of package of information should I give them? Most media professionals don't have a lot of time. A one-page fact sheet may be more effective than a fat press kit. Most media people don't enjoy being called directly. In fact, the thing they hate the most is the call asking, "Did you get my news release?" You circumvent that by making sure the news release you *do* send is so well constructed in terms of headline and presentation that it is *absolutely irresistible*. I see the most god-awful P.R. press releases every day.

ML: What makes them awful?

AC: They're dull. They're boring. The headline, if one exists, does not interest me in the contents in the slightest bit. The first paragraph doesn't say anything about why I should bother reading any further. P.R. is a craft. It requires a lot of know-how to understand the mind-set on the receiving end of your news release or story. In a typical media organization, you have a limited staff of people working very hard to meet deadlines. These people are under tremendous pressure. That's why I say don't waste their time, don't insult their intelligence, and be sure you're giving them something they can use.

ML: What kinds of materials are useful in a P.R. campaign?

AC: While it may be applicable in some cases, the big heavy-duty press kit is more a burden than a help. It's useful usually if you represent a client with a major research study, and you have to provide a lot of documentation. In most cases, you don't need anything more than a one-page news release. There isn't that much media space available to begin with, and if you deliver your story in the first two paragraphs, you're well ahead of the game. A good press kit has three elements: a fact sheet on the company and/or product, a bio of the key individual involved, and a ready-to-use canned feature story. These are essential starting points for any client. They set up the story.

ML: What about follow-up?

AC: There's no point to follow-up if you've done it right. The follow-up will come *from* the media *to* you. It's a fallacy that you must follow up. Ninety percent of the time you're going to piss someone off, anyway. Get the package right the first time.

ML: What's your conclusion about the nature of mass media and its effect on the public?

AC: Most people don't understand that news moves like wildfire. You have to get on the back of the tiger very quickly. You've got to ride it until the tiger gets tired and wants somebody else for dinner. Most stories have a shelf life of less than two weeks. We go from kidnapped children to some new environmental hazard to the latest skin rash in a month's time. The attention span of the public is very brief, so it's better to *create* news and be the trendsetter than try to catch up.

ML: What about the people who constitute the media?

AC: People have higher expectations of media professionals than they should. They're working stiffs like you and me, and must live with the internal politics of wherever they work. I've known thousands of them, and most are damn nice people who should be approached with the best possible story; then you should get out of their way in terms of whether they go for it or not.

ML: What do you mean?

AC: People don't understand that in the P.R. process, much of the time the answer is "no." It's like prayer. To some degree, P.R.—even in the best professional's hands—is a crapshoot. The story you've worked on for weeks can go right down the toilet because there's been a plane crash, a volcano has erupted, or the president fell on his tush playing golf. Any number of things can wash your story away, whether you've invested $2 in it or whether you've got $200,000 on the line. The job can be done beautifully but get nothing and nowhere because the world is turning and events overtake it.

Acknowledgments

So much gratitude, so little space.

I find myself in endless debt to many people for their inspiration and encouragement on this book.

Jeff Cohen, a tremendous support in creating this revised work. Jeff helped immeasurably and assists me in continuing to create the concepts that you are reading.

My office staff: Liam Collopy, Donna Dillard, Ali Duncan, David Goodman, Eric Heppding, Dawn Miller, Patricia Mora, Andrea Nicastro, and Monique Regalado, and the LCO Interns: Julie Brock and Janet Muradian, both of whom work hard and long with me, day-to-day, hour-to-hour, in running LCO in Los Angeles.

Blessed associates and friends, who assist, support, and encourage me when it is not always easy to do so: Peter Bart, Marilyn Beck, Adam Christing, Julie Craig, Richard Imprescia, Rob Jupille, Karen Karsian, Phil Kass, Arthur O. Levine, Patty Levine, John McKillop, Nancy Mager, Cable Neuhaus, Marissa Nicolaescu, Alyse Reynolds, Steve Shapiro, David Slon, David Weiss, and Lisa Yukelson.

Interns interested in working in Mr. Levine's Los Angeles office can contact his office at MLAsst@LCOonline.com.

About the Author

Michael Levine is the founder of LCO, which is among the entertainment world's most prominent and successful P.R. firms. Called "one of Hollywood's brightest and most respected executives" by *USA Today*, Levine has created P.R. campaigns for celebrity clients including Barbra Streisand, Michael Jackson, Bill O'Reilly, David Bowie, Michael J. Fox, Charlton Heston, Demi Moore, Suzanne Somers, George Carlin, Ozzy Osbourne, Jon Stewart, Robert Evans, and numerous others. He is the author of eighteen previous books, including *Broken Windows, Broken Business: How the Smallest Remedies Reap the Biggest Rewards*. www.MLevineOnline.com.

Index

It's Wrong for
Me to Love You:

Renaissance Collection

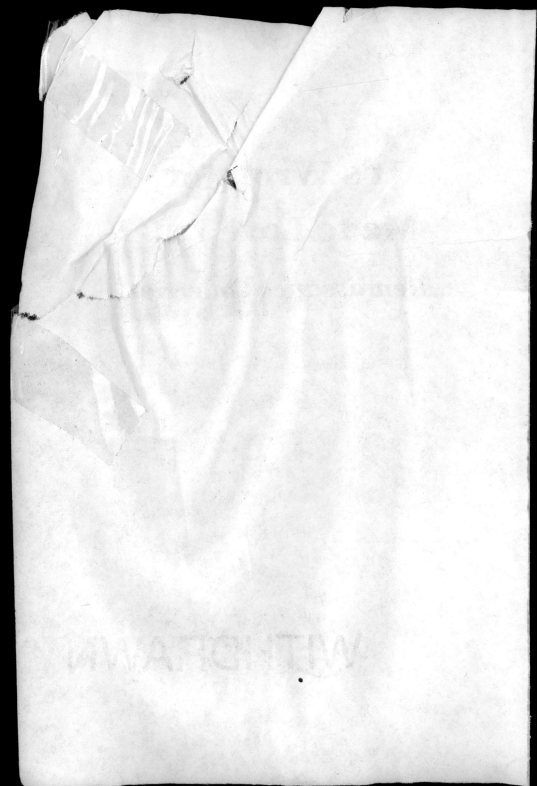

It's Wrong for Me to Love You:

Renaissance Collection

Krystal Armstead

www.urbanbooks.net

Urban Books, LLC
300 Farmingdale Road, NY-Route 109
Farmingdale, NY 11735

It's Wrong for Me to Love You: Renaissance Collection

ISBN 13: 978-1-62286-522-2
ISBN 10: 1-62286-522-7

First Trade Paperback Printing August 2017
Printed in the United States of America

10 9 8 7 6 5 4 3 2 1

Distributed by Kensington Publishing Corp.
Submit orders to:
Customer Service
400 Hahn Road
Westminster, MD 21157-4627
Phone: 1-800-733-3000
Fax: 1-800-659-2436

Acknowledgments

Because of my supporters' love and dedication to me, I have to dedicate this book to them.

Words cannot express how thankful I am for Racquel Williams and Carl Weber for taking a chance on me. I appreciate the opportunity to work with you and look forward to accomplishing greatness!

I would also like to take this time to give thanks to the following people who believed in me enough to read my writing before it was even published: Angela Vega, Wendy Palmer, Krystal Brackett, Sara Stephens, Charita Warren, Tanya Felder, Markiesha House-Woodson, Rhomesha Peterson, Danika Glass, Chaynia Dawkins, Coquenia Cooper, Mashawn Anthony, Brittany Derden, Yolanda Henderson, and Jamie Artis. You all took the time to actually read my thoughts. Your belief in me means more than you could ever know. I will *always* love you all!

Since I have been a published author, I have met some wonderful people! This wouldn't even be possible without them: Robin Michelle Watkins, Michelle Neal, Mesha Turner Latrese Washington (that's my cousin, y'all!), Nicki Ervin, Shonda Midgette, Octavia Carter, Elysia McKnight, Glenda Daniel, Kasey Smith, Shyalice Oates, Monique Franklin, Fallon Hampton, Allison Smith, Latonia Peterson, Natasha West, Monique Gray, and all of my reader homies in my reading group, "Krystal's Motivation"!

Acknowledgments

Thank you to my mother and father, Jennifer and Conrad Artis Jr. We have not always seen eye to eye, but you have always been there to support me. Nothing I can ever do can repay you both for all that you have done for me, but I promise to make you both proud!

This book is for my four beautiful children, Jada, Adrian, Jordan, and Angel. See, babies, dreams really do come true! This book is also for the missing pieces of my heart, my beautiful three stepdaughters, Jamie, Jasmine, and Anglie. I love you all like you are my own, even if you don't see it.

And last but definitely not least, my husband, James. I would not have accomplished this book without you. You are the motivation for *every* male character in this book! I put characteristics that I love about you in some, and characteristics that I hate about you in others! Without good, bad, happy, and sad times that we shared, I would have never been inspired to tell my story.

Thank you all for your support. Thank you, God, for the opportunity.

A'ight, y'all, *let's do this!*

Chapter 1

The Unexpected

Ne'Vaeh

I swear, we do some stupid shit when we're young and in so-called love. It's like the part of our brain that contains common sense completely shuts down, and the part of our brain that is completely delusional takes over. Whom can we blame? Our parents, who never took the time to make sure we didn't make the same mistakes that they did? Our friends, who couldn't wait for us to fuck up just so they could bask in our misery? The boy who made you love him when he knew that he wasn't the type of guy you should give your heart to? Or yourself, who should have known better?

My name is Ne'Vaeh Washington. Juanita Washington gave me that name because she said that when she gave birth to me, her life was the complete opposite of heaven. January 1, 2015, was the worst fuckin' day of my life. However, it goes back further than that. . . .

I was a freshman attending Howard University in our nation's capital. I was a straight-A student, the vice president of the Student Government Association, a member of the National Honor Society, and a soloist of the Gospel choir. I occasionally went out clubbing and drinking, and I may have smoked a blunt or two every now and then. For the most part, I kept my head in the books and didn't let anything distract me from my goals. I was determined to do something with my life, and I was determined to find love again, wherever it was.

Though I feared love and shied away from it, I had this burning, physical sensation of desiring it. I guess you can call it hunger. I mean, there was this boy who set my soul on fire every time that he entered the room. I'm telling you, he had me to the point where just one glance at him sent sweat trickling down my back. Just the thought of him made my mouth water. He looked so delectable that I would have done just about anything to get just one taste of him, just to see how he felt in my mouth. That was the way Aaron Whitehaven made me feel. The only problem was . . . He was my best friend's boyfriend, and I should have known better.

I only had one good friend. Her name was Charlene Campbell, Charlie for short, and she was the best friend I ever had. She was the total opposite of me. I was a short, petite girl with brown skin and dark, shoulder-length hair. I had a mouthful of breasts and barely a handful of ass, but Charlie? She was about five foot seven, with the perfect Coke-bottle figure, and legs and ass for days. She had long, dark brown hair and a toasted-almond complexion. Her skin always looked as if she'd just had a facial. She barely wore any makeup unless it was lip gloss, which drew attention to her plump, perfect, pouty lips. On her worst day, she looked better than most people looked on their *best* day. She looked, talked, walked, and even breathed like a model. Everyone wanted to look like her and live the life that she did, me included.

I'd known Charlie ever since the first grade, and she'd always been the most popular girl in school. I don't think there was a male athlete that she hadn't dated, fucked, sucked, kissed, or dismissed. She was my girl, but the way she played the field always bothered me. She never knew when to quit—that was, until Aaron made his debut. . . .

I'll never forget . . . It was a Thursday, spring semester of our junior year in high school, 2012. I was sitting next to Charlie, fourth period, in African American History, a class taught by the whitest of white men, Mr. Jimmy Porter. We were in class, laughing at Mr. Porter's jokes, which were actually funny for a change, when Aaron strolled through the classroom door.

Charlie grabbed my arm, her light eyes looking in the same direction that every girl in the classroom was looking. "*OMG*, look at *that!*" she whispered, digging her American-manicured tips into the skin of my forearm.

My eyes followed him as he strolled his way over to Mr. Porter to hand him a sheet of paper, probably a note from the principal, assigning him to our class. Aaron stood about five foot ten. He had a peanut butter complexion, and dark, wavy, close-cut hair. He was dressed in black and white, from his hat to his Nike shoes. He had the smoothest walk. The brutha had a swag that nobody could deny. I watched as Mr. Porter pointed in my direction, telling Aaron to sit in the chair behind me. My heart pounded in my chest as he looked at me. Our eyes met. I could feel my cheeks turning red. Aaron grinned as he walked toward me.

I braced myself as he sat down behind me. As he sat, it was as if every female in the class, single or not, turned in their chair to face him, Charlie included.

Charlie scooted to the edge of her seat and cleared her throat to get his attention.

Aaron looked at her.

"I'm Charlene, but everybody calls me Charlie." She smiled, sticking her chest out even further.

That's not all they call you, I thought to myself.

"What's up, shorty? I'm Aaron." His voice was music to my ears.

"And *this* is my BFF, Ne'Vaeh—heaven spelled backward." Charlie threw her pencil at me to get my attention. "Ain't that the coolest name you've ever heard?"

I felt a tap on my shoulder. My heart nearly shot out of my chest. I turned around in my chair to look into his eyes—those gorgeous eyes.

"Heaven, huh?" Aaron grinned.

"Your . . . Your eyes are green. . . ." I stuttered, not sure what else to say to someone who *had* to know how good he looked.

Charlie giggled. "So," she looked at Aaron, "what are your plans for tonight?"

The girl couldn't wait to get the first taste. She couldn't wait to sink her fangs into his neck. Two weeks didn't even go by and the two were already a couple. You wouldn't see one without the other. I never told her how angry I was with her for stealing his heart before I even had the chance to have a full conversation with him. I never told her that I wanted that boy more than anything.

They dated for over two years. In high school, they were voted most popular, most attractive, best-looking couple, most athletic, and they were chosen as prince and princess at the junior prom and fuckin' king and queen at the senior prom. Aaron made the basketball team in no time. Upon graduation, he received an academic *and* athletic scholarship to the University of Maryland, College Park. Charlie ended up at Morgan State University. I ended up at Howard University. As different as both Charlie's and my lives were, we tried to remain close. When she wasn't with Aaron, she was at my dorm in D.C. *talking* about Aaron.

As time went by, we spent more time on the phone and less time together. It seemed like the only time she came around sophomore year in college was so I could help her with her homework or study for exams. Her life was dancing, cheering, and Aaron. She was in love, and she wasn't letting him go. They were the perfect couple, and I was alone. Aaron wanted Charlie, and I wanted *him*. Damn . . .

***

There I sat alone in my dorm on a Friday night, the weekend of homecoming, fall 2014. I was supposed to be at the homecoming game, and I was supposed to attend the dance, being that I was the vice president of the SGA. I just couldn't bring myself to party that weekend, though. Charlie invited me to attend her homecoming at Morgan State a few weeks earlier, but plans had changed. Charlie's uncle had passed away that week, so she flew home to Texas where her uncle was going to be buried. She was devastated, and I felt for her. I lost my brother six years earlier, and I swore on my life that I would never attend another funeral.

Charlie and I had been texting each other on our iPhones that whole day. It was 8:30 p.m., and I sat at my desk typing on my Dell laptop when my cell phone rang.

I looked over at it and then held it in my hands. I didn't recognize the number, but I answered it anyway. "Hello? Ne'Vaeh speaking. . . ."

"What up, Heaven? What'cha been up to?"

My heart palpitated in my chest in sync with every syllable uttered through his lips. I couldn't believe it was Aaron's voice on the other end. He had never called me before. I could never go on double dates with him, Charlie, and whatever loser they'd try to hook me up with. I couldn't even look at the boy longer than a few seconds, because my eyes had a tendency to want to undress him. I went speechless for a second or two.

"Heaven, are you there?"

"Yeah . . . Yeah, I'm here. . . ." I stuttered.

"Good, 'cuz I am too. Come downstairs. . . ." He hung up his phone.

My mouth dropped open as I took the phone from my ear. I just sat there, staring at it. I felt like I was in the Twilight Zone. I couldn't believe he'd called. He never called. Up until that point, Aaron and I hadn't even had a one-on-one-conversation.

I put the phone down. I was dressed in a black tank top and black boy shorts, so I threw on some sweats, grabbed a hoodie, snatched my keys, and headed out the door. I was so anxious. I couldn't wait at the elevator, which seemed to be taking longer than normal. I shot down four flights of stairs and out the lobby of my college dorm.

There stood Aaron, leaned up against the side of the building. He was dressed in his gym clothes—a dark blue hoodie, baggy, dark blue sweatpants, and white Air Force Ones. He stood up from the building as he saw me walking toward him.

My heart fluttered in my chest as I approached him. I stood before him, arms wrapped around myself. My hair floated in the wind as it flew past us.

Aaron looked down at me as he licked his lips. "What up, Heaven? What's good with ya?"

Ever since the day we met, I don't think that boy ever called me by name, but I loved it. It was our thing.

I looked up at him. "*You* tell me. It's homecoming weekend. Why aren't you out with your friends?" I didn't understand why he'd driven over forty-five minutes to go see someone he hadn't so much as had a forty-five minute conversation with.

Aaron just looked at me.

I looked at him. "Why'd you come here?"

"You never go out with me and Charlie when we go out. I tried hooking you up with my boy, and you won't give a nigga a chance. You're cold, sweetheart." Aaron shook his head at me.

I resented that. "*I'm* cold? No, what's cold is you and Charlie trying to hook me up with a dude who was like twenty in the eleventh grade, eats with his mouth open, has six baby mamas, and who laughs at his own corny-ass jokes. His breath smelled like sweaty gym socks, and he wouldn't even supersize my fries when we went to Burger King because he said some lame shit about how he likes his women 'pretty in the face and slim in the waist'!" I rolled my eyes. "Where did you meet *that* idiot? *Y'all* were wrong for *that* shit."

Aaron threw his head back in laughter. "I swear, I didn't know any of that shit about him! I knew the dude had a few kids, but *damn!* Well, forget about Trey—what about Keon? He's a good dude, no kids, no baby-mama drama, and I hear he's been diggin' you since y'all were in the eighth grade."

I shook my head. "No way. Thank you, but *no* thank you. I appreciate your concern for my so-called love life, but don't even bother hooking me up with *anybody* else, because you apparently have absolutely *no* taste in men."

Aaron grinned. "I guess not. Hey, you can't be mad at me for tryin'. I just don't wanna see someone like you alone. . . ."

I looked up at him. "S . . . Someone like me? What do you mean?"

He avoided the question. "So, what'cha doin' tonight? Aren't you the vice president of SGA? You're supposed to be at the homecoming. If you're not gonna go to the homecoming, you should at least kick it with your boy, Aaron. Come kick it with me. . . ."

I was speechless. I didn't know what to say to him. I would have given anything two-and-a-half years earlier for him to ask me to hang with him. Just to be in the same room with him. Breathing the same air as him was too deep. I was in love with that boy, but he wasn't mine, and it broke my heart. The smarter half of me wanted to walk away, tell him I was working on a fifteen-page paper for my Humanities 101 class. However, the part of my heart that beat for him took over my body. He was Charlie's boyfriend—my *best* friend's boyfriend. That meant that he was off-limits. Untouchable. She was out of town, and he was alone.

"Why are you here asking me what I'm doing tonight? We never speak. You've never called me. You've known my number ever since junior year in high school. We never hang out. The only time you talk to me is when you're trying to hook me up with one of your lame-ass friends. So, I guess you're lonely tonight, and you needed someone to talk to since your girl's gone. Is that it? The only reason you came is because she's gone, right? Admit it." I had to be honest.

Aaron licked his delectable lips. "To be honest, yes."

He didn't beat around the bush.

My mouth dropped open a little. I didn't expect him to be *that* honest.

"What I'm trying to say is . . ." Aaron tried to correct the way his words came out. "There are some things that I need to talk with you about. I never get the chance to talk with you, because I'm not trying to make Charlie upset. We both know that her jealous streak is hell-a-crazy. I don't wanna come between you and your best friend, but . . ." Aaron took my hand in his, and my heart melted. "We need to talk. So, come for a ride with me."

I nearly lost my breath. I quickly slipped my hand from his. He had driven nearly an hour to see me—how could I look into those pretty green eyes and tell him no? "But . . . I'm not dressed. . . ." I whispered, looking down at my outfit.

Aaron smirked. "Neither am I. I just left the gym with my boys." His eyes traced my lips. "C'mon. We can just go chill, get something to eat, or we can go kick it over at my crib since my roommate is gone for the weekend. We can do anything you wanna do. We can go anywhere that you wanna go. I just got paid today, so you can chose wherever you wanna go, and I got you. Just come with me . . . please. . . ." Aaron pleaded, taking my hands again, holding both my hands in his.

My whole body blushed. I could feel his heart beating through the palms of his hands the blood rushing through his veins. He was just was nervous as I was. Aaron had more power over me than he knew. From that day we met in Mr. Porter's class, I wanted him. Now, there he was, asking me to go back to his apartment with him. Should I have gone out with him that night? No . . . but I did.

It was 10:30 p.m. when we arrived back at Aaron's three-bedroom apartment in Parkville. We had stopped at Taco Bell for a late-night snack and brought the food back to his cozy apartment. We sat at the bar, facing each other. I tried to hold my composure as he watched me eat. He had his eyes on every piece of food that slid through my lips.

I looked up at him. "What?" I blushed, licking the sour cream from my fingers.

"Y . . . You have a little sour cream on your lips. . . ." He put his hands on my face, swiping the sour cream from my lips with his fingertips.

I watched him as he licked the sour cream that he took from my lips from his fingers. Charlie had herself one sexy man, but for whatever reason, he felt the need to come to me. What wasn't she doing for him that had him coming to me that night?

Aaron kept watching my lips.

I looked at him. "Why do you keep looking at me like that?"

"What, I can't look at you?" Aaron's eyes searched my face. "I haven't seen you in months. . . ."

I tried not to smile. Over his shoulder, I caught a glimpse of a picture of Charlie on his refrigerator. I looked back at him. That picture snapped me out of my trance. I had no business there with him that night. "Why'd you drive so far to talk to me? Since *when* do me and you *ever* hang out, Aaron?" I asked.

Aaron cleared his throat. "I . . . ummm . . . I asked Charlie what she thought about marriage a few days ago."

I instantly lost my appetite. I placed the nacho that I was about to pop into my mouth right back in the bag. I looked at him as I wiped my fingertips on a napkin. I just knew that whatever he was about to say was something I really didn't want to hear.

"The thing is, as soon as the words came out of my mouth, I thought about you . . ." Aaron looked at me.

My heart jumped in my chest. "You . . . You thought about *me? Why?*" I was stunned. Definitely not what I expected to hear from him.

"I . . . ummm . . ." Aaron was nervous as hell. He was struggling to find the words to whatever it was he had to tell me. "I've been avoiding you, trying to hook you up with my boys, trying to spend as much time as I could with Charlie, trying my hardest not to look at you when you come around. . . . From the moment that I met you junior year, I wanted to ask you out. I wanted you bad as hell, but I didn't think you wanted the same thing, so I never approached you."

I nearly swallowed my own tongue. I hopped up from the bar stool, shaking my head, not believing my ears. "No, no, you can't be telling me this now, Aaron!" I wanted to cry and punch that muthafucka at the same damn time. "You're my best friend's boyfriend, and you're telling me right now—today—that you have feelings for me? Why the hell would you want me when you have someone as beautiful as Charlie? You have *got* to be joking! Is this some type of sick, cruel joke?"

Aaron got up from the stool, reaching for my hand. "Baby, calm down and just hear me out."

I pulled from him. "No! You shouldn't have told me this!"

"It doesn't even matter how I feel about you—it ain't like you feel the same way. It's not like you ever talked to me. You haven't so much as tried to carry on more than a three-word conversation with me. You don't look at me, you don't talk to me, you don't laugh with me, and you don't acknowledge me. I know I'm wrong for saying this, but I wouldn't have ever gotten to know Charlie if you would have taken some interest in me. You had to feel me staring at you the day we met. The fact that I was dancing with *you* and not her at our senior prom didn't ring a bell? I only got to know Charlie to get to know you, but you never let me," Aaron explained.

I wasn't going to let that boy make me cry. The words that came from his lips stung like a muthafucka. "So, what did my best friend say when you asked her to marry you?" I looked up into his face.

Aaron looked down at me. "I didn't ask her to marry me. I just told you that I asked shorty what she *thought* about marriage. I asked her if she could see herself spending the rest of her life with me. I asked her if she was still in love with me, and do you know what the girl did? She laughed at me. She said she was too young to be thinking about spending the rest of her life with anyone. She said she loved me, but marriage was the furthest thing from her mind. I felt stupid as fuck for even bringing the shit up—I should have stuck with my first mind and kept the shit to myself. She doesn't feel for me the way that she used to. At first, I thought she was just being cold because her uncle just passed away, but I know that wasn't it, because she left me that night and went out to the club with her girls. Yeah, I feel for the girl, but a part of me can't help but wonder what it would have felt like to be with you. That's why I call you Heaven. I know that heaven is what it would have felt like to be with you."

My heart fluttered in my chest. I wanted to be angry with him, but my heart wouldn't let me.

"Don't be mad with me, Heaven. I just have regrets. I've been with Charlie going on two years now, and I know I'm not who she wants to be with. I know that she isn't the girl who I want to be with either. I don't even know why we're dragging this relationship out, because it's not going anywhere. In high school, she was funny, she was flirty, she was sexy, she was popular, she was interested, and we looked good together. Knowing her helped me get on the basketball team as quickly as I did. Knowing her helped me get scholarships and grants to college. I think she used me just as much as I did her." Aaron paused a moment, then said, "She doesn't love me, Heaven, and I don't love her."

I shook my head. "Aaron, I don't need to be hearing this," I whispered.

"I'm sorry if I'm not supposed to be talking to you about any of this, but I couldn't hold in the way that I felt anymore. When I asked Charlie about marriage, I knew in my heart that I wanted her to say exactly what she said. Charlie and I don't belong together, but me and you? I know we could work something out." Aaron spoke softly.

My eyes began to water, and I knew the tears were coming. "You could have anyone in the world, Aaron—why would you choose me? Why would you choose your girlfriend's best friend?"

Aaron's eyes traced my lips. "Because you complete me."

I shook my head. "Complete you? You don't know *anything* about me."

Aaron grinned. "Your favorite color is blue. I know because every time you get dressed up, you wear royal blue all the way from your hoop earrings to your stilettos. Your favorite restaurant is IHOP. You always order scrambled eggs with extra cheese, turkey bacon extra crispy, two pancakes, and hash browns. You don't hang out with your girls as much as you used to in high school. You'd rather kick it in the library, in the farthest corner, just you and your Dell laptop. Your favorite candy is Haribo Gummy Bears—you go through at least two packs in a day. You were raised by your aunt and Miss Campbell. Your mom is in prison. You haven't seen your sister since you were thirteen. Your brother passed away. Your first boyfriend was a dude named Jamie—you dated him for about two years until he moved to Memphis, Tennessee, the summer before your sophomore year. You're shy. You keep to yourself. You're not easily persuaded. And you wish people would know the way that you feel without you having to open up your mouth to say a word. Now, wouldn't you say I know a *little* something about you?"

I just looked at him. He didn't hit the nail on the head exactly, but he was close enough. I don't even think Charlie paid me that much attention. For someone who only saw me once in a blue moon, he sure did pay close attention to details. "How . . . How did you know about Jamie?" was all I could say.

"I have my sources, but don't worry about all that." Aaron looked down into my face.

Jamie was my first love, my first kiss, my first hug, my first touch, my first everything. We made love for the first time before he left me to move to Tennessee. He took a piece of me with him when he left me, a piece that I thought I would never get back. I loved that boy *hard*. I never thought I would love anyone else again. It wasn't until Aaron walked in my classroom door that day that my heart began to beat again.

"Why didn't you just tell me how you felt about me back in high school, Aaron?" I asked.

"Everyone kept telling me that you were still in love with Jamie. I didn't wanna be the rebound nigga, so I did what any man would do—I went for what was available." Aaron licked his succulent lips. Oh, I wish he'd stop doing that.

"Well, you're about a year and a half too late, Aaron. You picked a fine time to tell me how you feel about me." Tears lined my lashes.

"Well, tell me something—how do you feel about *me?*" he asked.

I backed up a little. "What?"

"Stop being scared and just tell me how you feel about me. It's just between you and me." Aaron held my hands, pulling me closer to him.

My heart thumped against my rib cage. I slid my hands from his, backing away from him again. "I'll tell you how I feel. I *feel* like you could've told me how you felt about me a *long*-ass time ago! Maybe a good time would have been before you started dating my best friend! Or maybe before you started telling her that you loved her! Or maybe before you started having sex with her! Or better yet, before you became the strongest, longest, most faithful relationship that she's ever had! No matter what she may mean to you, I *know* that you mean the world to her! You're all she ever talks about, all she ever dreams about, all she ever brags about! She probably said that shit to you a couple of days ago because you scared the shit out of her when you brought up marriage. Charlie is beautiful, but she has been dogged out and has been played just like an average girl. Guys hit, split, and quit her ass just like they do everyone else! She thought you were different, but you're obviously not!"

Aaron frowned a little, though he didn't deny that what I was saying wasn't true.

"Okay, fine, you wanna know how I feel about you? Fine, I'll tell you. I've had feelings for you ever since I looked into those pretty green eyes of yours that day you stepped into Mr. Porter's African American History class our junior year in high school. I got lost in your eyes, and I still haven't found my way back. I hadn't felt that way about anyone but Jamie." I looked up at him. "After he left, it's like my heart stopped beating. It didn't beat again until I met you."

Aaron looked at me for a minute or two as he tried to find the words to respond to what I had just said. "Why-Why didn't you tell me how *you* felt?" He stumbled over his words a little.

"Because my best friend didn't hesitate to let every female know that you were hers and only hers. You were hers from the moment she spotted you in class that day. She's happy with you—happier than I've seen her with anyone. She's happy with you, so I'm happy *for* her. And if she knew how I felt about you, it would kill her." My eyes grew mistier with each second that I looked up into his face, so I looked away. "So, Aaron, if this is all you brought me here for tonight, you might as well take me back to Howard so I can work on my paper."

Aaron shook his head. "Nah, you're with me tonight, and tonight, my boy, Maxwell, is throwing a party. We don't gotta get all dressed up or anything—it's more of a get-together. You know, people drinking, dancing, playing cards, and shit. Just roll with me."

I looked up at him, into those irresistible eyes. Why didn't I just walk away, stick with my first mind, tell him to forget about me, tell him I couldn't be his friend, and tell him it hurt to know how he felt about me?

Instead of going with my better judgment, I went into his bathroom, threw on a little makeup, did a little something with my hair, and made sure my lip gloss was poppin'.

Aaron took me to his friend's party that night. My eardrums vibrated like a snare drum from the bass coming out of the stereo speakers. Chicks were throwing their asses, twerkin', grinding as hard as they could against the crotch of the males' jeans, sweating out their perms, dressed in next to nothing. The males were holding on for dear life to the women's hips as they were thrust back against the wall. Blunts were being passed around, along with alcohol of every sort. Cigarette and weed smoke filled the room. All in all, it was a typical frat party.

The party was a little too much for me, and I tried to slip away unnoticed, while Aaron was talking and laughing with his friends. He caught my hand just as I tried to sneak past him, and he pulled me back to him.

I looked up at him.

"Hold up, ma. Where you goin', Heaven?" He spoke over the music.

"Outside, where I can breathe and hear myself think. I need some air. Besides, I seem to be a little overdressed for this type of party." I rolled my eyes as a girl in a halter-top and what looked like fuckin' boy shorts walked past us. I looked back up at Aaron. "This ain't even my scene. I don't know why I'm here! Not to mention, there's a lot of people coming here that I know from Howard." I slid my hand from his.

"So?" Aaron took a sip from his cup.

"*So?*" I watched his lips as he drank. "What do you mean 'so'? You're not mine, so I have no business being here with you. You're dating Charlie, and everyone here knows it. What does that make me look like, Aaron?"

Aaron's friends looked at me.

Aaron lowered his cup from his lips. "Like you came to have a good time."

I shook my head. "I can't do this." I backed away.

"Hold up, shorty. Let's go outside." He took me by the waist.

We stood face-to-face outside on Maxwell's balcony. I wrapped my arms around myself. I looked up at Aaron as he drank the last sip of Hennessy from his cup. I shivered, hands tucked in the sleeves of my Old Navy hoodie.

Aaron looked at me as he tossed his cup in a small trash can in the corner of the balcony. "That hoodie is cute, but I know you ain't warm in it. You wanna wear my coat, shorty?" He didn't even wait for me to answer. He took off his coat and placed it over my shoulders.

"This is hell-a-awkward, Aaron," I whispered, looking up at him.

Aaron looked at me as he leaned over, resting his forearms on the balcony railing. "How do you think that *I* feel telling you everything that I said to you tonight? I feel stupid as fuck."

I looked at him. "So . . . How do you expect me to react to you now that I know how you feel? Aaron, you're with Charlie. That, alone, is hard for me to deal with. Now I have to deal with the fact that my best friend's boyfriend wants to get to know me better. And the worst part about this whole situation is that . . . I wanna get to know you too, more than you could ever know."

Aaron's eyes sparkled under the moonlight.

I laughed to myself, thinking of the lonely nights I spent thinking, dreaming, and yearning for Aaron's touch. "Do you know that I used to dream about you?"

Aaron just looked at me, his green eyes searching my face.

"I wanted you in the worst way, but I knew better. Not to mention my heart hasn't fully recovered from that summer before sophomore year when that jerk left me. Your friends weren't lying. It took me years to get over Jamie. Sometimes, I'm not really sure I'm over him, but I've learned to deal with the fact that he's never coming back." My vision was getting hazy. I tried to fight back the tears.

Aaron laughed a little. "So, you *are* still in love with him?"

I shook my head. "A heart never fully recovers from the pain of losing someone, Aaron, if that's what you mean. He left me when I really needed him. I never got any closure, but I'm good. When I met you, my heart started to feel something again. I think that you are amazing. I used to go to all of your basketball games. I didn't see anyone else out there on that court but you. The way you would glide across the hardwood floor of that basketball court looked as if you were floating on air." I leaned over the balcony next to him.

Aaron looked at me, his eyes searching my face. "You make me sound like a star."

"You *are* a star." I looked away from him. "Charlie doesn't know how lucky she is to have someone like you. And this right here, us talking this close, is teasing the hell out of me. I don't want a damn snack, Aaron—I want a whole *meal*."

Aaron laughed a little.

My eyes sparkled. "You laugh, but I'm dead serious. I'm in love with my best friend's boyfriend. Ain't *this* a bitch?"

Aaron looked at me. "Yeah . . . It is."

I really wanted to cry because the more I stood there next to him, breathing in the same air that he was breathing, the more I wanted him to be mine. I was in love with him, and that alone was wrong.

I looked back at him. "Can we get out of here? I don't care where we go. I just can't risk anyone seeing us together and word getting back to Charlie. I don't wanna hurt her," I whispered.

Aaron looked at me as he took his keys out of his pocket. "Yeah, let's roll out before I get too drunk to drive."

I felt awkward being alone with Aaron that night. No matter where we went, I felt uncomfortable. We ended up going back to his apartment. We sat in his weight room that night, dressed in a tank top and sweatpants. We talked about everything you can think of that people talk about when they're trying to get to know more about each other. I found out more about him that night than I had in the past two years I'd known him.

"I had no idea that you could cook!" I squealed. "That's so exciting! I can't believe Charlie never told me that! If I had a dude who could cook, bruh, I'd be telling everyone who *didn't have a man who* could cook that I had one who could!"

Aaron grinned, sitting down next to me on his exercise bench. He handed me a bottle of Lipton's green tea. "I was raised by my five aunts and grandmother—hell yeah, your boy can cook. You name it, and I'll cook it. I'll have to invite you over for dinner some time." He threw his left leg over the bench and sat facing me.

I blushed a little, holding my hoodie in my hands. "Aaron, this is the hardest thing I've ever done. I've been feeling you from day one. It was just a fantasy of mine to be sitting here, this close to you, breathing the same air, smelling your cologne, listening to your sexy voice. I could have never imagined that you actually wanted to know me the same way that I wanted to get to know you. I never would have thought you felt for me what I feel for you. I haven't felt this way in a long time. This is so wrong, but it feels so right. And all I can think about is you touching me."

Shit, I guess all Aaron needed was an invitation. He took the hoodie and bottle of tea from my hands and placed them on the carpet. He held my hips, pulling me closer to him, in between his legs.

My heart pounded in my chest, thumping against my rib cage. I hadn't been touched in four years the way that he touched me that night. "Aaron, no, we can't." I wanted to cry.

Aaron's said, "I can't keep my mind off touching you either. I wanna kiss you too—can I do that?" He held my face in his hands.

Before I could pull away from him, his lips were pressed against mine. His silky lips embraced mine, and

I nearly melted. His lips were so smooth and delicate. The insides of my thighs began to twitch and tingle, and I could feel my panties instantly dampen.

I pulled my lips from his, getting up from the bench as fast as I could. "Take me back to my dorm, Aaron! I'm not even supposed to be here!" I cried, rushing toward the door.

Aaron got up from the bench, catching me by the arm before I could reach the door to escape. He pulled me back to him.

I looked up at him as he held my face in his hands. My body was on fire. I dreamed of that moment, and there it was—a reality. A *cruel* reality. Tears slid down my face as he slid his hands around my bare waist. The warmth from his hands soothed my soul. He loosened the drawstring to my pants as he gently sucked on my bottom lip. He was killing me.

I pulled my lips from his and shook my head at him, my heart pounding and my lungs gasping for air. "Aaron, this is wrong—what are we doing?" I panted. "You have a girlfriend—she's my *best* friend! She took me into her home when I had no place else to go!" I could hear my cell phone vibrating in my purse, and I knew it was Charlie.

Aaron's eyes searched mine as he slid my pants over my hips. "Heaven, I apologize, but I've been wanting to do this for over two years—can I just touch it? That's all I wanna do."

I shook my head, my chest heaving in and out. I was breathing so hard, I thought I was going to hyperventilate. My lips were saying, "No, I can't do this," but my body language was screaming, "Yes, just *take* it, dude, *all* of it."

"That's it, Heaven, I promise." Aaron's eyes hungrily searched my face.

I looked up into his face, lips trembling, and body shaking.

He slid my panties over my hips, and they fell to the floor. I looked at him as he looked down at the Brazilian wax that I had done a few days earlier. He bit his lip as if he couldn't wait to get his hands in my pussy. He looked back up into my eyes, and then lifted my body up, wrapping my legs around his waist. He walked back over to the bench, holding me up by my thighs. He sat back down on the bench, gripping my thigh with one hand and the other hand gripping my behind.

"Why would you wanna start something that there's no way we can finish, Aaron?" I whispered, tears already sliding down my face.

"I ask myself every day why I didn't start *sooner*." His eyes focused on my face.

Tears continued to cascade down my cheeks. I shook my head, "Why are you doing this to me?"

"All I wanna do is touch you, shorty. That's it. I just wanna hear you scream. And when you come, I'll stop. I promise. So, will you scream for me?" He slid the index finger and middle finger of his right hand inside of me, making sure to swirl his fingers along the way, all the way, until his fingertips tickled my cervix.

Beads of sweat instantly formed along my hairline. "Aaron!" I moaned, grabbing on to his biceps with what little strength I had.

"How does it feel?" His hand rested on my behind and outer labia, as his fingers gently massaged the walls within me. The insides of my thighs were slippery wet, and fluid trickled down them.

"Why-why does something so wrong have to feel *so* good, Aaron?" I stumbled over my words, tears tumbling down my cheeks. I sunk my nails into his biceps. "Aaron, please stop. You have no idea what you're doing to me." My thighs began to tremble, and every blood vessel in my body began to twitch.

Aaron took his other hand and began to massage my clit.

My whole body trembled, and I screamed with delight.

"I'm not gonna stop until I feel that pussy come on my fingers, Heaven." Aaron gently kissed my trembling lips. He started to massage my clit a little faster and pumped his fingers in and out of me at the same time.

My whole body jumped, and the veins between my thighs pulsated. Aaron continued to rub and penetrate my insides with his fingers until I let out a sigh. I exploded from the inside out. My legs trembled uncontrollably against his waist.

Aaron stopped rubbing my clit but continued to penetrate my body with his fingers until I screamed and came all over again. The walls over my pussy caved in, pulsating around his fingers.

My body fell against his, and I laid my head on his shoulder, as my whole body pulsated. My vagina cried out in ecstasy all over his fingers. His whole hand was saturated. I cried on his shoulder. I lifted my head from his shoulder, looking up into his face. His fingers still rested inside of me. My sugary walls throbbed around his fingers.

Aaron slowly took his fingers from out of me; then he slid those exact same two fingers inside of his mouth. He sucked the sticky fluid of my vagina from his fingers, satisfied with its taste. "*Shit*," he whispered. "You taste just like I imagined you would."

Tears covered my face. I felt guilty as hell, and it was blatantly obvious that Aaron was ready for more. Though I wanted his hands, lips, tongue, and dick all over me, I knew what I was letting that boy do to me was wrong, *dead* wrong.

Aaron gripped my thighs tightly in his hands, as he licked his lips.

My lips trembled. "Aaron, this is wrong, and I want you *so* bad, but this is *so* wrong."

He started to loosen the drawstring to his pants as if he didn't hear me.

"Aaron!" I cried, pushing him, stopping him from loosening his pants. "Take me to my aunt's house *now!*" I got up from his lap, going over to where my panties and pants lay on the floor.

He sat there on the bench, catching his breath. He watched as I cried to myself, putting on my panties, then my sweatpants. I slid into my socks, then into my Nikes. I kneeled down to tie my laces.

Aaron got up from the bench and walked over to me.

I stood up, backing away from him. I could smell myself all over him.

He caught my hand, pulling me closer to him. "Heaven," he whispered to me.

Tears stained my face.

"Heaven, I love you," he whispered.

I cried aloud, pulling from him. I had been waiting over two years to hear him say those words to me, but when he finally said those three words, it hurt like nothing I'd ever experienced.

"Take me to my aunt's house *now,* Aaron! I'm not supposed to be here! Why did I let you bring me here? Why did I let you touch me like that? Why?" I cried. "Why am I in love with my best friend's boyfriend? This isn't supposed to be happening!" I pushed him.

Aaron looked as if he wanted to cry as well. He knew that what we did was wrong and that there was nothing we could do to take it back.

"Aaron, this is the *last* time that anything like this will *ever* happen!" I sobbed. "I don't wanna see you, I don't wanna talk to you, and I don't wanna know you!"

Aaron shook his head. "You don't mean that."

"I love you, and I'm not supposed to! You touched me, and you weren't supposed to! You're not supposed to love me when you're with my best friend, Aaron! We don't belong together! You got who you need! Forget about me—forget about us!" I pushed past him and walked out of the room.

Aaron dropped me off at my aunt Joyce's house that night. We didn't say one word to each other on the ride over. My mind was racing. I silently cried to myself, wondering how I could let Aaron touch me and kiss me the way that he did. He licked the juices from my vagina from his fingers. He tasted my insides, and he liked it. He enjoyed pleasing me, and no feeling had ever felt better. I couldn't erase the thought of it from my mind. I could still feel his fingers inside of me, and I could still taste his tongue inside of my mouth.

When we got to my aunt's house, I darted out of the car, slamming the door behind me, and I raced up my aunt's porch steps without even saying good-bye to the poor boy. I couldn't even look at him after what we'd done. I didn't have to knock at my aunt's door. She stepped out of her new black BMW, dressed in a black Gucci dress with matching stilettos. I knew she'd just gotten home from one of her many hot dates.

I stood there on the porch as she approached me.

"Baby, what's wrong?" she asked, and then looked across the yard at Aaron's maroon Chevy Impala speeding off the down the street.

I cried, throwing my arms over her shoulders. I cried my eyes out, burying my face in her neck.

Chapter 2

Closer

Ne'Vaeh

I sat down on the leather sofa in my aunt's living room the next morning. I didn't get any sleep the night before, and it was going to take a gallon of cappuccino to keep me awake all day so that I could finish my Humanities 101 paper.

My cousin Renée sat down next to me, handing me a cup of toasted almond cappuccino. She was a tall, sexy, brown-skinned girl with hazel-brown eyes and shoulder-length curly hair. Seemed like I was the only one not blessed with hips and ass. Renée looked like a got-damn stripper, her body was so bad. Women paid thousands to have a shape like hers.

She looked at me as I took the cup from her and held it to my lips with both hands. "So," she hesitated, "Mama says you came over late last night."

I nodded, taking sips from the mug.

"We're like sisters, Ne'Vaeh. You know you can always talk to me," she assured me.

I looked at her. She was right. When Aunt Joyce took my brother, sister, and me in for those months my mother spent in rehab, it was Renée who kept me from pulling my hair out. She was there to comfort us. If it wasn't for her, I would have never made it through junior high and some of high school. She never left me alone when I was feeling down. When I needed to talk, she was always there to listen, so I had to tell her about Aaron.

I turned to her as I placed my cup down on her glass coffee table. I took a deep breath to calm myself. "Well, you know Charlie's boyfriend named Aaron, right?"

Renée looked at me and nodded. "Hell yeah, I know him! He's the finest boy on the basketball team at College Park! His ass is gonna end up getting drafted! Charlie says there are already about two or three teams after his ass right now! What about him?"

I sighed, not sure how to tell her what Aaron did to me the night before. "He-He came to my dorm room last night. He said he needed to talk to me. He's *never* come by to talk to me. We've known each other going on three years, and we have *never* talked one-on-one."

Renée looked up at me. She scooted to the edge of her seat as if she were bracing herself for what I was about to tell her.

I hesitated. "He-He took me to his apartment. I wasn't feeling it, so we went to a party. I wasn't feeling *that* because too many people I knew started walking through the door. We ended up *back* at his apartment. No one was there but the two of us. And while we were there, he told me that he wishes he would have chosen me instead of Charlie." My eyes dampened.

Renée's eyes widened. "Ne'Vaeh, *tell* me that you didn't sleep with that girl's boyfriend!"

I hesitated. "No, but it was close enough."

"*How* close?" She folded her arms.

I looked at her. "He licked my pussy juice from his fingers—*that's* how far it got, Renée."

Renée shook her head in disgust, not really sure what to say to me. She was pissed—more like disappointed—at me. She looked at me. "Charlie loves that boy—you know how much that boy means to that girl! You let the nigga play in your pussy? Charlie is gonna kick ya ass!"

"I love him too, Renée!" I cried. "What was I supposed to do when he touched me? What was I supposed to do when he kissed me? What was I supposed to do when he told me that he loved me? I've wanted that boy from day one, and when I finally had him to myself—telling me that he felt the exact same way about me—what was I supposed to do? He knew what he was doing to me! He made it feel *so* right, when he *knew* it was wrong!"

Renée looked at me, her eyes sparkling. "You're my baby cousin, and I love you like you were my own little sister, so I'm just gonna have to say this to you: you are stupid as hell if you actually think that this situation is gonna work out in your favor. Your best friend's boy-friend—*really*, Ne'Vaeh? I'm twenty-six years old, and I have *never* seen a situation like this work out. Charlie's gonna end up hurt, Aaron's gonna end up hurt, and *your* ass is gonna end up hurt! You've been through so much shit in your life, and Charlie has been there through a lot of it to help you through it. And this shit is how you repay her? You're a whole lot smarter than this shit, Ne'Vaeh! I don't even know why you're crying."

Tears slid down my cheeks, but I quickly dried them away. "I don't wanna hurt Charlie. I told Aaron that I can't see him anymore. And I know that after what happened last night, I'll never be able to look Charlie in the eyes again. How could I do this to her? How in the hell did I fall for my own best friend's boyfriend?"

Renée shook her head at me. "Ever since Jamie left, girl, you have been totally lost. My girl, Kristina, said she saw him a few weeks ago when she went to visit her cousin at Memphis State. She said Jamie even asked about you."

I shook my head, heart palpitating in my chest. The sound of his name still sent blood rushing to my heart. "Can we *not* talk about Jamie right now, Renée?"

Renée sighed, getting up from off of the couch. "C'mon, cuz, let's go get something to eat. You know I can't talk about depressing shit like this too long. Let's go get our grub on."

I looked up at her, tears saturating my face.

She looked down at me and grinned. Renée's heart didn't know how to withstand pain, hurt, or anger. She wouldn't allow herself to feel any type of misery. Whenever she felt even the slightest twinge of any emotion that she couldn't handle, she'd snap right out of it. I loved how she was able to turn her emotions on and off like a light switch. She hated pain, and she refused to let herself experience it. She held my hand, pulling me up from the couch.

Renée called up a few of her friends that morning to join us at IHOP. They sat there laughing and talking about the crazy situations that they happened to get themselves out of that week. I, on the other hand, sat there pushing my food around on my plate, trying to figure my way out of *my* crazy situation.

Renée eased her laughing when she noticed that I wasn't eating. "I thought that was your favorite meal," she commented.

I looked down at the scrambled eggs with extra cheese, turkey bacon extra crispy, two pancakes, and hash browns that sat on my plate, untouched. Aaron knew what I ate for breakfast. He knew so much about me, when I barely knew him.

"Ne'Vaeh, food is *not* free. I paid nine eighty-nine for that meal. Shit, that's over three gallons of gas!"

Her friends giggled. Renée could literally "make a dollar out of fifteen cents." She was the cheapest person I knew. She brought her own food to the movie theater, used every drop of toothpaste, diluted hot sauce with water, and only bought clothes off the clearance rack. She was one of those girls who counted out seven fifty in pennies at the register. She was embarrassing, but homegirl was never broke.

I looked up at her. "I'll eat it, and if I don't, I'll pay you back. No worries."

"Ne'Vaeh, Charlie is supposed to be going with me tomorrow morning to pick up a few things for your party. I tried calling her, but she's not answering my calls. When is she coming back?" Kristina asked. Kristina was a pretty, brown-skinned, big-boned girl with a round face and deep dimples. She was in graduate school at College Park, maintaining a 3.8 GPA.

I looked at her. "She's supposed to be here tomorrow morning at eleven o'clock."

Renée looked at me. She knew that I hated the thought of Charlie coming back so soon. I didn't know how I was going to face her after what I'd done with her boyfriend.

Kristina looked at me, and then over my shoulder. She squinted her eyes to get a better look at what she had spotted. "Hey, isn't that Aaron?" she asked, pointing in the direction she was looking.

My heart fluttered in my chest as Renée and her friends turned in their seats to get a good look at the famous Aaron Whitehaven. I didn't even have to turn around to know that it was him. The whole restaurant clapped their hands and cheered for him and his entourage as they walked through the dining area.

Renée looked at me. She knew that I felt uneasy. "Girl, come with me to the restroom real quick."

I nodded, springing up from my seat. I turned around just in time to see Aaron walking right up to my table. I gasped, placing my hand over my chest as he walked up to me.

Aaron stood before me, dressed in a white Polo shirt, dark denim jeans, and fresh white Nikes. He looked fresher than a muthafucka, fine as hell, but the boy still wasn't mine.

"What up, Heaven?"

I was speechless, out of breath. My mouth fell open, but nothing came out.

"Oh, so you don't see the rest of us sitting here?" Renée's friend, Adina, rolled her eyes, popping a grape from her fruit cup into her mouth.

Aaron looked over my shoulder at our table, and then at Renée. "Hello, ladies. How's breakfast? Y'all bought enough food—damn, is there anything left for me and my boys?"

The girls giggled.

Renée rolled her eyes. "We were just about to bounce. We got a lot of business to attend to today. So, if you'd excuse us. . . ."

Aaron looked at me. "Can we go somewhere and talk?"

I shook my head, my bottom lip trembling. "I don't think that's such a good idea, Aaron."

"What do you have planned for today, ma?" he asked.

"Why you worrying about all that? Her plans ain't with *you*. She's comin' with me and my girls to Hair Expressions. Her birthday party is tomorrow, so a full makeover is on me. If you ain't payin', don't worry about where she's goin'." Renée folded her arms. There she was again, being her usual loud, talk-so-the-whole-wide-world-hears-her, smart-ass self.

"Damn, Renée—why you gotta treat the boy like that? He just asked the girl a simple question." Kristina shook her head at Renée.

"I'm just sayin', why's he worried about what she's doin'? He ain't goin' with us." Renée looked up at Aaron. "You need to be worried about what *Charlie's* doin'. My cousin is turning nineteen tomorrow. We're throwing her a big birthday party tomorrow. We still have a lot of setting up to do, and *you're* holdin' us up."

I sighed. I was turning nineteen, not really an age to look forward to. You're on your way out of your teens, but still not of legal age to drink. However, with cousins like mine, getting drunk was never an issue. Renée and her friends planned to take me to a club that Sunday night. I swear, Renée knew every bartender in Maryland, D.C., and Virginia, so getting drunk was *not* going to be a problem. I needed a drink. Shit, I could have used a whole *bottle*.

"Am I invited?" Aaron whispered to me.

"*Hell* no," Renée spoke up for me, irritating the hell out of me.

"Renée!" I exclaimed. "Damn, I can speak for myself!"

Renée looked at me, folding her arms, weight shifted on to her left leg. *Oh, so now you wanna just talk to him?* was written all over her face. I knew she wanted to call me out in front of him for getting loud with her, but she remained as calm as she could.

I turned to Aaron. "Aaron, today is really not a good day. My family has a lot planned for me, I have a term paper to finish, not to mention, *Charlie* is flying back in town in the morning, and I am supposed to be meeting her there. So whatever it is you need to talk to me about will have to wait until another day."

Aaron wasn't backing down. "C'mon, Heaven. You know we need to talk, and you know what we need to talk about. You're not gonna be busy all day and night, shorty—don't try to play me. If you don't come find me, I'm coming to find *you*."

I knew he wouldn't back down. From what Charlie told me about him, when Aaron had his mind made up, it was made up, and there was no changing his mind. The night before proved how determined he was to get what he wanted. I couldn't spend the rest of my day worrying about what Aaron had to say to me.

I turned to Renée. "Renée, I'll be right—"

Renée shook her head, cutting me off. "*No,* Ne'Vaeh! What the fuck! We have hair appointments! Whatever he has to say to you is irrelevant in this situation, and you know it! I had to book these appointments a fuckin' month and a half in advance! If we miss this appointment, Ne'Vaeh, I swear to—"

I cut her off, "Renée, please, stop, okay? I'll be right back. I promise."

I stood outside the restaurant, facing Aaron. I looked up at him. "Aaron, why did you show up here this morning?" I asked.

He looked down into my face. "Because I knew you'd be here."

I shook my head. "I mean, really, though? In front of my cousin and her friends? You know how much those bitches run their mouth about everyone's business but their own! I can't do this today with you today, Aaron." I turned to walk away from him.

He held my arm, pulling me back to him. "Heaven, please don't walk away."

I pulled from him.

"Just hear me out, shorty," he pleaded.

I looked up at him.

"I, ummm . . . I couldn't stop thinking about last night. I apologize if what I did hurt you, Heaven. I don't wanna hurt anybody. That's not what I'm here for. I'm here to be with you, sweetheart—I know in my heart that you're the one that I wanna be with."

My eyes sparkled.

"I'm sorry if me being in love with you scares you, but it's how I feel, and it was killing me to hold it in." Aaron reached for my hands, but I pulled away. He sighed. "C'mon, Ne'Vaeh, just hear me out."

Once again, tears slid down my face, but I wiped them away as quickly as I could. "I don't wanna hear you out because you're not hearing *me!* I can't have a relationship with my best friend's boyfriend, and you shouldn't even wanna *put* me in this situation! You should have kept this shit to yourself! You shouldn't be in love with your girlfriend's best friend!" The tears kept coming.

Aaron tried to dry my face, but I pushed him away. "Well, tell that to my heart, Heaven. You think I wanna feel this way about a girl who's like a sister to my girlfriend? How I feel isn't lust. I'm not just saying I love you just to be saying this. It took me over two years to build up the strength even to tell you how I feel, Heaven. And to prove to you that I'm not playing, that what I'm saying is real, I'm breaking up with Charlie tomorrow night."

My eyes widened, and my heart was pounding as if it were going to shoot straight out of my chest. "Wh-what did you say? You're gonna do *what?*"

"I'm gonna tell shorty it's over," he restated.

"On my birthday? And why would you do that to her when she just lost her uncle?" I exclaimed.

"Well, when do you suggest I tell her? Is there *really* a right time to tell someone good-bye?" Aaron's eyes searched mine.

I hesitated—I wasn't sure what to say to that.

"I can't be with someone when I'm in love with someone else. It's wrong." Aaron's eyes watered.

I just stood there crying. Charlie was there for me ever since we were six years old. My so-called mother, Juanita, was an alcoholic. She'd drink until she threw up; then she'd drink some more. When she wasn't drinking, she was mixing all sorts of prescription medication together. She'd pop pills all day long, which would put her to sleep for days at a time. All sorts of people would run in and out of our house. My sister even got molested and sexually assaulted in the process. Even after she was violated and my brother kidnapped, social services still didn't step in. In fact, my mother's doctor continued to prescribe her Percocet for her so-called back pain.

One night, Juanita drank so much and popped so many pills that she damn near lost her mind. She'd abused my brother, my sister, and me all of our lives, but that night, she beat my little brother so bad that he didn't wake up the next morning. My sister ran away that night, and my mother went to prison the next day. I haven't seen my sister since my little brother died six years ago. I was thirteen, Kevin was nine, and Autumn was sixteen at the time. Aunt Joyce couldn't take us in anymore. Uncle Sean—her husband at the time—was getting tired of my mother and her problems. Aunt Joyce cared about my mother and us more than she did about him and his needs. It was too much for him, and he couldn't care less if social services stepped in and put us in foster care.

Charlie's mother wasn't having it. Miss Theresa Campbell, a single mother of four children, took me into her home. They treated me like family. I came to the Campbell house with a book bag that contained a toothbrush, toothpaste, a hairbrush, a bar of Ivory soap, three outfits, and three pairs of underwear, two bras, two pair of socks, and a diary from Hallmark. Charlie got her mother's credit card and took me shopping for a whole new wardrobe. She spent her allowance on making sure my hair, fingernails, and toenails were done. No friend of hers was going to go around looking tore up from the floor up.

Charlie couldn't relate to what I was going through, but she knew her friend was hurting, and she did whatever she could to keep a smile on my face. There were nights when I cried myself to sleep because I missed my brother and prayed that my sister was somewhere alive. There were nights that I woke up from the same recurring nightmare that I had about finding my brother dead in his bed. Charlie would stay up with me, holding me in her arms, singing me to sleep. Charlie was my mother and my sister, and I couldn't forget everything that she had done for me. Aaron was everything to her. She swore she won her a trophy when she snatched Aaron up. How could I take her happiness when she did all she could to restore mine?

I looked up at Aaron, tears gliding down my cheeks.

Aaron looked down at me. "Ditch your people and ride with me."

I shook my head. I didn't even have to turn around to know that Renée was standing in the glass double doors behind me with her arms folded—I could feel her glare burning a hole in the back of my neck.

"I'll pay to have your hair done, Heaven. Please." His eyes traced my lips.

I shook my head. "Please don't break up with that girl, Aaron! She doesn't deserve this, and you know it." I backed away from him. "Aaron, I gotta go."

Renée and her crew walked through the doors to my rescue. Renée walked past me, linking her arm with mine. I looked back at Aaron as she pulled me off with her.

I sat at my computer that night, working on my Humanities paper. I was finally making progress when there was a knock at my dorm door. I stood up to get it. I thought it was my RA coming by my room to tell me to turn down the music, so when I answered the door, I didn't even bother to look through the peephole. I opened the door . . . and before I could open my mouth to say anything, Aaron walked through, the smell of Ralph Lauren cologne trailing behind him. He made his way over to my bed, sat down, and leaned back against the headboard, making himself at home.

I closed the door and leaned back against it. That boy was killing me oh so softly. . . . He knew it too.

"Aaron, what part of 'we can't do this' don't you understand?" I exclaimed.

"The 'can't' part," he grinned.

"And how the hell did you even get in here?" I asked.

"You know who I am, shorty—you think I really have to *ask* if I can get into a female's dorm? They just ask *me* who I'm there to see, and they let me in, baby girl."

I rolled my eyes. "Sweetie, you can't stay here. I have work to do tonight. I already know that I'm not gonna get any work done this weekend with my party goin' on and everything. I don't have time for this right now."

Aaron sat up in the bed, taking his hat from his head. He was dressed in South Pole—a white shirt and dark denim jeans. His Nikes were clean and scuffless. He was looking fine as wine, and he knew it too. "What do I have to say to get you to go out with me tonight? I mean, look at you—you got your hair done, nails done, toes done. You're looking too good to stay in, Heaven. Let's go to the club. We can go with a group of my friends so nobody will think we're there together, bae. C'mon."

I shook my head, walking over to my desk to plug in my laptop because the battery was dying. "Aaron, don't call me 'bae.' And you got a lot of nerve comin' here after what happened at IHOP."

Aaron reached for my hand and in an instant, I was sitting on his lap. My heart pounded in my chest as he slid his hands around my waist.

"I meant what I said when I told you that I can't be with Charlie anymore. I'm breaking up with her tomorrow night. I know you ain't tryin' to hear that, but it's the truth."

"You can do whatever you want, Aaron, as long as you don't break up with her because of me," I whispered. "We can't be together, so stop torturing me like this!"

Aaron's hands gripped my waist. "I shouldn't even ask you to be my girl when my soon-to-be ex-girl is your best friend. I'm wrong for that, and I apologize. When Charlie asked me out on that first date, I should have told her that I wasn't feelin' her, but that I was feelin' *you*."

I got up from Aaron's lap and turned to him.

He stood from the bed, looking down into my face.

I looked up at him. "We were wrong for what went down at your apartment, Aaron, and you know it. You are such a freak."

Aaron grinned, biting his lip. "And you like it too, don't you?"

"You know what you're doin' to me, Aaron—I don't have to tell you. I'm just asking you to *think* about what you're doin'." I looked into his eyes.

Aaron pulled me closer to him by my waist. "I *have* thought about it, trust me."

I blushed. "Slow down, Aaron, that's all I'm asking. Stop calling me, stop coming by my dorm, stop teasing me, stop looking at me like this, stop touching me like this. This is too much. So just keep your hands, your eyes, your hormones, and your thoughts off of me, Aaron."

"C'mon, Heaven, I promise I'll get you back here in time to finish your paper," he pleaded.

I shook my head, looking up into his face. "Sorry, Aaron, but no."

He sighed. "Heaven, okay, I'm just gonna be honest with you. Yeah, you know I wanna fuck the shit out of you. Yeah, I wanna kiss you, touch you, taste you, be with you. Just let me take you out tonight and let whatever happens just happen. I promise you that if you don't enjoy yourself with me tonight, I'll leave you alone. I won't call you, I won't text you, I won't e-mail you—I'll keep my distance. I'll back off."

My eyes glistened, and my heart raced. My mind kept telling me, *No, don't go out with that boy because he's nothing but trouble. Look at him, look how fine he is. He knows you want him. He knows his touch makes you weak. He knows his very presence makes your panties wet.*

But my heart—my heart wasn't trying to hear that shit that my mind was saying.

Aaron went to his car to wait on me while I got dressed. I threw on some stilettos, some skinny jeans, a spaghetti-strap shirt, and a dark denim jacket. I grabbed my purse and keys and darted out the door. I knew what I was doing was crazy, but I went along with it anyway. About ten of Aaron's friends met us at the club that night. There were so many people there that no one really noticed that I was there, sitting at the bar with Aaron. Aaron and his crew knew the owners of the club, not to mention the bartender was Aaron's best friend and roommate's cousin. So you already know the bartender kept the glasses full all night.

Aaron's friends were scattered throughout the club, having a good ol' time. Meanwhile, I sat there at the bar, trying to drown the thoughts of Aaron playing between my thighs from my head. It had taken me years to get over losing Jamie. I did everything that I could not to let anyone else into my heart, but there I was, my heart infatuated with even the mere thought of Aaron. He was amazing, perfect in every way. What did Charlie do to push him to me?

"Heaven, you good?" Aaron was grinning, sipping from his glass. "You having a good time?"

I nodded, taking a gulp of whatever sweet-tasting alcoholic drink the bartender gave me. "Umm-hmm."

I turned to him a little. "If Charlie didn't leave town this week, when were you gonna tell me about your feelings for me, Aaron?"

He didn't respond. He just drank from his glass.

I rolled my eyes. "Charlie must have really done something bad for you to build up the nerve to talk to me, Aaron. And don't try to blame it on the fact that she turned your idea of marriage down either."

Aaron just looked at me for a few seconds before responding. "She just wasn't you, that's all."

I shook my head. "You have to do better than that, Whitehaven." I pushed my bangs from my eyes.

Aaron sighed. "I just got tired of lying to myself, Heaven. I got tired of telling myself that I could make it work with her. I got tired of hearing about muthafuckas that she slept with. I got tired of getting into fights in the locker room with niggas who used to sleep with shorty. It would have been nice to know why she was so popular *before* we became official, know what I mean? How the fuck would you feel if you were dating someone, and every time you turned around, bitches were in your face, telling you how, when, and where they fucked your dude? You'd get tired of defending your relationship too. . . ."

I shook my head. Well, Charlie didn't actually give anyone a chance to tell the boy the truth about her. She cuffed the man thirty seconds after he walked into our classroom. He was "hers" thirty seconds into their first conversation. It wasn't my place to tell Aaron that his girl was Superhead, was it?

"When I asked around about you, everyone said you were a good girl. That after Jamie left, you put up this wall, shutting everyone out. When I asked about Charlene, muthafuckas got quiet. It wasn't until I got cool with Ashton that his girl, Alisha, started telling me the truth about the girl I was with." Aaron took a sip from his glass.

I looked at him. True, Charlie should have told him the truth about her history, but I mean—come on—Aaron was fine as hell. He was talented, smart, and charming. Everyone loved to be around him. Up until he approached me about his feelings, he was a one-woman man, despite all the hoes that were up in his face every day. Most girls would have done exactly what Charlie did—keep their past a secret.

"Nobody's perfect, Aaron. That girl changed for you. She would lie, die, and fight for you. Charlie loves you, you know she does." I took another sip, my glass almost on E.

"Nah," Aaron shook his head, "she loves dancin', kickin' it with her friends, partyin', cheerleadin', clubs, fame, attention, recognition, makeup, and shit." Aaron looked at me as I drank the last sip from my glass. "I'm glad you decided to kick it with me and my people tonight, Heaven. It's good to see you open up a little. That dude, Jamie, did some serious damage, ma."

"Excuse me," I signaled the bartender to come over. "I need another drink. Anything sweet." I looked at Aaron. "I'm *really* not in the mood to talk about him. In fact, I haven't talked about him in over four years, and I'm not about to start talking about him now with you—*especially* with you." The bartender slid me a Strawberry Daiquiri topped with whipped cream and a cherry.

Aaron watched as I plopped the cherry in my mouth, then started to drink from the glass. "I can hear your heart, Heaven. It needs someone." He shook his head at me.

I fought back the tears. I knew that I needed love, but Aaron belonged to someone else. He was right. I did need to talk to someone about my feelings. Charlie was always too busy to talk to. The only thing she was concerned with when it came to me was helping her pass. Renée was about the only one who didn't make me feel like shit when I brought up Jamie's name years earlier. I didn't hang around Alisha or her girls that often because they were always running their mouth about other people's business, and I didn't have the time to get caught up in their shit. My family members were more concerned with my education than with my heart. I didn't have anyone other than my therapist to talk to, and she didn't do shit but say "Hmm" while probably writing, *this bitch is crazy*" on her notepad.

Aaron looked at me, waiting for me to say something about Jamie.

I shook my head. "I don't know what to say other than I loved him, and he left me. I gave my heart to him, and he left me, Aaron. One night we were making love, the next day he was gone. All I know is when I woke up, he wasn't next to me. I woke up to his sister throwing my clothes at me, telling me that I had to get dressed and get the fuck out of her house. I was a few months shy of turning fifteen. True, I had no business having sex. But the look on her face when she told me that her brother deserved better than me is still imprinted in my mind. She always thought I was holding him back, that he lost focus when we started dating. No, he lost focus when his own family didn't support him or his dreams. I know you've seen him on TV, playing college football. He's doing the damn thing now. I don't know what motivation he has now, but I guess his sister was right—all he needed was to get away from me to complete his goals." Tears began to slide down my cheeks.

Aaron's eyes traced my face. "Nah, Heaven, there has to be more to that story."

I shook my head, drying my face. "Well, whatever it is, I hope the nigga is happy, because I'm miserable! I don't know how to love or be loved! It's been four years, and the only person I've managed to fall for is my best friend's boyfriend!" I put my glass to my lips, drinking it to the last drop.

Before I could wipe the whipped cream from my lips, Aaron held my face in his hands, wiping the cream from my face with his thumbs. Yet again, he licked the cream from his fingers.

"And cute little shit like that doesn't help, Aaron," I sighed, still holding the glass in my hands.

He laughed a little. "Heaven, I told you that I was gonna show you a good time tonight, and that's what I plan on doing. So, do you wanna dance with me?" He took a sip from his glass then set it on the bar.

I looked up at him as he licked the liquor from his lips. My favorite love song came on serenading the club at the very moment that he asked me to dance. My heart was racing, my lips and hands were trembling, and my stomach was doing fuckin' backflips.

Aaron grinned, taking the glass from my hands and setting it on the bar. He got up from his seat, then pulled me up from mine by my hands. He led me out onto the dance floor. As soon as we were in the middle of the crowd, he turned to me, pulling my body up against his.

We hadn't danced together since our senior prom, and even then, it wasn't to a slow song. I went to prom alone, and I didn't have anyone to dance with. Aaron grabbed me off the wall and took me out in the middle of the dance floor. I had to admit, he had the moves. He could dance his ass off. He loved to have fun. He was always smiling, and I always loved that about him.

That night at the club, there we were, hormones raging, hearts racing, palms sweating. Aaron gripped my hips in his hands, and I lay my head up against his chest, listening to his heartbeat. I danced with him until my feet hurt. I drank with him and his friends until I couldn't stand on my own. I hate to admit it, but I had a great time with Aaron that night. He didn't flirt with me, he didn't try to kiss or touch me inappropriately, and he didn't act as if we were anything other than friends. I hadn't opened up about my feelings for Jamie in years, and it felt good to talk to someone who actually gave a damn about my feelings.

I enjoyed myself a little too much that night, because it wasn't until around 2:30 that morning that I decided that I had had enough. I accidentally grabbed the wrong set of keys that night when I left my dorm room—I grabbed my spare car key instead of grabbing my room key. There wouldn't be anyone at the front desk of the dorm to let me in at that time of night. I had no choice but to go back to Aaron's crib with him.

Chapter 3

Getting into Heaven

Ne'Vaeh

The last thing I remember from that night is waking up on Aaron's sofa. I pushed my hair from my face, looking up to see Aaron asleep on the couch across from me. I peeled myself from the sofa. My head was throbbing. My shoes and jacket were off. I stood from the couch only to fall straight back to the floor, hitting my knee on the damn corner of the coffee table. I didn't let out a peep, but the sound of me knocking against the table and falling to the floor woke Aaron from his deep sleep.

His eyes opened. After seeing me on the floor, he instantly sat up from the couch and got up, making his way over to me. He helped me from the floor, even though I was trying to push him away. "Too much fun last night, huh, Heaven?" he smirked, helping me back to the sofa.

I looked at him as I pushed my hair from my face. "I bumped my knee on your fuckin' coffee table," was all I could think of to say.

Aaron laughed aloud. "Which knee—this one?" He started rubbing my left knee with his big, warm, strong hands.

My whole body blushed, and I pushed his hand away. I looked up at him. He was dressed in a wife-beater and gray sweats. He smelled as if he had just stepped out of the shower, like fresh Irish Spring.

"What-what time is it?" I asked.

He looked at me, then down at his watch. "It's 7:30."

"Someone should be at the front desk at the dorm to let me in around 8:00, so maybe we should get going. I have to get dressed. I have a long day. I had a little too much to drink last night, and my head is pounding. My party is tonight, so I have to do something to get rid of this migraine," I said, watching Aaron's eyes trace my lips.

"Let me fix you some breakfast before we roll out, shorty." He got up from the sofa.

I sighed, slowly getting up from the sofa, careful not to bump my knee again on the way up. "Aaron, please, just—"

"Don't act like you're not hungry." Aaron made his way over to the refrigerator. "It won't take me long to hook up some French toast, eggs, and bacon, shorty."

We sat side by side on Aaron's couch that morning eating breakfast. The French toast was amazing, made from scratch. The eggs had been scrambled just right, and the bacon was crisped to perfection. We both sat there eating, not saying a word to each other. I looked up at Aaron, just when his tongue slid across his silky lips, licking away the maple syrup that coated them. Instantly, thoughts of Aaron sucking my pussy juice from his fingers flashed through my mind.

Aaron felt me looking at him. "Is the reason why you haven't slept with anyone these past four years because you've been waiting on me, Heaven?"

My heart jumped in my chest. "What? What makes you think that I haven't slept with anyone?"

Aaron smirked, looking up at me.

My whole body blushed. "You know, you're real fuckin' arrogant, Aaron." But it was true. Though I knew I couldn't have Aaron, I wanted him badly. I found myself comparing him to everybody who tried to get my number. If a man didn't walk, talk, think, act, or even smell like Aaron, he didn't have a chance.

Aaron grinned. "I'm just sayin', Heaven. A nigga can just tell."

I rolled my eyes. "For your information, I *have* slept with someone before, Aaron. I told you that shit last night. Yeah, it's been a few years, but I'm in *no* way waiting on you to take my virginity. That was taken years ago, *thank you*, Mr. Ego."

Aaron laughed a little then continued eating.

I sat there, eating nervously. He knew he was driving me crazy. He knew that I wanted his lips all over mine. He knew that I wanted him to fuck the shit out of me. I tried my damnedest to remain calm, but my emotions were draining through my pores. My palms began to sweat. My limbs began to tremble. It soon became difficult to swallow.

Aaron laughed a little watching me struggle to cut the French toast into little pieces. He took the fork from my hand and started cutting the French toast for me. He looked up at me, turning to face me, and he held the fork up to my lips.

I shook my head.

"Open your mouth, shorty," he whispered.

My lips trembled as I opened them, and he slid the moist French toast through my lips. I chewed and swallowed hard as I watched him eat from my plate.

Aaron looked at me as he licked syrup from his lips again. "You know I can't stop thinking about that night I touched your pussy, Heaven."

I shook my head, holding my hand over my heart. "Please, Aaron, no, I'm begging you not to do this." He was driving my hormones up the fuckin' wall. "You did such a good job last night of *not* bringing that up. Please, don't bring it up now."

"Your pussy was so tight, wet, sticky, and sweet. That fat pussy tasted like butterscotch . . . shit. Got a nigga's dick hard just thinking about it."

I snatched my fork back. "C-can we *not* discuss this right now? What are you doing, and *why* are you doing it to me? You know you need to stop."

Aaron grinned as his cell phone rang in his pocket. He took it out, looked at it, touched the screen to answer it, then held it to his ear. "Yo?" he answered.

I looked at him.

"Where you at, nigga?" He looked down at his watch; then he looked at me. "Nah, Charlie's not here, but I *do* have company. . . ."

My heart pounded in my chest.

"A'ight, nigga, you just make sure you have my bottle of Grey Goose that you and your fuckin' cousins drank up the other night. Ha-ha, my ass. Have my shit when you get here, a'ight?" Aaron pressed "end" on his phone, then set his phone on the coffee table. He looked at me.

I looked at him.

"My roommate is on his way over with some friends. Said he'd be here in fifteen. We probably gonna fire some shit up, shorty. Not sure if you get down like that or wanna be here for that, but—" He stopped talking, seeing me reach for my purse, shoes, and jacket.

I stood from the couch.

Aaron looked up at me. "Where are you goin' so fast?"

"Back to the dorm. You said that your roommate, Ashton, was on his way over. He and Charlie are like best friends! I don't care what y'all are smokin' on. I don't wanna be here when I'm not even supposed to be here with you." My eyes searched his. "Not to mention, Charlie's flight will be in soon, and Renée is supposed to be picking me up in a few hours to get ready for the party."

Aaron shook his head, standing up from the couch. He reached for me, but I pulled away. He sighed, shaking his head at me. "I just want to say Happy Birthday, baby."

My eyes moistened over. "Thank you."

"Come upstairs with me to my room real quick before you leave—I got somethin' for you."

I shook my head. "Dude, no!"

He grabbed me by the hand anyway, pulling me out of the living room and up the stairs to his room.

Aaron's room was warm and cozy. His bed was dressed in a chocolate-brown and olive-green comforter and quilt. His headboard, footboard, nightstand, desk, and dresser were cherry wood. Posters of his favorite sports stars and beautiful Victoria's Secret models were all over his walls. It was nice to see a black man actually have pictures of *black* women on his wall. He had all of the latest electronic gadgets, from his 42-inch flat-screen TV, to his PlayStation, to his laptop, to his desktop computer, to his stereo system—*everything* was up-to-date.

I looked over on his nightstand, and walked over to it, picking up a picture he had in a frame of Charlie and me together. We were all hugged up, posing, on the day of JV cheerleading tryouts, freshman year in high school. I have to admit, we were looking pretty fly that day. I laughed to myself.

I looked up at Aaron as he walked over to his closet. He must have had fifty boxes of Jordans stacked on top of his closet shelf, and I don't think he could even fit any more clothes in there. He bent down to pick a gift bag off the floor of his closet. Then he stood back up straight and turned around, walking toward me with the bag.

I looked at him as he held up the sparkly bag. I set my jacket, shoes, and purse on the floor, then took the bag from his hand.

My whole body blushed. "Wha-what's in the bag?"

Aaron grinned, biting his lip, as I reached into the bag.

First, I grabbed a gold box that contained a pair of platinum hoop earrings. Then I pulled out a red velvet box that had a platinum "Heaven" charm hanging from a platinum necklace. Two diamond-studded angel wings enclosed the name.

I looked up at him, tears already sliding from my cheeks. I reached in the bag to pull out a tight-fitted, thigh-high, Coogi sweater dress with a hood, size five. My eyes widened. That dress was three-hundred-fifty bucks at the mall! I know Coogi is a nineties thang, but I loved Coogi, and he knew it too. That gift bag had to contain at least $800 or more worth of gifts.

I looked up at him, not even knowing what to say except, "Why? Why would you spend all of this on me? It's too much. I can't accept this." I started to put everything back in the bag.

Aaron caught my hand.

I looked up at him, tears racing down my face by now.

Aaron shook his head. "Your cousin already told me that I wasn't invited to your party, shorty, so this is the least I can do, since I can't be there."

"Are you kidding me?" I dried my tears, but more followed right behind them. "The *least* you can do? I can't afford things like this. A Coogi dress? I saw this dress at the mall last week, *wishing* I had a dress like this. I couldn't even afford to try the dress on!"

Aaron laughed a little to himself.

I looked up into his face as he held my face in his hands and dried my tears. "Why do you have to be so fuckin' amazing?"

"Are you gonna wear this to your party? Do you have shoes to match the dress? If not, I can go get you some." Aaron's eyes searched mine.

I blushed a little and shook my head. "No, you've done enough. Thank you. I'm sure I can work out something."

"So, you like everything? I don't have such bad taste after all, huh?" Aaron smiled, taking the bag from my hands.

My heart beat stronger for him in my chest as he took the bag and removed the dress from it. He placed the bag on the floor, threw the dress over his shoulder, then pulled me closer to him by the belt loops on my jeans. After that, he started to unsnap my jeans.

I caught his hand. "Whoa, what are you doing?"

"Try this on for me. I wanna see you in it. I can't see you in it tonight, so I just thought I'd get to see you in it now." His eyes traced my bare shoulders.

I sighed. What could it hurt? Whether I was dressed or undressed, Aaron was going to think what he was going to think. It was obvious the man had a vivid imagination. He saw me in the dress before he even gave it to me. He knew my size just by looking at me. He'd never seen me in a dress that tight, but he knew I'd like it.

I unzipped my pants and stepped out of them. I slipped my shirt over my head and tossed it on the floor.

Aaron pulled me closer to him by the elastic waist of my panties, but I put my hands on his chest, pushing him away. He laughed a little as I snatched the dress from his shoulder.

I turned around and walked over to the full-length mirror on his wall. I could feel his eyes roam all over me. I pulled the dress over my head and slid it over my breasts, waist, hips, and over my butt. I looked at my reflection in awe. I looked hot. The V-neckline was low, showing the right amount of cleavage. The dress hugged me in all the right places. I turned around to Aaron, who was already walking toward me.

"So-so what do you think?" I whispered as he pulled me closer to him by my waist.

He gripped my dress in his hands. "I got Magnums, shorty," he whispered back. "I mean *lots* of 'em."

I tried to back away, but he was gripping my dress tight. "You know, just because you bought me a dress doesn't mean you're gonna get some pussy, Aaron. I just wanted to throw that out there."

"So then, what's it gonna take, shorty?"

I shook my head. "Aaron, don't do this, please. I have to go. Thank you for everything, but you *know* this is wrong."

He let go of me, and I pulled the dress up and over my head and walked back over to the bag and my clothes on the floor. I placed the dress back in the bag and picked my jeans up off the floor.

Aaron walked back over to me. "Heaven, ever since that night we kissed, all I can think about is putting this dick inside of you. I keep imagining what my dick going in and out of that pussy must sound like. Yo, I wanna make that pussy *cry*. Shorty, there are so many things I wanna do to you," he had the nerve to tell me.

I started to cry again, about to slide my feet into my pants when Aaron grabbed my arm and took the pants from me, tossing them back to the floor. I tried to pull away from him, but he pulled me closer to him.

"Heaven, you *know* I want you." His eyes glistened. "I mean, not just in this way, but in *every* way."

I looked up at him, lips trembling, as he slid his hands up my back. He unhooked my bra. I shook my head, trying to back away from him, but he moved with me. "Aaron, this is wrong! You *know* this is wrong!"

He held both straps to my bra, pulling the straps from my arms, and from my body. "Heaven, you can't tell me that you don't want me as much as I want you. You *know* you want this dick."

I did. I *did* want the dick, but I still tried to resist him.

I reached for my bra, but he tossed it over in the pile with my jacket, shoes, and purse.

"Aaron, we can't do this," I cried as he slid his shirt over his head, then pulled the drawstring to his pants. He dropped them to the floor then stepped out of them.

Aaron pulled me closer to him. In an instant, I was in his arms, legs wrapped around his waist, and he was carrying me over to his bed. He lay me down on his bed, his body hovering on top of mine, and he gently kissed my lips.

My body melted in his arms. He felt so good. Every hair on my body stood straight up. Every inch of my body was burning hot. My clit was throbbing. My pussy was already dripping wet.

I held his face in my hands, pulling my lips from his. I looked into his face. I could feel his heart beating against my breasts.

"Please, Heaven, I need this. I need you." He gripped my waist in his hands. "If you never wanna see me again, just please, be mine for this one moment." I could feel his dick through his boxers.

I looked into his eyes as he sat up and reached for his nightstand drawer. My body trembled. Aaron stood from the bed, dropping his boxers. I watched as he bit open a Trojan, then slid it on his thick, long, hard, curved penis. He didn't give me a choice. He didn't hear my cries. My body language was all he paid attention to.

I sat up from his bed as he tugged on the reservoir tip of the condom to make sure there was enough room for his semen. That thing was *huge,* and there was no way that I could brace myself enough to be able to handle it. I shook my head as I tried to get up from the bed. "Aaron, we can't do this to her!" I cried out.

Aaron held my thighs, pulling me toward him, causing me to fall back on the bed. He quickly slid my panties from my body, down my thighs, over my calves, and past my ankles. He tossed them on the floor then climbed on top of me. "Heaven, you already knew when you came in this room that I wanted this pussy. You already knew what was gonna happen," he whispered, gently kissing my lips.

"Aaron!" I screamed out, as he held my body against his by my hips. "Wait wait *wait!* I can't—I can't do this!" I cried, feeling like I was going to have a heart attack.

Aaron gently kissed my neck as he gripped my thighs. He didn't hear my cry for him to stop. "Can't" wasn't in his vocabulary. "No" wasn't a word he understood. He was going to take my pussy, no turning back. He knew I wanted his body, even though I was terrified.

"Sshhh," he whispered as he reached down to hold his dick and slide it into me.

I shut my eyes as tightly as I could and gripped his biceps.

He pushed his way through me, stretching my vagina like a speculum.

Before I could scream out in agony, his lips were caressing mine. I dug my nails into his back as tears slid down my cheeks, soaking his pillow.

Aaron slid himself all the way into me. He stopped kissing me, then looked into my face.

I looked up at him and watched as he eased his way out of me, snatched off the condom, tossed it on his nightstand, then slid his way back inside of my wet pussy. He didn't even ask whether I was on birth control.

I cried, "Aaron, what are we doing?"

He started to stroke, and my soul was on fire. He dug deeper and deeper into me. He kissed my lips as he brought my vagina to tears.

"Heaven, I love you. Shorty, I knew you would feel like this," he whispered in my ear.

I just cried, locking my legs around his waist.

It felt too good, too amazing. I was floating on air.

"*Got-damn. Shit.*" His body became moist. "So, *this* is what Heaven feels like."

I screamed out in pleasure, holding on to him.

Just when he threw my legs over his shoulders, about to work the shit out of my pulsating pussy, the door to his room flew open.

"Eh, Aaron, where is the—" His roommate Ashton and his girlfriend Alisha were standing in the doorway, mouths dropped open.

"Got-damn, muthafucka!" Aaron yelled. "Don't you knock?"

"My bad, A!" Ashton was shocked and embarrassed as he slammed the door closed. There was a pause, then loud whispers. "Oh, what's up, Ne'Vaeh?" Ashton hesitantly said.

I cried out as I pushed Aaron off me. I heard Ashton and his girl whispering between themselves as they walked away from the room.

Aaron sighed as he got up off me, sitting on his bed. He reached for me to help me up off the bed, but I pushed his arm away. "Heaven, baby, I'm sorry," he whispered.

I looked at him, tears brimming, threatening to spill over. My pussy was still throbbing. We barely got it in that morning, but my pussy was already sore. Though I was angry and embarrassed, I couldn't help but think about what my body would feel like had we gone all the way to the finish.

"You're 'sorry,' Aaron? *Sorry?* Your fuckin' roommate and his girl just walked in on us fuckin'! I know both of them! I've been going to school with Alisha since third grade! You think she doesn't know that your girlfriend is my *best* friend? Do you really think that she's not gonna say anything to Charlie? She fuckin' *hates* Charlie! And forget Alisha—what about *Ashton?* He grew up with Charlie! He's gonna tell her!" I cried, getting up off the bed.

Aaron watched as I went over to my clothes and rushed to put everything back on. He didn't know what else to do except put his clothes on as well.

I put my clothes on in a minute—tops. Aaron stood there in his clothes as he watched me slide into my shoes and slide my arms through my jacket's sleeves. I picked up the gift bag and walked up to him to hand it back to him.

Aaron looked at me as if he was hurt. "What are you handing me this for, shorty?"

I shook my head, tears rolling down my face. "This doesn't belong to me. It was a great thought. It was a wonderful gift. I don't deserve anything like this."

Aaron shook his head. "Shorty, I can't take this back to the store. This stuff is nonrefundable, Heaven."

"I don't care what you do with it, Aaron, I just can't take it. Give it to Charlie or some other girl, for all I care! And stop calling me 'Heaven'!" I cried.

Aaron shook his head, taking all of the gifts out of the gift bag, and taking my large purse from my shoulder.

I tried to get my purse back from him, but he pushed me away.

He shoved the dress and jewelry down in my purse. He looked up at me and handed my purse back to me.

I snatched my purse, putting the strap back over my shoulder.

His eyes glistened as he reached for me, but I pulled away. He knew that I was hurt, angry, and embarrassed out of my mind. He also knew that I loved each and every inch of him that morning. He had entered my soul that day as well as my heart. I was in deeper than I wanted to be. He reached for me again, pulling my body up against his. "Shorty, they won't say anything, I can promise you that," he assured me.

I shook my head, tears saturating my face. "I can't believe I let you do this to me! I'm smarter than this! I know better than this shit! Aaron, why didn't you just stop when you heard me *crying* for you to stop?"

I shook my head, looking up into his face. "I can't even be mad at you. What was I thinking, coming to your bedroom, when you made it perfectly clear two days ago that you wanted to get me naked? I'm so fuckin' stupid."

"Baby, nobody thinks any less of you." Aaron dried my face with his big warm hands.

I looked into his face. "But I think less of *myself*, Aaron. What am I doing here?" I cried aloud.

"This is where you wanna be. This is where you *need* to be." Aaron placed my hand over his heart, then placed his hand on top of mine. His heart beat strong against his rib cage. "You feel this? *You* did this to me, shorty. Not Charlie, not anybody else but *you*."

My heart skipped a few beats. I slipped my hand from under his. "I-I have to go, Aaron." I didn't know what else to say.

"Let me at least drive you back to the dorm. It's the least that I can do," he suggested.

I backed away from him, shaking my head. "No, no, you've done enough. It's obvious that we don't need to be alone together. I'll just catch the bus back." I turned away from him, about to walk toward the door when Aaron pulled me back to him.

I looked up at him as he pulled me close, up against his chest, and he gently kissed my lips. My knees grew weak. My stomach was doing all sorts of twists, flips, and somersaults.

"I love you, Heaven. I'm sorry, but I love you," he whispered in between kisses.

I held his face in my hands. He held my waist in his hands. I could feel his pulse through his lips, through his hands, through his skin. I was lost in the moment . . . that was, until there was a knock at the door to his room.

"Umm, Aaron, uhhh, ya girl, Charlie's on the phone," Ashton hesitated through the other side of the door.

I cried aloud in Aaron's mouth as I pulled my lips away from his.

His eyes glistened. "Baby, I'm sorry," he whispered.

I opened the door, rushed past Ashton down the hallway, and raced down the stairs. Just when I opened the door about to rush out into the cold, Alisha was finishing a Newport, on her way back into the house.

She grinned at me as she flicked the cigarette butt into the grass. "Where you off to in such a hurry, Cutie?" She exhaled smoke through her nostrils. Just like Aaron, I don't think she'd ever called me by my name ever since I met that girl.

"I'm gonna miss this bus if I don't hurry." I was nearly out of breath. "You know how them fuckin' bus drivers will have you chasin' their ass down the street."

"I know that's right. These bus drivers around this muthafucka are ratchet as hell. I'll give you a ride." Alisha's looked at me. "It's too fuckin' cold to be waitin' on a damn bus. Fuck *that* shit. And what you look like walkin' up them bus steps in fuckin' stilettos?"

I hesitated.

"C'mon, I'm headed in your direction anyway. I gotta go to my mom's crib to get a change of clothes. Your cousin invited me to your party—I gotta go get cute. I know your shit is gonna be off the chain tonight! I can't wait!" Alisha grinned, nudging me in the shoulder.

My eyes glistened. I just knew she thought I was a damn slut for fuckin' my own best friend's boyfriend.

Alisha rolled her eyes, pulling me by the arm off the porch along with her to her car. "Girl, c'mon, and stop actin' childish."

We cruised down 495 in her burgundy Dodge Charger, on our way to my dorm. I needed to attempt to get some sleep before my cousin picked me up at noon. She was supposed to be taking me to lunch with the family and with Charlie who felt like family. My intentions were to meet up with Charlie at the airport at 10:00, but after what happened that morning with Aaron, there was no way that I would be able to face her that soon. I had to get myself together. My emotions were running wild. My mind and heart were racing.

Alisha glanced at me while she was driving. She was probably *the* most popular girl from middle school all the way through senior year in high school. She was dark-skinned with long, sleek, shiny black hair. She had the prettiest smile and the smoothest skin. Not to mention, she was thick as hell and had an ass like *whoa!* which made her a favorite among the guys. She and Charlie always bumped heads. Neither of them were fans of the other. Alisha always called Charlie the blue-eyed devil. She had been accusing Charlie of sleeping with Ashton junior year after homecoming. Ashton and Charlie both denied it, but Alisha knew in her heart that the man she had with since seventh grade had been unfaithful. She'd found an earring similar to one that Charlie had lost around the same time, in the backseat of Ashton's car. She even found an empty condom wrapper in Ashton's pants that night. She was in love, but she was no fool.

"You know, I never liked Charlie, right?" Alisha stated.

I looked at her, eyes puffy and all.

She grinned a little, glancing over at me.

I shook my head, knowing that she was trying to make me feel better, but I was in no mood for jokes. "Alisha, I'm *really* not in the mood. Please talk your shit about Charlie some other time, okay?"

She glanced at me. "So, you're embarrassed because me and my man caught you fuckin' *Charlie's* man this morning, huh?"

I didn't say anything. I just gazed out of the window.

Alisha sighed. "Not that you owe me—or anyone else for that matter—an explanation, but . . . Did you sleep with Aaron to get back at Charlie for something?"

I looked at her, shaking my head. "No. What has Charlie ever done to me?"

Alisha ignored the question. "Do you like Aaron?"

I shook my head. "I don't just like him, Alisha, I *love* him."

"Then you didn't do anything wrong." She glanced at me.

My eyes widened. "How could you say that? Charlie *loves* Aaron!"

Alisha smirked. "Are you serious? You have no idea, and I'm not gonna be the one to tell you."

I looked at her. "What do you mean?"

Alisha laughed a little. "Let's just say that Aaron is the farthest nigga from her mind right now. I told Aaron back in high school that he should've hollered at *you*, but no, he had to listen to his boys, who told him that you were still stuck on Jamie. Aaron told me back then that he liked you. Maybe *I* should have been the one to tell you. I don't even know why you're crying about this shit. You should be happy!"

There the tears were, freely flowing down my face again. "Happy? You're trippin'. I don't care what you say, Alisha—I'm wrong for this shit."

"Well, I tell you what, I know *Aaron's* not feeling bad about it. He's been talkin' about breaking up with Charlie for weeks. He talked to the girl about marriage, and she dissed him. He probably was just sayin' the shit to see what she said, but that's beside the point. She doesn't care about him. Probably only got with the boy because she knew that *you* were feelin' him first." Alisha glanced at me again.

I shook my head. Why was everyone bad-mouthing my best friend? "She's not even like that, Alisha. We must be talking about two completely different Charlies. The Charlie that *I* know has been my best friend ever since elementary school. When no one else took the time to be there for me, she was there. My mother murdered my brother and beat my sister until she ran away. Haven't seen my sister in six years, and though I miss her, Charlie has done one hell of a job playing her part. Charlie has always been supportive, and she's always had my back. She feels like family to me, and for me to go and do something like this to her . . ." I fought back the tears. "I don't even deserve to have her as a friend."

Alisha shook her head at me. "You'll find out soon enough, Cutie. She's not the girl you think she is. I'll just leave it like that, because I already know that whatever I say, you're not gonna believe me."

I just looked at her. Alisha was always the gossip queen of our clique. I didn't have time for her drama today. Whatever she had to say about Charlie didn't matter at that moment.

I sat nervously in my dorm room that day around noon. It took me at least two hours to find something to wear. I hung the dress that Aaron gave me on a hanger on the knob of my closet door. I must have walked past that dress fifty times before breaking down and deciding to put the muthafucka on. I slipped the dress over my head, pulling it down past my waist, and over my hips. Then I slipped my feet into a pair of burgundy stilettos, glossed some burgundy lipstick over my lips, and slid the strap to my matching Coogi purse over my shoulder. My hair still managed to stay intact. All I had to do was separate the curls a little with my fingers. I looked at myself in my full-length mirror. I was lookin' good, but I felt like shit.

I sat there shaking my leg nervously when my cell phone vibrated on my lap. It was a text from Renée, telling me that she'd pulled up outside my dorm, and for me not to take all damn day because the family was waiting for me at Venus, a soul food restaurant owned by my cousin, rapper and superstar Darrick "D-Allan" Allan's ex-wife, Jade Abdula-Matthews. It was an honor that she would even let all twenty-five of us dine at her restaurant on such short notice, let alone free. She was in town for the week, and I couldn't believe I was going to get the chance to meet her. Seeing her around usually meant that Cousin Darryl, Darrick's fraternal twin, would show his face. I didn't see much of him these days. He'd taken a break from producing records and went straight to working with film. He was married to Anastasia Jones, one of the hottest singers, dancers, and choreographers there was. She was phenomenal, and I hoped that she would show up at my birthday party as well.

"I cannot believe you missed your own birthday breakfast this morning." Renée rolled her eyes at me as I got into the passenger seat and closed the door behind me. "You had my ass up at seven-thirty this morning, and I don't wake up that early unless I'm goin' to work."

"Sorry, girl." I looked at her, "I didn't wake up until almost eleven."

Renée looked at me as we drove off, out of the parking lot, away from my dorm. "Oh, yeah, I forgot—you *did* say that you were working on that term paper."

I glanced at her. I had forgotten all about that damn paper. I would be pulling an all-nighter this weekend to finish it, that was for damn sure.

"And your girl, Charlie, called me, telling me that she had been trying to call *you* all morning. Her flight just got in a few minutes ago. Their flight was delayed this morning, and she didn't want you showing up to the airport when she wasn't going to be there. She said she would be at the hotel around one o'clock to help set up."

My heart began to race in my chest. I couldn't face her—there was no way I could face that girl after what I'd done. I shut my eyes as tightly as I could, trying to fight back the thought of Aaron's lips pressed against mine. I could still feel his warm dick inside me.

"Cute dress." I felt Renée looking me up and down.

I opened my eyes, my heart nearly popping out of my chest. Damn, that bitch never misses *anything,* always peepin' shit. Ol' nosy ass. "Huh?" I gulped.

"What? Don't 'huh' me. The dress—it's awesome!" Renée laughed a little. "The perfect party dress!" She looked at me again. "Wait a minute. I saw that dress at the mall. That freakin' dress was like $400! Where the hell did you get that kind of money to spend on a dress, when you're not even working full time?"

I swallowed hard. "Girl, you know I'm broke as hell. It was a birthday gift."

Renée glanced at me. "A birthday gift? Whose nose do you have *that* wide open for them to get you a dress that cost damn near half a grand?"

I remained quiet. She got on my damn nerves always figuring shit out.

The girl slammed on her brakes in the middle of traffic.

My heart nearly stopped in my chest as the car behind us slammed on its brakes to avoid hitting her. I swore my damn heart slammed against my rib cage. "Damn, Renée! You're gonna give me fuckin' whiplash!" I squealed. "Are you fuckin' crazy?"

Cars were honking their horns as they passed around Renée's stopped vehicle.

She gave them all the middle finger as they drove by her, cursing her crazy ass out. "Man, fuck them." She looked back at me, her light eyes searching the expression on my face for clues as to who could have bought me the dress. "Aaron." She pointed in my face. "Aaron bought you that dress? And those earrings! And that necklace?" She covered her mouth. "I mean, fuck! The necklace says 'Heaven' on it! Who the fuck is the only one who calls you that? That is a *dead* giveaway!"

I put my hand over my heart in agony. I couldn't bring myself to talk about what happened that morning, but cuz was forcing me to talk to her about it. "Please, Renée—please start this car before someone runs us off the road."

Renée shook her head at me, "What did you do to him?"

My eyes widened. I looked at her. "What? What did *I* do to *him?*"

Renée finally came back to her senses, put the car back in gear, and began to drive down the street again. "What did you do to get that muthafucka to buy you a dress *that* sexy and *that* expensive? Did you suck his dick or something?" She gasped. "You fucked him, didn't you?"

I shook my head. "No."

Renée looked at me, pursing her lips.

"He fucked *me.*" I sank back in my seat. "He fucked me *good* too, Renée."

Renée shook her head, "O-M-muthafuckin' G! I can't believe this 'Jerry Springer,' 'Love and Hip-Hop' type shit! You should have given him the dress back!"

"I tried!" I exclaimed. "I tried to give it back, but he wouldn't let me. When he kissed me, I told him to stop. When he undressed me, I tried to push him away, but he just . . ."

Renée glanced at me. "So, the muthafucka just forced his shit on you? The muthafucka just *took* the pussy? That nigga *raped* you, Ne'Vaeh!"

I shook my head at her before she got into her head that Aaron raped me. "Renée, see, that's *not* what I said. I knew what I was doing when I went to his room, I knew what I was doing when I tried on the dress, and I knew what I was doing when I got naked in front of someone who made it perfectly clear that he wanted to have sex."

She just continued to shake her head. She was pissed off.

"Renée, I love him." I started crying.

She sighed, frustrated with me. "Girl, *why?* You are too smart and too beautiful to want anybody's leftovers, no matter how muthafuckin' fine he is or no matter how much money the brotha is about to be making in the very near future. You have so much potential. There are so many men that want you. I've seen the kind of men that approach you, and I've seen you turn each and every one of them down. And for who? A man who belongs to someone else? Ne'Vaeh, *why?*"

I look at her, tears trickling down my face. "I loved Aaron the very moment that I ever laid eyes on him. I was going through *hell,* and Aaron looked like an angel. There was a connection to that boy from the start. I had no idea that he felt the same way that I did until just two days ago. For almost two years, I have been holding in the fact that I was in love with him. He barely looked at me, and I thought he didn't notice me. I thought he didn't care. I thought he would never see me. As bad as I feel for letting my emotions overrule my common sense . . . I just couldn't stop him from kissing me, touching me, undressing me, and loving on me. I hadn't been touched in four years, Renée! If it wasn't for Ashton and Alisha walking in on us this morning, I'd probably still be in his bed, in his arms."

Renée's eyes widened. "They walked in on y'all fuckin'? Ne'Vaeh, sweetie, you're in for the rudest, most fucked-up awakening, I'm sorry to tell you. I'm telling you, sweetie, stay away from that man. You had your fun, you got laid, you woke the pussy up from her nap, you got some dick, but it's morning. So, 'as you slept the night away' with Aaron, you both 'forgot to face one simple fact'—he belongs to someone else—and that someone else is your best friend. The same best friend who took you in when your mama abandoned you, and you didn't have a fuckin' pot to piss in. She's back in town, so the next time that you decide to visit his bed, remember that Charlie sleeps in that bed too. Charlie gave you a home. I suggest you keep that shit in mind the next time you decide to wreck *her* home."

I cried because I loved Aaron, but . . . I respected Charlie just as much, if not more. She was like a sister to me. I couldn't hurt her when all she'd ever done was try to protect me from hurt. I loved Aaron, but he belonged to Charlie. What was I supposed to do when *my* heart belonged to Aaron? He was going to break up with her. I believed him when he told me that he would do it at my birthday party. He hadn't talked to me in over two years, and as soon as he got the opening to tell me how he felt, he jumped for the chance. He was serious. As if my life wasn't hectic enough, I had to go and make things even more complicated.

Chapter 4

Gonna Fuck Him

Charlene

"Here, honey, let us help you with those bags. Why are you carrying these bags by yourself? Heather, come carry these bags for your sister. Jorge, come hold this." Aunt Stacen took my Coach carry-on bags and purse from me, passing them off to my little sister and brother.

I sighed, rolling my eyes. "C'mon, Aunt Stacen, really? My *purse?* I can't carry my own *purse?* I'm pregnant, not crippled. Got-damn, people, stop treating me like I'm fuckin' handicapped." I took my purse back from my sister.

"Charlie!" my mother exclaimed. "Watch your mouth!" My mother pranced over to the baggage conveyor belt in her Chanel sandals. "We're only trying to help. Keep acting like you don't need anybody. In a few months, when this baby comes, you're going to wish you weren't so bitchy to the people who were just trying to look out for you." Mother grabbed her Gucci suitcase from the conveyor belt. She looked at me, her blue eyes searching my face. She was so disappointed in me, but I was more disappointed in myself.

Mama hadn't said too much to me since she found out that I was pregnant. I took the pregnancy test one day in my sister's bathroom, and carelessly, I left the applicator on Heather's sink. Mind you, my baby sister is thirteen. Mother happened to walk into Heather's room and found the applicator, and you know she went *straight* off on my sister. I had to tell her that the pregnancy test was mine; then she went straight off on *me*.

My eyes began to water. "Mama, I'm sorry. It's these hormones. I'm trippin'. I appreciate your help, but you know how I am."

Mama's eyes searched my face. "So, when are you going to tell Aaron about this baby?"

I looked at her, my heart skipping a few beats. Tell Aaron? I dreaded the thought because I was too young for a baby. I'd already planned to get an abortion when Mama found the applicator, but Mama made it perfectly clear that it was my mistake, and I wasn't going to make the baby pay for something that I did. I also dreaded the idea because I knew in my heart that Aaron wasn't the father of my baby. Let me tell you how I pretty much played myself. . . .

It was August 15, about two weeks before sophomore year in college started for the fall 2014 semester. My girls from the cheerleading squad and I took a trip to Miami just because. Sometimes, we took trips just to unwind from all of the hard work that we had been doing throughout the year. We did everything from tournaments, to fashion shows, to community service, to football games, to basketball games, to TV appearances. We deserved to relax and unwind. We all needed a relaxing getaway under the sun. Especially me—I just needed to get away *period*.

I needed to escape Maryland. I needed to get away from the responsibility of babysitting Ne'Vaeh, plain and simple. Even though we were in separate colleges, my mother and the rest of the family still expected me to keep up with Ne'Vaeh. They felt sorry for the girl. It was more than sympathy. They loved her as if she were their own, especially my father's side of the family. My father died of a heart attack when I was six years old. My sister was just born, and my mother was devastated. I knew Ne'Vaeh's pain of losing someone that she loved. Ne'Vaeh lost a brother, a sister, a mother, and never knew her father. My father was everything to me. Losing him did serious damage to my heart and to my life. No one bothered to notice. From the moment Ne'Vaeh stepped into my life, she'd won my family's heart. When her mother went to prison for killing her younger brother, my mother stepped up to the plate and took Ne'Vaeh in. Ne'Vaeh's mother, Juanita, used to be best friends with my mother when they were in high school, according to my grandmother. They were the original Salt-N-Pepa. My mother was white, and Juanita was black. Whatever happened to split the two apart, no one talked about it, but I'm pretty sure it had something to do with a man. It always does.

The squad arrived in Miami at 1:15 p.m. that day. I was so happy to get away from Maryland, away from Ne'Vaeh, and away from *Aaron*. Yes, I know, Aaron is wonderful. He is the epitome of the perfect man—someone *else's* man. He didn't love me. It was obvious that he was in love with someone else. He tried his damnedest to love me, but he couldn't, and I desperately wanted him to. He was a great guy, don't get me wrong, but there was absolutely no passion in our relationship. Sure, we looked phenomenal together. Every night out together felt like a Red Carpet event, but whenever we made it back to our separate apartments, he stayed on his side of the bed, and I stayed on mine.

Aaron didn't pay me attention anymore. We made "like," not love. He had the most amazing sensuous lips, yet he never kissed me. He had the softest hands, yet he never touched me. Whenever we had sex, I'm pretty sure he didn't even reach orgasm. After a few strokes, sometimes, he would just get up and go to the bathroom. When we had sex, it was like he was thinking about someone else the whole time. Sometimes, he would just stop, pull out, and go to sleep. Nothing I did turned him on. I showed up to his apartment one night with nothing on but Burberry stilettos, a Burberry raincoat, and a black lace thong from Victoria's Secret. Do you think he cared? No. The nigga took one look at me as I opened my coat, and said, "Charlie, its thirty-two degrees outside. Are you trying to get sick?" Yep, he wasn't cheating on me . . . but it was sure to come.

I needed to get fucked, if not loved. My trip to Miami was going to help that shit happen. There was always something going on in Miami. That night, there was going to be this huge college football party at a hot new club in Miami Beach. I stepped off the plane that afternoon with one thing on my mind—fuckin'. Aaron and I hadn't had sex in over three months. I needed a fling, a one-night stand, a hit it—split it—and—quit it. I didn't give a fuck, just something to let me know that someone actually wanted to spend some sort of time with me. Men hit on me all the time, but I wanted *Aaron* to want me. I wanted him to need me, but he didn't, and I was tired of it.

"Ladies, we're going to the College Football Fiesta tonight at nine-thirty," Alisha announced to all fifteen of us that afternoon in the lobby of the Hilton Hotel. "I have three limos picking us up at nine-thirty *sharp*. Dress to impress, divas, because some fine, hot, sexy, soon-to-be-drafted-into-the-NFL men are going to be there tonight!"

All the girls cheered, whooped, and hollered.

I looked up at Alisha and rolled my eyes at her.

Why I had to be cursed by ending up at the same college on the same cheerleading squad with that bitch, I don't know. Yeah, I slept with a lot of guys in my day, but she had in her head that I had sex with her boyfriend, Ashton. Ashton and I grew up together and lived next door to each other, until my mother moved when I was twelve years old. Though he might have had feelings for me, he never told me so, nor treated me like anything other than a sister. I was wild, I was loose, there was no taming me. Ashton didn't have time for that shit. He tried to keep me out of the trouble that I always seemed to be searching for. I would party *hard*, even to the point where I'd get so high and so fuckin' drunk that I would wake up in places, having no idea how I got there. Imagine waking up sore and buck naked, lying next to a man, woman, or men and women you didn't even know. Yeah, that was your girl. Ashton would often come to my rescue. He saved me from wild fraternity parties on *many* occasions.

I started having sex at the age of thirteen. I lied about my age to a nineteen-year-old guy who was in college. I can't even remember dude's name. All I remember is the feeling. He adored me, he admired me, and he lusted after me. I didn't realize then the muthafucka was a pervert. All I cared about was the fact that he lusted after me. The guy blew up my phone for weeks, looking for some more of me. I ignored his phone calls. He wanted some sort of relationship, as sick as that sounds. I just wanted a rush.

I believe that between the ages of thirteen and sixteen, I had to have had sex with at least fifty or more guys, all ages, sizes, and colors. I had a reputation. I was good at what I did. I was trying to fill the empty space in my heart with something—anything. I was afraid to love, even though I desperately wanted it, and when I met Aaron, I knew I had to change. I didn't want to be that girl who was great at giving lap dances, who was great at giving head, who could eat your girl's pussy, who could take on four guys at a time. I can't even begin to tell you the amount of shit me and my girls got into with men and women of all statuses in life. I'm talking senators, doctors, lawyers, judges, *every* muthafucka who held some type of political position. And this is while we were only in high school. I couldn't be tamed, but that day that Aaron stepped into my classroom junior year in high school, I knew it was time to change. I wanted Aaron from the moment that I met him. I knew I had to have him. He was beautiful, he was talented, he was sweet, he was amazing, and he was sexy as a muthafucka. I didn't give a damn who else wanted him. He was going to be *mine*. I was determined. Thirty seconds into our first conversation, I asked him out on a date.

I introduced Aaron to Ashton junior year in high school, and they clicked from the start. I was so excited when they decided to be roommates. I had my "brother from another mother" and the man who I loved with every inch of me.

Aaron treated me like royalty when we first met, which had my emotions soaring high. I didn't know much about Aaron, but what I did know was that he was from a very wealthy family. His parents lived back in California, so he stayed with his aunt, who was in the military, right up until he moved in with Ashton. I didn't know why his relationship with his parents was so strained, but he didn't want anything from them or anything to do with them. Aaron was an amazing basketball player, destined to achieve greatness. I knew I could help him get to high places in no time. I introduced him to college basketball coaches and college scouts from all over the country, some of which I had slept with, of course. I got him a great job working with my uncle at an engineering company. I introduced Aaron to a life he wouldn't have known otherwise. He held me on a pedestal for the first six months or so into our relationship.

That was, until he discovered who I was. No one gave a damn about my sex life until Aaron came along. He made me want to change. I wanted to forget my past, but no one else wanted me to forget. Almost everyone—including Alisha—decided to put me on Front Street in front of Aaron. They couldn't wait to let him know the name of every guy and girl I screwed around with in college. They told him about my adventures in the boys' locker room. They told him about my fling with the art teacher. They told him about the time I was caught giving head to the assistant basketball coach in the boy's bathroom. They told him about the three-month relationship I had with Carla, this beautiful Puerto Rican girl who was a sophomore in college—she knew how to eat pussy until your toes curled and eyes rolled to the back of your head. They even told him about the group sex tape I was in on my sixteenth birthday. Aaron was disgusted. We almost broke up, but he gave me a chance. Though he didn't leave me, he was no longer the same. He hadn't touched, kissed, looked at, or spoken to me the same since he found out the truth about me, and I started hating myself.

That afternoon, I snuck away from the squad and went out on the town on my own. I didn't feel like going to the spa with them, listening to them brag about all the shit their men bought for them. I walked along the sandy beaches of Miami, did a little shopping, and got my nails done. Then I went out to eat. I sat alone at a small restaurant, just staring at my cell phone. Aaron hadn't called or texted me *once* to even see if I was okay or that I made it safely into town. Ne'Vaeh had called at least six or seven times, though I ignored her calls. I rolled my eyes every time the phone rang and her name appeared on the display. She loved me like her sister. She adored me. I loved her too, but I hated her just the same. It was as if my family replaced my father with her. It seemed as though my mother took her in to help distract her from missing my father. I resented Ne'Vaeh for throwing all of her weight on top of the weight that I already carried. I was responsible for that girl, and I hated it. I needed a life outside of her. She had me trapped. I tried my hardest to avoid her in college, but she'd find her way to me. Man, that week in Miami felt like freedom.

"Charlene Campbell, got-damn, I *know* that ain't you!" a familiar, deep, sexy voice exclaimed over my shoulder.

I looked up to see Jamie "Memphis" Green looking back at me. I stood from the table in shock as he turned my body around to face him then threw his arms around me, squeezing me oh so tight. Oh my God, his body was so soft and warm. And he smelled so good.

Jamie Green was Ne'Vaeh's first and only boyfriend. She was in love with that boy, from the top to the bottom of her heart. It nearly killed that girl when he left her back in high school. There he was, standing before me, tall, milk chocolate, handsome, delectable, looking good enough to eat. His hair was close cut. His eyebrows and goatee were perfectly trimmed. He was dressed in a clean, crisp, white T-shirt and ankle-length khaki shorts. Fresh Air Force Ones were on his feet. I could see how chiseled his body was through his shirt. He looked a-maz-ing, *got-damn.*

"Oh my goodness! What the fuck!" I covered my mouth, giggling.

Jamie laughed a little.

"OMG, how you've grown up! You're not Li'l Memphis anymore!" I watched him smiling. "Boy, what are you doing here?" I exclaimed.

"I'm here with the football team. You know I'm at Memphis State right now, right? I'm sure you seen me doing my thang on TV." Jamie smiled, showing his dimples, pearly whites and all.

I looked at him, rolling my eyes, shaking my head, "Humph, still cocky, I see. I have my own life, Jamie. Don't nobody got time to be watching your conceited ass on TV."

Jamie laughed a little. He had the most gorgeous smile. He was still sexier than a muthafucka, and he knew it too. "So, what are *you* doing here?" he said as he licked his lips.

"Vacationing with the squad. You know we've been doing it big since freshman year in high school." I smiled up at him.

Jamie looked around for the squad. "Where they at? Who's here with you now?"

"They went to some spa. I had to get away from them. *Alisha's* the captain of my team. Yeah, you *know* I'm hatin' that. I ditched the crew. I'm here on my own," I responded.

"You wanna kick it with your boy today? I mean, if you're not too busy. You look busy."

My heart skipped a few beats. I didn't know what to say except, "I have a boyfriend."

Jamie laughed a little to himself. "I have a girlfriend— what's your point?"

I looked up at him. "My point is I don't think it's appropriate to be alone with you, Jamie. You might not be good at keeping your hands to yourself. I've heard about you. You know it's a small world. Cheerleaders talk. And most of their talk is about you and your dick." I looked him up and down a little, pursing my lips.

"Oh, it's like that, huh? I haven't seen you in, what, three-and-a-half or four years. We've known each other since second grade, shorty, and you can't come chill with me, get some lunch, go to a movie, or hit up a mall real quick? That's fucked up." Jamie held my hand, pulling me a little closer to him.

I looked up at him. His intentions were probably very innocent, but shit, *mine* weren't. He looked too hot and too damn tasty. If wherever he took me to didn't have a lot of people there, oh yeah, I was gonna fuck the *shit* out of him.

"We need to talk, catch up, and shit. I miss y'all, man. My niggas are having a barbeque at my man's beach house around six o'clock; then they're heading over to that college football party at this club. Call your girls, tell 'em to meet up with you. My team would love to see your girls, man." Jamie grinned, still holding my hand.

I looked up at him. I really wanted him to ditch his crew, take me back to his hotel room, and fuck my pussy *dry*. I should have been thinking about Ne'Vaeh at that time and how much she would have loved to hear from him. When he left her, she cut off all contact with him. It was his choice to move to Memphis to live with his father. He didn't have to go, but he did, and she felt abandoned.

I should have been thinking about her, but I was only thinking about my own needs at that time. Someone finally wanted to spend some time with me, and I wasn't about to pass that up.

Of course, Alisha had something to say about Jamie's invite. She sat down alongside me on a bench outside of the beach house belonging to Jamie's friend that evening. I'd never seen such beautiful scenery. The man's house was so peaceful, so serene. It was as if Jamie's friend, Alonzo, lived on heaven's beach.

"I cannot believe that you just *happened* to run into your best friend's ex, almost 1,100 miles away from home." Alisha laughed to herself, crossing her legs, showing those fat-ass thighs the niggas loved oh so much.

I rolled my eyes at her. That bitch always had something smart to say to me. "Look, just because you're captain of this team doesn't mean you're captain of my fuckin' life, Alisha," I snapped at her.

She laughed aloud. "Whoa, let me keep my opinions to myself then! All I'm saying is that when you saw Jamie, the first thought on your mind should have been Ne'Vaeh, and not yourself. She loved that boy with all of her heart back in the day. She cried for nearly two years over him leaving her, or did you forget that?"

I looked at her. A twinge of guilt stung my heart. I couldn't care less about Ne'Vaeh when I ran into Jamie. All I cared about was my own selfish, horny needs. Jamie was making me feel the way Aaron used to make me feel. Aaron had made me feel like royalty when we first started dating, and I needed that old feeling back, even if it was from my "sister's" ex-boyfriend.

"He's been all over you since we've been at this party." Alisha couldn't help but notice. She looked at me, her brown eyes searching my face for remorse. When she found none, she shook her head. "I don't give a fuck how you feel or don't feel about Aaron, but *Ne'Vaeh* loves you like a sister, Charlie. The kind of friendship y'all have doesn't come around that often. You really wanna fuck that up by fuckin' with her heart? I don't too much care for you, and you know that, but Ne'Vaeh is good people. You've known the girl since third grade. Don't do this shit to her like you did to me. . . ."

Alisha made tears fall from my eyes. I dried them as fast as I could. The bitch fucked up my relationship because she thought I was fuckin' her man, Ashton. Okay,

I will admit one thing: I sucked his dick. It was more of helping him out than it was sexual. He was about fourteen years old. We were chillin' in his room, doing homework as usual. We were watching some movie that had a sex scene in it, where a woman went down on this guy. Ashton looked at me, asking me how it felt. I told him I didn't know because I wasn't a guy, but if he wanted to know what it felt like, I would show him. I sucked him off for five or ten good minutes before he busted in my mouth. I went to the bathroom, brushed my teeth, and that was it. We never talked about it again. I'm sure he never told her about it, though I figured he asked her to do it to him the same way that I did.

I couldn't care less about what Alisha had to say about what I chose to do with my life.

"I've done a lot of wild shit in my time, but I never fucked any of my friends' men, and I didn't fuck yours, Alisha. You didn't have to go telling Aaron all about my past, because it was none of your fuckin' business. Thanks to you, Aaron won't fuck me, touch me, kiss me, talk to me, or fuckin' *look* at me!" I stood up from the bench.

A slight grin grew across her face. "Why are you mad at me—because *you* chose to be a ho in high school? Be mad at yourself, shit. *You* should've never fucked with my man, Charlene. I told you I was gonna get you back."

"Trust me, bitch, if I wanted Ashton, I'd be with him, believe that shit! You worry about your fake-ass life and stay the *fuck* out of mine." I stormed away from her and passed Jamie, who stood alongside his friends near the grill.

Jamie caught my arm and pulled me to him, looking at the dried-up tears on my face. "What's up, ma? What's wrong?"

I looked at him, tears lining my lashes. "I'm not feeling this. I'm leaving. Y'all have fun with the squad. Trust me, that sexy li'l Puerto Rican chick named Lailah, the skinny white chick named Nicole, and Rita, that thick-ass, dark-skinned chick will fuck you *and* your team's brains out. Have a fuckin' ball." He loosened his grip on my arm, and I walked away.

I went inside the house to grab my jacket and purse. It was about 7:15. The night was still young. The party was just getting started, and Alisha had to start fuckin' with me, fuckin' up my mood.

The door slid back and in came Jamie. I looked at him as I slid my purse over my shoulder.

"Wanna talk about it, shorty?" he said softly, his eyes searching my face.

I shook my head, "Nah, not really. I don't know what I was thinking, going on a trip with Alisha's ol' hatin' ass. I'm taking the first flight up out this bitch tomorrow morning, believe that!"

Jamie laughed a little. "You gonna let Alisha chase you away from a good time, shorty?" He shook his head. "Nah, man, you can't go. How long were you supposed to be here in Florida?"

I looked at him, "A week. Why?"

"Because I'm not ready for you to leave yet. . . . You could stay with me for about four days." Jamie looked into my face.

My heart jumped. "With-with you? Seriously?"

He nodded. "Why not? I have a few television appearances this week, but that's about it. I'm free. We leave in five days. I wouldn't mind the company. I'm staying at my cousin's house on the other side of the beach. He let me stay in it for the week, while he's away on business. I'm all by myself, shorty. C'mon, stay with me."

I looked up at him, hormones jumpin', and pussy already starting to throb in my panties. "You promise not to touch me?"

Jamie laughed to himself, "Yo, I don't make promises that I can't keep."

"Whatever, Jamie. I just need to get out of this house *now*. Alisha is gonna make me fuck her ass up. Always talkin' shit." I looked up into his face.

"Let's roll, then, shorty. I'll try to be on my best behavior. You shouldn't look so good if you don't want anybody to touch you. I'm just sayin'." Jamie looked down into my eyes.

Boy, he was turning me the hell on.

I rolled my eyes, trying to play off my attraction to him. "I can't believe I'm actually contemplating your offer. I know better than this."

Jamie grinned a little.

He took me back to the hotel to get my luggage. Then he took me to a movie that night. We sat close, shoulders touching. His hand rested on my knee as we ate popcorn out of the same bucket, laughing at the same parts, and getting upset at the same parts. It felt like a real date. He treated me as if he cared about me. He knew I was hurting about something, and he did everything that he could to make me smile. When his phone rang, he didn't even look at it to see who it was. I was his number one focus at that moment, and I needed that desperately.

We sat on the steps outside of his cousin's beach house that night smoking, drinking champagne, and eating fresh fruit. I was feeling *real* nice. The wind blew through my hair. I loved the salty, yet sweet smell of the air.

Jamie laughed after reminding me of our many memories in middle school. "Man, we had some crazy times back in middle school, shorty! I don't even know how the fuck I passed! My ass was foreva' skipping school and shit!" He took a hit from his Newport 100. "Remember Mr. Nelson's art class? We used to throw paint at that nigga! And remember smokin' weed in the back of the gym?"

I slid the cigarette from his lips, then put it to mine.

Jamie looked at me and grinned.

"Those were some good times, boy!" I laughed, "Those were the good ol' days. Those days are *long* gone. I'd give anything to get those old days back, I'm tellin' you." I took a sip of champagne.

Jamie exhaled deeply. "Shit, you ain't *never* lied."

There were a few moments of silence.

"Are-are you happy?" Jamie hesitantly asked.

I looked at him, shaking my head. "No. Not really. This time right here with you is the happiest I've been in a *long* time," I admitted. "You?"

Jamie shook his head, taking his cigarette back from me. "I thought I wanted this life, but it's not what it's cracked up to be. I got muthafuckas thinking they control me and shit. I got my manager, then the agent, then the coach, then my endorsers, then my professors, then I got my family asking me for shit when they ain't ever did a *got*-damn thing for me. I love playing football, don't get me wrong, but I don't have time to enjoy the game anymore. Everything is happening so fast. Endorsement deals, television appearances, muthafuckas asking to write a book about my life, radio interviews, magazine photo shoots, parties—it's almost unreal. You know, I've been through so much bullshit in my life. I don't have the support from my family—shit, if you even wanna call them backstabbing, dysfunctional muthafuckas *family*. My dad tries to be supportive, but you know he's sick, which is the whole reason why I moved back to Memphis."

I looked at him, shaking my head. "I never knew that, Jamie." I'm pretty sure Ne'Vaeh didn't know that was the reason that he left either.

Jamie nodded. "Yeah, shorty. I wanted to get to know my father before he . . . ya know. Basically, what I'm saying is that I don't have the support that I need to keep myself motivated to make it through all of these changes and to stay focused on my goals. If it weren't for my coach, teachers, and all y'all believing in me, I would be back on the streets. Coach Jackson believed in me, working the shit out of me to improve on my skills. I have everything that I could ever want, and more except—" He stopped.

I looked at him.

He looked at me, his brown eyes sparkling under the moonlight. "I have this girl who wants all of the perks of this lifestyle, but isn't willing to deal with all that *comes* with this lifestyle, ya feel me?"

I rolled my eyes. I knew what the hell that meant. "You're cheating on her, huh?"

Jamie laughed aloud. "Is *that* what you call it?"

I just looked at him. "Really? Sticking your dick in a bitch who's not your girlfriend? Yeah, honey, that constitutes cheating. Y'all niggas kill me."

Jamie took a hit from his cigarette. He shook his head. "I just can't see myself with one woman."

I shook my head. "No, you just haven't found the woman that you want yet. You haven't found that *one* woman yet who makes you wanna settle down."

"I had a girl once who I just knew I wanted to be with foreva'." Jamie shook his head to himself.

I looked at him.

He looked at me. "So-so, how is she?"

I knew Ne'Vaeh's name would come up sooner or later. I wanted to avoid that subject, but I should have known Jamie well enough to know when he wanted to vent about the past. So, I let him vent.

"She's still Ne'Vaeh. All school, no play. Since you left, niggas don't stand a chance with her. She talked about you for two years straight after you left. She was really hurt. Took her a minute, but she learned to deal with the fact that you weren't coming back. I know you stopped calling because she never returned your calls, but I think you should call her sometime. She hasn't forgotten you, and I think she would wanna hear from you, boo." I sipped from my champagne flute.

Jamie shook his head. "Nah, shorty wouldn't wanna hear from me. She's mad at me for leaving her. Shorty, you know, she's the only girl I ever loved. Everybody else—the girl I'm with now, included—was just a substitute. I never forgave myself for leaving her to stay with my dad, but . . . I had to go. My father came looking for me. He knew I needed him. Ne'Vaeh couldn't understand where I was coming from because she was tired of people abandoning her. I didn't mean to fuck shorty up the way I did, but I had to do what I had to do for *me*. This girl I'm with now . . . shit, I tried to love her, but you know how it is. Your mind can't tell your heart what to do, you know what I'm sayin'?" Jamie's eyes sparkled.

I nodded, taking the rest of champagne left in the bottle to the head.

Jamie looked at me. "So what about you?"

I glanced at him before popping open a bottle of gin. "What *about* me?" I opened up a bottle of orange juice. I shook my head, not really in the mood for talking about my nonexistent love life.

"From what I can remember, you're not that much different than me, shorty." Jamie blew smoke through his nostrils.

I rolled my eyes, pouring a little gin in my orange juice. "People *can* change, Jamie."

"*Can* they?" He flicked his cigarette out into the sand, then sat back against the stair rails facing me.

I nodded. "Hell yes. I met someone in high school. *He's* the reason I wanted to change. I *had* to change. He saved me from myself. I mean, damn, you remember the old me, right?"

Jamie laughed aloud. "Is this a trick question? You *really* want me to answer that?"

I rolled my eyes, watching him laugh at me. "Yeah, okay, it's obvious that you do. Yes, you're probably the *only* guy on the football team that I didn't fuck, and that was only because I have known you all my life and because you were Ne'Vaeh's man."

Jamie smiled a little.

"I had a few issues going on back then, I'll admit to that. I craved attention, fame, recognition, and dick. It wasn't until junior year of high school that I met Aaron." My eyes started to glisten while I was thinking about him. "I didn't give a fuck *who* else wanted that man. The moment I saw him, I knew he was mine. I didn't even give the nigga a chance to ask me out—I asked him out on a date within the first thirty seconds of our first conversation!"

Jamie shook his head at me, taking the orange juice bottle from my hand. "Yeah, that's typical Charlene Campbell."

"I just go for what I want, Jamie—you know how I do," I whispered, taking the bottle back from him.

"So, what's the problem now?" Jamie watched as I took a gulp of orange juice.

I swallowed hard, holding the bottle firmly in both hands. "From the moment I met Aaron, I knew I wanted and needed to change. I gave up my whole lifestyle the moment I set eyes on him. I erased all the male contacts in my cell phone that weren't family members, I threw away all my provocative clothes, I took all of my revealing pictures off of My Space and Facebook, I had some of my nude tattoos removed, and I threw away my homemade porno tapes. I did a *major* transformation. I didn't leave a trace behind of who I was before we met . . . or so I *thought,* anyway." My eyes swelled up with tears.

Jamie already knew the deal. "Hatin'-ass bitches."

I nodded, "Shit, niggas, too. Nobody wanted me to forget that life. They let Aaron know *every*thing about me from day one. At first, he didn't let what they were saying bother him because he knew that people make shit up when they don't want to see a person happy. But more and more people approached him about me, and he started to question me. As long as I was that slutty, fuck-you-and-your-friends, fuck-you-and-your-girl cheerleader that I was, everything was all good. As soon as they saw that I wanted to change because I met a man who *made* me wanna change, oh, all hell broke loose. I made a lot of mistakes. I did a lot of shit that I had no business doing with a lot of men who were already in relationships with some girls that I knew. I have changed drastically, but nobody supported me except for Ne'Vaeh. I know I was an embarrassment to that girl, but she never turned her back on me."

I exhaled deeply then continued. "Alisha's bitch ass told Aaron *everything* about me. She's pissed because she thinks I fucked Ashton. Okay, yeah, I sucked his dick back in the ninth grade, but that was it. Okay, maybe I fucked up, but I didn't deserve this shit! Just when I meet a guy who I want to be with, my past comes back to haunt me. Aaron hasn't left me yet, but it's coming."

Jamie shook his head, "Nah, shorty. If he wanted to leave you, he would have left when he first heard the shit. How long you been with him?"

"It'll be three years in January," I replied. "Not long enough to think that he's gonna stay with me. He won't touch me, kiss me, fuck me, look at me—*nothing*."

"Everybody has problems, shorty. No relationship is perfect." Jamie took a pack of Newports out of his pocket.

"I miss him . . . I miss *us*." I took a sip of orange juice. "I want the old Aaron back. The one who used to hold me, kiss me, make love to me, see me. All he sees is the old me. I'm not that girl anymore, Jamie. I *swear* I'm not that girl anymore." Tears started to slide down my face, and I quickly dried them. "Oh my goodness, I'm sorry. You don't wanna hear this bullshit."

Jamie put a cigarette to his lips and lit it. He shook his head, inhaling. He exhaled smoke from his lips and nose. "Nah, shorty, you're good. I'm here to listen."

I shook my head, taking another sip of alcohol. I was getting tipsy as a muthafucka. "My life is *not* how I want it to be right now. Your life seems so calm and peaceful. Look at this beach. Oh my goodness."

Jamie smirked, "Peaceful? No, my life is *not* peaceful, shorty. Are you serious? I *never* get to chill like this. If you hadn't come over here, shit, my homeboys would be here, bringing about seven or eight groupies with them. I would be in the hot tub right now fuckin' about three or four females. Shit is hard work."

I rolled my eyes. "TMI, Jamie. *Seriously?* Who wants to hear some shit like that?"

Jamie laughed a little. "Just keepin' it one hunnid."

I rolled my eyes. "Whateva, Jamie. That orgy shit is old and played, I'm sorry. After awhile, you'll get tired of itchin' and going to the gynecologist every other week. *Trust* me."

Jamie laughed a little to himself.

It was quiet for a few seconds.

He sat there looking at me, watching me drink. "So," he hesitated, "when *is* the last time you and your man— Aaron, is it—had sex?"

I looked at him. "Like three months ago."

Jamie's eyes grew huge. "Whoa."

I nodded. "Yeah, I know, right? And even longer if you're talking about *good* sex. Shit, when we *do* have sex, he doesn't even kiss me, touch me, or look at me. He just bends me over, doesn't even want to see my face. He hits it then quits it. I can't even remember the last time that we spent time together like me and you are doing right now. I can't even remember what his lips feel like on mine." My eyes watered again.

Jamie looked at me. He heard the pain in my voice. He reached over and took the orange juice from me before I could take another drink.

I dried the tears that began to fall again.

Jamie stood up, pulling me up with him. He pulled his shirt over his head.

I looked at him, my drunk heart pounding in my chest.

"Let's go for a swim." He pulled me closer to him by my shirt and started to unbutton it.

I just looked into his face as he removed my shirt from my body. "A swim?"

Jamie grinned as he unbuttoned my pants, his hands grazing against my belly button ring. He undressed down to his shorts and began walking past me, Polo boxers showing. "C'mon, shorty." He walked off the porch, across the sand, to the water.

I watched him undress all the way to this boxers. My heart raced in my chest as I undressed down to my violet Victoria's Secret push-up bra and low-rise panties. I walked down the porch steps and across the sand and stood in the wet sand, the water washing up against my feet. I was a little scared to go into the water any deeper, though I had been thinking about wading in that water *all* day, if you know what I mean.

Jamie signaled me to come in farther. "Feels good, right?" he whispered as I walked toward him.

The water was above his waist, and just below my breasts.

I faced him, tears lining my lashes. "What would your girl think if she knew you were alone like this, with a half-naked girl as fly as me, on a beach?"

"Shit," Jamie grinned, "she's probably sending me a text right *now* that says, 'your ass better not be alone on a beach with some little bitch'!"

I smiled a little. "You're a trip. . . ." I was terribly nervous. I knew where the night was going, and at that moment, I wasn't so sure I was ready to go there. I was starting to miss Aaron, and I was starting to think about how Ne'Vaeh must have felt when she was alone with Jamie. He was so charming and so charismatic. Everything he did felt good. He was so sexy, his skin looked so soft, and his lips looked so moist. Jamie was still the same old Jamie. He was who I used to be two years before. He had no problem getting a girl into bed with him. He was so smooth. He knew all the right moves.

I looked up at him. He wasn't even thinking about his girl or Ne'Vaeh. "You didn't even tell me your girlfriend's name. She must not mean that much if you can't even tell me her name."

Jamie grinned. "Why you wanna know her name? You want her number too, so you can call her and tell her where I am and what I'm doing? While we're at it, how about you give me Aaron's number, so I can call him and tell him that I have his girl here with me and what I plan on doing with her in just a few minutes."

I laughed nervously. He always was a smart-ass. "All I'm saying is that I remember how much in love with Ne'Vaeh you were back in high school. You can't tell me that you don't miss her or even think about her."

Jamie looked at me. "I try my best not to think about her too much. I have a girl—*Pamela*—now. I'll admit, I do find myself thinking about what could have been, but . . . but who *doesn't* do that shit?"

My eyes sparkled. I wished someone felt that way about me. "Do-do you still love her?"

Jamie's eyes sparkled back. "I haven't talked about shorty in years. I want to keep it that way, Charlie, you feel me?" was his response. He loved her. I could hear it in his voice and the way he kept trying to avoid the topic of her. He just didn't want to admit to himself that despite all the women he'd had in his life, his heart still belonged to Ne'Vaeh. A woman he hadn't seen in four years.

"Well, I love Aaron. I'll admit my life wasn't right for a long time, and my past is just coming back to kick me in the ass, but I just want someone to look at me and see me for who I really am, and what I really need. Aaron never saw me. He never saw past my looks. He never saw my heart. He never tried and as soon as he heard about—not *saw*—a side of me that he didn't like, he turned his back on me. Like I said before, he hasn't left yet, but the time is coming." I lowered my head.

Jamie shook his head, looking down at me.

I shook my head back. "He's ready to give up on me, and I wish the muthafucka would just dump me instead of stringing me along. I'm so tired of feeling this way, Jamie. I wanna be happy. I wanna feel good about life."

"What did you come here for tonight, outside of leaving the party before you beat Alisha's ass?"

I just looked up at him.

"Did you come here to talk about Aaron or to forget about that muthafucka for a few days?" His hands slid around my waist.

My heart skipped a beat. I looked up at him. "Jamie, I haven't slept with anyone *but* Aaron in over two years, since the very day I laid eyes on him. But yet, when he looks at me, all he can see is that girl who slept with hundreds of people. I know I fucked up, Jamie. I know I don't deserve someone like him. But I just need him to see the person that I am now. Why can't he see me, Jamie? Me, just me!" I cried.

"C'mon, shorty, don't cry." Jamie tilted my chin so our eyes could meet. He tried to dry my tears, but I took his hands from my face.

I shook my head. "Jamie, I'll be okay."

He ignored me because he knew I needed affection. He surrounded me in his arms. He gently kissed my neck, and my whole body trembled. I could feel his heart beating against my chest. His body was so silky, smooth, and warm, and oh, he smelled so good. His muscular arms were so strong. His body was amazing. He held me close against his body. I could feel his dick rising, poking me in the stomach.

Jamie sucked on my neck until I couldn't take it anymore. I giggled, trying to pull away, but he wouldn't loosen his arms or his lips, and I laughed aloud.

"Jamie, stop!" I squealed.

He laughed, removing his lips from my neck.

I dried my tears of sorrow, which had turned into tears of joy. "Oh my goodness, Jamie! You still know how to make a girl smile even when she's upset. But you *did* promise me that you'd keep your hands to yourself, and you didn't keep your promise."

He looked down into my face. "No, I said that I would *try* to be on my best behavior. I tried to keep my hands to myself. I swear I tried. But listening to you talk about what your man's not giving you is only giving me ideas of what I would do if I had the chance, and since you're here with me, I *do* have the chance."

I so needed the affection that he was giving me. I needed someone to make me smile and make me laugh, even when times were bad. I hadn't seen Jamie since I was fifteen, and here he was, four years later, making me feel like no time had passed between us. He'd never crossed the line, never hit on me. He never so much as even looked at me in a sexual way. And despite how my life was back then, he never judged me or called me out of my name.

I looked up at him as he lifted my body up, wrapping my legs around his waist.

He held me close against his body. "It's just you and me tonight. Nobody else is here with us. My girl, Pamela, isn't here. Your man, Aaron, isn't here, and your best friend and my ex-girlfriend, Ne'Vaeh, isn't here. It's just us. I think we could both use a vacation away from stress. I think you came here because you wanted to get fucked."

I blushed a little, not wanting to admit that I needed some dick. A girl who used to know how to make a nigga come in his pants just by dancing with him needed to get laid? I was ashamed of myself. I had completely changed for Aaron, and where did it get me? I was still being judged as if I were that same girl, so what was the point of changing?

"I can't lie," Jamie gently kissed my lips. "When I ran into you today, seeing how fine that ass was lookin' in those tight-ass jeans, yeah, I wanted to hit it. But once we started talking, and I could see that you were in pain, I knew what you needed more than anything was to feel some affection. I want to make you feel good, Charlene. I've known you since elementary school. You've made mistakes. Shit, we all have. You're human, shorty. You've grown a lot too. I can see that. You've changed for a muthafucka, who can't even see that. He didn't know you like I knew you, shorty. I see you, Charlene. I *really* see you. You're *more* than beautiful. You're a woman who owned up to her past and made an effort to change.

So even if that muthafucka can't see you, *I* see you, Charlene."

Tears slid down my face as I felt Jamie unsnap my bra.

I helped slide it from my arms and held it in my hands. I nearly lost my mind as he kissed my breasts, sucking my left nipple into his mouth. He sucked on my nipple until my pussy started throbbing.

I held his head in my hands, running my hands across his smooth, low-cut fade.

He kissed all the way up to my lips, and I nearly lost my mind as his lips touched mine. He held me tighter against him. We nearly ate each other's lips off at that moment. I hadn't been kissed that way in so long. I needed him, *all* of him that night. He ran his fingers through my hair. He tugged on my hair just a little. He gripped my behind as he carried me back toward shore. We made it halfway across the beach to the house, when he got down on his knees and laid me on the sand, hovering over the top of me. He gripped my thigh in one hand and slipped my panties down with the other. I helped slide them off my body. Then I helped him slide his wet boxers off.

Jamie lay down between my legs. He didn't waste any time sliding his hard dick inside of my extremely wet pussy. I sunk my nails into his shoulders as his tongue penetrated my lips, and his dick penetrated my soul. Our wet thighs slapped together as he pumped in and out of me.

"Jamie!" I screamed out, "Please . . . fuck me," I cried.

"Your pussy feels so wet . . . so warm. . . . *Fuck*, this shit is good," Jamie whispered between kisses. His body shivered as he pumped deeper inside of me.

I held on to him as he dug into my soul—and then abruptly pulled out of me and sat up.

I sat up, nearly out of breath. I looked down at his dick. It was still nice and hard, covered in my pussy juices. He didn't bust yet, so why did he stop?

"Wh-what's wrong? Oh my gosh, why did you stop?" My chest heaved in and out, as I watched him pick up his boxers, along with my panties and bra.

He looked up at me and held my hands, pulling me up off the wet sand. "C'mon." He led me to the house.

We walked up the steps into the beach house. Jamie tossed his boxers and my underwear on the couch. I stood there naked as I watched him walk over to the stereo to turn it on. The sounds of R&B singer Jamie Foxx flowed through the speakers.

I smiled nervously, eyes already full of tears, as Jamie walked over to me.

He looked down into my face as he held my hips, then gently kissed my lips.

I cried in his mouth. His hands, his lips, and his body felt so good up against mine. He backed me up against the wall, lifted my body up, and I wrapped my legs around his waist.

Jamie braced my body up against the wall as he slid himself inside of me and began to grind to the music. I moaned as Jamie sang in my ear. With every stroke, my pussy spit fluids down his thighs. His dick was saturated.

"How does it feel, Charlie?" he moaned, pumping harder.

I sighed. "Like fuckin' magic," I cried out passionately.

"Tell me you like it." He pounded to the rhythm of the drums in the song.

"I *love* it." I dug my nails in his shoulders.

"If I taste that pussy, would you put your lips on this dick? Your lips are so thick and juicy. I wanna kiss those lips between your thighs like a muthafucka, shorty. And I want these lips" Jamie gently kissed my lips, sucking on my bottom lip just a little, "on this dick. I know that shit would feel good as fuck, and I promise to make that pussy purr over and over in my mouth. Can we make that happen tonight?"

I burst out in tears. I loved every bit of the way that Jamie was making me feel inside and out that night, but I was angry at the same damn time.

Jamie watched the tears slid down my face. He stopped stroking me but still held my legs around my waist, bracing me up against the wall. "Do you want me to stop?"

I couldn't stop crying enough to respond to him.

Jamie pulled himself out of me, then lowered my feet back down to the floor. He looked down into my face, his body still pressed up against mine. "Why are you crying? What am I doing wrong?" he whispered.

I looked up at him, shaking my head. "What? No, Jamie, you're not doing *anything* wrong. You're-you're doing everything just right, just perfect. I wish I had more of this each and every day."

Jamie knew what the problem was. He wasn't Aaron, and he knew how much that I wished that he were. I was in love with Aaron, yet Aaron was far from being in love with me. And I was there making what felt like love to a man that my own best friend once loved with all of her heart for years.

Jamie held my face and dried my tears. "Charlie, 'til this day, you are still one of the hottest, finest women that I have ever met."

I shook my head, rolling my eyes. "Whateva, Jamie, you don't have to flatter me."

He shook his head, "Nah, nah, I'm not just saying that. Man, all them niggas in middle school and in high school wanted your ass. And it wasn't because you was fuckin' some of them, shorty—it was because they was in love with you. You're sexy, smart, talented, and you're beautiful. Your lips, eyes, hair, skin, ass, thighs, shit, your pussy—*everything* about you is sexier than a muthafucka. If I wasn't constantly on the road, didn't already have a girl, and if your best friend wasn't my ex, I swear to you that I would do whatever it took to make you mine. You know I couldn't care less about your nigga, right?"

Tears trickled down my face.

"I've known you since elementary school. I don't give a fuck about your past. You're a beautiful person, Charlie, real talk. We've been friends for a long time, before it even came down to this moment. That nigga, Aaron, is crazy. If he doesn't love you the way that you want him to love you, maybe it's time that you let him go and stop wasting your time. And stop crying. The Charlene Campbell that *I* know never cried over no nigga. You know better than that shit, ma."

I looked up at him as he backed up and pulled me to him by my hands. He turned my body around then held me by the waist, grinding his body up against my booty. I began to grind my booty and hips up against his dick, in time to the music.

He kissed my neck, rubbing his hands across my stomach, hips, ass, and between my legs. I gyrated my hips up against his dick until precome began to drip from the tip.

"*Shit,*" he moaned, turning my body around to face his.

I looked up into his face.

Jamie held my hands, leading me into the bedroom. He sat down on the bed, pulling my body in between his legs. I sat down on his lap, swinging my legs around, facing his body. I lifted my ass a little, holding his dick, easing it inside of me. I looked down into his face, and he looked up at me, biting his lip. He held on to my hips as I began to bounce on his dick. It was the perfect size . . . not too big, not too long, not ginormous. It was just right, and it curved to the left just a little.

Jamie gripped my waist, damn near digging his nails into my skin. He moaned as I rode him. "*Charlene.*" Jamie called out my name as I locked my knees around his waist and rode him until he couldn't take it anymore.

He held my waist, signaling me to stop before I made him come. We quickly switched positions. He lay me down on the bed, lying between my legs.

My tears saturated the pillow as Jamie began to dig deep into my pussy as if he was digging a hole, digging for buried treasure. Deep sex, yeah, that was what I needed. Jamie pumped in and out of me. I gripped his ass in my hands.

I was just about to come. Jamie felt my body begin to moisten and the walls of my pussy begin to tighten. Then, he pounded harder. I cried even more as my body jerked. We came together, as he bit down on my neck.

All Jamie's weight fell on me as his heart beat strong and steady in his chest. I held on to him as tightly as I could. His body felt so warm against mine. I inhaled his scent. He smelled so good.

Jamie buried his face in my neck. "*Damn . . . Baby?*"

"Hmmm?" I fought back the tears, loving the sound of his voice in my ear.

"How many more days do I have you?" He gently kissed my neck.

Just when I was about to answer, I heard my cell phone ring in my purse. The ring tone was my favorite old-school song, "Come Talk to Me." It was Aaron.

"Aaron!" I whispered excitedly, butterflies fluttering in my stomach.

Jamie laughed a little to himself as he pulled out of me.

I couldn't get to my phone fast enough. I almost tripped over my own two feet. "Hello?" I answered the phone, damn near out of breath.

"*Hey, baby, what's up?*" Aaron's voice was music to my heart.

"Nothing much. Just chillin' with my people. Ran into a few old friends." I laughed nervously.

"Sorry it took me all day to call. I had basketball practice, I had to work, and then I went out to get some drinks with the fellas. You enjoying yourself? I mean, are you behaving yourself?" I could hear him exhaling, which meant he was smoking. I hated that. Aaron hid his health from the team, but he hadn't outgrown his asthma. He just had a doctor who knew he was good at playing basketball and didn't want to ruin his career.

I looked up, watching Jamie make his way to the bathroom. I knew I was making him feel uncomfortable. "Ummm, yeah, of course, I'm behaving myself. I haven't whooped Alisha's ass yet, if that's what you mean. She's still breathing, so everything is all good."

Aaron laughed a little. *"So, how long are you gonna be in MIA?"*

"A few more days." My eyes glistened. I was starting to feel a little guilty because he actually sounded like he missed me.

"When you get home, Charlie, we need to go out and have some fun. I'm tired of working twenty-four-seven, not spending any time with my girl. I wanna take my baby out and show her off. When is the last time that we went out and had some fun?"

I smiled a little to myself as I began to cry. "Like four months ago." I could hear people talking and the faint sound of music playing in the background. "Where are you?"

He hesitated. *"In the restroom at Purple Panties."*

I rolled my eyes, drying my face. Purple Panties was a new strip club that the basketball team went to on a damn near daily basis. I knew most of the hoes who worked up in there, and they damn sure didn't make all that money they made by just dancing. Those bitches got buck-ass naked onstage, damn near fucked dudes onstage, and went with about two, three, or even four guys to the "champagne room." I don't give a fuck what Chris Rock said—there *is* sex in the champagne room.

"Oh my goodness, Aaron, you know I hate when you go to that fuckin' club. Please wash your hands when you leave there if you touch any of those girls." I reached for my bra and panties. "And do *not* take your ass in that champagne room, do you hear me?"

"Hey, Charlie, I gotta go. I'll give you a call tomorrow, a'ight?" Aaron acted as if he didn't hear my comment.

I sighed, "All right, Aaron. I love you, baby."

I waited to hear an "I love you" back. But I waited in vain.

"Talk to you later, babe." He hung up.

I just sat there on the floor, phone still to my ear. The tears started rolling again.

"Everything all right, shorty?" I heard Jamie's voice behind me.

I took the phone from my ear, quickly drying my tears. I stood up, turning around facing Jamie. He was dressed in his wife beater and Ralph Lauren boxers.

I nodded, faking a smile as I slid back into my bra and panties. "Everything's all good," I whispered.

"You in the mood for another drink?" Jamie walked past me, over to the kitchen area.

"Yeah, sure. I could use a drink or two." I ran my fingers through my hair anxiously. I went over and sat at the bistro table, watching Jamie as he took out a bottle of Grey Goose from the fridge.

"Jamie?" I called out.

He looked at me as he reached into the cabinet for two glasses. "What's up?"

"Thank you for tonight," I whispered. "I really needed this."

He looked at me and smiled a little. "Did I warm you up enough to go back to your man?"

I looked at him, shocked that he would imply that I actually used him. "Oh, so, you think I used you? That's not what this was, Jamie. You have a girl like I have a man, so before you wanna go throwing up those types of comments—"

Jamie laughed, cutting me off. "Shorty, I'm just sayin', though, you couldn't get to the phone quick enough. Pamela has been blowin' up my phone all day long, and you haven't seen me answer the phone *once*. As a matter of fact, you haven't seen me check my phone *once* to see who it was. I just know it was shorty because she calls me three times back-to-back, then texts me about three times back-to-back, then sends me a message on Facebook about three times, then calls again back-to-back for about an hour straight. The girl blows my phone up when I don't answer. I have a life outside of her, man. Aaron's ass didn't call you all day, and as soon as he did, you nearly broke a toe trying to answer the phone. What did you expect me to say?" Jamie sat down at the bar next to me. "You sprung, shorty. The nigga's got you *sprung*."

I hesitated. "So, maybe he does, okay? I guess I'm still looking for something that's not there. I need him to need me, and he doesn't." I shrugged.

"Shit, it is what it is, shorty." Jamie popped open the bottle. "And if it's not, well, then, shit, it's just not. And you don't need that shit. You deserve love, Charlene. You don't deserve bullshit. It's about time you start realizing your worth. You fine as a *muthafucka*, Charlene. You deserve so much better." He poured me a glass then poured a glass for himself.

I took the glass.

Jamie held up his glass to toast me. "To five days together. No worries. No drama. No boyfriend. No girl-friend. No bullshit. No *crying*. Just fun, smoking, drinking, shopping, and fuckin'. Just you and me. Fuck everything else. A'ight?"

Tears lined my lashes. I nodded, holding my glass up to him. "I'll toast to that."

The week went by fast, *too* fast. I didn't want it to end. Jamie and I went out on the town. I went with him to just about all of his TV appearances that week. I went with him to two parties. We went to four or five movies that week. In public, we were old friends catching up. But in private, shit, we were like two lovers who had spent months apart. We had sex at least three or four times a day. I ended up staying with him the entire week. He wasn't lying when he said that he was a celebrity. He made time for me when he really didn't have the time, and it felt great. We were inseparable that week. I was having a great time, and I really didn't want to leave him. He had my body on fire whenever he touched me. He sparked a flame inside my soul that Aaron hadn't even bothered to tend to. I felt with him what I wanted to feel with Aaron. Jamie was more than a friend at that moment. I waded in waters too deep, and I was drowning in it.

Chapter 5

Deeper

Charlene

I met back up with the cheerleading squad just in time for our flight to leave.

Alisha folded her arms as I walked up to the squad. She tapped her Prada shoes against the terminal floor. "Well well well, look who finally decided to grace us with her presence. If it isn't Queen Charlene," she hissed.

I rolled my eyes, flipping my hair over my shoulder. "Alisha, I am not in the mood for your shit today, so you need to back the fuck off."

"For real, Charlie, where have you been?" Kelissa asked. Kelissa was a short, petite, brown-skinned girl with long hair and hazel eyes. She didn't too much care for Alisha either, but she always took her side to avoid confrontation. "Half of the clubs that we wanted to get in wouldn't even let us in without you, the 'Redbone Bombshell.' You wanna fill us in on where you were?"

I looked at Alisha. They all stood there waiting on me to respond. I shook my head. "Last time I checked, my daddy was dead and my mama was in Maryland. I'm grown, and I don't have to answer to none of y'all bitches. I went and spent some time by myself. I had to get away from y'all to avoid opening up a can of kill-a-trick on a few of y'all, okay?" I rolled my eyes.

"Excuse me," I heard a sweet, gentle female voice call out over my shoulder.

I turned around to see bright, Colgate-clean teeth gleaming at me. She was the color of soft caramel, with long, dark, silky hair and bright brown eyes. Her lips were full and glossy. She was about five foot five, with a Coke-bottle figure and dressed very classy. She wore a white button-down shirt, tight smoky-gray pants, and a gray scarf around her neck. She smiled at me, handing me a brown leather wallet. "Sweetie, you left this in the cab. I was just about to get in when I saw it in the backseat. You were in such a hurry. I don't think you heard me calling out to you."

I hesitated, taking the wallet from her. "Thanks, hon. Oh my goodness, girl, my *life* is in this wallet!" I laughed a little.

Alisha pointed at her. "Hey, you look real familiar."

The young lady smiled. "Yeah, some of you all do too."

"Wait a minute, I know you." Lailah, the Puerto Rican cutie in the squad, stepped forward. "You're captain of the cheerleading squad at Memphis State! I saw you doing your thing at one of y'all's basketball games in Charlotte last year when I went to visit my cousin last season! Your team has mad skills! Y'all make that shit look effortless!"

The young lady shook her head. "No, we just work our ass off. We have our flaws, trust me. We just know how to dress it up a little on the court." She looked at me. "I know who you are too. Seen you at a few competitions. I think my boyfriend even said he went to school with you."

I looked at her, and my heart skipped a beat, for what reason, I don't know. Seems like my body caught on to the situation before my mind did. "School with me? What did you say your name was?"

She smiled, holding her hand out to shake mine. "Oh my goodness, I'm so rude. I'm Pamela Rhodes, trying to be Pamela Green, if you know what I mean."

Alisha loved the expression on my face. She laughed a little. "Green—as in *Jamie* Green? Yes, girl, I went to school with him freshman year in high school. Shit, Charlene here practically grew up with him. How *is* he doing?" Alisha elbowed me a little, waking me up from my daze, and forcing me to pick my jaw up from the floor.

"Great! He's here on a few television appearances. We took separate vacations. Thought I'd surprise him. I'm here with my parents for a few days." Pamela smiled sweetly. "I'm sure y'all have seen him and his teammates."

"Oh, I thought that was him at that basketball party about a week ago. Nope, didn't say much to him, though. Charlie, did you speak to him?" Alisha grinned at me.

The squad giggled.

I shook my head nervously. "Girl, I probably wouldn't recognize him if I did. Haven't seen him in years, but when you do see him, tell him I said hi."

Just when I thought the situation couldn't get any worse, we all caught sight of Jamie and a few of his teammates walking toward us. You should have seen the look on his face when Pamela went running up to him, jumping into his arms. She was happy to see him, not even stopping to wonder why he showed up at the airport when he didn't even know she was arriving. She was there to surprise him, and he was there to say good-bye to me.

Jamie looked over her shoulder at me, as she hugged him around his neck. We never exchanged numbers. I planned to leave things the way they were, but apparently, he wanted something more. We both agreed that week was just that week—something we both needed—well, maybe me more than him. I didn't see a need to get his number, since I was going back to Maryland to deal with my own situation. Up until that point, I wasn't even feeling bad about cheating on Aaron with Jamie, especially after Aaron called me from the strip club and couldn't even tell me he loved me over the phone. However, when I saw Pamela hugging Jamie as if he was the most important person in the world to her, I felt like a true slut. She held on to him the same way that Ne'Vaeh once held on to him. I couldn't help but think that sleeping with Jamie was the worst thing I could have done to a woman who didn't deserve that.

"Shorty, what's up? What are you doing here?" Jamie was as shocked to see Pamela as I was shocked to see him show up at the airport.

Pamela let go of Jamie, slapping him in the shoulder playfully. "Sweetie, my mom came here to visit my aunt, who's having a baby in a few days. I just wanted to surprise you! You must've been real busy since you weren't returning any of my calls!" Pamela looked over at me and saw me staring straight back at Jamie. She looked at Jamie. "What are you doing here, Jamie? I didn't tell you I was flying in."

Jamie looked at me, then back at Pamela. "Oh . . . My homies wanted to come wish the ladies luck this coming basketball season. A few of the girls from the squad showed up at the party the fellas threw at a club last week. They was just stopping by to give their number to a few of the ladies on the squad. Ain't that right, fellas?"

They nodded behind him, agreeing and spread out, walking up to the ladies on my squad.

One of Jamie's teammates stepped to me, handing me a folded-up sheet of paper.

I took it from him, grasping it in my hand while glancing at Jamie over his shoulder.

Pamela looked at me. "What was your name again? Charlene, is it?" She turned to Jamie. "Jamie, this is Charlene. She said she went to school with you."

Jamie nodded, "Yeah, we did." He looked at me. "You were friends with Ne'Vaeh, right? Tell her I said what's up when you see her."

I nodded, clearing my throat, "W-will do."

Pamela pulled on Jamie's arm. "Sweetie, we need to get going. My mother is waiting. Tell your friends you'll catch up with them later. It was nice meeting you all."

Passengers boarding flight IG F8122, please report to the passenger service center at this time.

"Well, that's us, fellas." Alisha hugged and kissed one of the players on the team. "It was nice meeting some of y'all and reuniting with a few of y'all! The party was off the fuckin' chain! Until the next party, y'all!"

The girls hurried over to the flight attendant to hand over their boarding passes.

I couldn't move. My feet were planted on the ground.

Jamie looked back at me as Pamela locked arms with him, leading him away from the passenger terminal. He winked at me, and my heart melted.

"C'mon, Charlie!" Kelissa grabbed my arm, pulling me off to board the plan.

We stuffed our carry-on bags in the compartments above our head and sat down in our first-class seats. Just when I sat down at the window, finally able to breathe again, Alisha sits her big butt beside me.

I looked at her, rolling my eyes. "I thought Karla was supposed to be sitting next to me, Alisha."

"We switched seats, boo. I thought I would enjoy sitting next to you." She grinned.

I looked at her. I smelled a blackmail coming on. "What the fuck do you want, Alisha?"

"I know you fucked Jamie, Charlene Campbell." She glared at me, pointing at my face with her American-manicured pointer finger.

"And how the fuck—"

Alisha put her hand in my face, cutting me off. "Don't try to play me, bitch. You walk different, talk different, skin glowing and shit. And I saw the way he looked at you. You fucked your best friend's ex-boyfriend, and instead of being ashamed, you're actually falling for the nigga."

I hated that bitch, but she was right. "Like I said, Alisha, what the *fuck* do you want?"

"I want you to quit the cheerleading squad," she grinned.

My eyes widened. "You must have lost your fuckin' mind if you think I'm going to give up something that I have been working my whole life for!"

Alisha couldn't care less. "You have until homecoming game to give up your pom-poms, boo, or I'm telling Ne'Vaeh. And it's as simple as that."

I shook my head at her. "You have no proof that I slept with Jamie, the same way that you have no proof that I ever slept with Ashton's ass, trick."

Alisha looked at me as if she wanted to smack me in the face for even bringing up Ashton's name. "I don't? Back in high school, you had niggas callin' their girl 'Charlie' every time their girl gave them head, and why? Because you were giving them niggas head. You had them niggas asking their girls to swallow that shit, and why? Because *your* nasty ass was swallowing that shit. When I gave Ashton head the first time, the nigga called me 'Charlie,' and why is that, bitch?"

I sat back in my seat, looking out the window. I couldn't even deny what the bitch was saying. "I'm not quitting the team. I don't give a fuck what you say. You have no proof of that shit you talkin'." I looked back at her, my eyes glistening. "*No* proof."

"What's on the note Jerry handed you? Did you even *look* at it?" Alisha asked.

I hadn't looked at it, and I didn't even realize that I still had it in my hands. I hesitated. What did I have to lose by opening the note? I unfolded it.

Alisha leaned over to take a peek. *"I can still feel your lips on it. Until the next episode. 901-761-3228, Jamie G."* She looked at me.

I looked up at her, swallowing hard. That nigga Jamie, boy, I tell you . . .

Alisha was disgusted. "Ol' nasty-ass bitch. Still suckin' dick. You a dick-sucker. You'd probably suck mine too, if I had one."

"Shut up, Alisha." I rolled my eyes, folding the note back up. "Keep talkin' shit."

"Homecoming game, Charlie." Alisha shook her head at me.

It was the second week of school at Morgan State, and we were behind on cheerleading tryouts. I was going through my own personal issues and really wasn't in the mood for being one of the judges on the panel that chose which girls were worthy of being on our cheerleading squad. I had an eye for talent, which is why I was on the panel, but I really wasn't feeling it that day. Alisha had already warned me that I only had a few months to come clean about my affair with Jamie.

Four weeks had passed since Miami, and I found out just a few days before tryouts that I was pregnant. I wasn't exactly sure how I was going to deal with the situation. I'd avoided any contact with Ne'Vaeh, and I made it a habit to seduce Aaron from the very day that I found out that I was pregnant. If I decided on keeping the baby, I had to get the timing right. Aaron kept his promise of trying to spend more time with me. However, it wasn't until the night that I found out that I was pregnant that I finally came around to sleeping with him. Though I loved the attention from Aaron, a part of me couldn't help but wish that I was back on that beach with Jamie.

"Girl, are you all right?" Dana, the assistant cheerleading coach, nudged me in my shoulder that afternoon at tryouts.

I snapped out of my daze. "I'm good." I looked up into her pretty brown eyes, faking a grin. "I'm good."

Her eyes searched mine. "Mm-hmm. Well, we need to make a decision. We should have had a decision like *yesterday*, and your ass is sitting over here daydreaming. We have games and tournaments coming up in like two weeks, and we don't even have our squad together yet. I'm tired of UMBC and Howard showing us up. I wouldn't be surprised if some of them bitches from College Park show up here today, *just* because they know we're having tryouts. Alisha is *pissed*, okay? And I really ain't trying to hear her mouth today."

I looked over at Alisha, who was in the middle of the basketball court, choreographing the cheers for the tryouts.

I rolled my eyes. "Man, fuck Alisha, okay?"

Danita, who sat to my left, laughed a little. "Girl, we have been dealing with y'all's drama since middle school. How long are you two gonna let that old shit dictate your lives?"

I looked at Danita, who seriously needed to get those thick-ass eyebrows tweezed before she wanted to try to check somebody. "'Old shit'? *Please,* okay? She is *still* trippin' off of that shit with Ashton. *Her* ass is the one who can't leave the past where it is. She's been accusing me of fuckin' her man for the past five years. . . ."

Dana looked at me. "Well, wasn't it *you* who told me that Ashton ate you out in the ninth grade?"

Danita burst out in laughter.

I elbowed her then looked back at Dana. "What? I *never* told your ass no shit like that! I told you that I sucked *his* dick. *Please* get your facts straight. See, that's how rumors get started. Sucking a boy's dick doesn't mean that he reciprocated the favor, *nor* does it mean that there was any penetration involved. Alisha wasn't suckin' his dick to his satisfaction, so, hey, he came to me."

Danita rolled her eyes. "Okay, *Superhead,* and you wonder why the girl can't stand you. She loves that boy. Call it what you want, but *sex* is sex. Suckin' and fuckin' are the same damn things, if you ask me."

"Well, nobody *asked* your ass, Danita." I rolled my eyes.

Danita shook her head. "Alisha can destroy you, and you know it. Fuckin' with someone's man in any type of way is suicide. Trust me. Y'all *know* that I know." Danita pulled back her hair that covered her left ear. You could still see where the doctors sewed her ear back to her damn head.

In the eleventh grade, Danita got into a fight with this Puerto Rican chick named Marcia. Marcia was the hottest, most talented dancer of the senior graduating class that year. Danita was fuckin' Marcia's boyfriend, Carlos, nearly six months before Marcia caught the two. She'd seen Carlos's car parked in front of a Motel 6. She went to the front-desk clerk to ask what room he was in. The clerk barely got the words "room 206" out before Marcia rushed off to the room. She got to the room, damn near out of breath, but as calmly as she could, she knocked on the door. She heard a woman's giggle behind the door. She knocked again then stood to the side of the door so the person wouldn't see her through the peephole. Danita's stupid ass opened the door, sticking her head out. As soon as she turned to see Marcia's face, it was too late. Before the bitch could run back inside and slam the door, Marcia grabbed her by her hair. If the housekeeping cart hadn't blocked Marcia from throwing Danita's ass over the railing, Danita's ass would have been dead. Before Carlos could even make it out of the room, Marcia had pulled out her got-damn knife and cut Danita's ear slap off.

I shook my head at Danita. "That's your crazy-ass life, Danita. Not mine. Nobody told you to fuck Marcia's man. She's the only girl in a family of eight boys. You knew she'd fuck your ass up on sight, no questions asked. You lucky she didn't throw your ass over the railing, you crazy bitch."

Danita laughed, shaking her head at me. "All right, Charlie, keep talking that shit. That might be you one day."

I rolled my eyes. "Please, Alisha ain't shit but talk. I knew Ashton all my life. We're just friends, regardless of whether Alisha wants to believe me. I ain't got shit to prove to her, and I *damn* sure ain't got shit to prove to y'all bitches, either."

Dana shook her head at me too. "Well, whatever. All I'm sayin' is that as bitchy and as loud as Alisha can be at times, she is cool people. Best damn captain that we could ever have on our team. You know she's leaving us in January to be a Laker Girl, right? She's going places. Where the hell are *you* going?"

I should have known that she would stick up for Alisha. I mean they *are* cousins.

I rolled my eyes.

Dana thought I was a slut too. The only reason she even hung around me was because I had connections. The reason why she really didn't like me was because she liked Ashton but never had the chance to be with him because he was with her cousin, who was "going places." Shit. Who gave a damn? Okay, *I* gave a damn. I was pregnant and scared as a motherfucka. My mom tried to convince me not to have the abortion, but at that point, I wasn't so sure. Hearing that Alisha was living her dreams was tearing me the hell apart. My reputation had gotten the best of me. I was turned down from damn near every dance audition that I went to because there were at least two judges on each panel that I'd got into it with in high school because of cheating with their man, or they were friends with the person whose man I slept with. Nineteen and my life was already shot to shit. I had no idea how I was going to get my life back. What was I going to do with a baby? Jamie's baby at that?

"You know what?" I got up from the table, but Danita grabbed me, pulling me back down. I pulled from her. "That shit with Ashton was five fuckin' years ago. We were kids. Yeah, Alisha was fuckin' him, but she wasn't *suckin'* him. So he came to me, his best friend, who, at that time, would do *any*thing for him. Yeah, I was a ho back then. Yeah, I fucked and sucked the whole basketball team! Are you happy now? Y'all can judge me if you want, but that is the past. I've changed. I moved on, and I am *not* that girl anymore! I've been with Aaron since January, junior year, spring 2012. It's almost fuckin' 2015 and y'all hoes are *still* talkin' about the same old shit! Y'all bitches helped Alisha make my life a living hell, and yeah, maybe I brought it all on myself. Aaron barely wants shit to do with me! I damn near have to rape the boy to get him to have sex with me now!"

Dana laughed a little.

I glared at her. "Oh, you wanna laugh, do you?"

She straightened up. "My bad, you're right. It's not funny. And you're right, we're wrong as hell."

"If I wanted Ashton, I could have him. Alisha needs to let that shit go and stop putting ideas in everyone's head about me." I shook my head in disgust.

Danita looked at me, tapping her pencil on the table. "Oh, okay, so I guess she's wrong about Jamie too, then, huh?"

I damn near swallowed my tongue. "Wh-what?"

"She *said* she guesses Alisha is wrong about Jamie too, then, huh?" Dana was always a fuckin' cosigner.

Danita nodded. "Alisha said that you went missing from the squad for the whole week y'all were in Miami. Said you may have been chillin' with Jamie the *whole* damn time. Wasn't Jamie your bestie's man a few years ago?"

Just when I started to answer Danita, stomping and chanting echoed throughout the gym. We looked up to see about ten girls, dressed in tight blue, tiny T-shirts and black leggings steppin' across the hardwood floors, forcing our squad and the girls trying out for our squad out of the way. Hair flippin', booties poppin', hips gyratin', flips, twerkin', feet stompin'—shit, they were *killin'* it—and made our squad look like beginners. It didn't take me long to notice the big dark blue "M" embroidered across their breasts. My eyes widened. It was the Memphis State cheerleaders.

My heart pounded in my chest as about ten dudes wearing blue and white sport coats made their way into our gym, standing back up against the wall. I looked back over at the cheerleaders, who were seriously showing us up, and I saw Pamela dancing in the center of the squad, chanting her ass off. I looked back over at the ten guys standing up against the wall, only to see Jamie staring straight back at me. My heart skipped a beat. He winked his eye at me.

I looked over at Alisha, who stood, posing with her arms folded across her chest. She looked back at me . . . and winked her eye at me too.

I shook my head at her as the Memphis State cheer-leaders' showdown came to a close. Our squad had no choice but to clap for them, even if it was a forced clap. We could hate if we wanted to, but we had to admit they had skills. I'm pretty sure the girls who were trying out for our team wished they went to Memphis State.

"Well well well, looky here." Alisha walked up to Pamela, who stood with her hands on her hips in front of her squad. "If it isn't Pamela."

Pamela grinned, breathing heavily. "What's up, girl? You know we had to pay y'all a visit to show y'all how the South gets down and dirty."

Alisha nodded. "Oh well, that *was* dirty as hell, show-ing up here when we have tryouts going on. What are y'all doin' here anyway?"

"My baby is in town visiting his sister." Pamela signaled Jamie to come over.

Alisha looked over at me, signaling us to come over too.

I shook my head, but Dana and Danita each took an arm and pulled me up from my chair. "O . . . M . . . G," I whispered, with my hand over my chest.

Dana laughed a little, letting go of my arm, making her way around the table. "It's showtime, ladies."

We made our way to the middle of the floor, just in time to meet Jamie and his boys.

"So, how long do y'all plan on staying here?" Kelissa approached the Memphis State athletes. "Shit, y'all know y'all can't leave town without us showin' *y'all* asses up at the Q party tonight."

Pamela and her squad nodded. She grinned, teeth looking like she just hopped out of the dentist's chair. "Well, we're here all weekend. We could use a little practice for nationals. We don't mind putting y'all skills to the test at your *own* school!" Her team laughed along with her.

"Well," I finally caught my breath. "It has been nice watching y'all kick our asses today, but I gotta get going. I still haven't gotten all of my schoolbooks for the semester, so . . . I'll holla . . ." I turned to walk away.

Kelissa caught my arm. "Charlie, we're supposed to be going shopping, girl! I don't got shit to wear to the Q party tonight!"

I glanced at Jamie, then looked back at Kelissa. "Girl, I'll catch back up with you. I'll call you when I leave the bookstore."

I hurried off to the bathroom before the chunks started to rise in my throat. I just knew I was going to throw up all over the floor. I could feel my stomach burning, and I could feel the tension building in my chest. I burst into the stall, kneeling down over the toilet, and instead of vomit spewing from my mouth, tears spilled from my eyes instead. How could I have been so stupid? I knew in my heart that I was in love with Aaron, but when I saw Jamie standing there in his letter jacket, looking good enough to eat, my body was on fire. There I was, pregnant with his baby, knowing good and damn well that there was no way I could keep his baby *and* keep Aaron without telling Aaron that he was my child's father.

I did end up going shopping with Dana, Danita, Kelissa, and Lailah that evening. They were pressed to get dresses with our school colors, orange, blue, and white. I ended up buying a tight, backless, royal blue minidress. I wasn't in any mood to go to a fuckin' Q party. The fraternity party scene was played out to me. Not to mention morning sickness was kicking my ass twenty-four-seven. I played it off as best as I could, but even the squad knew something was up when I didn't want anything to drink later. They danced their asses off that night, paying the Memphis State crew back for making us look bad at tryouts.

I sat at the bar, cheering from the sidelines. Jamie sat with his crew at a far corner of the club. I can't tell you how many muthafuckas were drooling over me that night. Some were hot, some *really* not. I *was* looking good in my D&G dress. My hair was slicked up into a bun. Silver hoop earrings hung from my ears. My makeup was flawless. The stilettos I had on made it look like I had legs for days. Despite how good I knew I looked, I wasn't in the mood for anybody being all up on me, smelling like sweaty balls and liquor.

Jamie caught sight of me as I took a sip from my ginger ale. I set my glass down on the bar table and quickly got up as I saw him rise in his chair. I wasn't sure where he was off to, but just in case the nigga decided to be bold and talk to me in a room full of people in front of his girl, I made my way to the bathroom.

I stood at the mirror, set my purse down, and took out my cell phone. Aaron hadn't called me once that night. Ne'Vaeh had called several times, and I had yet to return her calls. I had only looked that girl in her face about two times over the course of four weeks, and it was only because I needed help studying for calculus. I hadn't seen her since I found out that I was pregnant. There was no way that I could face her after what I had done. If I was any type of friend, I would have called the girl and told her that Jamie was in town. However, the selfish part of me actually was glad that he showed up when he did. I had to find a way to talk to him about my situation. I never called him once in those four weeks. In fact, I threw away his number the day that he gave it to me at the airport.

"So, that's how you do a nigga, huh?" I heard a deep male voice over my shoulder.

I looked up to see Jamie standing in the door to the ladies' room. My eyes widened as I backed up against the counter in shock. "Jamie, what the fuck are you doing in here? Are you *seriously* bringing your ass into the ladies' room like somebody isn't gonna walk up in here and see your ass?"

Jamie grinned as he approached me, looking down into my face. "Why didn't you call a nigga?"

I looked up into his face, eyes coated in tears. "You need to get out of here before someone sees us, Jamie! What if your girl walks the fuck up in here? How are you gonna explain this shit to her?"

Jamie reached and opened the door to a stall, and he went in, pulling me in with him by my dress. I pulled away from him as he closed the stall door behind him.

My heart pounded in my chest as I pushed him in his. "You have *some* fuckin' nerve showing up to my school with your girl and shit, Jamie! You don't love Pamela, that's cool. But I am actually in love with Aaron, a man who has a hard time trusting me because of shit like this!"

Jamie looked down into my face. "We have known each other since elementary school. Took us damn near twenty years to finally sleep together. We spent a whole week together. It wasn't just about sex. We're friends, shorty, *more* than friends."

I shook my head. "I don't know what we are now, Jamie, but we're not friends. Your girl is out there, Jamie. What would she say if she knew about this? I have a boyfriend. Jamie, we *just* had sex this morning! You don't see anything wrong with fuckin' Pamela, then turning around that same day fuckin' somebody else?"

Jamie gripped my dress in his hands and slid it up, exposing my panties. "I haven't *touched* Pamela since the day I touched you, shorty," he whispered.

Tears slid down my face. He knew just what to say. He knew just what I wanted to hear. He knew just what I needed in my life.

I shook my head, lips trembling as he unbuckled his belt, unbuttoned his pants, and dropped them to the floor. Only Jamie Green would actually have the nerve to have sex in a public bathroom, in a club where his girl was just a few steps outside the bathroom door.

I tried to resist him as he held my hips, lifting my body up, wrapping my legs around his waist, bracing my body against the door of the stall. I could feel him pulling his dick out through the hole in the boxers. He didn't take my panties off; he just pulled them bitches to the side and pushed his way through.

I squealed a little bit as he bit down on my neck and began to work the hell out of me, digging into me like a shovel. He gripped my thighs as I held on to his shoulders, trying to hold in the screams.

Jamie moaned, "Charlene, *shit*." He whispered my name, thrusting his pelvis. He worked me as if we were dancing to the music outside the door.

My pussy held on to his dick with all her might. Though she was wet as a muthafucka, she was gripping for dear life. She held on to him as if she never wanted to let him go. When I came, my body fell limply against his. He held my body against the door and worked me until my legs went numb. When he came, he let out a long sigh in my ear. Our hearts pounded against each other's chest, and he just held me for a moment. He looked up at me, and I looked down into his face as he pulled out of me and gently let my body down to the floor.

I pulled my dress down as he pulled his pants up.

Tears slid down my face as I watched him buckle his belt.

Jamie dried my tears and gently kissed my lips. "Damn," he whispered. "I swear, your pussy feels good as a mutha-fucka. Feels like the best place on earth to be, shorty."

I gently pushed him away, then opened the door to the stall. Just when I walked out of the stall, Alisha and Kelissa walked into the bathroom. My heart literally stopped beating, and I froze in my tracks.

Alisha stopped in the doorway when she caught sight of me. She was in as much shock to see me walking out of the stall, with Jamie following behind me, as I was to see her walking in the bathroom on us.

Kelissa wasn't paying us any attention at first, too busy digging in her purse. "Girl, I can't believe my period had to come on tonight of all—" She abruptly stopped talking when Alisha held her hand up to her face. Kelissa looked up at us. Her eyes widened. "What the . . . Charlene? *Jamie?*" she squealed.

Alisha shook her head, folding her arms across her chest. "Fuckin' in the fuckin' bathroom? Y'all cheating muthafuckas couldn't get a room somewhere?"

Jamie laughed a little. "What's up, Alisha?"

Alisha glared at him. "Y'all are some triflin' mutha-fuckas. Pamela is out there lookin' for your ass, Jamie." Alisha looked back at me. "And Ashton just called me, saying him and Aaron were on their way here. And quit all that got-damn crying, Charlie! Your ass wasn't crying when you were fuckin' that nigga! No, wait, I take that back. I heard how he does. The dick put you to tears, huh, bitch? Ol' nasty, trashy, sleezy, classless—"

I rolled my eyes, drying my tears from my face. "Shut the fuck up, Alisha."

Kelissa shook her head at me. "Charlie, what are you doing? Jamie fucks *everybody!* Y'all in here fuckin' in the bathroom and shit, when his girl is right out there on the fuckin' dance floor? This shit is fucked up! You haven't changed since high school, Charlie! You want people to look at you differently, but you're *not* different! Alisha never lied about you, dummy! Your reputation doesn't *need* words! I *told* Aaron he couldn't turn a fuckin' ho into a housewife! I *told* him he couldn't tame a bitch who had a pussy hole that was miles long!"

Before I could get in her face, Jamie pulled me back. "Hold up, hold up. Y'all comin' down real hard on somebody like y'all shit don't stink. Alisha, didn't you pay the judges at Charlie's last audition *not* to choose her, even after she was already chosen?"

I looked at Alisha. "What's he talking about?"

Alisha glared at him.

Jamie nodded. "Yeah, Charlie, *you* were supposed to be a Laker Girl, not this bitch."

Before I could even reach out to strangle the shit out of Alisha, Kelissa got in the way. I pushed her out of my way, but Jamie pulled me back by my arm.

Alisha laughed aloud. "Hey, it's not like you would be able to keep the job anyway due to your . . ." she pointed at my stomach, "little *situation*."

Both Kelissa and Jamie looked at me.

I shook my head at her. I should have known that bitch would have eyes on me at all times, even at the fuckin' hospital. I should have known she would look at my hospital records after we had our physicals for cheerleading the week before school started. If that bitch opened her mouth, I was going to knock her got-damn teeth out.

Alisha grinned. "See, at first, I was going to lay *all* your shit bare in front of the whole school, in front of the whole squad, in front of Aaron, in front of Ne'Vaeh. But then I found out from a friend of mine, who works as a physician's assistant at the University of Maryland, that you might have a little *situation* that might just prevent you from dancing or cheering for Morgan

State—or *any* state, for that matter, for a long time."
Alisha approached me, getting all in my grill, just daring me to touch her. "I was going to be the one to hang
your ass, but I thought I would just stand by and let you
hang yourself. Oh, I am *really* going to enjoy watching
this shit."

I pushed her out of my face. "Alisha, you got one more
time to get in my face."

Jamie pulled me back again.

Kelissa shook her head. "I don't know what the hell
Alisha is talking about, and I *really* don't wanna know
either. All I'm saying is a lot of people are going to get
hurt. I'm sorry I said that shit to Aaron about turning
a ho into a housewife, because I'm no one to judge, but
Aaron is a great guy, who anyone would love to be with.
Jamie, on the other hand," Kelissa rolled her eyes over to
him, who stood there nonchalantly with his hands in his
pockets, "has groupies lined up and down the East Coast."
She rolled her eyes back over to me. "You're wasting your
time with him. And you're gonna ruin a good friendship
and a relationship in the process. You're too pretty to
be *this* fucked-up in the head. I'm gettin' up outta this
bathroom before Pamela comes in here." Kelissa threw
her hands up, walking out of the bathroom.

Alisha walked over to the mirror to take a look at her
flawless face and smooth her edges down with her hands.
She looked at my reflection in the mirror.

Jamie looked at me. "Shorty." He grabbed my hand.

I looked at him, tears lining my lashes. I slid my hands
from his. No matter how much I couldn't stand Alisha
and the rest of the girls on the squad, I knew they were
right. I shook my head at Jamie, putting my hand in his
face before he said another word. "Jamie, please, just go."

Jamie looked over at Alisha, who stood at the mirror,
arms folded across her chest. Jamie shook his head,
then looked back at me. "What you do with your life is

nobody else's business, shorty. There's no ring on my finger, and there's no ring on yours. Until Aaron puts a ring on it, you can do whatever the fuck you like. All I'm saying is . . ." he kissed me on my forehead, "you deserve better than what he's giving you."

My lips trembled as I watched Jamie walk out of the bathroom. I didn't want to break down and cry again in front of Alisha, but I couldn't hold back the tears.

Alisha sighed, going into the bathroom stall, and tearing a wad of toilet paper off a roll. She walked up to me, handing me the tissue.

I looked up at her, reluctant to take it from her hands.

She nodded, shoving the tissue in my hands. "Stop all that punk-ass crying. And here, clean your face, Charlene—we have a lot of appearances to make tonight."

I dried my face, shaking my head in disgust. I couldn't believe I was destroying my life, all over the need of attention, love, and affection. If I hadn't been such a ho, maybe Aaron wouldn't have treated me as such. He wasn't cheating on me at the moment, but he was cold, and it was only a matter of time before he found whatever it was that he was looking for. What I was looking for in Jamie, I had no idea. Jamie was a playa. Everyone knew that shit. He was arrogant and conceited, but he was compassionate, loving, and charismatic. He knew just what to say. He knew just where it hurt. He knew just where to touch. He was everything that I needed in Aaron.

"I know how you feel, Charlene." Alisha went back over to the mirror and dug through her handbag.

I walked up to the mirror, standing alongside her. "How could you possibly know how I'm feeling right now, Alisha?"

Alisha looked at me, shaking her head. "You don't think I know what it's like to be with a man who doesn't show you any kind of attention? Whose eye is always on another girl? Who wishes that I was someone else? Do you think *my* life is perfect? You were just the first bitch to screw around with my man, but you damn sure weren't the last!"

I just looked at her, not sure what to say.

"Nothing I do to that muthafucka in bed has topped whatever it is that you did to him. I know in my heart that Ashton loves me, but for a man as fine as him, one woman just isn't enough." Alisha shook her head again.

I didn't know what to say, except, "Alisha, why don't you leave him?"

Alisha looked at me as if I were crazy. "What? Ashton is going to medical school. He's going to be a doctor, making all kinds of bread. He's been good to me in ways that no one can imagine. All men cheat. I haven't met one who doesn't . . . except *your* man. And that's why I'm so pissed at you, Charlene! You think I don't need to be loved, held, touched, and fucked from time to time? Ashton would rather go to the strip club than to spend time with me! He's a *man*, Charlene. They disappoint us sometimes, they hurt us sometimes, they make mistakes sometimes, but if you do right by them, they'll eventually turn around. You wanted to pay Aaron back for not loving you and look what you did to yourself. Pregnant by your best friend's ex-boyfriend."

I cried harder.

Alisha shook her head at me. "Does she even *know* he's in town? Or did *you* want all of his time? Does the nigga even know you're pregnant with *his* baby?"

I shook my head. I couldn't even look her in the face. "I'm not keeping it, Alisha."

Alisha's eyes widened. "Not keeping—" She couldn't even get the words out. She shook her head at me. "So you're just gonna get rid of it and act like this shit between you and Jamie never happened?"

"What do you expect me to do, Alisha? I have worked my whole life to become a dancer! You stole my chance with the Lakers, and it's all good because I'll get another chance. I can't have this baby, Alisha." I dried my tears.

Alisha glared at me as she shook her head. "You always were a selfish little bitch. Everything is all about you. Whether or not you keep this baby, your problem is not going away. I suggest you tell your boyfriend and your best friend the truth before it's too late. Y'all need to stop playing before someone fucks around and gets hurt."

Why didn't I listen to Alisha? While we were at a party in downtown Baltimore that night, I heard one of Jamie's old teammates mention that he was staying at the Hilton downtown. I don't know what inside of my heart, mind, and body told me to go to him that night, but I did. I wasn't even thinking about the fact that Aaron was blowing up my phone or that Jamie might have had company that night. I was tired of thinking about Jamie. When I slept with him in Miami, I had no idea that I would fall as deep as I did.

There I was, at three-thirty in the morning, knocking on the door to Jamie's hotel room. The door flew open, and a bitch dressed in nothing but Jamie's tank top answered the door.

The bitch grinned, flipping her blond hair over her shoulder. "Yes, may I help you?"

I immediately went into defense mode. "Did I *ask* for your help? I'm here to see Jamie."

"Shorty, who's at the door?" I heard Jamie's deep voice coming from down the hall.

I pushed past the bitch, walking into the hotel room. And there were three other females sitting on the couch, smoking, drinking, all dressed in next to nothing. A few of Jamie's boys were sitting at the table playing cards, drinking, and smoking too. Jamie came down the hallway from the bathroom. He stopped in his tracks when he saw me standing there in the living room, arms folded, eying the groupies on the couch.

"Shorty, what's up?" He approached me. "What'cha doing here at three-thirty in the morning? You know your man's probably wondering where his girl is."

"And what about Pamela? Does she know y'all got all these hoes up in here and shit?" I looked around at everyone. "I don't think she'd be too happy to know that her man is out here fuckin' bitches and shit when you probably have her waiting for you in another hotel room!"

Jamie laughed to himself. He knew I was jealous. "You need to clear your mind about somethin', Charlie?"

I shook my head at him. "You told me that you hadn't touched Pamela since the day that you touched me, but what you *didn't* tell me was that you were fuckin' *other* bitches! True, you don't owe me any explanation, but I thought I actually meant something to you, Jamie! This here proves that I don't. You made me feel special, and I'm pretty sure that's how you got these hoes to come here to see you tonight." Tears welled up in my eyes and slid down my face.

Jamie's eyes glistened. "Charlene, you already know my lifestyle." He grabbed my arm before I could walk away. "Shorty, you *have* a man. What are you doing here questioning me about what I do, when you're not even supposed to be here?"

I just looked up into his face, lips trembling and speechless.

"What do you need me to do, shorty? We got a room full of people and you talkin' to me about shit I don't think you want everyone to know about. Do we need to talk in another room or what?" Jamie's eyes traced my lips.

I hesitated as he grabbed me by the hand.

Jamie and I stood face-to-face in one of the bedrooms in the suite. I was angry with him when I had no business even being there.

"Where's your man at, Charlie?" Jamie's eyes searched mine.

"At his place, calling me every ten minutes or so," I whispered, drying my eyes.

"So, what are you doing here? Why are you not at his place, cuddled up with him? You don't need to be here. You don't need to see this side of me." Jamie shook his head at me. "Go home, Charlie."

I shook my head. "You knew what you were doing when you pulled me in that bathroom stall today. You knew from the moment that you touched me that my body was yours. I can't even have sex with Aaron without thinking of you, Jamie! My body is addicted to yours, even though my heart belongs to him. Whatever this is that you're doing, it has to stop. If we're just friends, then that's all we're gonna be, Jamie. From here on out, we're just friends, and nothing else. I can't deal with this kind of confusion. You either want me or you don't. There is no got-damn in between with me!"

Jamie nodded, eyes sparkling. "I feel you."

I turned to walk away from him when he pulled me back to him. I looked up into his face as he kissed me. My lips trembled in his.

Jamie's lips let go of mine. "Just a friendly reminder that you *are* special and the fact that you had to come to me to find that out says a lot about the nigga you're with." Jamie's eyes searched mine. "You need to leave that muthafucka. You deserve better than this. Better than having to go to someone else, just to feel some sort of affection. There's someone else out there for you, shorty. It's not me, it's not him, but it's somebody."

I wanted to tell Jamie then that I was pregnant with his baby, but how could I, when he was basically telling me that there was nothing between us but sex? I should have taken Jamie's advice about leaving Aaron alone, to find someone who truly valued me, but I couldn't. Not just yet. One way or another, I was going to have the man that I wanted, and at that point, I wasn't even sure who that man was.

Chapter 6

Trapped

Charlene

The week before homecoming, Aaron took me out to a fancy restaurant. No friends, no teammates, just the two of us. It had been awhile since he had taken me out on a date. I still hadn't seen Ne'Vaeh face-to-face and had only spoken over the phone to plan her birthday party. I was a little over two months pregnant and not sure when I was going to tell Aaron. I still maintained my figure, and the only thing on me that had gotten any bigger at the moment were my breasts. I knew Aaron noticed it because he couldn't stop staring at them.

That night at dinner, Aaron asked me what I thought about marriage. It scared me out of my mind. I knew that I was pregnant with Jamie's baby. I knew that he would be pissed if he found out the baby wasn't his, and I knew he would leave me if he found out. All I could think about was Jamie at that moment and how I was going to tell him. The last thing on my mind was marriage, and it wasn't because I didn't want to marry Aaron, because I did. It was because I knew I was in the wrong, and I didn't deserve to marry him. I knew I broke his heart when I told him that marrying him was the last thing on my mind, that my career was more important than us, and that I wasn't even sure if he was the guy I wanted to marry. Maybe a small part of me was trying to push Aaron away before he left me. Maybe a small part of me wanted to make my situation easier.

That same week, my uncle passed away. My family and I flew to Texas to attend his homecoming. I was devastated. Uncle Carlito was my favorite uncle and my father's little brother. He was the youngest of ten children. He stayed with us until I was about thirteen years old. He was more like an older brother to me, than he was my uncle. He taught us how to play soccer, how to fight boys, how to fire weapons, how to fish, how to make a campfire. . . . He was going to be missed. I hated the fact that I couldn't see his face and talk to him about my problems. I was avoiding him throughout my entire pregnancy because I knew if I called him on the phone, he would hear in my voice that something was wrong. Rest in peace, Uncle Carlito.

I had finally started talking to Ne'Vaeh again, or at least texting the girl on a regular basis. Two months had gone by, and I hadn't contacted Jamie, nor had he reached out to me. However, the day I arrived back in Maryland from Texas, I got a call from Kelissa telling me that Jamie was going to be in town for the week. Why she felt the need to tell me, I had no idea. And why I couldn't contact Ne'Vaeh *or* Aaron the day I arrived back in Maryland, I didn't know either. Neither one showed up to the airport to meet me as planned. Neither were answering their phones, either. I had to contact Renée, Ne'Vaeh's cousin, just to know what was up. Once I had arrived in Baltimore, I agreed to meet Renée at Venus around one o'clock to help them finish decorating for the party.

I got in a cab that afternoon, as my sister and brother placed my bags in the trunk. My whole family was going to a family get-together at my aunt's house. I planned to meet Aaron for lunch, but he wasn't answering my calls. I tried calling Ne'Vaeh to wish her a happy birthday, but she never picked up her phone either. I asked the cabdriver to take me over to Aaron's crib. I was going to shower and change before heading to Venus. My flight was already late, and I knew that by the time I got to Venus, they would probably be finished setting up the ballroom for the party. Renée told me that the family was meeting there around twelve-thirty for Ne'Vaeh's birthday lunch. She was really hoping I'd show up in time to eat with them, but I wasn't in the mood to converse with Ne'Vaeh's fake-ass family. Renée and her family were cool, but the rest of the family never supported her because of the way they felt about her mother. Why they decided on showing up years after the fact, I had no idea.

I could smell the Purple Haze in the air as I stepped out of the cab, upon arriving at Aaron and Ashton's apartment. I rolled my eyes as I walked around to the trunk of the cab to get my bags from there. Aaron and his friends were so busy sitting, smoking, and laughing on the balcony that they didn't even notice that I pulled up. Ashton strolled out of the front door of the apartment building just in time to help me.

"What's up, sista?" he called out, running up to meet me at the cab.

"Hey, Ashton." I smiled at him as he approached me.

He kissed my cheek. "Girl, let me get those."

"Thanks, boo." I sighed. I looked up at Aaron as he passed a blunt to Amina, this light-skinned chick who made it a habit to show up to the crib whenever she knew weed was involved. I wasn't really sure what to think of her. I wasn't really worried about Aaron sweatin' her. He didn't even seem to have an interest in red chicks, myself included. Every poster on his wall of a model was either brown or dark-skinned.

"Well, I see why Aaron hasn't been answering his phone." I rolled my eyes. "How long have they been here? Have they been out here smoking *all* day?"

Ashton looked at me as he closed the trunk. "Nah." He put the strap to my overnight bag over his shoulder and pulled the handle on my suitcase so he could roll it down the walkway. "How was your trip?" he asked.

I looked at him, shaking my head. "Saw a lot of family I haven't seen since I was like four or five. Had some laughs and a whole *lot* of tears. You know how much I loved Carlito. He was like a father to me. He will be missed."

Ashton nodded. "Yeah, shorty, I know. I wish I could have been there with you, but I just got this job down at the hospital and—"

I cut him off. "Please, Ashton, you don't have to apologize." We started walking toward the apartment building. "You have always been there for me. I didn't want anyone seeing me falling out, crying over Carlito's body in that casket anyway. I don't even wanna talk about it."

We got to the building, and Ashton opened the door to let me in. We walked up a flight of stairs to his apartment, and again, he opened the door for me. The smell of butter and cinnamon smacked me in the nose the moment we entered the building and nearly suffocated me upon walking into the apartment. "Oh my goodness . . . *Mmmm.*" I followed the smell into the apartment. "Y'all niggas were cooking French toast this morning?"

Ashton shook his head, carrying my luggage into the apartment. "Shit, not me. You know I can't even boil water."

I looked at him, setting my purse on the coffee table. The apartment was so nice and tidy, smelling like Pine Sol and carpet cleaner, which was *so* not the usual. Usually, their apartment smelled like sweaty gym socks, cigars, and Newports. "Damn, so y'all cooked *and* cleaned? Y'all must have had company over."

Ashton set my luggage alongside the coffee table. He looked at me, then came over and sat by me on the sofa. "Nah, shorty, I ain't had shit, and I ain't cooked shit. And I damn sure didn't clean this apartment. Shit, niggas come in this bitch all day fuckin' up shit. Eating up all the snacks. Most of the time, Aaron has the whole basketball team up in this bitch. Alisha helped Aaron clean a few days ago. Guess she got tired of shit lying everywhere."

I rolled my eyes. "Ashton, why the fuck you lyin'? Alisha wouldn't clean up after y'all grown-ass men."

He just looked at me.

I really didn't even want to know. Alisha admitted that Ashton was slinging his dick around the tristate area. As much as Alisha got on my damn muthafuckin' nerves, I had to admit that she was beautiful. Her body looked amazing. Weren't too many teenage women who had big breasts, a tiny waist, a phat ass and thick thighs. She looked like a stripper. Alisha dissed niggas left and right for Ashton, and meanwhile, he was playing the field.

I rolled my eyes. "I'm not even gonna ask. Y'all niggas make me sick. How much pussy does one nigga gotta have? Y'all always claiming hoes ain't loyal; then you turn around and do shit to *make* her not be loyal to your sorry ass!"

Ashton laughed to himself. "So, you think it's *me* who's cheating on my girl?"

I looked at him, feeling like I was talking to Jamie. "Ashton, do we *really* even have to play this game right now? As much as I can't stand your girl, a nigga would have to be real stupid to even *look* at another girl, when they have a girl who looks like that! Alisha is a knockout! Ashton, why would you cheat on her?"

He looked at me. "Charlie, it's not cheating when your girl knows about it. You don't have to understand what me and my girl have going on, because that's *our* thing. I don't have to answer to you or anybody else. I use protection. I wrap my shit up. If I'm gonna give into my weakness from time to time, I play smart about it. I might bring a girl or two over, give them the dick, then I send her 'bout her business, simple as that. I know my worth, and I know these chicks around here make a career out of getting pregnant by athletes and doctors and shit. I'm going to college to play ball, *and* I'm going to medical school. I really don't give a fuck if you think I'm triflin' or not, Charlie. I *love* Alisha, and the last thing I wanna do is hurt her. We can't have sex, shorty, which is why we *don't* have sex."

I looked at Ashton, a little puzzled. "What do you mean you 'can't' have sex?"

He looked at me, shaking his head. "Just forget it, yo. Let's just leave it at that, shorty. I've said too much already. We *all* have our secrets. There are skeletons in everyone's closet, including *yours*."

My heart skipped a few beats. "Wh-what is that supposed to mean, Ashton?" I stuttered.

He just looked at me for a few seconds. "I think that's a conversation you need to be having with Aaron. I try not to get in grown folks' business."

I shook my head. Alisha and her big-ass fuckin' mouth. "Ashton, I love Aaron, okay? If I tell him about Jamie, he'll leave me alone with this baby! A baby that I don't even want! A baby that I am *so* not ready to have!"

Ashton looked confused. "Jamie? Jamie who? I didn't say anything about no 'Jamie.' And you're *pregnant*? What?"

I was stunned into silence. He wasn't even talking about Jamie. The expression on his face proved he had no idea what in the hell I was talking about. Alisha had kept her big-ass mouth shut for once, and I had opened mine too soon.

Ashton's looked at me. "Charlie? What are you talking about?"

I sighed. "Ashton, yes, I'm pregnant. About eleven weeks pregnant."

Ashton wasn't even sure what to say. His brown eyes searched my face. He shook his head at me in disbelief.

I started to cry because I was in a fucked-up situation, though there was really no use in crying. I created the storm, yet I was the one upset when it started to rain. Man, that Karma is a mean bitch.

Ashton thought to himself for a minute then looked at me, watching the tears slide down my face. The look on his face changed from disbelief to *I-know-what-the-fuck-you-did*.

"Charlie, Alisha mentioned this morning that she was going to surprise Ne'Vaeh with someone from her past tonight at her birthday party. I have known shorty for a long time, and I know that there's only two people that she might want to see right about now, and that's her sister who ran away six years ago or Jamie *Green* who left her about four years ago. Is *that* the Jamie you're talking about, Charlie? Tell me *he's* not the Jamie you're referring to, shorty."

I dried my tears. I couldn't even look Ashton in the face, but I could feel him looking at me.

Ashton put his hands on my face, turning my face toward his. "Charlie, look at me. Tell me what's goin' on. C'mon, shorty, I'm your boy."

I shook my head, taking his hands from my face.

"Eh, yo, what's goin' on?" Aaron's voice shook both of us.

Ashton got up from the couch.

I sat there, drying the tears from my face.

Ashton laughed the tension off. "Nuthin', bruh. Your girl was just curious about why you didn't save her any French toast this morning. You know that's her favorite, man."

Aaron looked over at me. He saw my wet cheeks. He wasn't buying it. "Uh-huh. Charlie, meet me in the bathroom, a'ight?"

I nodded my head, unable to look up at him. I stood from the couch, watching Aaron's back as he walked back toward the bathroom. I began to dig through my luggage for a pair of jeans and a ribbed tank top.

I could feel Ashton's eyes on the back of my neck. "Charlie, you're really not gonna tell me what's going on?"

I shook my head in frustration, standing back up from my luggage, clothes in my hand. "Ashton, just drop it, okay?" I started to walk toward the bathroom when he grabbed my arm. I looked up at him.

Ashton shook his head. "You might not wanna tell me what's goin' on, but trust me when I tell you that you aren't the only one who has some explaining to do." He let go of my arm.

When I stepped into the bathroom, Aaron sat on the edge of the bathtub smoking a cigarette. The shower water was running. The smell of Caress soap filled the bathroom, and I knew Alisha hadn't left the apartment too long ago. I tried to hold my breath, and not breathe in the smoke.

"Please," I coughed, "could you put that shit out? You have fuckin' asthma, Aaron, and I know second-hand smoke kills too. . . ."

Aaron exhaled smoke from his nose before tossing the cigarette in the toilet. He looked higher than a mutha-fucka as he watched me undress. Though he looked fine as hell in his wife beater and sweats, I couldn't help but notice he wasn't dressed to leave the house.

"Are you going to Ne'Vaeh's birthday lunch *or* her birthday party tonight, Aaron?" I unsnapped my bra, pulling it from my arms. My breasts popped out of my bra like biscuit dough popping out of a biscuit canister. Damn, I needed a bigger bra. In two months, my breasts had gone from just barely a C-cup to a damn D-cup.

Aaron's eyes were fixated to them. He didn't take his eyes off them the entire time I undressed. "Nah, I wasn't invited."

I rolled my eyes, sliding off my panties. "Aaron, I would like to *not* have to dance alone this year at Ne'Vaeh's party. You know every time Renée throws a party for anyone, she has that damn couple's dance." I climbed into the shower.

He sighed. "How was Texas, shorty?" He brought up another touchy subject to avoid the touchy subject that we were already on. For some reason, Aaron never went to any of Ne'Vaeh's parties. I shouldn't have been surprised that he didn't want to go to this party.

"Shitty as any funeral would be, Aaron." I stood under the shower, rinsing my hair before applying floral-scented shampoo to it. "Don't try to change the subject, Aaron. Why the hell do I always have to go to this girl's birthday parties by myself? What do you have against her? You don't like my girl or something? You're always avoiding her or any conversation about her." I lathered the shampoo, massaging my scalp with my fingertips. "You never like any of my friends, Aaron!"

"Charlie, I have nothing against your girl. I just don't go where I'm not invited, shorty. It's that simple. But if you want me to go with you, all right, I'll go. What time are you going to her party?"

I rinsed my hair. "Well, I was supposed to be there a few hours ago." I washed my face. "Speaking of a few hours ago, I was blowing up your phone all morning, and you didn't answer. As a matter of fact, I called both you *and* Ne'Vaeh, and *neither* of you answered."

Aaron was silent, *too* silent.

"So, you have no words, right?" I began to lather soap all over my body.

He sighed. "Charlie, you wanna talk about not answering calls, huh? Why did you avoid *my* calls the entire week that you were gone? Why did you laugh when I mentioned getting married? And why didn't you tell me that you were thinking about transferring to Miami?"

I looked up to see Aaron peeping at me from behind the shower curtain. He always did answer a question with about two or three questions of his own. That was his way of reversing the blame. I wasn't in the mood for his games when I was already feeling really shitty.

"Look, Aaron," I rinsed the suds from my body, "I was going through a whole lot in Texas. I didn't feel like talking to *anyone*." I turned off the shower. "When you asked me what I thought about marriage, I had just found out that my uncle passed away. I was in my feelings, I was emotional, and I wasn't thinking straight. Of course, I love you and would love to be your wife someday, but now isn't the time." I wrung out my hair.

"I applied to colleges outside of Maryland because I'm sick of this place. I cannot seem to get away from my past, and I'm tired of it getting thrown in my face. The University of Miami was the first college to accept me. The only person I even mentioned it to was Dana's big-mouthed ass. I didn't think it even mattered to you one way or another. You could give a fuck if I stay here. Your mind always seems to be on everything else *but* me, Aaron. You don't care if I leave Maryland. You probably wouldn't even notice." I stepped out of the shower onto the rug.

Aaron made a face at me as if he didn't know what in the hell I was talking about. He watched me grab a towel and wrap it around my body. "Charlie, where is all of this coming from? The fuck you mean I wouldn't notice? How the fuck could you think I don't care if you leave and go to Florida?"

I looked at him. "Aaron, we both know this relationship is in no way what it used to be. You don't have to pretend to love me anymore. You stopped loving me when Alisha and the rest of her bitches told you about my slutty past! Yeah, I was a freak. Yeah, I fucked everybody! Yeah, I was a ho! Yeah, you deserve better!" I squealed.

Aaron sighed. "Charlie, I can't do this shit. . . ." He ran his hands over his head, frustrated as hell at the way that I was acting.

I looked up into his face. "Can't do what, Aaron? It's like every time we have a conversation, you avoid telling me how you really feel! You don't wanna go with me to Ne'Vaeh's party, and I need to know why."

Aaron looked at me. He took a deep breath. "Charlie, I gotta do this. I know it's not the right time, but then again, it's never the right time to tell someone that it's time."

My eyes grew misty. "Time for what, Aaron?"

He didn't say anything. He just turned and walked out of the bathroom.

I followed behind him, grabbing his arm. He pulled away from me. "Time for *what*, Aaron?"

Aaron stood against the hallway wall. He couldn't even look at me.

My heart thumped against my rib cage. It was time to say good-bye. I could see it in his face. We both knew it wasn't going anywhere. We both knew it was over. He wanted to make the first move. I couldn't let him leave me without an explanation. "Why, Aaron?"

He still couldn't look at me. "I just don't feel the same way that I used to feel about you, and it doesn't have shit to do with what Alisha or her friends said about you. It's just me, Charlie."

I shook my head. "Hell nah! No, it's not you. It's someone else. Who is she?"

Aaron finally looked up at me. "Does it really matter, Charlie?"

I pushed him in his chest. "Yes, it fuckin' matters! I want to know why the only man who I have ever loved isn't in love with me anymore! There has *got* to be someone else! You don't kiss me, you don't hold me, and you won't fuck me! I have to basically get you drunk or act like I'm one of those got-damn strippers to get you to touch me!" I pushed him again. "Fine. If you wanna be free, just go! I can take care of this baby all by my damn self!"

Aaron looked at me, catching my arms and stopping me from pounding on his chest. "What did you just say?"

I looked up at him, tears sliding down my cheeks. The words had just exploded out of my mouth. I wasn't even thinking. I sure as hell didn't plan to tell him until I couldn't hide the pregnancy anymore. The look on his face when he heard the words come out of my mouth broke my heart. I wasn't sure if he was concerned or if he was hurt at the fact that the woman that he wanted to leave was pregnant with his baby. Regardless, I had thrown a wrench in whatever plan that he had.

"I'm pregnant, Aaron," I cried.

He let go of my arms. He just stood there stunned and looked at me. "How long have you known about this?"

I dried my tears. "Oh, what does it matter? This doesn't change the fact that you want to leave me, Aaron! I'm too young to have a baby! I don't even want this baby, and you want to leave me to take care of it alone?"

Aaron shook his head at me. "You knew about this baby when I asked you what you thought about getting married? You have been acting strange as hell for about two months, Charlie, and it's because you knew you were pregnant and you weren't even gonna tell me? Why, Charlie? Why would you keep this shit from me?"

"Because I didn't wanna have this baby!" I yelled, walking past him into his bedroom.

Aaron followed behind me. He stood in the doorway as he watched me dig through his dresser drawers for a bra and panties.

"The day I went to the abortion clinic to get rid of it, my mother showed up, cursing out everyone at that clinic! She made everyone there feel like shit! I didn't wanna have a baby in this situation, Aaron! I'm in love with a man, and I'm pregnant with a baby that's not—" I stopped talking, then looked up at him. "That's not wanted."

Aaron's eyes glistened. "A baby isn't in my plans right now, Charlie, but that doesn't mean you have to kill it either. I'll take care of what's mine, shorty. That includes you *and* the baby."

I broke down and cried. "Aaron, please don't leave me!" I sat at the corner of his bed, turning my back to him. I couldn't even face him. How could I when I basically just stopped the man from leaving me because he believed that the baby inside of me was his? I was wrong, and I knew I was going to pay for it one way or another some day.

Chapter 7

A Bitch Named Karma

Charlene

By the time I made it to Venus, Ne'Vaeh's entire family was there. The restaurant was covered in blue and silver balloons. I should have known that a few cameras would be there. Superstars Darryl Allan, Anastasia Jones-Allan, and Jade Abdula-Matthews were in the place. Darryl barely came to Maryland after he moved to the ATL years ago. It wasn't until a few years back that Ne'Vaeh even knew that Darryl Allan was her cousin. She found out on her sixteenth birthday when we went to one of Anastasia's concerts in D.C. Renée introduced us to Darryl Allan backstage. He said that he found out from his grandmother that Ne'Vaeh's mother was his mother's half sister. Ever since he found out Ne'Vaeh was his cousin, he made it his business to look out for her whenever she needed it. Though she had a hard time adjusting to the fact that she had a cousin that was a celebrity, they still kept in touch. Most people would have been milking the shit out of their multimillionaire cousin, but not Ne'Vaeh. The girl could sing her ass off, but she never told Darryl about it. Couldn't have been me, shit.

Ne'Vaeh was looking *very* sexy that day in her Coogi dress. I know Coogi was the nineties look, but she was making it look real fly. She was bringing Coogi back. The dress hugged her in all the right places. She was a short li'l girl, but that minidress and those heels made her look at least five foot eight that night. Her makeup was flawless. Her skin was glowing. She sat at the far end of the table, between Renée's mother and Anastasia Jones-Allan. Ne'Vaeh looked a little tense. She barely hugged me back when I hugged her that afternoon. She looked like something was bothering her real bad. She sat there, chin in hand, with laughter all around her.

I swear, every time Anastasia or Darryl opened their mouth to say anything, a damn camera was flashing. The media has no damn respect for privacy.

"So, Ne'Vaeh," Anastasia set her wineglass down, "I heard from your cousin, Renée, that you have an *angelic* voice. I've been looking for a background singer for *months*. So, any time you wanna show me your skills, let me know. And any time you want a break from school, come holla at'cha girl." Anastasia winked her eye at Ne'Vaeh.

Ne'Vaeh laughed to herself, shooting Renée a quick glare. "Thanks, cuzzo, but *no* thanks. I'm going to college, then to law school. Singing in the choir is something I do to keep God in my life when I'm not in church."

Renée's eyes widened. "'No thanks'? What the . . . girl the fuck's wrong with you? Are you crazy? *Anastasia Jones-Allan* just ordained you her got-damn backup singer! Hell yes, Anastasia, she'll rock the fuck out of that microphone! Mama, I'm sorry, but your niece has some issues that I needed to set straight!" She put her hands up, surrendering before Miss Joyce got in her ass about her language.

We all laughed a little.

I looked at Aaron, who leaned back in his chair, looking a little uncomfortable to be there with us. I elbowed him to sit up in his chair, but he didn't budge. I rolled my eyes at him.

"So, cuz, tell me why I don't see a man sitting at your side today." Darryl chimed in with his wife. Miss Joyce elbowed Darryl in his rib cage. "What? Aunt Joyce, I'm just sayin', look at her. My cousin is *beautiful,* with a *capital* B. So why doesn't she have a man?"

Aaron finally sat up in his chair, as if he was waiting to hear the answer to the question as well.

Ne'Vaeh glanced at Aaron. She laughed nervously, looking at Darryl. "Wow, really? What's this? Embarrass-the-hell-out-Ne'Vaeh-on-her-birthday? Gee, thanks, cuz."

Ne'Vaeh's cousins laughed a little.

Darryl made a face. "Nah, cuz, what? I'm just concerned, shorty. You look sad as hell on your nineteenth birthday. I haven't seen my baby cousin smile in *years.* I just know your family and friends have some fun planned for you tonight. I'm only gonna be able to party with y'all for about an hour tonight. And while I'm here, I wanna see my cousin have some fun. I don't wanna see you sitting alone on your special night, cuz."

The family nodded in agreement.

Ne'Vaeh's eyes glistened. "I appreciate that, Darryl. And I'm *not* alone—I have y'all here with me today." She grabbed Anastasia's hand in hers and cameras flashed. "Oh, goodness, that's annoying. Cuz, could you please tell them to stop taking fuckin' pictures? How do y'all live like this? *Sheesh.*"

Anastasia smiled, squeezing her hand. She signaled the camera crew to get lost with her other hand.

"Lunch was amazing, Jade. And thank you all for coming." Ne'Vaeh tried to fake a smile. She looked over at Aaron. "Even those who weren't invited."

I looked at Aaron.

Aaron grinned at her, nodding in agreement, winking his eye at her. It was the first time that he had smiled all day. That moment really had me feeling some type of way. I wasn't sure what to think.

Lunch was awesome. There was nothing better than freshly cooked seafood, dessert, and wine for an afternoon meal. Ne'Vaeh tried her best to enjoy her much-needed time with her family. After lunch, her family members presented her with their gifts. Darryl, Anastasia, and Jade stuck around for a little while. Aaron left to go pick up his bonus check from work. And a few of the family members left to get a few more things for the party. That afternoon, those remaining presented Ne'Vaeh with her gifts. She was in tears opening them all. She got everything from an iPad to a Rolex. Darryl handed her the last gift. It was a gift from her mother. Ne'Vaeh finally looked at me that afternoon. It was the first time that her mother had reached out to her in six years. She got up from the table, then hurried off to the bathroom.

Renée rose from her chair. "Oh, poor baby . . ."

"Wait," I rose in my chair too. "I'll go get her."

"Ne'Vaeh, sweetie?" I crept into the bathroom, hearing Ne'Vaeh sobbing in one of the bathroom stalls.

"Please, Charlie, leave me alone, okay?" she cried.

I sighed, approaching the stall where her voice was coming from. "Well, I can't do that, hon. You have a room full of people who are *so* happy to see you today." I opened the door, seeing Ne'Vaeh sitting on top of the toilet seat. I grabbed a wad of tissue from the roll and started dabbing her cheeks. "Ne'Vaeh, oh my goodness, you're going to ruin your makeup! You look gorgeous! Please, stop crying before you ruin this masterpiece called 'your face'!"

Ne'Vaeh laughed a little, taking the tissue from my hands. "Please, Charlie, let me sit here alone and cry, okay? I really don't feel like talking."

"Sweetie, your family came from all over the U.S. to wish you a happy nineteenth birthday. I know your mother was the last person you wanted to wish you a happy birthday, but, hey, that's life. Full of surprises, some good, some fucked-up." I leaned up against the wall of the bathroom stall.

Ne'Vaeh looked up at me, "Charlie," her lips trembled. "It really hurts being alone."

I shook my head, "Sweetie, you know Darryl didn't mean any harm by what he said."

Ne'Vaeh nodded. "I know he didn't. But he reminded me of how lonely I am when he brought up the fact that I don't have a boyfriend. I know he didn't mean any harm, but that didn't make it hurt any less. I'm nineteen years old, and I haven't found love. Love *never* loves me like it's supposed to! I can never have what I love, or love always ends up hurting me. I'm sick of this disappointment. I'm so sick of this pain. When is it *my* turn to be loved? I wanna be loved too, Charlie! Not the kind of love that hurts, but the kind of love that heals old wounds. That makes you smile even when you're mad. That you don't have to show where it hurts because he already knows. That knows when I need him to hold and comfort me. And that lets me know with every waking moment he can't live, breathe, eat, sleep, *exist* without me." Tears slid down her cheeks again. "Charlie, I *need* love. My mother *hated* us with every inch of her soul. She hated life. When she failed at taking her own life, she took my little brother's. Your mother saved my life. My aunt Joyce saved my life. And for that, I will always love them both. I have not one mother, but I have *two* mothers." She handed the small gift box from her mother back to me.

"And neither one of their names is Juanita Washington. Fuck that bitch."

My eyes glistened. Ne'Vaeh was in so much pain. I could hear her pain in her voice, and I felt so guilty inside for what I had done. Jamie was just what she needed at that moment. He was amazing. Though a part of me had started to fall for him, I knew what I was feeling was mainly lust. He was sexier than a muthafucka, he knew the right things to do, he knew the right things to say, and he knew just where it hurt. Everything that Ne'Vaeh said that she needed, Jamie was the man to give it to her. Though I had started to develop feelings for him, a small part of me hoped that Jamie showed up to her party tonight. She needed him. She needed him *so* badly.

"Okay, babe, let's clean you up, then go back out there with your family to enjoy the rest of your lunch. You got your makeup bag?" I pulled her up from the toilet seat, taking her by her hand over to the bathroom sink.

"I'm so sorry for breaking down like this." Ne'Vaeh continued to cry as I dabbed her face with Kleenex. "Maybe I drank too much."

I swept her hair from her face. "Where did you put your purse so we can fix this makeup?"

Ne'Vaeh pointed to the drawer. "Renée said she put some makeup in the drawer this morning for me. I guess she knew I would cry when I saw Juanita's gift."

I dug in the drawer for some mascara, concealer, and pressed powder. "We just need to touch you up a bit and we're good."

The tears just kept rolling down her face, which made it impossible to apply any makeup. Black tears slid down her cheeks.

I sighed. "Sweetie, trust me, I know how you feel. Love hurts like a muthafucka. I wish I didn't feel the way about Aaron that I do." I didn't want to turn the conversation to me, but I wanted her to know her life wasn't the only one that was a wreck.

Ne'Vaeh looked up at me, her tears slowly subsiding.

"Our relationship has changed. Hasn't been the same since Alisha's bitch ass outted my past. I act like everything is so perfect between me and Aaron, but it's not, girl. For a long time, we didn't kiss, touch, hug, fuck, or look at each other—*nothing*. It wasn't until like two months ago that we actually started having sex again after going without it for like three or four months straight." I looked at Ne'Vaeh and the expression on her face.

She held her stomach, looking like she was about to throw up. She braced herself up against the bathroom sink.

"Are you okay?" I asked her.

She nodded, tears lining her lashes. "Yeah, I guess I'm a little queasy from all that wine I drank."

I sighed. "Well, I could use a drink or two or *three*. Aaron and I almost broke up this morning."

Ne'Vaeh looked at me. "W-what? *Almost* broke up? What is 'almost broke up'?"

I shook my head, "Yeah, girl, I believe he had a whole speech down too. He was about to give me this whole never-the-right-time-to-say-good-bye-but-I-gotta-make-the-first-move-Chris-Brown shit." I laughed a little to hide my pain. "Well, that was until I told him that I was pregnant."

Ne'Vaeh put her hand over her heart as if she was about to have a heart attack. The girl nearly stumbled over her own two feet.

I caught her before she fell up against me. I helped her over to the vanity seat. "Whoa, Ne'Vaeh, are you okay?"

Her whole face flushed. She didn't respond. Her body was completely limp. I braced her body up against the wall, then hurried to the bathroom entrance to call for help. Renée was the first to enter the bathroom. Anastasia, Jade, the aunts, and the few female cousins that were in the restaurant rushed in behind her.

"Go get some water, ma!" Renée rushed over to Ne'Vaeh's limp body over on the vanity seat. She held her cousin in her arms. "Oh my goodness!" She struggled with all of her might to hold back any tears. "What happened, Charlie?"

I was stunned. I had never seen Ne'Vaeh pass out before. "I-I don't know! We were just talking, and she fainted! She fell up against me! What's wrong with her? I have never seen her pass out before!"

"She was diagnosed with heart failure a few months ago, Charlie." Miss Joyce came back with the water, handing it to Renée. "She had numerous surgeries as a child. She was born with several holes in her heart, sweetie, and the left side of her heart isn't pumping properly. We really shouldn't have even let the poor girl have any wine today. Oh my goodness—that present from her mother—I don't know what we were thinking."

"Heart failure?" I was shocked. I had no idea, and Ne'Vaeh never mentioned anything to me about having any health issues. All those times she went in for surgeries growing up, I thought she was getting her tonsils or her appendix removed. I knew she said her heart was broken, but I didn't know she meant it literally.

"Miss Joyce, we were only talking." I shook my head, watching Ne'Vaeh's aunt try to help resuscitate her.

Anastasia sat on Ne'Vaeh's other side, fanning her. "Well, whatever you said to the child had to have been something serious for her to just pass the hell out!" She looked up at me, dark, luminous lashes surrounding her brown eyes. "What were y'all talking about? What did you say to her?"

Jade took her cell phone out of her purse. "Should I call the ambulance? I mean, she looks really bad, y'all!"

Renée looked up at me, curious about what I said to her cousin that would make her pass out cold. "*Well?*"

I swallowed hard. I really didn't want to tell them about me being pregnant, but the cat was already out of the bag. "I don't know what I could have said to upset the girl! Nothing I said to her was really that devastating that she would fall the fuck out! We were talking about her mother, about love, about me being pregnant with Aaron's baby."

"Lawd." Renée sighed, shaking her head at me, patting Ne'Vaeh's cheeks to make her come to. "C'mon, baby, please . . . Snap out of it, cuz."

"Like I said, do we need to call 911?" Jade repeated frantically.

Renée looked at me, shaking her head as if I had done something wrong. "Nah, sweetie, no ambulance is needed. She'll be fine. I guess baby girl just heard some news that she wasn't ready for, that's all."

Ne'Vaeh came to. As soon as she opened her eyes, looking into Renée's face, she started bawling her eyes out in her cousin's arms.

Renée sighed, her eyes growing misty. "Okay, everybody out. I got it from here."

Everyone, me included, was stunned. We wanted to see if Ne'Vaeh was okay, but Renée was adamant about us leaving them alone.

"C'mon, now, everybody get the fuck *out!*" she exclaimed.

I just stood there alongside the sink, watching everyone exit the bathroom.

Renée looked up at me, rolling her eyes, "OMG, Charlie, what part of 'get the fuck out' didn't you understand? The 'get,' the 'fuck,' or the 'out'? You always were kinda slow!"

I made a face at her. Ne'Vaeh had been living in my house for years, and I couldn't hear whatever conversation the two of them were going to have? I was just as much family as anyone else there was. Hence, the fact that I was invited to the *family* luncheon.

"Look, Renée, I'm the one who made her pass the fuck out! I don't know what I said to upset her, but I need to be here to comfort her." My eyes grew misty, watching Ne'Vaeh bawl.

Renée shook her head. "Nah, sweetie, you really don't need to hear this. Please, let us talk alone."

I put my hands up, surrendering. I had lost that battle. Renée wanted me out of their business, so I stayed out of their business.

Needless to say, the party was turned *all* the way up that night. Seemed like the ballroom was filled beyond capacity, once everyone found out that Anastasia Jones and Darryl Allan were in the spot. The celebrities were there for a good hour and a half before leaving that night. By then, everybody was already tore up, even Ne'Vaeh, who sat alone at the bar. She had recovered physically from the incident that happened earlier, but mentally, I'm not so sure. I wasn't sure what was going on with her, and I was afraid to ask. I sat at a table with Dana, Danita, Kelissa, Monique, Raya, and Kai, keeping an eye on Ne'Vaeh, making sure she didn't drink too much. It was almost time for the couples' dance. Renée would pick a random love song and have the DJ play it to calm the mood a little bit. She made her way over to the DJ, and Aaron had finally made his way over to me.

Kelissa grinned. "Yeah, ladies, it's about that time. Let's go find our men."

They got up from the table, making their way out onto the dance floor just in time for my favorite song, "You Gotta Be." My heart nearly jumped out of my chest. I absolutely loved that song, but I knew someone who loved it more. I looked over at Ne'Vaeh, who sat, face in hand, in tears. I looked back at Aaron.

Aaron looked at me. "What's up, shorty?" He spoke over the music.

I leaned over and whispered in his ear, "Please, go dance with her."

Aaron looked at me, then over at Ne'Vaeh. He shook his head, looking back at me. "Nah, Charlie. Trust me. She doesn't wanna dance with me."

I nodded. "Please. Look at her. She needs it."

Aaron hesitated before getting up from the table. He made his way over to the bar. He whispered in Ne'Vaeh's ear, over her shoulder. Ne'Vaeh turned around in her chair, stood up, and pushed Aaron out of her way before walking past him.

I stood in my chair. *What the hell?*

Aaron grabbed her arm, pulling her back to him. She tried to pull from him, but he pulled her close, surrounded her in his arms, and the girl started crying her eyes out up against his chest. Though I couldn't hear what Aaron was saying, I know I saw him mouth the words, "Baby, I'm sorry" in her ear. Now, what the dude was sorry about and why he was calling her "baby," I had no fuckin' idea. However, something in my heart wouldn't let me pass off that moment as nothing. Before I could make my way over to the two, someone grabbed my arm.

I turned around to see Jamie Green looking me dead in the face.

My heart fluttered in my chest. "Jamie, what the hell are you doing here?" I exclaimed, forgetting that Kelissa mentioned that he was in town.

Jamie smiled, platinum teeth gleaming. "Shorty over there invited me." He pointed over to Alisha, who was over by the loudspeaker, dancing with Ashton.

I glared over at her. Alisha caught sight of me looking at her, and the bitch winked at me. Ol' messy-ass bitch. I knew Ashton said that she planned to invite someone from Ne'Vaeh's past as a birthday surprise, but the day was already hectic enough. I didn't have time for drama. Yes, Ne'Vaeh needed Jamie, but by the looks of things, I wasn't so sure Jamie was who she wanted.

I looked at Jamie, then back over to the bar where Aaron and Ne'Vaeh were supposed to be. I had lost sight of them. I searched the room with my eyes until I caught sight of them on the dance floor. The two were more like hugging than dancing. They were barely moving. Looked like the two were both crying to me. What the fuck was going on?

I looked up at Jamie. "I need your help," I said as I leaned over and whispered in his ear.

Jamie nodded. "What's up?"

I pointed over to Aaron and Ne'Vaeh on the dance floor. I looked back up at Jamie. His eyes were coated in tears. I'm not sure how he felt seeing the love of his life hugged up with another man, but I knew I was feeling some type of way watching the love of *my* life hugged up with another woman. Though I had walked myself into that situation when I asked Aaron to comfort her, I didn't like what I was seeing. Something was telling me that this dance was not just a dance.

"I take it that's your man, huh?" Jamie looked back at me.

I nodded. "Yeah. I guess."

"So, why is *she* dancing with *your* man?" he questioned my logic.

"She needed it, Jamie. The girl is hurting. You should have seen her today. She's been crying and moping around *all* damn day." I looked up into his face. "I told my man to dance with her because I thought she needed to feel *someone's* arms around her. She needs love, Jamie."

"Who's love? *Aaron's?* I thought *you* needed his love." Jamie looked back at the two on the dance floor.

I looked over at them. Ne'Vaeh lifted her head from resting on Aaron's chest. She looked into his face, and he looked down in hers. He dried her tears. I watched as his eyes searched her face, as if he wanted to kiss her, but instead of kissing her, he swiped his thumb across her lips. Oh, I was *so* done. That was enough. There was something going on.

I was about to step out onto the dance floor when Jamie caught my hand. I looked up at him. Oh, I was mad. Aaron never touched me or held me the way that he was holding her. He cared for her. He hadn't so much as spent five minutes of his time with that girl; yet, there they were—close enough to kiss. I was ready to fight—ready to beat a bitch's ass over my man—heart problems or not.

"Charlie, be easy. Damn! You stay ready to fight someone." Jamie looked down into my face.

My eyes widened. "What? *Look* at them! Do you see what *I* see? That nigga *never* touches me like that!"

Jamie grinned a little bit. He leaned over and whispered in my ear. "How can you really be mad at them, shorty, for dancing, when we *both* know that a lot more than *dancing* happened between us?"

I looked at him, coming to my senses . . . just a little bit. I was already fragile, and I knew that Aaron wanted to break up with me. I had trapped him with a baby that he didn't even know wasn't his. "Jamie, I *don't* want him dancing with her." I was furious.

Jamie held my hand, leading me out onto the dance floor. Ne'Vaeh's back was turned to us as we approached them on the floor. Aaron caught sight of us walking toward them, then loosened his grip from Ne'Vaeh's hips. She turned around to see Jamie approaching her, me following close behind him.

It took her a few seconds to register who he was and when it registered in her mind, I think it registered in her heart as well. Her lips trembled. She looked up at Aaron, who was looking right back at her. His temples twitched a little.

"Aaron, it-it's Jamie." She talked over the music, looking back up at Jamie. "Jamie," she whispered to herself, looking at her long-lost love.

Jamie held her hand, pulling her to him. "Happy birthday, li'l Ne'Vaeh." His eyes glistened under the ballroom lights.

Ne'Vaeh slid her hand from his, then looked at me. "What's going on?"

"Surprise!" I heard Alisha's voice over my shoulder. She ran up to Ne'Vaeh to hug her around her neck.

Ne'Vaeh wasn't sure how to react. I'm sure the last person she expected to see was Jamie. She hadn't seen him or talked to him in four years. She had just learned to deal with the fact that Jamie was never coming back to Maryland—and there he was, standing there before her, looking like a sexy piece of milk chocolate.

"Look who I found, honey!" Alisha glanced at me, then looked back at Ne'Vaeh. "All the way live, from Memphis, Tennessee!"

"Jamie, what are you doing here?" Ne'Vaeh was obviously upset that no one bothered to ask her how she felt about seeing Jamie again after so long.

"Just came by to see what was up with my first love. I must say, shorty, you are looking fine as a muthafucka in that dress. C'mere, shorty. Give me a hug. Let me hold you." He pulled her close in his arms.

Ne'Vaeh broke out in tears.

Aaron looked crushed. He watched Jamie holding her, gripping her waist in his hands. He watched Ne'Vaeh crying in his arms.

Ne'Vaeh pulled from Jamie, pushing him off her. "Four years, Jamie! I haven't seen your ass in *four fuckin'* years, and you think you can just stroll up in here like you didn't just up and leave me?"

Jamie just looked at her, not sure what to say.

Ne'Vaeh looked at Alisha. "How could you all do this to me today? On my muthafuckin' birthday!" She stormed off past us, pushing her way through the crowd of people.

Alisha sighed. "Well, *that* didn't go as planned."

"Yeah, shorty, you *think?*" Aaron shook his head. "I don't know why women don't think before they do shit. How do y'all figure she wanted to see this muthafucka?"

Jamie had to laugh at the fact that Aaron was talking about him as if he wasn't standing right there.

Alisha rolled her eyes. "Whatever, Aaron. Fine. Y'all want me to take the blame for how she feels, as if *y'all* don't have shit to do with this? Okay, I'll take the blame. This is *my* fault, so *I'll* go get her." She hurried off to find Ne'Vaeh.

There I stood, between Aaron and Jamie. Aaron looked at Jamie. Jamie looked at him. Aaron knew what Jamie once meant to Ne'Vaeh. By the look on Aaron's face, I wasn't so sure what Ne'Vaeh meant to *him,* but it was obvious by the way he looked at Jamie that he didn't appreciate him ruining their sensual moment.

"What's good, Aaron?" Jamie grinned. "I heard a lot about you, man."

"Well, I haven't heard shit about you, nigga, other than the fact that you smashed the girl, then bounced." Aaron was defensive.

Jamie laughed a little. "Hold up, homie. Forgive me if I'm wrong but, uh, you seem a little offended that I'm here. Now, if Charlene is your girl, why does me coming here to see *Ne'Vaeh* got you feeling some type of way?"

I pulled Aaron away from Jamie by his arm. It didn't take much to piss Aaron off, and from what I remember about Jamie, he was on the same page—Anger Management 101.

Aaron pulled from me, getting back in his face. "Muthafucka, I don't gotta explain a *muthafuckin'* thing to you. Anyone can see that Heaven has been through enough bullshit. Your ass hasn't stepped foot in the girl's life in four years; then you pop up out of the blue like she's supposed to greet your ass with open arms?"

I looked up at Aaron. Since I've known him, he's always called that girl 'Heaven,' and it always bothered me, though I never said anything.

Jamie looked at me. *He* knew it bothered me. He looked back at Aaron. "What do you know about 'Heaven'? Why is 'Heaven' any of your concern, Aaron? I don't see her here with anybody. Is she here with *you?* Because I thought you were here with *her*." He pointed at me. "You wanna explain to your girl here why you're in your feelings about a girl—who's *not* your girl?" Jamie grinned. "You have a woman as fine as Charlie, and you worried about her best friend? Fill her in on that, my nigga."

Aaron looked at me, his eyes glistening, temples twitching. "Charlie, I told you that I didn't wanna come to this party. I knew it was gonna be some shit. If you wanna stay here and reminisce with your friends, cool, but I can't do this shit." He walked past me.

"Aaron!" I tried to grab his hand, but he pulled away, making his way through the crowd, and out of Venus. "Oh my goodness, this night couldn't get any worse!"

Jamie shook his head at me. "Shorty, you got bigger problems than you know."

I looked up at him. "What do you mean?"

Jamie looked at me. "There's a reason why he calls her 'Heaven,' shorty. Seems to me like 'Heaven' is where he wants to be." Jamie walked past me toward the bar.

I just stood there in the middle of the dance floor, heart pounding. I wasn't going to make any assumptions until I found out from the horse's mouth. I was feeling guilty for my own actions, which probably had me questioning Aaron's. Aaron never so much as brought up Ne'Vaeh's name, unless he was trying to hook her up with one of his friends. I had no idea why he all of a sudden cared about her feelings. He'd been calling her Heaven from the day he met her. If he wanted her from day one, then why did he take *me* out instead of her?

Would you believe that Ne'Vaeh left her own birthday party? Turns out, she asked Renée to take her back to Howard. Jamie stayed until the party was over. Aaron went wherever he went and didn't answer any of my phone calls. I stayed until one o'clock when the party was officially over. The girls invited me to the club with them, and I agreed, though I was in no mood to party. I knew Jamie would be at the club with the whole damn football team. Judging by the fact that his phone didn't ring or vibrate all night long, I'd assumed that things were over between him and his girlfriend. I didn't have time for any more drama. I had problems beyond repair. Aaron was in his feelings about Jamie's encounter with Ne'Vaeh, and I was in my feelings about Aaron's encounter with Ne'Vaeh. Something was going on, and I was going to get to the bottom of it.

Just as I was about to leave Venus with the girls, Ne'Vaeh's aunt runs up to me with Aaron's coat. "Sweetie, Aaron left this at the table this afternoon. . . ." She handed me his coat.

I thanked her, taking the coat from her.

Just when she handed me the coat and walked away, what looked like a receipt fell from the coat pocket.

"What's that?" Danita asked as she bent over to pick the piece of paper off the floor. "Looks like a receipt." She handed the receipt to me.

I looked at it. It was a receipt from the new Vintage Urban Hip-Hop Outlet at the mall. The shit in that store was too damn expensive for the average person. I shopped in the store from time to time when I felt like splurging, but it had been a few months since I stepped foot inside that store.

Dana took the receipt from my hand. "Three hundred seventy-eight dollars and forty-two cents, Coogi Sweater Dress with Hood?" She looked at me after reading the receipt.

I looked at her, taking the receipt from her hand, reading it for myself.

"Didn't that receipt come from *Aaron's* pocket?" Danita asked.

Dana looked at me. "I haven't seen you wear no damn Coogi sweater dress with no damn hood. As a matter of fact, you don't even *wear* Coogi. Who the fuck *still* wears Coogi?"

My heart started to pound in my chest. I knew who did. That funky bitch.

Kelissa looked at me. She knew too. "*Ne'Vaeh* had on a Coogi sweater dress with a hood tonight."

Tear instantly lined my lashes. I looked at Danita.

Danita shook her head. "I told you. That bitch Karma always shows up just in time."

Chapter 8

Drink a Little Bit

Ne'Vaeh

"Ne'Vaeh, sweetie, you need to pull yourself together. Do you really want him to see you like this?" Renée exclaimed.

I was hurt. I cried like a baby in my cousin's arms that afternoon, in the bathroom at Venus. I couldn't believe that Charlie was pregnant with Aaron's baby. I mean, Aaron and I had *just* had sex that morning. He'd just told me that he was breaking up with her. He'd just told me that *I* was the one who made his heart beat. The fun had just begun—and then it was over, just like that. I hadn't felt so lost, so hurt, so confused, so angry since Jamie left me some four years earlier. I hated love, and obviously, that bitch hated me.

Renée held my face in her hands, drying my tears. "You need to dry these tears because there is really no use crying over this! Baby, didn't I tell you that this would happen? Didn't I? Why are you so shocked? Why are you falling out in front of the damn girl? Why are you not owning up to the fact that *you* are the other woman, *she's* not? I told you that your weekend fling wouldn't last, boo! I know you love that boy. Trust me, I know what love looks like, but he is *hers*, do you hear me?"

I shook my head at her. "Why doesn't love . . . love me, Renée? Why does it always hurt me? He doesn't love her, Renée! He loves *me!*"

Renée shook her head back at me, still holding my face in her hands. "Sweetie, his love for you isn't gonna stop that baby from being born. It's not gonna change the fact that your best friend is in love with that boy, despite how you feel about him. Y'all had two years to get this shit straight. If the nigga loved you like he says he does, he wouldn't put you in this position. If he loved you the way he says he does, he would'a manned up and asked you out in high school. It's too late for you two, boo. You gotta move on."

I looked up into her face, tears dripping from my face, on to her hands. There was no denying that my cousin was right. I was in love with Aaron for two years and had to live with the fact that he was with my best friend every day. Once I finally got the chance to spend some time with him alone, it only took him two days for him to have me sprung. The fact that Aaron and Charlie were together was devastating enough. The fact that there was a baby in the picture took away my consciousness. As soon as the words came out of Charlie's mouth that afternoon, my whole body completely shut down. I didn't know how I was going to live, knowing that Charlie was going to give birth to a part of Aaron. Anastasia's offer to move to Atlanta and possibly sign on to her record label was looking pretty damn good right about now.

I could barely think straight the rest of that night. The liquor was taking over me. I drank until I could barely move. I sat at the bar in Venus, sitting alone at my own birthday party. Tears slid down my face as I sipped from a bottle of Budweiser.

"Heaven, will you dance with me?" I flinched at the sound of Aaron's voice over my shoulder.

I jumped up from the barstool. I wanted to slap him dead in his face, but instead, I pushed past him. "Get the fuck away from me, Aaron!"

He grabbed my arm, pulling me back to him.

I looked up into his face, shaking my head. "Aaron, go back over there and dance with your baby's mama!"

Aaron shook his head, pulling me closer to him, surrounding me in his arms.

I buried my face in his chest. "How could you do this to me?" I sobbed. "You said you loved me!"

"Baby, I'm sorry." He whispered in my ear, "I'm sorry you had to find out like this."

I lifted my head from his chest, looking up into his face. "Aaron, what is it you want from me? We can't be together when you're having a baby with my best friend!"

Aaron looked like he was on the verge of tears, but he manned up. He let go of me and took me by the hand, out into the middle of the dance floor, where we faced each other. He grabbed my body by my hips and brought me closer to him. I slid my arms over his shoulders as Aaron looked down in my face. His lip was trembling. He didn't know what to say. His words came out in tears. I cried aloud, burying my face in his chest.

"Heaven, I love you. This doesn't change that. I'm sorry. I swear, I didn't know," he whispered in my ear, drying the tears from my face. "I'm not ready to be a father, especially to a girl I know I don't wanna be with. I wish that *you* were the one having my baby, shorty. You know I'd rather be with you, Heaven, don't you?"

I looked up into his face, my heart fluttering in my chest.

He looked down into mine, his eyes searching my face. I thought he was going to kiss me, right in front of everyone. To top it off, the drunken part of me actually wanted him to . . . but he didn't. He just held my face in his hands, drying my tears. His thumbs grazed against my lips.

"Aaron, you-you are *so* wonderful. And I wish I would have told you sooner," I whispered, looking into his face as he put his hands back on my hips.

I looked up at him, watching the look on his face change from remorse to frustration. He let go of my hips, and I turned around to see Charlie standing there, arms folded, alongside . . . It took a few seconds to realize who the man beside her was because my whole body seemed to go numb. Flashbacks of middle school raced through my mind. Flashbacks of the happiness, sadness, pain, anger, and loneliness flashed through my heart. There I was, staring in Jamie's face again after four years. He looked amazing, like a model fresh off the cover of *GQ* magazine. He stood there, dressed in all white from head to toe. His skin was smooth, chocolate, and flawless. When he held my hand, I could feel his pulse. I snatched away before my soul connected with his again. He had left my heart to fend for itself, then, out of the blue, he pops up at my birthday party four years later. In just three days, my life was turned upside down. I went from being lonely to being confused, to being angry. I had no choice but to leave my own party.

I didn't make it halfway up the sidewalk when Alisha comes running behind me. "Cutie, where are you going?" She caught up with me.

I turned around to face her. I wanted to slap her dead in her face, but instead, I cursed the bitch out. "Why the *fuck* would you invite Jamie?"

"Oh, sweetie," Alisha grabbed me in her arms and hugged me. "I didn't mean to hurt you, I swear! I just thought you needed to see him. I ran into him a few months ago in Miami. One of his teammates gave me his number. A few weeks ago, I called him and told him that I wanted to surprise you. It wasn't easy getting him to come. He said you wouldn't wanna see him. I guess he knew more than I did. I thought you would at least be a little happy to see him, Cutie. I didn't know you would be this hurt." She let go of me.

"He-he looks so *good. Why* does he have to look so fuckin' good?" I sobbed.

Alisha laughed a little. "I know, boo, I *know*."

"I found out today that Charlie's pregnant." I dried my tears.

Alisha just looked at me, not really sure what to say. She hesitated, "S-she told you that she was pregnant?"

I nodded, "Yeah. She said that Aaron and her were about to break up this morning until she told him that she was pregnant with his baby."

Alisha giggled a little. "Aaron's baby, huh? That's funny as hell."

I didn't see anything at all humorous about the situation. "Alisha, you know how I feel about him! You saw us fuckin' in his bedroom! Charlie is like a sister to me, and this was the *last* thing that I wanted to do to her! My cousin's wife asked me to go on tour with her, and I'm seriously considering it. I can't stay here anymore. It was bad enough loving Aaron when I didn't know how he felt about me. Now that he told me how he felt and he *showed* me how he felt, there's no way I can live with this. I couldn't breathe when Charlie told me that she was pregnant with Aaron's baby, Alisha. I passed the fuck out right in front of her! When I woke up, I was looking right into the face of the person who *told* me that I was only going to end up hurt! I straight up ignored her—and look what the fuck happened!"

Alisha shook her head. "Girl, you need a drink."

I looked at her, wiping my tears that just wouldn't stop coming down. "Alisha, I drank enough for at least ten people tonight."

"Hey, cuz!" Renée came scurrying down the sidewalk in her heels. "Where do you think *you're* going? Oh my goodness, did you see *Jamie's* fine milk-chocolaty ass up in there?"

I shook my head. "Girl, you just answered your own question with another question. I gotta get outta here."

Renée looked frustrated. "Ne'Vaeh, why are you gonna let your emotions run you from your own birthday party? Do you know how long it took me to plan this shit? Do you know how much *money* I spent on these decorations? You lucky Jade Allan let us get this spot for free, or I would kick your ass right about now!"

I put my hand in her face. "Renée, I had a long day. I need to get the fuck outta here. Now either one of you are gonna drive me back to Howard, or I'm gonna walk. I'm sure some perverted muthafucka will be glad to pick me up and give me a ride."

Renée rolled her eyes, grabbing me by the arm. "You are too damn dramatic. C'mon, but I'm not taking you home, boo. I know *just* the place."

We ended up going to a late-night karaoke bar. I was in no mood to sing, but I always did enjoy watching people making a fool of themselves, trying to keep up with words to songs that they'd never heard. It's funny as hell watching an old white guy rapping to Lil Wayne. The shit you see in Baltimore.

The three of us sat at a corner booth in the far corner of the club, eating vodka Popsicles, the bartender's specialty. It was really strange to see Alisha hanging out without her little entourage.

"That bartender looks real familiar." Alisha pointed over to the light-skinned bartender.

Renée nodded, taking a bite of the Popsicle. "She's Amina, my best friend's little sister."

Alisha shook her head, "Nah, I know her. She comes over to Ashton's crib every now and then to smoke with the crew. As a matter of fact, she was over there today." Alisha looked at me. "She came over to the crib after *you* left."

She just had to remind me about that morning. I sank back in my chair. "See, I was just about to thank y'all for taking my mind off my stupidity, but never fuckin' mind, Alisha."

Alisha laughed a little. "Girl, I don't even know why you're trippin'. I mean, besides the fact that you think Aaron got your girl pregnant."

I looked at her. "What do you mean I 'think' Aaron got her pregnant? You know what, Alisha? I'm not even gonna get into this shit with you. Let's just chill and get some more drinks. Matter of fact, I'll go up to the bar and get us some. What y'all drinkin'?"

Renée looked at me, looking like she wished she hadn't invited instigating-ass Alisha to come. "Girl, just get me a rum and Coke."

"Make that two." Alisha winked at me.

I rolled my eyes, getting up from the table. I made my way over to the bar. The place was crowded. The bar was surrounded with people, but Amina caught sight of me and signaled me to come to the front of the bar.

"Hey, sweetie!" Her red lips formed a smile. "What'cha drinking?"

"Three rum and Cokes, please." I sat on a stool at the bar.

Amina looked at me as she mixed the drinks. "You're lookin' real nineties fly in your Coogi today."

I grinned a little. "Thanks, boo."

She smiled, setting the drinks on a small tray. "Girl, a mutual friend called a few minutes ago. I hope you don't mind that I told him you were here."

I looked at her. "Friend? What friend?"

"So you just up and leave your own party, Heaven?" I heard Aaron's voice over my shoulder.

I looked up to see him looking down into my face, his green eyes glistening under the bar lights. I hopped up from the stool, turning around to face him, my heart flickering in my chest. "Aaron, I'm not with this shit tonight. Y'all muthafuckas already ruined my birthday party! Now you're here to ruin the only peace I've had all fuckin' week? Why would you show up here?"

Aaron pulled me to him by my hand. "Shorty, can we go somewhere and talk?"

I slid my hand from his. "No! What is there left to talk about, Aaron? You're having a baby with my best friend! What is there left to discuss?" I walked past him, heading out of the bar. I really couldn't have the whole bar in my business.

Aaron followed behind me. "So you're just gonna ignore me? You're just gonna walk away from me?" He grabbed me by the arm once we got outside of the club doors.

I pulled away from him then pushed him in his chest. "Aaron, why are you doing this to me? I told you this morning when you kissed me that this was wrong! That touching me, kissing me, making me feel like I was someone special was *wrong!*"

"Ne'Vaeh, is this muthafucka bothering you?" I looked up to see Renée walking out of the bar. Alisha came close behind.

I looked back up at Aaron. "No, he was just leaving."

Aaron looked at me.

Renée walked over to my side, hands on her hips. "I can't believe you would bring your ass here! Now, it's bad enough that you took advantage of this girl when you knew how she felt about you, but then you have the nerve to *still* pursue her after she just found out that you got Charlie pregnant?"

Aaron looked at her as if he was really losing his patience with her. Every time she saw him, she had a nasty attitude. "Look, Renée, you need to stay out of this shit. Now, I'm trying to respect my elders, but you keep overstepping your boundaries."

Renée's eyes widened. "*Elders?* Oh, so now I'm old? Overstepping *my* boundaries? Nigga, you have me *fucked* up! Muthafucka, *you* overstepped your boundaries when you fucked my cousin when you knew you had a girl!"

Alisha had to step in. "Whoa. Hold up now. I mean, she had a part in this too, while you're talkin' all this shit to Aaron. He didn't force her to have sex with him!"

Renée looked Alisha. "Oh, really? Let's see." Renée looked at Aaron. "Aaron, did she tell you no?"

I pulled Renée from him before she got in his face. "Renée, please, just leave it alone."

Renée pulled from me, stood her ground, and got right up in Aaron's face. "I asked you a fuckin' question. *Did* she tell you no?"

Aaron's eyes glistened. He looked at Renée then looked at me. "I know I was wrong, but I had to have her."

I rolled my eyes. Renée was always in my business, and I had to admit, it was pretty fucking aggravating at times. "C'mon, y'all, let's just end this conversation before we take this too far."

Renée was already fired up, and there was no stopping her. "You are a triflin'-ass muthafucka! You know the girl hadn't had dick in like four fuckin' years! You knew it wouldn't take much to get into her panties! You could have had any girl you wanted, so why would you choose your girl's best friend? Why?"

Aaron just looked at Renée. He had had enough of her. "So, God hired you to be my judge, right? How the fuck are you gonna judge me *or* your own cousin when the nigga you dealin' with *now* has a fuckin' girlfriend *and* a fuckin' baby on the way? How the fuck is a side chick gonna try to give relationship advice? Get the fuck outta here with that bullshit, ma."

Alisha just stood there, sipping her rum and Coke from a straw, with her eyes lit up like she knew some shit was about to go down.

"Why are you bringing this shit up? What you got going on with my cousin has nothing to do with me!" Renée pushed him in his chest.

"Well, the way I feel about your cousin doesn't have shit to do with you either!" Aaron exclaimed, trying his best not to push her ass back.

"The hell it doesn't! Why are you out here talking to her? There's no way that y'all can be together when that girl is pregnant! I'm not gonna let you string my cousin along!" Renée turned to me. "Ne'Vaeh, sweetie, please use your head! What do you think is gonna happen to you if you continue to mess with Aaron? He claims he loves you now, but how do you know how he'll feel once this baby is here? How do you think Charlie will feel once she finds out that you've been fuckin' her man behind her back?"

I looked up at Aaron. Everything in my mind was telling me that the way I was feeling was wrong, but my heart had no common sense whatsoever.

"Heaven," Aaron grabbed my hand, "I didn't mean for any of this to happen. I swear I didn't know that Charlie was pregnant! You know I was gonna break up with her this morning. I was gonna end it until she told me that she was having my baby. I didn't want this. I'm not ready to be a father. In my family, most of the men had unplanned children with women who they didn't plan on being with. Even my own father. He married my mother at seventeen because she was pregnant. My father is from England. His family is big on reputation. When you get someone pregnant, they expect you marry the girl."

I looked at Aaron, my heart pounding in my chest.

"Aaron, no!" Alisha exclaimed. "You're gonna let your parents tell you who you need to marry? You're a grown-ass man! No, don't do this! Not with Charlie! I'm telling you!" Alisha looked at me. "Ne'Vaeh, say something!"

I shook my head. What could I say? I was wrong in all types of ways. I deserved for Charlie to be pregnant with Aaron's baby. I deserved for her to jump the broom with him right in front of my face.

"Heaven, I have to do the right thing. I wasn't raised to walk away from my responsibility. I love you. I have never loved *anyone* the way that I love you. I should have stepped to you in high school. Baby, I'm sorry." He held both of my hands.

"Well, it is what it is. And it's already done." I slid my hands from his.

Renée held my arm. "C'mon, Ne'Vaeh, let's go back inside. Let him go."

I turned around to walk back inside the bar.

"Heaven," Aaron called my name.

I turned back around, heart racing, a sharp pain in my chest.

"If it's all right with you, I wanna finish where we left off this morning." Aaron's green eyes shone under the streetlights. "Heaven, we may never have this opportunity again. So come with me. *Fuck* your cousin *and* what she has to say about it."

I looked at Renée, who stood there with her arms folded across her chest.

She shook her head at me, pretty much done with my heart and me at that moment. Then she threw her hands up, finally surrendering. "Fuck what *I* have to say about it? You know what? I'm done. If all you want from this boy tonight is sex, then I'm not gonna judge you. Go ahead. Fuck his brains out. All I'm saying is Charlie *is* gonna find out. I just hope Aaron is worth the drama that she's gonna bring, because you *know* the bitch is gonna bring it. Karma goes *both* ways, cuz. You just remember that shit." Renée stormed back inside the bar.

Alisha looked at me, not really sure what to say. She looked at Aaron. "I told you to tell her how you felt back in high school, Aaron. This shit is gonna get messy, *real* messy." She turned around and walked back into the bar as well.

I turned to Aaron, looking up into his face.

His cell phone rang in his pocket. He ignored it, looking down at me instead.

"Aren't you gonna answer it? You already know it's Charlie callin' you, wondering where you're at. You can't just ignore her calls, Aaron." I shook my head.

"She'll be all right. I got something I gotta do. I may never get this chance again." His eyes grew misty. "I know I'm wrong, Heaven, but I'm really feeling some type of way about Jamie showin' up here to your party. I know you're not my girl, but you're not his either." His eyes hardened. "Charlie didn't like the way that I was defending you, and I really don't give a fuck, Heaven. *She* should have been defending you. She knows the nigga broke your heart, yet she and Alisha thought it was cool to invite the muthafucka to your birthday party."

"I don't think Alisha meant any harm by inviting Jamie. Why she invited him, I'm not sure, but I don't think her intentions were to hurt me."

"My agent's cousin owns the Courtyard Marriott in Alexandria. Some friends are there now, throwing a party in the ballroom. We can go there, show our faces, get a dance in, have a few drinks, then bounce. I plan on gettin' drunker than a muthafucka. I ain't gonna be able to drive, shorty. My manager reserved me a suite in his name—we can go chill there. I need to stay there for a few days to clear my head. I need to think. I need to figure out how I'm gonna tell my aunt and my parents." Aaron ran his hands across his head anxiously.

I shook my head, looking into his shimmering eyes. "Look at the mess we've made, Aaron."

I didn't know the kind of family that Aaron was raised in, but apparently, everyone else did. Even Alisha knew his parents would want Aaron to marry Charlie to "protect his reputation." It took me until our high school graduation to finally meet his family. His father was a handsome white man from England. His mother was breathtakingly beautiful. Her bronzed skin looked as if the sun had kissed it. She was Arabian and Senegalese, and one of the most beautiful women that I had ever met. I saw instantly where Aaron got his green eyes. Her eyes looked straight through you to your soul. She couldn't care less about me when she met me at our high school graduation, but she immediately took to Charlie.

Aaron's parents lived in California. When he got into some sort of trouble, hanging out with the wrong crowd, they sent him to live with his father's half sister, who was an officer in the army, stationed at Fort Meade. From what I knew about his family, I wasn't exactly the type his family would have accepted. I wasn't "paper bag" light or from a rich, prestigious family. I was the brown-skinned daughter of a poor drug addict, who didn't know which one of many lays fathered her three children.

I was put in a pretty tough spot. I was in love with a man who was untouchable in every aspect. It was obvious by the look on Charlie's face when she mentioned being pregnant that Charlie was afraid of losing Aaron. I had no idea their relationship was a mess. I hadn't been around Charlie or her friends in years to know anything about the rumors that caught Aaron's attention. From the moment the two had started dating, I'd tried to keep my distance. My heart had been sealed shut for years before Aaron came along. Jamie had ruined every man's chance at breaking my heart. I swore the day that he left me that I would never fall in love again. However, from the moment I looked into Aaron's eyes that day in my African American History class, my heart was his.

There we were, cruising down the street in Aaron's candy-painted maroon Chevy Impala. The late-night slow jams played on the radio. The fact that it began to rain didn't help brighten the mood either. My cell phone was on vibrate, but it was ringing off the hook. Family members were blowing up my phone, calling, texting, leaving voice mails. Even Jamie happened to get ahold of my cell phone number. The dude left three voice mails, and I deleted each one of them, without listening to the messages. Alisha called, Renée called, even Darryl and Jade called. The only one who I expected to call hadn't called even once. Charlie was feeling some type of way about me that night. I knew it wouldn't be long before I would have to deal with her wrath, regardless of whether she knew something was going on.

I couldn't handle any more drama from anyone that night. I looked over at Aaron, about to ask him exactly what friends were going to be at this party. Aaron was deep in thought, temples twitching. I knew he was angry with himself but probably angrier with the family tradition that he would be forced to follow. I grabbed his hand in mine, kissed it, then held it up against my chest. I wanted to tell him that everything was going to be okay, but I wasn't so sure how things would turn out myself. All I knew was that Aaron and Charlie were going to be married, and I was going to have to watch.

We got to the party within an hour and fifteen minutes. The parking lot was packed. It was about 11:00 that night. To be honest, his friends' party was a lot better than mine was. I at least felt welcome at their party. There was no drama, no family asking me why I didn't have a man, no presents from Juanita, no pregnant best friend, no cousins making me feel guilty about my feelings, no old boyfriend, no tears, no pain, and no heartbreak. We drank, we danced, and we had a great time. I made it through three slow dances and three Long Island Iced Teas before Aaron had to call it a night. I don't think he could take any more skin-to-skin contact that night without wanting to undress me.

Chapter 9

The After-Party

Ne'Vaeh

We made our way down the hotel hallway toward the suite that Aaron's coach and manager reserved for him that night. Aaron's hand trembled as he slid the key card into the key slot. He opened the door, and we walked in. I was in awe walking into the hotel suite, which was more like a two-bedroom apartment. Fresh roses were in every vase. Scented candles were scattered around the living room, down the hallway, and all over the kitchen. The hotel room smelled like the cleaning crew had just left. The carpet smelled like Carpet Fresh, the wood floors in the hallway looked like they'd just been mopped, and the furniture looked like it had just been polished. I felt like I was on my honeymoon, and I wasn't even the one who was about to get married.

Suddenly, I felt like shit.

I turned to Aaron as he slid my jacket from my shoulders.

He tossed the jacket on the sofa. "Shorty, I am drunk as *fuck!*" He laughed a little.

I nodded in agreement. My vision was a little blurry, and I could barely stand up straight. "Yeah, boo, I had a little too much to drink myself. Not to mention all the weed that you and your homeboys smoked around me got me feelin' like *I* was the one chiefin'!"

Aaron smiled a little. "It's been a long day. I mean a *very* long day. I'm staying here for a few days because I ain't trying to go back to my apartment. I don't wanna deal with Ashton's mouth or run into Charlie. You can stay with me for a few days if you want to, shorty. You know you need a break."

I sighed. I did need a fucking break. Not just from school, but from "Mama" Renée. She was always on my ass about *every* decision that I made. Not saying that I didn't need it, but just like Aaron said, her life wasn't up to par to be talking about anyone else's. "What about a change of clothes, Aaron?"

"I already got you." He grinned. "There's an outfit in the back room for you. You know, some sweats, a tank top, a pair of Reeboks. C'mon, shorty, let's get in the shower."

He was too amazing, and the more I was around him, the more I hated my life. I never got what I wanted or what I needed. Everything that I wanted seemed to be out of reach. There I was, alone in an expensive hotel with my best friend's soon-to-be-fiancé. I wanted that boy more than I've ever wanted anything. It was hard to enjoy the moment when I knew it wasn't going to last forever.

"So, you just knew that I'd give in and come here with you tonight?" I looked up into his face as he grabbed me by the waist, pulling my body up against his.

Aaron licked his lips. "Nah, but I was hoping you would ditch your cousin and roll with me. She's miserable, shorty. Any decision that you make, she'll have something negative to say about it. Let's just enjoy the moment. We can drink a little bit more if you want. We can get in the hot tub. We can fix something to eat. Whatever you wanna do, it's totally up to you tonight, Heaven." He gripped my dress in his hands.

Our eyes held their gaze as he slid my dress up over my head then tossed it on the sofa. I stepped out of my heels. Then he held my hand, leading me down the hallway to the bathroom. The bathroom was huge, about the size of my old bedroom at Charlie's house. Large, scented candles surrounded the huge tub, which was in the center of the bathroom. Everything I needed to take a shower sat in a basket on top of the sink's countertop—bath sponge, vanilla-scented bath wash, shampoo, a bar of soap, face wash, washcloth, and towel.

"H-how did you know what my favorite body wash is, Aaron?" I exclaimed.

Aaron smiled at me before walking over to the shower. "You remember the other day when I had you in my weight room, and I was playing in your pussy? Well, I still remembered the scent you left on my fingers. It smelled like a mix between vanilla and butterscotch. I couldn't find butterscotch at the store, so I went with vanilla."

He knew just what to say to get my adrenaline pumping and my hormones raging. Even though he had me feeling some kind of way about him, my emotions were overpowered by the guilt of being infatuated with my best friend's boyfriend. I stood there, barely able to move as Aaron slid back the frosted glass door, then turned the shower on. Steam immediately filled the bathroom.

My heart pounded in my chest as he sat down on the toilet seat to untie his shoes. He kicked them off, then slipped his shirt over his head, tossing it on the floor. He pulled off his tank top, then stood up to unbuckle his pants. He looked up at me, noticing that I wasn't undressing along with him.

He walked over to me and pulled me closer to him by my hands, snapping me out of my "what-the-fuck-am-I-doing" daze.

"Heaven?" He looked down at me.

I looked up at him, bottom lip trembling. "M-maybe we shouldn't do this, Aaron," I whispered. "Haven't we done enough already?"

Aaron shook his head, letting go of my hands, removing the belt from his pants. "Nah, we haven't." He unbuttoned his pants, dropping them to the floor. I watched as he slipped off his socks, then his boxers. He looked down at me as he slid his hands around my waist, then up my back to unhook my bra. "Just forget about everyone else. Right now, it's just you and me. Charlie doesn't even *exist* right now, if you ask me."

The steam in the bathroom caused my curls to go limp. My damp hair hung just below my shoulders. Aaron gently kissed my lips, running his hands up and through my hair, yanking it just a little. My body was on fire, and I felt light on my feet. I would say that I was floating on air, but I was really floating on weed and alcohol. I had been drinking nonstop all day, and my body was feeling it. I didn't have the strength to resist Aaron that night, and he knew it too. I grabbed the body wash, loofah, shampoo, then followed him into the shower. I'd barely lathered my hair or body when Aaron turned around to face me. My whole body trembled under the showerhead that night. I was feeling all types of emotions, mostly heartbreak.

Aaron held my face in his hands, looking down intently. "Heaven, baby, I know you're upset with me."

"Yes, I am, Aaron! If you wanted me in high school, you should have just said so!" I exclaimed. "I would have done anything you would have asked me to! I was in love with you from the very first moment I saw you! You were *so* beautiful! Oh my goodness, Aaron, if you would have asked me back then, I was *so* ready!"

Aaron sighed, shaking his head to himself. "Shorty, I had no clue. You barely even *looked* at me! I got with Charlie because I didn't think I had a chance with *you*."

I shook my head, looking up into his face. "Well, now, you have the girl of your parents' dreams. The woman your mom and dad would want you to be with. She's having your baby, whether or not you like it. I love you, I really do, but you belong to Charlie! I don't know what is going wrong in y'all relationship, but I promise, I am *not* the answer."

Aaron shook his head in disagreement. "Nah, shorty, you *are* the answer. I have loved you for almost three years but was too afraid to get rejected by you. Shorty, you were so mean and stuck-up in high school!" He laughed a little.

I blushed. "No, Aaron, I was *not* mean or stuck-up. I was just hurt. Someone who I loved hurt me when he left me, so I kinda kept my guard up. But you broke down my walls, Aaron. Like now, for instance. I'm naked in a shower with my best friend's soon-to-be husband, and for what? To get heartbroken all over again?"

"I never meant to hurt you, Heaven. Just when I decide to tell you how I feel about you, Charlie tells me she's pregnant. I mean, she told me *right* when I was about to break up with her, shorty. The girl wasn't even planning to tell me because she didn't plan to keep the baby. But as soon as I tell her it's over, yo, shorty drops the news on me."

I continued washing my hair. "Well, Aaron, any woman in her right mind would say just about anything to keep you."

Aaron looked at me as he continued to lather his body in Lever 2000. "I can't stand the fact that your dude, Jamie, is here. The nigga had me ready to pop off in that bitch tonight, I'm tellin' you. He knows the way I feel about you. Even hinted to Charlie that I was a little 'too concerned' about him coming to see you."

I looked up at him.

Aaron looked down at me, pulling me closer to him. His body was so silky, so smooth, and so warm. "I missed out on my chance of being with you the way that I wanna be with you, which is why I brought you here tonight. If I can't have you forever, I thought I should at least get to spend some time with you for just a little while." His heart beat rapidly against mine. He gently kissed my lips, and I nearly melted in his arms. His kisses soothed my soul, instantly taming my heart and my mind.

"Let's just—" I whispered in between kisses. "Let's just go to bed. I just want you to hold me, please. That's pretty much all I can handle tonight."

He lifted me up in his arms, wrapping my legs around his waist as he opened the door to the shower and walked out, carrying me out of the bathroom.

We were soaking wet, suds dripping everywhere. He carried me into the master bedroom, sat down on the bed, then lay back, holding me against his body. He gently kissed my neck as I buried my face in his. Having sex was the furthest thing from either of our minds at that point. I think we were both too drunk to perform that night. Our drunken asses fell asleep right there, wet as hell.

I awoke early that morning to the smell of pancakes, bacon, and eggs. My head was pounding. For a minute I forgot where I was until I sat up, looking around at the hotel room, remembering the events that had happened the night before. I looked over at the alarm clock on the nightstand. It was 6:15 a.m. I had class that morning at 11:00, and I had to finish my term paper, which was due the next day.

A white robe sat on the chair in the corner of the room. I got up from the bed then walked over to the chair to put it on.

"Aaron?" I called as I walked down the hallway to the kitchen.

There he stood over the stove, in his tank top and boxers. Oh my goodness, the boy had a body on him. He was chiseled and cut as if someone had carved him out of stone. He was a little cocky, yes, but in an adorable kind of way. The more I looked at him, the sadder I became. He wasn't mine, and he was supposed to be, and that shit was eating me up.

He looked over at me as I sat down at the kitchen table.

Two wineglasses, both filled with orange juice, an ice bucket with a bottle of champagne, ketchup, syrup, salt, and pepper sat on the table. I was in awe. I looked up at Aaron, shaking my head at him. "Oh my goodness, what time did you wake up to do all of this?"

Aaron grinned. "Man, you look beautiful when you wake up in the morning."

I rolled my eyes. "Aaron, please. I know I have the breath from hell right now, and my hair looks like a bird's nest." I ran my fingers through my tangled hair, which was still damp. "I look like something from *The Nightmare Before Christmas* right about now."

Aaron laughed aloud. "Girl, you're somethin' else! Never did know how fine you are." He walked over to me with two plates stacked full of food and set the plates on the table.

Bacon, eggs, pancakes, sausage, and hash browns were on my plate. He was too much.

Aaron looked at me as he handed me a fork and a knife.

I took the utensils from him. I knew from the moment we started eating that I wasn't going to make it to class that morning.

"Do you have classes today, Heaven?" Aaron dug in.

I nodded, cutting my pancakes into small pieces.

"You goin' or you hangin' out wit'cha boy today?" he asked, already knowing the answer to that question.

"I don't feel like facing the world just yet, Aaron," I whispered back.

He agreed. "Me neither, shorty."

"But I *do* have a term paper that I really need to work on today. I've been trying to get it done all weekend." I looked up at him.

"There's a laptop in the other room, shorty. Everything you need is right here."

I dried the tears that slid down my cheeks. Yeah, I'm a crybaby. Get over it. "I don't wanna waste time crying or feeling sad. Just once, I would like to feel happy and loved, even if it's only for a day or two. Let's talk, let's laugh, and let's drink. Today, I'm yours. So whatever you wanna do, just ask, or better yet, just do it."

Aaron grinned. "A'ight. Let's hurry up and eat."

Aaron lay on the bed watching TV as I blow-dried, then flat ironed, my hair that morning. He wasn't lying when he said that he had everything that I needed for me at that hotel. He bought me a full change of clothes and sexy lingerie. I stood at the mirror admiring myself in the silk burgundy bra and panties that he bought me.

Aaron looked up at me as I unplugged my flat iron.

I walked over and sat beside him on the bed.

He pulled me closer to him by my hips. I knew he was scared of where his life was going. I knew he had no clue about what he was going to say to his family about Charlie. I don't think it was so much the baby that bothered him. I think it was more of the fact that since Charlie was pregnant with *his* baby, he would be forced to marry someone who he wasn't in love with.

"I got a call a few days ago, shorty, from my agent. He said that there were a few teams that wanted me. It was just a matter of which team offered the most on my contract." He looked into my face.

My eyes lit up. It was the best news that I had heard all weekend. "That's great! Wow, so, which team do you wanna go with?"

He shrugged. "I don't know. It all depends on Charlie now. I would like to go with LA, or overseas, but we'll see." He swept my bangs from my face.

I smiled, happy as hell for that boy. "That's amazing, Aaron! I'm so happy for you. See, I *told* you that you were a star!"

Aaron laughed a little to himself. "A star, huh?"

I looked into his face. "You don't seem too happy about this, Aaron. Why don't you sound happy about joining the NBA? Your parents would be so happy for you!"

He shook his head. "Nah, not really. I haven't even told them. As a matter of fact, my parents thought I was going to school to be a doctor. My father even had medical schools picked out for me already, shorty. Hanging out with the fellas from the basketball team is what got me kicked out of school in California. I got caught selling drugs for my homeboy back in South Central."

I shook my head. "Aaron, why the hell were you selling drugs? And why the fuck were you even hanging out in South Central? Word around town is your father is some sort of royalty, and your family has money for centuries to come!"

He sighed. "I know, Heaven. I wasn't the one selling drugs. It was my homeboy. He was from the hood. He was gonna be the first in his family to graduate high school and go to UCLA on a full athletic scholarship. The nigga had skills. I knew that if I took the rap for him, my father would just pay my way out and send me to another school or some shit. My boy, Timothy, didn't have it like that. He didn't have a chance. Now, he's in UCLA, doin' the damn thing, making damn near straight-As. His family is proud, while my parents can barely look at me. And the fact that Charlie is pregnant isn't gonna help fix the situation either. I'm basically fucked."

I wasn't sure what to say. I had no idea that he had so much going on. "Ummm, do you really have to tell your parents that Charlie is pregnant?"

Aaron laughed a little. "Heaven, my parents are gonna know the only reason I'm marrying Charlie is *because* she's pregnant. They know I don't love that girl. If I don't marry her, that will be one more thing they'll be disappointed in me for."

"Everything that you do isn't gonna make someone else happy. I learned that a long time ago when I would do everything in the world to try to make Juanita smile when she was depressed." I swept my hair from my face. "There were times when she wouldn't get out of bed for weeks. There were times when we had to beg family members for food because sometimes, the only thing we had in the refrigerator was baking soda and Budweiser."

Aaron's eyes searched mine, a sympathetic look swept across his face.

"Juanita hated us, Aaron. My little brother and my older sister were the best siblings anyone could ever have. I loved them so much. I would get the shit beat out of me for trying to stop Juanita from beating my brother, all because he kept stealing money out of her purse to go buy food from the corner store. My sister was beautiful . . . legs, hips, and ass for days. She had long hair, caramel skin, light eyes. I think every one of my mother's boyfriends molested her, and my mother never gave a fuck. She probably traded my sister for drugs. Who knows? All I know is only *one* of her boyfriends tried me," I hated to admit.

Aaron's temples twitched. "What did the nigga do to you?"

I looked at him. "Let's just say I made it out of the house alive that night. About the only thing Juanita ever taught me to do was how to fire a gun. One night, when her boyfriend tried to climb into my bed naked, I reached under my mattress, pulled out the gun, and shot the muthafucka right between his legs. My mother came home that night to find an ambulance and the police outside of our home. She never forgave me for that night, even though I told her that he tried to rape me! She drank herself into a deeper and deeper depression. She watched another boyfriend rape my sister, and the bitch ended up killing my brother. Aaron, I have been through hell!" I shook my head, stomach in knots. "If it wasn't for Renée or for Charlie, I wouldn't be here talking to you right now. I would have blown my brains out the day my brother was murdered!"

Aaron held my hands, kissing both of them. He wasn't sure what he could say that could take away any of the pain that I still felt inside.

I looked at him. "Jamie helped me through a lot too. We grew up together. We only dated for about two years. He was my best friend. A huge part of me died when he moved to Tennessee to live with his dad. He just up and left me, not really saying good-bye. I had lost so much, Aaron. I lost my father who I never knew, I lost my mother who never wanted to know me, I lost my brother who loved me with all of his heart, I lost my sister who couldn't handle what had happened to her, and I lost Jamie who was my sunshine after the storm."

Aaron's eyes traced my lips.

"I'm sorry for talking about this. I said I wanted to be happy today, and here I am bringing up the past. Aaron, it's just that I need love. I don't want your pieces. I have been getting bits and pieces of people all of my life." My eyes searched his. "Don't I deserve to be happy, Aaron? Don't I?"

Aaron gently kissed my lips. "Yes, shorty, you deserve the world."

I looked into his face as he kissed my lips again. "Oh my goodness, my heart could have really used your touch back then. I seriously doubt that you would have left me feeling as if love doesn't exist. Everything about you is love, Aaron. I wish I would have felt some of this sooner."

Aaron's eyes traced my lips once again. "I don't know what Jamie's reason was for leaving you, but that nigga was crazy to leave someone like you. I would have protected you. I would have done whatever I could to make sure I kept a smile on your face, Heaven. I would do anything I could to repair your heart. You would have been happy with me, Heaven, I promise you that." He ran his fingers through my hair. "I'm not even gonna lie. The only time you would feel a little pain would be when I was drillin' that pussy. I would have fucked the *shit* out of you in high school . . . shit, probably middle school too!" He smiled a little.

I shook my head, drying my tears. "You're so stupid," I laughed.

"I'm serious, shorty. You deserve to be happy. I wish I wasn't so intimidated by how I knew you felt about Jamie. You were so *fine*, so pretty, so cute. I tried approaching you in school, but every time we were face-to-face, I lost my nerve." Aaron held my hips. "If I would have known that you were feeling me too, this whole situation would have been avoided." His lips caressed mine, his hands gripping my hips. "C'mon, enough of the talkin'. Let's put in some work."

I stood from the bed, unhooking my bra.

Aaron slid my panties past my hips, across my thighs, down my calves, and from my feet. He slipped his tank top from his head and pulled his boxers off. He scooped me up in his arms, wrapping my legs around his waist, laying me down on the bed, his body on top of mine. We kissed passionately until he couldn't take it anymore. He reached for a condom from the nightstand. I watched him tear it open, then slide it on. I held on to him as he slid his way inside of me. I bit down on his neck as he dug through me. He had a fist full of my hair, and he tugged on it a little. My whole body was burning hot. It didn't take long before we both broke out in a sweat.

My pussy was so wet. Aaron's heart beat against my chest. He took my breath completely away at that moment. All I could do was take in his air. He pumped my pussy until it was dry. I felt my cervix shift in all sorts of directions. I whimpered and I cried as he dug into me. I gripped his ass in my hands as he stroked my body. Just when I couldn't take it anymore and begged him to stop, I could feel his dick throbbing inside of me. And then, all his weight fell on top of me.

We had sex that entire afternoon. I needed it, though the entire time we spent together was pointless. Kissing him, touching him, holding him, suckin' on him, fuckin' on him, stroking him, riding him. . . . It was all pointless. I knew he loved me. He had to. He knew he would have to deal with Charlie as soon as he saw her. He had been avoiding her calls since the night before. Meanwhile, Renée, Alisha, and damn near the whole dance squad was blowing up my phone. People I hadn't talked to in years were calling, asking me why I hadn't shown up to class. I think I even got a call from one of Aaron's teammates. I knew then that everyone was calling me just to see where Aaron was.

While Aaron slept that afternoon, I worked on my term paper and finished it within two hours. At about 2:30, Aaron awoke from his nap and went to the grocery store to pick up a few items. I guess the boy wanted to seduce me with his cooking. He made shrimp pasta, rolls, salad, steak, and potatoes. Oh my goodness, the boy made love to me with his cooking. I had already been sipping on Siren Songs all afternoon, and I was drunk as hell. We laughed, we drank, we smoked, and we ate. Then we had sex. A *lot* of sex.

Aaron and I had sex on a chair out on the balcony. We had sex on the kitchen table. We had sex on the recliner. We had sex in the hot tub. He had sex in my mouth. I had sex in *his* mouth. We had sex in the shower. I was too drunk to remember if there was another round after that, that afternoon. All I knew is that I woke up on the bathroom floor, condom wrappers stuck to my back. My whole body was sore. I could barely drag myself up off the floor. I could barely walk. I could feel my pussy lips throbbing, swollen between my legs. Needless to say, yeah, he murdered the pussy. I peeled the empty condom wrappers from my skin, tossing them in the trash can. My sweatpants and tank top sat in a corner. I walked over, picking them up off the floor.

"Aaron?" I called out, walking down the hallway, pulling my tank top over my head. As I slipped into my sweatpants, I felt a breeze coming from the living room. The smell of a Newport hit me in the face. Aaron was outside smoking on the balcony.

He looked up at me as I slid the door open wider to go outside to join him. He grinned at me as I sat down. It was dark out. The moon sat high in the sky.

"What time is it?" I asked, sitting across from him.

"It's 9:30." He exhaled smoke from his nostrils. He saw me squirming a little in the chair, trying to figure out a way to sit that was comfortable. "You all right, shorty?"

I looked at him, trying not to show any signs of pain on my face. "Just trying to get comfortable. The pussy is a little swollen."

He laughed a little, leaning back in the chair, the very chair that we had sex in. He didn't look too happy. He looked like something was bothering him.

I hesitated. "Do you want to be left alone? I mean, I can go back inside if I'm disturbing you."

Aaron shook his head as he exhaled smoke through his nose. "Nah, you're good. I'm just thinkin', that's all."

"About?" I swept my bangs from my face.

"You." He put his cigarette out in the ashtray.

My heart palpitated in my chest. "What about me?" I asked.

"What's gonna happen to you? I mean, what are you gonna do?" He sat up in his chair.

I was confused. "Do about what, Aaron? What do you mean?"

"I called Charlie." He ran his hands across his close-cut hair.

I suddenly felt like shit again.

"Told her that we needed to talk in the morning." His eyes grew misty.

I got up from my chair, about to head back into the hotel.

Aaron got up from his chair and grabbed my arm, pulling me back to him.

I pushed him off me.

He exhaled deeply. "Heaven, we knew this was coming. Did you really think I was gonna be able to face her without having to explain to her where I've been these past few days?"

"Aaron, whatever you decide you wanna do with her, that's your business. I really shouldn't be, and I really don't *wanna* be hearing this." My voice trembled.

Aaron tried to fight back the tears. "It's not fair to myself, Charlie, or the baby to marry someone who I am not in love with, just to save my family's reputation or so that the person who my parents think is the 'perfect fit' for my family can inherit their money. Charlie's not stupid, shorty. She's been blowing up my phone since I left your cousin's restaurant last night. The only reason why she even agreed to meeting me in the morning is because she has a doctor's appointment tomorrow and wants me to go with her."

I was so hurt hearing him talk about her. There was no use in crying over him. There was no use in being mad at the situation. He wasn't mine to begin with. The past two nights with him didn't change that.

"Charlie couldn't care less about my family's tradition. She might say fuck me *and* my got-damn family tomorrow when we speak. She already cursed me out over the phone! After I get her to calm down, and if she wants to get married, then I'm calling my parents."

I laughed a little. "*If* she wants to get married? *Really,* Aaron?"

He looked confused. "What do you mean?"

"Charlie *loves* you, Aaron. I don't give a fuck *what* you do. The girl is in love with you. Now, she might hate *me* after this, but *you?* No, boo-boo, she's not going anywhere any time soon. I really think you could get away with murder right about now and the girl would probably say 'the muthafucka deserved it.'" I swept the bangs from my face. "So, go 'head, and pick your girl out a nice ring. Something at least three or four karats—probably princess cut—most likely in a platinum setting. You know Charlie hates gold or anything too flashy. But I'm pretty sure that your family has some sort of ring that they pass down through generations, huh?"

Aaron looked surprised that I talked about his situation so calmly.

I shrugged. "What do you want me to say, Aaron? The sex today was *beyond* amazing. I can barely feel my legs right now!"

Aaron laughed a little, though I know he was hurting inside just as badly as I was. "Yeah, that pussy *still* has a nigga dazed."

"But despite how good it feels to be with you, we know this is wrong. This is it. After tonight, it's back to reality." I sighed, hair blowing in the wind behind me.

Aaron hesitated for a minute, as if he had something to say, but didn't know how to say it.

I looked up at him. "What?"

He looked into my face. "I found out today why your boy Jamie is here for a week."

I looked up into his face, heart pounding against my rib cage. I shook my head. I really couldn't care less why Jamie decided after four years to show his face back up in Maryland. I knew I wasn't the reason why he showed up. He had missed four of my birthdays already. I knew I couldn't have been the reason he'd come back.

"Word on the street is his new agent works out of Baltimore. Come May, your boy will be drafted into the NFL. I heard the Ravens want him, but that's just what I heard." Aaron looked at me, waiting for a reaction.

I was highly upset. "What the hell does that have to do with me? I don't give a fuck what team Jamie ends up playing for. His life is not my concern anymore; hasn't been for four years, Aaron."

Aaron knew I was hurt by the entire situation. Jamie was the last person I wanted to see, let alone hear about. "You gonna meet up with him this week, shorty?"

I was getting really irritated with the whole subject. "Aaron, why are you asking me about Jamie? Why are you even bringing him up, that's what I wanna know?"

"I'm just sayin', shorty, what are you gonna do the rest of your life? Be alone?" His eyes glistened. "You know it pains me to say this shit, but maybe you should give dude a try. The way he got all defensive at your party proves the dude still has feelings for you."

My lips trembled. I fought back the tears. "The only thing worse than being alone is to even *think* about being with him! I can't even believe that you're suggesting this!"

"You just said last night at your own birthday party, in front of your cousin, that you weren't lonely, but we all know that's bullshit, Heaven. You wanna be with somebody. You want love. Even before I knew that Charlie was pregnant, and I told you that I would leave her for you, you pushed me away. You're afraid to get hurt, and that's cool, but someday, your heart has got to give." Aaron pulled me closer to him by my hands.

I looked up, shaking my head. "Aaron, today, you kissed my lips—the ones on my face *and* the ones between my legs. You massaged my shoulders, my back, my butt, my thighs, and my feet. You sucked on my fingers, my neck, my shoulders, my nipples, *and* my clit. You gently pulled my hair. I put scratches on your back. I wrapped my legs around your neck while you tongue fucked my pussy. I came in your mouth, and you came in mine. We took a shower together. You ran your fingers through my hair. You made my pussy cry just as you said you would. Tears of joy trickled down my thighs. Aaron, we made long, wet, passionate, hot, sticky, sweaty, nasty, crazy, drunk *love*."

"Yeah, it felt like magic, that's for damn sure." Aaron shook his head to himself.

I slid my hands from his. "If I can't feel the way I felt with you today *every* day, then I don't wanna feel that way at all. I don't know what I'm gonna do, Aaron, but moving on to someone else isn't gonna heal my heart. You have me wide open, like literally. The fact that Jamie is coming back in town doesn't change the fact that he left me four years ago, without looking back. He never came to visit, let alone wrote me any letters. I could give a fuck if Jamie is here or not. He's toxic, and I'm not going anywhere near him."

"Heaven, the reason why you're still hurting over dude is because you still love him. If you didn't, it wouldn't hurt so badly. You'd be like 'fuck it, fuck *him.*'" Aaron's eyes maintained contact with mine as he spoke.

I shook my head. "Aaron, I *really* don't wanna talk to you about Jamie, okay?"

He nodded. "A'ight. I'm sorry for bringing him up, but you're gonna have to face the dude sooner or later. Can't run from dude for too long, and I already know it won't take a week before he comes looking for you. You didn't see the look on his face when he confronted me about you. Dude still has feelings for you."

I sighed. "I need a drink." I ran my fingers through my hair anxiously.

Aaron grabbed my arm, pulling me closer to him. "Nah, let's get in the hot tub again." He looked down, eyes tracing my lips.

I nodded, heart pounding in my chest as he held my hand, taking me back inside. He had my heart ready to explode. His touch, his kiss, his voice, his smell, his very presence drove me crazy. Aaron had me like Kia up in that bitch. Dude licked, sucked, and fucked my *everything.* I rode that dick that night as if I was never going to get that dick again, literally. Charlie made sure of that. The sad part was that Aaron was right about Jamie. He'd come for me eventually. It's funny how niggas don't want you until they see someone else is interested in you.

Aaron didn't take me back to the dorm until early the next morning. At about 7:00, we got up, got dressed, and ate breakfast. I felt like I was on death row, eating my last meal before an execution. I already knew I was about to face the firing squad that morning. I had been avoiding Renée since the incident at the karaoke bar. She was bound to show up at my dorm that morning. I had a 10:00 Humanities class. I wasn't sure what time Aaron had to be in class, but he sure as hell looked like he wasn't in the mood for anything educational that day either. He must have gone through about half a pack of cigarettes that morning. I've never seen him smoke that much.

"You're not going to class today, Aaron?" I asked, watching him light up another Newport.

He looked at me, shaking his head. "Nah. I'm about to hit the gym, then roll up on shorty. She's got a 10:00 appointment this morning. Depending on how that goes, I might show up to my 1:00 Physics class." Aaron watched me as I folded the Coogi dress he had bought me. "I don't think I got the chance to tell you how good you looked in that dress."

I looked up at him.

"Shorty, you looked *good* in that dress. Fine as a mutha-fucka." His eyes searched mine.

I blushed a little. "Thank you, Aaron."

"You got everything?" he asked, walking toward the door.

No, I didn't have everything. I didn't have my head together. I didn't have my emotions together. I didn't have my dignity. I didn't have my pride. I didn't have my self-esteem. I didn't have my strength. I didn't have *him*. I was a complete mess. I had no idea how I was going to recover mentally, physically, or emotionally.

I shrugged. "I guess so, Aaron." I placed my dress, heels, jacket, and the toiletries that Aaron bought in the bag that the clothes I was wearing came out of.

Aaron approached me, handing me the clean pair of panties and bra that I had on the night of my party.

I took them from him, lips trembling as I placed them in the bag. I couldn't even look up at him. "I had a *really* nice time, Aaron. I can-I can still feel you all over my body. I can still feel you inside of me."

Aaron tilted my chin so our eyes could meet, and he gently kissed my lips, sucking on my bottom lip just a little. "No matter what happens from this day forward, just remember, Heaven, that I will always love you. *Always.*"

Aaron dropped me off at my dorm room that morning. When I opened my mouth to tell him good-bye, tears and pain came out instead. He leaned forward to kiss me on my forehead, then on my lips, then on my wet cheeks.

My lips trembled as he gently kissed my lips again. I held his face in my hands as his lips caressed mine. He felt so wonderful, so amazing, and so comfortable. I loved him. As brief as our encounter was, it was going to take every ounce of strength I had to give up and walk away from him. It took everything in me to pull my lips from his that morning. I didn't want to let him go.

Aaron held my hands to his lips, softly kissing them.

"Heaven, everything is gonna be okay," he whispered.

I struggled to smile. "My heart has been broken into so many pieces. Too many pieces to pick up, too many to count, too many to put back together. Kind of like dropping a vase on the floor—even when you put a shattered vase back together, there is always a piece missing, even if it's the tiniest piece." I dried my face because it was time to stop crying. "How can I mourn the loss of something that was never mine to begin with? I have no choice *but* to be okay with this. I ruined my own chances at a relationship with you. I shouldn't have been so shy and insecure. Charlie is *beautiful!* I didn't think I could compete with her! I never thought you would choose someone like me over someone like her!"

Aaron shook his head. "Heaven, you are sexy as hell. Your chocolate skin tone is mouthwatering, yo. Yes, Charlie is a beautiful woman aesthetically, but the connection was never there, and we both know that."

I shook my head at him. I couldn't handle being in his presence any longer. "Charlie loves you, Aaron. So you're just gonna have to learn to love her back, for the sake of this soon-to-be beautiful baby. See you around, Aaron." I couldn't get out of that car fast enough. Oh my goodness, why didn't anyone tell me that love would hurt this fuckin' bad?

Chapter 10

The Reunion

Ne'Vaeh

I dodged the firing squad for a few days, and I mean just a *few* days. I sat in a far corner of the library that Friday, studying for a statistics test I had that afternoon. I mean, I was just sitting there, minding my own damn business when a pair of size six-and-a-half heels comes stomping across the lobby of the library. I sank back in my chair, trying to bury my face in my notes, acting as if I didn't see Renée's crazy ass stomping toward me, like Ms. Sophia from *The Color Purple*.

"Okay, so now you're gonna not only ignore my mutha-fuckin' phone calls and texts, but you're gonna sit there, lookin' like you haven't slept in days, acting like you don't see me standing here in front of you too? Ne'Vaeh, act as if I won't get loud up in this muthafucka if you want to! You *know* I know how to get you and me both barred from somewhere! Act brand new if you want to, boo-boo!" Renée's voice already started to rise.

I rolled my eyes, looking up at her from my iPad. "Oh, hey, girl. What's up, Renée?"

Renée's eyes widened. "'*What's up?*' What's up? No, what's up with *you?* I've been worried sick about you *all* fuckin' week! Why have you been ignoring my fuckin' calls? I know you seen my texts! *And* I sent you like twenty messages on Facebook!"

My eyes filled with tears. She was right when she said I looked like I haven't slept in days. I hadn't. I hadn't had any sleep since I fell asleep that Monday night in Aaron's arms. It took everything I had every morning that week to crawl out of bed. I must have taken a whole bottle of sleeping pills. I'd had a prescription for sleeping pills ever since the day I found my brother's body lifeless in his bed. It took years to fall asleep without seeing his face. Now, here I was, unable to get Aaron's face out of my head. I couldn't get my mind to register the fact that I wasn't around him that week. In my mind, I could still smell, taste, hear, feel, and see Aaron.

I couldn't even say his name aloud without crying. I thought about him every second. I couldn't help but wonder how his conversation with Charlie went the morning he dropped me back off at the dorm. I kept one of the towels from the hotel, the towel that he dried off with after we got out of the hot tub. Oh, it smelled just like him. I draped the towel across the pillow on my bed, burying my face in it, crying in it every night. I hadn't even spent a week alone with Aaron, but the time that I did spend with him had embedded memories in my mind, heart, body, and soul. I could still feel him kissing me, touching me, biting me, sucking me, inside of me. I can admit, yeah, I was sprung. I had no idea how I was going to get over him, but I had no choice but to move on, and I was probably going to need counseling to do it.

I looked at Renée. "I really didn't feel like talking to anybody, okay? My fuckin' birthday was a fuckin' disaster. I'm gonna have to start going back to my damn therapist, just to get over the events that occurred that night. And you know I hate that bitch."

Renée sat down at the table across from me. She was dressed in a tight sweater that showed a little too much cleavage, and tight black denim jeans. She always did dress to impress. I don't even think that girl owned one pair of fuckin' sweatpants. Even when we went to the gym, she would find the shortest shorts. They might as well have been panties, and the tightest, tiniest tank top to put on. Always had to be the sexy one in the crew. You would have never thought by looking at her that she was pushing thirty because she fit right in with the teenagers.

"So," she looked at me, "how was the *after*-party?"

I looked at her, not sure really how to respond. I figured when all else fails, play dumb. "*What* after-party?"

Renée pursed her lips. "Bitch, don't make me slap the shit outta you."

I rolled my eyes. "Renée, you know, there are three rules to business. Number one, I mind my business. Number two, you mind *your* business. And number three, stay the *fuck* outta mine."

Renée laughed aloud. "Oh, okay, I see, using my own shit on me, huh? So, you got dicked-down by Mr. Whitehaven, and now you think you're a full-fledged woman? Okay, I got you. Well, I just thought I'd let you know that Charlie knows about your little love affair."

I just looked at Renée, my heart beginning to speed up.

Renée nodded, "Yeah, she found the receipt for that damn dress you had on last weekend in Aaron's jacket pocket. He admitted that he bought the dress, those damn earrings, *and* that necklace that you *still* have on for your birthday. He didn't admit to her that y'all slept together, but Charlie isn't stupid. The nigga was MIA from Sunday night until Tuesday morning. She knew where the fuck he was at. She knew where the fuck *you* were at. She has connections, Ne'Vaeh. You just remember that."

Tears slid down my face, but I quickly dried them away.

"Girl, I must say, though, Charlie slapped the living *shit* outta that muthafucka when he showed up that Tuesday morning!" Renée laughed to herself.

I looked at her, putting my iPad down. "How do *you* know this?"

She looked at me. "Because I was there, honey."

"Since when do you start hanging around Charlie?" I asked.

Renée shook her head at me. "Since *your* ass stopped answering your fuckin' phone, and I needed to find out where the fuck you were! Charlie is more pissed than a muthafucka at you! But for some reason, and I can't quite put my finger on it, she hasn't beat your ass yet. Or at least attempted to. I mean, as much as I'm pissed at you, I wouldn't let anything happen to you."

My heart was racing. "What-what happened after she slapped him, Renée?"

Renée shrugged. "I don't know. All I know is that she planned to take me with her to her appointment because she really wasn't ready to face Aaron. When he showed up, her ass blanked out on him—she was kicking, screaming, and slapping him! It took her cousin, Tyra, and me to pull her off Aaron! She fell to the floor crying, and the funny thing is that Aaron started crying too. I don't think the dude was crying over her being upset with him. I think he was crying over what happened with *you*."

Thoughts of Aaron's stroke flashed through my mind.

"Aaron asked us if we could give them some privacy for a few minutes. We stepped outside. Twenty minutes later, Tyra went back in the house to make sure everything was cool. She came back outside and said . . . Well, let's just say that he said something *and* did something that the girl needed to get over it." Renée knew she was telling me everything I didn't want to hear, but she continued talking. "Yesterday, Charlie and a few of her chicks from the squad showed up to my house with a few invitations."

I looked at Renée, heart pounding harder than ever in my chest. "Invitations to what, Renée?"

"The engagement party, Ne'Vaeh! The bitch is having the party Thanksgiving Day!" Renée exclaimed. She reached in her purse and pulled out a beige, sparkly invitation, handing it to me. "Here."

It had my name on it. I laughed a little. I knew Charlie was going to invite me just to rub it in. If she knew about my three-night stand with her boyfriend, she sure as hell was playing it off really well. She hadn't called. She hadn't come to hunt me down at school. She hadn't tried to fight me. She hadn't showed any signs that she knew about anything that happened between her fiancé and me. Yeah, she had plans for me.

"Well, *that* ruined my day." I laughed at Charlie's ignorance, handing the invitation back to Renée.

Renée shook her head at me. "Sweetie, I know this shit is devastating, but you gotta do what you gotta do to move on. I'm pretty sure you fucked that muthafucka's brains out those days you were with him in Virginia. And no sooner than a few hours after he's home, he's back to fuckin' *Charlie's* ass! It's sad that you're in love with this dude and know nothing about him or his stuck-up-ass rich family. I know that boy loves you. Shit, *Charlie* knows that boy loves you! But they are having a baby, and they are getting married, and that's that."

I sat back in my chair, mind racing in all sorts of directions.

"So, with that being said, *Jamie* also gave me an invitation to give to you." Renée reached into her purse again, pulling out a purple and gold invitation.

I looked at her, rolling my eyes, taking the invitation from her hand. "Renée, I can't even believe you're handing me this shit. What is this?"

"An invitation to *Jamie's* Ravens' party! It's tonight at ten-thirty! Don't tell me you haven't heard the dude just signed with the Ravens yesterday! Yeah, come spring, he's training with the Ravens!" Renée was definitely more excited than I was to hear that Jamie was coming back to town.

I shook my head, looking at the bitch as if she'd lost her fuckin' mind. "I'm not going to this shit. This invitation is just as fucked up as Charlie's invitation!"

Renée shook her head back at me, "Well, boo-boo, you *will* be ready to roll at ten o'clock tonight when I come back to get you. And if you're not, I swear to goodness, I will tell Jamie which dorm room you stay in. You know the muthafucka is fine. One of these thirsty bitches would let him in your dorm!"

I rolled my eyes, handing the invitation back to her. "Renée, that's fucked up! My heart is in no condition to go out to no fuckin' party, especially a party where Jamie Green's ass is gonna be! He broke my heart! You think I really wanna go around him right now?"

Renée sighed. "Girl, you gotta let it go. I know it's too soon to say some shit like that to you, but it's reality. You got the chance to be with Aaron for a few days. You got the chance to feel what it was like to know that he loves you. I know that feeling was snatched from you too soon, but I *told* you to leave that situation alone! Jamie Green is back, the boy you used to love with all of your heart. He's leaving Sunday to go back to Memphis to finish his semester in school; then he's back in Baltimore. He personally gave me this invitation to give to you, which means he wants you to come."

I fought back any old feelings that I may have felt for Jamie. "I really don't give a fuck, Renée. And you're wrong for doing this to me!"

Renée got up from the table, "Okay, whatever, Ne'Vaeh. I expect to see you waiting outside your dorm tonight wearing something purple and sexy. The party is at Purple Panties. We gonna have a ball, girl!" She came around the table to hug me. "Everything is gonna be okay, boo, you'll see."

Seemed like nothing fit right that night. It was too soon to be going to a got-damn party. It was too soon to have any fun. It was too soon to see Jamie's face. I prayed that the club would be so crowded that Jamie wouldn't be able to spot me. He knew everybody, so I knew the club would be crowded beyond capacity. Renée must have called me a million damn times that day, just to make sure that I was getting ready. She even sent over our cousin Jennel to do my hair and makeup. I was in no mood to be pretty, so I could give a damn if I wore a wife beater and sweatpants. Jennel flat ironed my hair, put makeup on my face, and even brought over a sexy, tight, purple dress with matching heels for me to wear. The bitch even brought me a purple silk bra and bikini panties set. Why the hell did I need to match my underwear with my damn clothes? I don't know whom Renée called herself trying to impress. I couldn't care less how Jamie thought I looked. That muthafucka.

"Done! I sure can beat a face!" Jennel said, after applying the last coat of mascara. She smiled, dark eyes searching my face for any flaws with my makeup. "Girl, I am a *beast* in the cosmetic department! Not that you needed any makeup with your perfect-skin-havin' ass, but yeah, you look like a beauty queen!" She gave me a hand mirror.

I grinned a little, looking at my reflection in the mirror. I admit, she *did* have skills, but I wasn't in the mood to go out anywhere. My smile quickly faded. "Jennel, I am *not* in the mood to go out tonight." I handed the mirror back to her. "Y'all know how Jamie did me. *Why* would I wanna celebrate with him? And you know this whole being drafted-to-the-Ravens thing is bullshit, right? Jamie doesn't even *like* the Ravens! Remember when he said they were dried up—he used to call them the Baltimore *Raisins!*"

Jennel shook her head, putting all of her makeup back in her Chanel makeup case. "Girl, shut up. Renée means well, and you know it. She is your *biggest* fan. Always has been, always will be. You're like a sister to her, the little sister she never had! A bunch of us ran into Jamie last night at the mall. He told her to bring everybody out to the club tonight for his party. *You* were the only one he had an invitation for. The only reason we are gettin' in is because *you* got an invite!"

I sighed. "Why did she have to match my underwear with my outfit? What the fuck kind of party do y'all have me going to?"

Jennel laughed aloud. "Girl, *you'll* see!"

Renée, along with about ten of her friends, picked me up that night in a stretch Hummer. Renée always rolled deep, if you haven't noticed. All of her friends were dressed to impress, looking like a bunch of black Playboy models. Renée was excited to see that Jennel had done such a good job with my hair and makeup. She went on and on about how I was going to win. Win what? I had no idea.

Once we got to Purple Panties, we stepped out of the limo. The line was wrapped all the way around the damn building. I didn't want to skip everyone, because I really didn't want to go to the party in the first damn place. But Alisha's ass was already standing in the door, wearing a skimpy silk purple dress that barely touched the bottom of her butt cheeks. You could see her purple push-up bra and thong through her dress. Her long hair was swept up into a bun. She squealed when she saw the thirteen of us walking toward her, prancing down the red carpet. She nudged the security guard, whispering something to him. He looked at us, then unhooked the rope, letting us in.

Alisha quickly rushed over to me, throwing her arms around me. "Cutie, you made it!"

I faked a smile. "Hey, girl."

"Ooohhh, look at *you!*" Alisha smacked me on the butt. "Look at the rest of y'all, lookin' like a bunch'a raisins with all that got-damn purple on! C'mon, girls, we got a few booths in the back of the club." She grabbed my arm, pulling me behind her, leading me into the club.

Alisha led us through the crowded club over to the section in the back of the club where a few other girls in the squad were sitting. Most of the girls were just dressed in purple stilettos, purple sequined bras, and boy shorts. Others were dressed in white, glowing under the white lights. Our crew spread out among the booths.

"What's up, ladies? Let's get these drinks flowing!" Kristina exclaimed. I hated going to the club with her because her drinking almost always led to a fight.

"Hey, y'all missin' a few dancers, aren'tcha?" Renée put her arm over my shoulder.

I looked at her, rolling my eyes. She was referring to Charlie, who was the only dancer that wasn't there at the moment. I looked at Alisha to see her reaction. Alisha laughed a little, shooting me a quick look. "Girl, you know Charlie hates this damn club, but there's no way she'd let Aaron come here unaccompanied tonight. She knows Jamie's party is tonight. She knows anybody who's anybody is gonna be up in the spot tonight, including Cutie."

My heart skipped a beat or ten. I sighed. I really was in no mood for any bullshit tonight. "Look, the only reason

I came to this damn club is because Renée talked me into this bullshit. Now, I'm not with the damn reality TV, drama shit tonight. So, if some shit is about to go down, y'all can just take me back to where the fuck you picked me up at."

Alisha took me by the hand, leading me to the corner booth that she was sitting in. "Girl, chill, no worries. You know we got your back. We're here to have some fun, get drunk, get crunk, and get *fucked* up!"

I sighed, sitting down next to her at the booth. "I'm tellin' you, any shit, and I'm out."

"Girl, whateva. Stop trippin'. Eh!"

Kelissa hollered across the room, taking a wad of one-dollar bills out of her bra, "Where them strippers at?"

Yeah, it did get live in Purple Panties that night. The party was jumpin' before Jamie and his crew even showed up. The strippers stayed in our section most of the night. Many admired Alisha's dancers. They were sexy, they were fit, they were flexible, and they were fashionable. Strippers didn't have shit on the Morgan Girls.

Alisha was right. Charlie *did* show up with Aaron that night around eleven-thirty. I had already been drinkin' a few Long Island Iced Teas, so their presence didn't bother me the way it would have if I had been sober. The two split up at the door. Aaron went over to what I call the basketball section, and Charlie made her way over to her squad. I remained as calm as I could when she came over to my booth and sat right across from me. My heart nearly shot out of my chest, but still, I remained silent.

"What's up, Charlie?" Renée turned to her in her seat.

Charlie looked at Renée, eyes sparkling under the club lights. "What's up?" She looked at me. "Can we talk in private?"

Before I could open my mouth to say anything, Renée opened hers. "Nah, she's cool right *here*. Anything you can say to her alone, you can say in front of us. Ain't gonna be no *shit* tonight. We came to chill."

Charlie rolled her eyes at Renée. "Renée, mind your business. Look," she looked at me, "I ain't here for all that. Me and you have been friends for a long time, Ne'Vaeh, and I'll be damned if I let a man come between us."

I just looked at her, lips trembling, not sure what to say.

She put her hand up, showing off the huge rock on her finger. The ring nearly blinded all of us girls who sat with her at the booth. She grinned, watching the hurt expression on my face. "Ya know, when I found the receipt to that dress you had on at your birthday party in his pocket, the first thought in my mind was beating your ass right in front of him. When I called him for three days straight and he didn't answer, I tracked him down. Turns out, a few people saw him at the Marriott Hotel in Virginia with you. Again, I plotted all sorts of ways to end your life in my head. My own best friend fucked my man." Charlie laughed to herself. "After all that I have done for you, you're gonna go and fuck with Aaron? What makes you think that he would leave me for something like *you?*"

"Charlie, you really need to back the fuck off." Kelissa stood from the table.

Charlie laughed. "I mean, really, you got my engagement party invitation, didn't you? Didn't anyone tell you that groupies get nothing but the dick? Groupies get no love, bitch. You should know that. You *were* Jamie's groupie for two years, *weren't* you?"

Renée almost went across the table on Charlie's ass, but Kristina and I pulled her back. "Bitch, you better watch your mouth before I wrap your ass around one of these muthafuckin' poles! Who the fuck do you think you are? You got my cousin fucked up! You got some nerve steppin' to her like this! Did Aaron tell you that they fucked? Did you hear that shit from *his* mouth? If not, then you need to back the fuck up. Me and you already talked about this earlier this week. You need to let the shit go."

Charlie looked at me. She was so angry that her lips and jawbone were trembling. "I wanna hear the words come out of *Ne'Vaeh's* mouth."

All eyes were on me. What difference did it make what I said? She had in her mind the way that she felt about me. According to her, I wasn't shit but one of the many girls who were drooling over an athlete. She knew Aaron loved me. I saw it all over her face. She knew the only reason they were getting married was because she was pregnant. She knew he didn't love her and probably never would, and she hated me for that. To hear her say those words to me stung like bees. Yes, I was wrong for what I had done, but it wasn't as if I went after her man. Aaron came after me, even when I told him no. But what use was it to explain that to Charlie, when she already had in her head that I was a groupie after her man?

I laughed a little to cover the pain and embarrassment that I was feeling. I really didn't feel like stooping to her level that night. "You know, it really doesn't matter what I say to you right now, because you have in your head that something happened between us. In your mind, you think I'm some random chick who fucked your man behind your back. You won, Charlie. You're having his baby, and you're getting married, and you get to do the shit right smack in front of my face. Yeah, he bought me a dress. I tried to give it back, and he wouldn't take the shit back. Yeah, he told me that he had feelings for me, and I told him there was no way that we could be together when his girlfriend was my *best* friend. Did he tell you that, while you're over here calling *me* a groupie? If you think I fucked your man, if you think I want your man, if you think your man wants *me*, then why are you marrying him?"

Charlie's lips trembled.

I shook my head. "You let everyone here know the first time you laid eyes on Aaron that he was yours, and that hasn't changed. Whatever you think happened between me and Aaron doesn't change that either. I won't deny that I have feelings for him. That may be inappropriate, but I missed my chance, so congratulations on the baby and on the engagement, Charlie."

Charlie looked at me, face red as hell. "You got me *fucked* up, Ne'Vaeh. If I catch you so much as *looking* at him the wrong way, I will *kill* you, girl. Do you hear me? I'm not fuckin' stupid, Ne'Vaeh, so don't think for one fuckin' second that you can play a playa! Stay the *fuck* away from him." Charlie got up from the table and walked away, shouting, "See you at the engagement party, *groupie*."

Everyone looked at me like I had been touched by an angel.

"Girl, I thought she was gonna dust the *floor* with your ass!" Kristina exclaimed.

Renée shook her head at me. "Y'all bitches crazy! I need another drink."

I looked at Alisha. "See, that's the shit I'm talkin' about, Alisha. I didn't come here to be called a fuckin' groupie. A muthafuckin' *groupie?* After fuckin' and suckin' hundreds—no—*thousands* of dudes *and* females in high school, she has the nerve to call *me* a fuckin' groupie?"

Alisha shook her head. "Man, don't even sweat Charlie. She's got problems bigger than you fuckin' her man, *trust* me."

That little conversation put a small damper in my night, but the party continued, and I soon found out why Renée was so adamant about me wearing purple panties. At around twelve-thirty, purple lights flashed all around the room, and every lady in the club, except for me, who was clueless about what was going on, and the strippers, who were already naked, of course, stripped down to their purple panties.

My heart pounded in my chest. "What the fuck is goin' on?" I asked Dana who didn't even have on a bra but just purple thongs. Titties and ass cheeks were flappin' *everywhere.*

"Girl, we about to do the pole-dancing contest! How could you *not* know about this?" Dana looked me up and down. She rolled her eyes. "Girl, I almost forgot how lame you were. Always got your nose buried in some book somewhere. You never get out. If you did, you'd know that on Fridays, the guests at the club compete with the strippers to see who's got it and who doesn't. Tonight, the winner gets a date with Jamie G.!"

I rolled my eyes. "Been there, done that shit, so I'll pass." I sat back in the corner booth, sipping on my daiquiri.

Every—and I mean just about *every*—woman up in the club took center stage that night, working the hell out of that pole. Asses shakin', twerkin', bouncin', droppin', poppin'. I know them dudes were lovin' that shit. I, on the other hand, was regretting my decision to come out tonight.

After the last dancer hit the stage, Jamie's childhood friend and teammate at Memphis State, Jerry King, got onstage. "So, is that it? No more titties?" he asked.

"No, that's *not* it!" The Morgan Girls pointed to me.

My eyes widened, and I shook my head frantically as Renée and Alisha pulled me up from my seat. "Oh, hell nah!" I squealed.

"Jerry King, baby, we have another one!" Alisha pulled my arm, pulling me behind her up to the stage.

A stripper held out her hand, helping me onto the stage. I stood alongside Alisha, the strippers, and Jerry.

My heart pounded in my chest. I looked over to the corner of the room where Jamie sat in the VIP section with his teammates. He was grinning from ear to ear. I looked around the room and caught sight of Aaron and his teammates in the basketball section. Aaron just sat back in his chair, leaned back, smoking and looking at me as if he couldn't believe I let the girls talk me into coming to Jamie's party. Charlie sat right on his lap, arms folded, looking at me as if she wanted to cut me.

I swallowed hard as a stripper attempted to untie my dress from around my neck. I turned to her, stopping her from doing that. "Hold up, now. Get your got-damn hands off me." I put my hands up. "Nah, I don't strip."

The crowd booed.

Jerry laughed into the microphone. "Well, then, what *do* you do, shorty?"

As I took the microphone from his hands, I looked down into Renée's face as she stood at the front of the stage, cheering me on. Then I looked at Alisha who was standing beside me in her bra and panties. She nodded at me to do what she knew I was about to do.

I took a deep breath, putting the microphone to my lips and I started to sing. *"I've been drinkin', I've been drinkin' . . ."*

The crowd went wild as I sang a cappella to the only sexy song I could think of at the moment. I didn't intend on singing it, but that was the first song that came to my mind because I could still feel the coldness of the kitchen floor on my back. I could still feel Aaron's lips all over me. Every time I closed my eyes, I could see him sucking the wine from my lips. I'm pretty sure Aaron knew I was singing that song to him. He couldn't help but grin before he got up and walked out of the club, Charlie following behind him.

The look on Jamie's face let me know that he knew I was singing to Aaron as well. He grinned, shaking his head at me, but he clapped and cheered along with everyone else. I couldn't finish the song fast enough when Alisha and Renée cheered me on, grabbing on me, hugging me as if *they* had just struck gold or something.

"This is *my* cousin, y'all! *Whew!*" Renée squealed at the top of her lungs. "Hollywood, here we come!"

I rolled my eyes as she dragged me offstage and back over to the table with the dancers. Everyone cheered me on, talking among themselves. Though I was in the choir, I'm pretty sure most of them had no clue that I could really sing. They thought the only thing I could do was homework. Dana sat there stunned.

"Humph, not so lame *now*, am I, Dana? Choke on *that* shit, bitch." I rolled my eyes at her as I sat down at the corner booth with Renée and Alisha.

"Girl, I know Charlie wants to whup your *ass* right about now! She knew you were singin' to her man! And look at *Jamie's* fine ass over there droolin'!" Kelissa laughed aloud.

The football players picked their favorite ten girls from those who danced that night and lined them up onstage. Just when I thought I was out of the running, Jamie called me to the stage. I was reluctant to get back up there, but Renée . . . Man, that bitch just wouldn't give up. She practically dragged me up onstage and stood beside me, arm around me, preventing me from running back off the stage. The winner was chosen, and guess who won the date with Jamie Green? Yeah . . . me.

After the humiliation was over, I sat alone at the bar.

"Why are you sittin' over here alone, shorty?" I heard Jamie's voice over my shoulder.

I rolled my eyes at him as he sat down next to me. "Because maybe I *want* to be alone, Jamie."

He laughed to himself. "So, where you wanna go on our date tomorrow night?"

"I don't know, but do you want me to tell you which part of hell that *you* can go to?" I took a sip from my rum and Coke.

Jamie laughed aloud. "Shorty, do you really hate me *that* much?"

I didn't answer. My eyes were drenched in tears. It took all my strength to hold the tears back. "What are you doing here, Jamie?" I managed to say.

"What do you mean?" he asked.

I looked up into his face. Oh, I had almost forgotten that face. I had almost forgotten how just one look, one word, one touch from Jamie could just set my soul on fire. He was so sexy and so charming. He was so fuckin' arrogant too, and a small part of me always liked that about him.

"What do I *mean?* Jamie, you could have picked any team you wanted to go to. I'm pretty sure that the Ravens aren't the only team who wanted you, right? Don't try to play me like I'm stupid." I took a sip from my drink.

He shrugged. "Shorty, you're the first person to know how much I hate Maryland or anything to do with this muthafucka, but shit, they need a nigga like me on their team. Who else they got on their team that can play like me?"

I rolled my eyes.

"Nah, the Ravens weren't my first choice, but trust me, they *are* payin' your boy quite a bit of bread. But honestly, this was my opportunity to come back to Maryland, so I took it. I already bought a house here, shorty, in Southern Maryland. You wanna see it tomorrow night?" His eyes searched mine.

I looked at him. "No, not really, Jamie. You know good and fuckin' well that every last one of those girls onstage

tonight did a hell of a lot better stripping than I did singing! Those girls got completely naked for you, basically
having sex with that pole! And you chose me *why?*"

Jamie laughed to himself. "Man, I missed you, shorty."
He signaled the bartender to fix him a drink. "I almost
forgot how muthafuckin' sexy you are. I almost forgot
how beautiful your voice is. I heard your cousin's wife
offered you a job singin' with her. Man, you crazy as hell
for not takin' her up on her offer. Do you know how *big*
Anastasia is right now?"

I looked at him, watching him as he took a sip from
his glass. It would have been easier to hate him if he
wasn't so damn nonchalant about my attitude. I believe
he knew it was a front for being hurt. He knew I still felt
something for him, but he knew I was mad at him for
leaving me. He knew what I had been through in my life.
He knew that he left me when I needed him the most. He
knew it wasn't going to be easy gaining my trust back.

Jamie looked up at me. "To answer your questions
about these girls twerkin' their asses off for me onstage,
that shit was just for show. I've seen every last one of
these girls who showed up tonight naked. If I wasn't the
one havin' sex with them, trust me, I *saw* them having
sex with someone else."

I rolled my eyes. "Yeah, they say you turned into a ho."

He laughed aloud. "Nah, I guess I just wanted a li'l
appetizer while I was waiting on the main course."

I couldn't help but laugh at his ignorance. "What
desperate kinda woman would wait around for you until
you got tired of fuckin' groupies, Jamie? I hope you don't
think that I was sitting around waiting on you, because I
wasn't, asshole."

"Oh, trust me, shorty, I know."

I looked at him, my heartbeat starting to accelerate in
my chest. "No, you *think* you know."

Jamie smirked. *"Think* I know? Shorty, do you think I'm stupid? Man, the muthafucka couldn't leave this club fast enough once you started singin' to him."

I rolled my eyes. "Singin' to *him?* What makes you think I was singing to Aaron?"

Jamie grinned. His grill was gleaming under the club lights. "You ain't gotta lie to me, Ne'Vaeh. My man seen your ass with dude at the hotel, shorty. You must'a really put it on him. Probably got the dude having flashbacks of whatever it is that you did to the muthafucka. Remember, I have *been* with you, so I know the magic you can do. You put your heart in it."

I just sipped on my drink, heart pounding in my chest. "I don't know what the fuck you're talking about, Jamie."

Jamie nodded, eyes sparkling under the club lights. "Yeah, you do, shorty. I'm sorry that I hurt you, okay? But you didn't have to go and fuck with Charlie's boyfriend. You think she don't know that you was with her man at the hotel for all those days, shorty? Sleepin' with your best friend's man, shorty? She's been your rider for *years,* Ne'Vaeh. Fuckin' her man, and then havin' the nerve to sing to dude in her *face? That's* fucked up."

I looked at him. "Fucked up? Are you serious? First of all, this shit is none of your fuckin' business! Second of all, he came after *me, not* the other way around! And third, if *you* would have never left me, he would have *never* gotten to me! Never!" I got up from the stool, nearly stumbling over my own two feet. Yeah, I was drunk as fuck, and I really didn't want the jerk to see that I still felt some type of way about him. Up until that point, *I* didn't even realize that I still felt anything toward him. I forced myself to forget Jamie and the feelings that I once had for him. Apparently, my heart hadn't gotten the message.

Jamie got up from the bar, taking the glass from my hands. "Shorty, you shouldn't even be drinkin', man.

What the fuck, yo? Since when did you start drinkin'? Since when did you start dressing like this? Since when did you start going to strip clubs? Since when did you fuck your own friend's boyfriend? Are you high, yo? You've been smokin' too? Man, this is not the Ne'Vaeh that *I* used to know."

"Well, I know I'm drunk, but if I remember correctly, *you* invited me to this club, Jamie!" I pushed him in his chest. "Yeah, I drink, I smoke, and I go to the clubs every now and then. Do you think I meant to fall in love with Charlie's boyfriend? I waited for you, Jamie! I hadn't had sex in *four* fuckin' years! So before you go thinkin' I turned into some fuckin' ho when you left, I didn't! I fell in love with Aaron, yes, but he pursued *me*, not the other way around! You wanna judge me, then go ahead, Jamie. But remember, *your* shit stinks too, muthafucka! You and Charlie wanna sit here and judge me, but if I can remember correctly, you two were professional hoes back in high school! There wasn't a guy Charlie *hadn't* fucked back then! And *you* started having sex around the age of thirteen! Charlie was the one sleeping around, chasin' niggas before Aaron came along, but *I'm* the groupie? Jamie, she called me your fuckin' *groupie!* A groupie?" I laughed aloud. I was so pissed off.

Jamie shook his head at me. "Shorty, you're drunk. Let me take you home."

"Was I really your groupie, Jamie?" I looked into his face.

He shook his head, lookin' down at me. "You gonna let what Charlie said to you out of anger have you questioning what you *know* you meant to me?"

"What I *know* I meant to you? Are you serious? Jamie, you left me the day your father came in town! You didn't even say good-bye! You just left, then tried to explain to me over the *phone* why you left me! You talked me into having sex with you, when you knew I wasn't ready; then you just up and bounced!" I pushed him in his chest.

Jamie sighed. "There's more to it and you know it, shorty. My father was sick. He had just come into my life. I hadn't seen him since I was about three years old. He needed help. He needed me to stay with him. My father, who I had never known, wanted to get to know me, so I left. I tried explaining the situation, but you wouldn't listen. I know you needed me, but my father needed me too. What was I supposed to do?"

I didn't know his father was sick. He never told me. He never mentioned anything about his father coming to get him. When he called me on the phone and tried to explain why he left me, I really didn't even give him the chance to explain. All I knew was that when I woke up the morning after we had sex, he wasn't lying next to me. Whatever reason he had for leaving me alone in his bed, staring at an empty closet, I couldn't have cared less back then.

I shook my head at him. "Follow your heart, which is exactly what you did."

Jamie shook his head back at me. "Ne'Vaeh, you know what you meant to me back then. I have known you since we were in day care. We were the *best* of homies for years before we started dating, shorty. Yeah, I messed around with a few females before we started officially dating. Yeah, I had a few girls still trying to holla, even when they knew me and you were dating. Yeah, I know I didn't make it easy for you to be with me. Yeah, I know I left you when you had a lot goin' on, but I had a lot goin' on too, shorty. You meant the fuckin' world to me."

I shook my head, trying to walk away from him, but he grabbed my arm, pulling me back to him. I looked into his face.

Jamie's eyes searched mine. "I had a lot of pressure comin' from all angles back then, so don't think I just up and left you because I wanted to leave. I never knew my father, and he was askin' me to come and stay with him. He was sick and doctors were saying he wasn't gonna make it past a year. It was a blessing that Pops lived a lot longer than doctors said that he would. He's hangin' on by a thread, but he's still here with me. Ne'Vaeh, you know, I have never had the support I needed from my family. You may not have had your mom's support, but you had support from your aunts, your cousins, and Charlie's family. Shit, even Darrick Allan and his wife have been helping you ever since he found out that y'all were related. I didn't have that shit, Ne'Vaeh. I always had to work ten times harder than anyone else to have anything, and you know that."

I looked up into his face.

Jamie held my face in his hands. "I'm goin' through a lot right now, shorty, and I need you, Ne'Vaeh."

My heart jumped in my chest. I took his hands from my face. His touch always sent a jolt of energy straight to my heart. My heart and mind were already in conflict enough. I didn't need Jamie confusing me any more than I already was. I turned to walk away.

Jamie caught my hand, pulling me back to him just when the DJ played "Heart Attack." "C'mon, shorty, let's dance." He held my hand, leading me out onto the dance floor.

I tried to pull from him, but he pulled me close against his chest. Oh my goodness, his smell was still intoxicating. He wrapped his hands around my waist. I was reluctant to glide to the music along with him, but he really gave me no choice. The people around us, cheering us on, really didn't help much either. Seemed as though every guy followed suit, grabbing a girl, bringing her out onto the dance floor. I wrapped my arms around Jamie's body, just in time to see Charlie and Aaron coming onto the dance floor. That damn song was the perfect theme song to my emotions at that moment. I felt like I was having a heart attack. I could feel Jamie's heart beating in his chest. I could hear the air circulating in his lungs. Aaron caught sight of me in Jamie's arms. Our eyes met for a few seconds before looking away.

"Shorty, I missed you," Jamie whispered softly in my ear, lips grazing against my skin a little.

Chills trickled up and down my spine. I looked up at him. I had to get out of there. Aaron's presence was something I really couldn't handle at the moment, and there I was, embraced by Jamie's arms, still feeling like I was in Aaron's.

Jamie looked down at me, looking at the uncomfortable expression on my face. He looked up, in Aaron's direction. He laughed a little to himself. "So, you're in love with your best friend's boyfriend? How's that working out for you?"

Oh my goodness, he always had such a smart-ass mouth. What really made me mad about some of the rude shit he said was that there was always some truth to his statements.

"Why do you say the shit that you say, Jamie? Are you laughing at my pain?" I shook my head at him, looking up into his pretty brown eyes.

Jamie shook his head. "Nah, shorty, I'm not laughing at you. I'm pissed when I really shouldn't be. The nigga would have never even gotten the chance to steal what was mine if I wouldn't have left you here. I should have taken you with me. I must've been real stupid thinkin' that one of the finest girls in our high school was gonna sit around, waiting on me, trying to figure out whether I was ever gonna come back. I just thought that I held the only key to your heart, but I guess you had a spare."

I knew Aaron was watching me. I could just feel him staring at me, but I refused to look. I quickly dried my face. I started to feel pressure in my chest, but I tried to ignore it. "I shut everyone off when you left, Jamie. I didn't want anything to do with love. Love feels like a fuckin' heart attack, especially when the one you love leaves you when you need him most, when the one you love is in a relationship with someone else, or when the one you love kills your brother!" I held my hand over my heart, feeling the room beginning to spin around me. My knees started to tremble, and my body grew weaker. Suddenly, I couldn't breathe.

Jamie looked down into my face, feeling my weight on him as my knees gave out from under me. "Ne'Vaeh, shorty, are you okay?" He held my body tightly up against his.

I shook my head, words slurring. "Help me."

Chapter 11

His Place

Ne'Vaeh

The next thing I remember, I was waking up to the sound of beeping. I was in a triage in the emergency room. A nurse stood over me typing on a computer. I looked to the right to see Renée, Alisha, Jamie, Kristina, and Kelissa. I sat up in the bed. Renée rushed over to my side once she saw that I was awake.

"OMG, cuz!" She threw her arms around me. "You scared me, passing out on the dance floor! Twice in one week, Ne'Vaeh? You gotta start taking care of yourself!"

I looked over her shoulder at Jamie, who sat in a chair looking right back at me, eyes dampened.

"I'm okay, Renée," I whispered.

Renée let go of me, looking into my face. She shook her head. "No, sweetie, you're not. You haven't been taking your medication, you've been drinkin' your ass off all week, and you've been stressed! I should have never taken you to that fuckin' party. I'm sorry! I don't know *what* I was thinkin'!"

I looked up at the nurse. "Ma'am, I'm fine. Can I please go back to my dorm?"

The nurse looked at me, shaking her head. "No, honey, I'm afraid the doctor is admitting you for further testing.

Your blood pressure is extremely high. Sweetie, you're already aware that you have a weak heart. You *have* to take it easy. You have had numerous surgeries to repair the holes in your heart, but your heart is still weak. Your left atrium isn't working properly, which puts even more pressure on the right side of your heart. We're ordering a stress test for you in the morning. Depending on the results, that will determine on how long you will be here. Sweetie, the blood is not flowing through your heart properly. Your friends sitting here with you now really care about you. They brought you here tonight. Just be thankful they did."

My eyes watered as I sat back in the bed. I knew my health was coasting downhill. I often ignored my doctors. I had stopped taking the heart medication and started drinking. My heart was broken, literally. Story of my fuckin' life.

The nurse left the room after getting a technician to start an IV. I was admitted to the hospital that night and moved to another room. Kristina and Kelissa had to leave that morning around 4:30, but Renée, Alisha, and Jamie stayed. I really need to be alone and wasn't in the mood to talk to anyone, but they wouldn't leave me. My stress test was that morning. It was abnormal. Apparently, my heart was still weak, even after numerous surgeries. See what I mean—once the heart is broken, it can never be completely repaired.

Renée was so upset, she couldn't stop crying. Alisha tried to console her. Jamie sat on the sofa, leaned back in the chair, not really sure what to say to me. The doctors debated whether to keep me in the hospital for a few weeks, or send me home under a nurse's supervision. The only problem was that home was my college campus dorm room.

"Ne'Vaeh, I think you should move back in with me." Renée dried her face. "I'm moving into a new apartment this week, and we should move in together. You need someone to help you with your medication."

I shook my head at her. "No, I don't, Renée. The doctors just said that I could stay here in the hospital for a few weeks to be monitored. I really don't wanna stay in an apartment with you. I don't feel like dealing with you and that dude of yours making out and damn near fuckin' in front of me, Renée!"

Renée shook her head at me, drying her tears. "Ne'Vaeh, me and Russell ain't that fuckin' bad. Okay, so we may kiss and touch a little, but no clothes ever came off in front of you!"

I rolled my eyes. "Renée, I'm *not* moving in with you!"

"I don't give a fuck what you say, Ne'Vaeh. By the time you leave this hospital, your shit is gonna be at my mama's house!" she exclaimed.

I sat up in the bed, furious with her. "Renée, oh my goodness! I am so sick and tired of you acting like you're my fuckin' mom! You're *not* my mother! Got-damn, I don't *need* a fuckin' mother! I need fuckin' space! I am so tired of everyone telling me what I need! I'm tired of everyone telling me what they think I should do! How about everyone get their lives straight before they go trying to straighten up mine! You can't undo the holes in my heart, Renée! The damage has already been done! You're twenty-six years old. You need to worry about trying to get and *keep* a man instead of trying to live vicariously through your nineteen-year-old cousin! I love you, Renée, but you are *smothering* me! I don't need a fuckin' babysitter! I need you to back the fuck off! Get a life of your own and stay the *fuck* out of mine!"

Renée's eyes swelled up with tears. She stood from the chair.

Alisha grabbed her arm. "Renée, she didn't mean it. It's all these pain meds they have her on." Alisha looked at me. "Nobody could really be *that* ungrateful after *everything* that you've done for her. Cutie, what's wrong with you?"

I didn't mean to make my cousin cry. "I appreciate everything, Renée, you know I do. But you have to stop trying to run my life," I exclaimed.

"Life? You call this a *life?* You sittin' here, heart bleeding over your best friend's boyfriend! He used the girl to get to you, instead of steppin' to you like a real man!" Renée exclaimed. "You push everyone away in your life who gives a fuck about you! I may be a little hard on you. I may be a little overprotective of my baby cousin. I may push you to be the very best that you can be. I know I'm not your mother. Shit, your damn *mama* isn't your fuckin' mother! I helped raise you, Ne'Vaeh, so don't you *ever* in your fuckin' life disrespect me again!"

"I'm sorry!" I apologized.

Renée dried her face. "I'm goin' to your dorm room to get your shit. Now you can either give me the key now, or I'll just go home and get the copy I made a few months ago."

"Renée?" Jamie spoke up.

"What?" she snapped, going over to the nightstand to pick up her purse.

Jamie looked at me.

I looked up at him.

"She can stay at my crib."

Renée's eyes lit up. "With you? Aren't you goin' back to Memphis tomorrow?"

Jamie shook his head. "Nah, I mean, I don't *have* to go, shorty."

Alisha rolled her eyes. "Jamie, please. Why you wanna stay here in Maryland three months before you're supposed to be here? You tryin' to keep tabs on Ne'Vaeh or somethin'?"

Jamie just looked at her, not feeling the need to respond.

"Mr. Panty Dropper, won't your groupies be mad if you have a girl living up in your house? Oh no, forget the groupies—what about Pamela, your *girlfriend?*" Alisha folded her arms.

I looked at her. Oh, she was "Team Aaron" all the way. She never really cared for Jamie too much. She always thought he had too many hoes.

Jamie laughed to himself. "You know, Alisha, you always were a fuckin' instigator. You know it was over with Pamela months ago."

Alisha rolled her eyes. "Whateva, nigga. I just call 'em how I see 'em. You want Ne'Vaeh to stay with you, why? Just so you can keep an eye on her? Just so you can make sure she doesn't go tiptoeing back to Aaron?"

"Shorty, you need to mind your own fuckin' business. I know you don't like me, and I really don't give a fuck. But this isn't about me. This isn't about you. It's about *her.* I haven't seen shorty in four years, and the day that I actually get to talk to her again, she passes out in my arms, man. Come to find out she stopped taking her heart medication. Alisha, *I* was the one who held her hand six years ago before she went into heart surgery. *I* was the one who held her hand in eighth grade when they told her that her heart was failing. I cried *for* her because she was too numb to cry about it herself. She's been hurt her entire life by the people that she loved the most, myself included." Jamie sounded sincere, as if he really cared about me, as if he was really sorry for what he had done.

I bit my lip to keep from crying out.

Jamie looked at me. "I just wanna be here for you, shorty. I already have two live-in nurses scheduled to move in the house this week, preparing for my dad to get here tonight. He was sick of Memphis and wanted to come up here a few months early. You're welcome to stay, shorty. You won't even know I'm there, I promise. This is the least I can do, shorty. C'mon."

I looked at Renée.

She nodded. Of course, she would be all for it. She always was a fan of Jamie's. To tell you the truth, if she was a few years younger, she probably would've been all on him. "I see no problem with that," Renée shrugged.

Alisha rolled her eyes. "Oh my goodness." She grabbed her purse. "Renée? *Really?*"

Renée rolled her eyes back, going over to my purse to get my dorm room key. "What the fuck you mean 'really'? Yeah, *really*. What, you expect *Aaron* to drop by and take her back to his crib? How would Charlie feel about that? A man who'd fuck his girl's best friend is *no* fuckin' hero. I don't see anything wrong with Jamie helping Ne'Vaeh. They have known each other forever. Yeah, he left her, but now he's back, just in time. She needs him."

I looked at Jamie.

"Y'all muthafuckas crazy! 'She *needs* him'? Are you serious? I don't think she's gonna need a house full of bitches every night! This isn't sweet, high school, popular Jamie. This is star quarterback, fuck-you-you-you-*and*-you Jamie! Y'all are making a huge mistake!" Alisha exclaimed.

Jamie couldn't care less about Alisha's attitude problem. "I just wanna take care of you, Ne'Vaeh. Fuck that shit Alisha's talkin' about. I've known you since we were in day care, shorty. I know I haven't been here in a while, but I'm here now. I'm not trying to disrupt your life or control your life in any way. I just wanna be here for you. Can I do that?"

I hesitated, not sure how to respond.

Renée looked at me, hoping I'd respond to Jamie before he changed his mind. "C'mon, cuz, say something! The doctor says that you need help. We're here to help you. You have a weak heart, you have fluid around your heart, and you can't keep trying to take care of yourself *by* yourself. You don't have to when you have friends who love and care about you." Renée's cell phone rang in her purse. "I know that's Mom calling." She looked at me. "Just let me know where you want me to take your stuff. I'm gonna head over to your dorm tonight to pack everything up. On Monday, I'll go talk to your professors to let them know what's going on. I have all the medical paperwork that they need. I'm going to see how they can accommodate you while you're on bed rest these next few weeks." Renée came over to kiss me on the forehead. "Love you, cuz. I'll call you later." She looked over at Jamie. "Take care of my baby, will you?"

He nodded.

Alisha sighed, getting up from the chair. "I'm sorry to ruin the moment, but there are two people in Maryland that I don't trust, and that's Charlie's and Jamie's triflin' asses. So if I were you, I wouldn't trust Jamie. I'm sorry, Cutie, but you know I'm team Aaron all the way. Jamie is nothing but trouble. I'm tellin' you, Charlie has plans for you, and I'm warning you, her plans include *him*."

Renée rolled her eyes, pulling Alisha by the arm. "Okay, Alisha, you said what you had to say, so let's go. Later, guys."

Alisha and Renée left the room, leaving Jamie and me there alone.

We sat there in awkward silence. I had so much to say to him, but had no idea where to start. I'd forced myself to forget about Jamie over the past four years. It hurt like hell being in his presence, seeing his face again.

"Jamie, my heart is broken, literally," I whispered.

He just looked at me.

"I'm really—I mean, *really*—vulnerable right now. I haven't been taking care of myself for some time. I've done some things that I normally wouldn't do, because I'm tired of being lonely. I'm stubborn, I know. I just have been doing things my way, on my own, for so long. My heart is really confused right now, so whatever you do, don't play games with it. This heart of mine refuses to let you break it again. I don't wanna love you again, Jamie. My heart can't take it." I shook my head at him.

Jamie looked at me earnestly.

"If I stay with you for a little while, it's just as a houseguest. I'm not your girl; you're not my man. Just keep doin' you, groupies and all." I dried my tears. "It is what it is, Jamie, so don't try to make it something that it's not. I don't wanna love you, so don't try to make me," I whispered, watching him gathering my personal belongings. He wasn't really listening to me once he heard that I agreed to go home with him.

Needless to say, Jamie's home in the countryside was spectacular. It didn't feel anything like being in Maryland. I felt so at home, so at peace, so comfortable. His home looked like it sat right in the middle of the Garden of Eden. There were gardeners all around the home, planting flowers, watering the grass, trimming the hedges. He had an outside pool, tennis court, basketball court, a pool house, and two guesthouses behind the mansion. Jamie had about seven sports cars and two antique cars lining the driveway. He finally did it, and I hate to admit it, but I was really proud of him. He wasn't lying when he said he didn't have it easy. His life was just as painful as mine was.

Jamie had to leave the hospital while I was waiting to be discharged. He had one of his nurses pick me up at the hospital that afternoon. She was about twenty-four years old, sexy, cute, brown-skinned, shapely, and dimply. Her name was Helen. She was going to be my personal nurse for the next two weeks. I rode to Jamie's mansion with her in her new black 2015 Mercedes-Benz, probably paid for in full by Jamie. Helen didn't say much to me until we pulled up into Jamie's driveway and she saw the awestruck look on my face as I stared out the window in wonder at Jamie's world.

"So," Helen's voice broke my trance, "*you're* that lady that's making it hard for everyone else? Wow, it's nice to finally meet that special someone who keeps Mr. Green from settling down."

I looked at her. "Wh-what?" I was still stunned by my surroundings, including her.

Helen grinned, one dimple piercing her left cheek. "I've seen a lot of girlfriends come and go. I've been working for Jamie for the past two-and-a-half years. Jamie is a pretty closed book. He doesn't open up to anyone. Pamela Rhodes was his last girlfriend. They dated for about a year. She loved that boy, despite all of his women, but she got tired of competing with those women and with football. I must say, you're the first girl who's ever lived with him."

I shook my head frantically. "Helen, no, we're not living together. Oh my goodness. My cousin thinks that I need someone to make sure I take my medications. The doctors wouldn't let me leave unless I was under a nurse's supervision. Jamie volunteered to let me stay here for a while until I was released from bed rest."

"And why do you think that is?" Helen took off her seat belt.

I looked at her.

She looked at me. "You've known Jamie a long time?"

I nodded, my eyes growing misty, tears already lining my lashes. I hated reminiscing. "Yeah, ummm, since we were about three years old. He stayed with his aunt and older sister on Fort Meade. He spent the school year here in Maryland, and the summer and holidays back in Memphis. We were, umm . . . He was my best friend. It hurt when he left me. I loved him for a long time."

A sympathetic look swept across Helen's face. "Well, the fact that he's here says a lot. He wasn't supposed to even move back to Maryland for another three months, and he wasn't supposed to move into this house until around March. He completely changed his life plans to include you, sweetie, so please remember that."

I looked at her. She felt some type of way about me. I wasn't crazy. She was more than Jamie's father's nurse. She had feelings for him. "You know, you're one nosy nurse," I whispered, taking my seat belt off.

Helen laughed a little. "Oh, sweetie, I'm *much* more than a nurse. You shall see." She popped the trunk open to her car, then opened her door to help me out.

I sighed, running my fingers through my hair. "What the *fuck* was I thinking coming here?" I said aloud to myself as I opened the door.

Helen closed the trunk. I heard the sound of tiny wheels rolling against the concrete. She pushed a wheel-chair over to my side.

I looked up at her.

She smiled, holding out her hand to help me out of the car. "Your chariot awaits."

I sighed, taking her hand, as she helped me out of the car.

I felt like I was in a fancy hotel room. Maids brought me fresh warm towels. They washed my clothes and even brought me pajamas to put on. African maids washed, brushed, and styled my hair. The Jamaican cook brought my plate to my room. Jamie even had a massage therapist give me an hour-long massage. Helen sat with me while I had my back, shoulders, arms, and legs massaged. My blood pressure was watched all through the day. I wasn't doing well. It was nowhere near going down.

It was 8:30 that Saturday night. I lay back in the bed, eating fresh fruit, watching reruns of *Martin* on the 42-inch, flat-screen TV. Renée had been texting me all day and messaging me on Facebook. Charlie unfriended me on Facebook and blocked me from looking at her page. Aaron messaged me on Facebook. "I miss you." That's what he had the nerve to say. I tossed my cell in the corner of the room, sighed, and ran my fingers through my hair. It was raining cats and dogs outside. It matched my situation, because it was raining cats and dogs in my life.

There was a knock at my bedroom door.

"Come in." I sat up in bed.

The door slowly opened, and Jamie entered the room. I could smell his cologne from the door. He was dressed in all blue from head to toe, looking like he was about to head to the club. He was blinged out from his ears to his wrists.

I sighed as he walked into my room.

"What's up, shorty?" he asked, coming over to the bed, sitting down at my side.

I looked at him, not really sure what else to say but, "Thank you."

Jamie looked at me, nodding. "No need to thank me. It's the least I can do. You deserve someone to take care of you. You deserve the best, and I'm here to give it to you."

I looked him up and down a little. He looked just like a bottle of vintage wine. Time sure did change that boy for the better. I hesitated, "You gotta date or something?"

Jamie laughed. "A date? Nah, I had to meet my agent in D.C. You know I dress to impress wherever I go, shorty. I haven't changed that much." He looked at me. "You had a bath? You eat good? Helen treating you right?"

I nodded. "Yes to all of the above."

Jamie's eyes searched mine. "I started not to come in your room. I promised you that you wouldn't know I'm here, but my dad is flying in from Tennessee in a few hours on a medical plane. I just wanted to make sure you were okay with meeting him. He's been asking about you."

I wasn't really sure what to say to him. His father was the reason that he left me.

Jamie held my face in his hands, knowing that hearing about his father was going to have me emotional.

I pushed him off me. "Don't touch me, Jamie!"

He instantly put his hands up. "I'm sorry." His eyes glistened.

There was a tap at the bedroom door before Helen entered the room. She grinned when she saw Jamie sitting there with me. "Time for your meds." She came over to my side with a glass of cold water and a medicine cup full of pills. She handed them to me and watched as I swallowed all the pills, washing them down with the entire glass of water. She nodded at me as I handed her the empty glass and pill cup. "Don't you two have a date tonight?" she asked.

I looked at Jamie, who sat there laughing to himself. I looked back at Helen. "Ummm, my blood pressure is already high enough. Don't get me started, okay?"

Helen grinned. "Well, to get the ball rolling, I found something." She reached into her pocket and pulled out a photo, handing it to me.

I looked down at the photo, immediately covering my mouth in astonishment. It was a picture of Jamie, my sister, my brother, Jamie's cousin Fred, and his cousin

Janet at my eighth birthday party. My pretty lace dress was covered in dirt. I think Jamie and I had gotten into a fight that day over a game of tag. He was always claiming someone cheated whenever he didn't win at a game. He always was a sore loser. Regardless of my soiled dress, I was happy. There I was, on Jamie's back, legs wrapped around his waist. We all had the biggest smiles on our faces. We were happy. My mom had OD'ed the night before and was not at my party, but Aunt Joyce threw the party for me at her house. I don't know why Charlie wasn't there, but I do remember that the biggest present on the table was from her: my Barbie Dream House.

"Oh my goodness, Helen! Where did you find this?" I exclaimed.

"Oh, in one of Jamie's photo albums. There's a lot more of these in the family room." Helen glanced at Jamie. "Well, I'm going to head out to the guesthouse to get some sleep before Mr. James Green shows up and shows out." Then she exited the room.

I just sat there with the picture held tightly against my chest, over my heart. Tears slid down my face. "Oh my goodness, this picture brings back *so* many memories!" I cried to myself.

"I never meant to break your heart, shorty." Jamie responded, after watching me embrace the picture.

I looked at him, drying my face, heart beating strong in my chest, even though I could feel it trembling. I shook my head at him. "Jamie," I handed the picture to him, "I told you no reminiscing. No more confusion, okay?"

"I just wanna help, shorty. I'm supposed to be at an event tonight in Baltimore. I'm late actually. My agent, Rodney, is gonna kill me." Jamie laughed to himself.

"Then maybe you should go. You have your career to think about. Your staff will take care of me. This hasn't been your job for four years, Jamie," I whispered.

He looked at me. "But *I* wanna take care of you." He placed his warm hand on my thigh.

A surge of energy soared through my body. His hands were so strong, so warm, so gentle, so soothing. My heart was racing. No, no, I couldn't let him get to my heart. I pushed his hand off my thigh.

"J-Jamie, you-you should go. Please," I begged him.

His eyes searched my face. "Do you remember our first kiss?"

I looked at him, my lips trembling. Why was he torturing me?

Our first kiss was in my aunt's backyard. I was thirteen. That was also the night Jamie wanted to try "other" things. He snuck me into his room at his older sister's house, at around 1:00 in the morning. He asked to shave my coochie. I was so scared, but let him do it. I wasn't ready for sex. We were too young. But when he asked to kiss my pussy, I let him, not knowing what he actually meant. He kissed it all right—he sucked it, licked it, and he chewed on it. He made my pussy explode in his mouth. I didn't have a problem feeling on him, jacking him off, or sucking on him. That was our thing. Before we officially started dating, we were having oral sex. That was our way of being intimate for about three years. Yeah, I was young and in love with that boy.

"How could I forget?" I rolled my eyes, playing off the fact that I still held on to that kiss.

"Shorty, you know I have been with a lot of girls, but none of them felt quite like you. I miss your lips, your hands, your skin, your touch." Jamie licked his lips. "I know I can't take anything back that I have done, but I mean it when I say that I *miss* you. I don't know what I have to do to make it up to you, but can I just start by taking you on a date? I know you can't leave the house, but I have something set up in a room down the hallway."

I shook my head. He already had my whole body trembling. I wasn't sure how much more of him I could handle tonight. "Jamie, no, I can't. This is already too much. I can't handle any more surprises."

Jamie held my hand, gently lifting me from the bed. "Nah, shorty, I think you'll like this surprise." He felt my hand trembling in his. "Want me to carry you?"

I hesitated as he scooped me up in arms, carrying me over to the wheelchair. He wheeled me down the long hallway to another room. He opened the door, and we went inside. It was a recording studio. My mouth dropped open as he shut the door behind him.

"A *recording* studio, Jamie!" I exclaimed.

He laughed to himself as he helped me out of the wheelchair. "Just another one of my moneymakers. I have a few artists already scheduled to record records starting next week, shorty. I would love to get *your* voice recorded."

I shook my head. "No, Jamie, I don't think so."

He chuckled. "Shorty, don't act like you're shy. You just sang in front of hundreds of people last night at the club. Not to mention you're the star soloist in the Gospel choir at your school. You should do something with that voice. C'mon, shorty. I even wrote a song for your cousin, D-Allan."

I laughed a little. Of all the skills Jamie had, writing wasn't one of them. He suffered from dyslexia. Fortunately for technology, Jamie made it through school by talking into a microphone connected to his Mac desktop computer to complete his homework assignments, projects, and book reports. If he did write a song, he probably used the microphone on his cell phone to write it. As hard as it must have been for Jamie to adjust to a life without being able to read, his memory was amazing. I would help him memorize book reports in school. I'm talking book reports ranging from five to ten pages. The boy had skills.

"Okay, let me hear it." I sat in a chair in front of the equipment.

Jamie looked at me. "Why you gotta laugh, yo? You think that I'm lyin'?" He sat in a chair, facing me. "Why would I lie about writing a song for someone, shorty?"

"I wanna hear the song." I looked at him.

He sighed. "Okay, shorty, you got me. It's not finished because I can't get the hook down."

"Well, what's the song about?" I hesitated.

He looked at me. "About this girl that he loved but lost because he did something stupid. The song describes everything that he likes about the girl, from her hair all the way down to her toes. Any nigga who's been in love with a girl can feel me on this song."

I looked at Jamie. "So, *this* is why you brought me into your studio? To help you with lyrics to your song? I'm really not in the mood for any singing tonight, sweetie."

He grinned, turning on his equipment. Everything lit up. "Do you remember our first dance?" he asked.

I looked at him, heart fluttering in my chest, as my favorite song started playing.

Our first dance was when I was fourteen, the summer before tenth grade, at Jamie's fifteenth birthday party. The song was "Slow Down." I held on to him tight. He held my hips, gripping my dress in his hands, and he whispered in my ear, telling me that that night, he wanted to make love. He knew I wasn't ready, but he said he would take care of me. That he wouldn't hurt me. That night over at his sister's house, in his bedroom, Jamie talked me out of my panties. I cried the entire time. He practically ripped my panties off that night. I bled all over his sheets. I must have had a hundred hickies all over my body. He kissed and sucked all the way from my forehead to my pinky toe. Our bodies were drenched in sweat and tears. He sucked my nipples, neck, back, stomach, thighs, and clit until they were throbbing. My body was sensitive to touch for weeks afterward. We cried in each other's arms that night. No birth control, no condoms, no contraceptives. Getting pregnant was the furthest thing from my mind. I think I even *wanted* the boy's child at that young age, that's how sprung he had me back in high school. The very next morning, I woke up to an empty room. He was gone and that was the last time that I saw his face up until my nineteenth birthday.

"How could I forget our first dance? That was also the night that we made love for four hours straight. The very next morning, you left me, Jamie!" I exclaimed.

Jamie dug in his pocket. "Yeah, I left with these." He took what looked like pink silk cloth out of his pocket.

I snatched it from him. "What the hell is—" I stopped when I held it in my hand, noticing what it was the panties I'd worn that night. I blushed, handing them back to him. "Jamie, that's gross. Why the hell do you still have these?"

He laughed.

I rolled my eyes, trying to play off my embarrassment. "Another pair to add to the collection, huh?"

He shook his head. "Nah, what collection? I took this pair from you so that I could always remember that night. I felt like I was in heaven with you, shorty. I didn't wanna leave you, baby, I swear I didn't. My sister woke me up that morning, cursing me the fuck out about having you in my room. We were both drunk, butt naked, and lying on *top* of the covers! My dad was outside waiting. I didn't get a chance to explain. I didn't even get the chance to shower or pack. My sister had my shit downstairs, in two black duffle bags. Not only was she tired of me getting into trouble, but my dad wanted to know me too, so she sent me to stay with him."

"I cried for *two* whole years after you left, Jamie. I really missed you." I shook my head at him.

"I missed you, too."

"I waited for you as long as I could. Four years, Jamie—four long-ass, muthafuckin' years! You made me feel like I was special that night, Jamie. You held me, you kissed me, you touched me, you made love to me—then you just left! It took a long time to shake the sensation of you kissing me and humpin' me. I felt you inside of me for a long time. You remember the way you beat it up, Jamie." My eyes searched his face. "You didn't care that I was a virgin. You ignored my whimpering and crying. You were *not* gentle at all."

Jamie laughed a little. "Hey, I waited all of my life to get it, shorty. I wasn't playin' no games, was I?"

I shook my head at him. "Jamie, this is not a joke."

Jamie's eyes traced my lips. "I also knew that I was leaving and I probably would never get it again. I cried in your arms that night, Ne'Vaeh. I wasn't crying just because you felt amazing—I was crying because I knew I was leaving you when you needed me the most."

My chest began to hurt. I stood from the chair. The song was bringing back hurtful memories. It was bringing back moments that were bittersweet. Moments that I wasn't ready to relive. "Jamie, can you just turn this song off? I can't do this." I tried my hardest not to let the memories of us make me break down and cry over him. "I really don't wanna relive the past, okay? I told you at the hospital that you need to keep the sentimental shit to yourself."

Jamie stood from his chair and reached for my wrist, pulling me to him. "Ne'Vaeh, you have to forgive me."

I shook my head. "I don't have to do *anything* tonight. And don't you have some place to be, Jamie?"

Jamie nodded, pulling my body up against his. "Yeah, right here." He looked down into my face.

I looked up into his face, lips trembling. "I'm . . . I'm supposed to be in bed."

Jamie grinned a little. "Well, let's go then."

I shook my head, but Jamie scooped me up into his arms. I thought he was taking me into his bedroom, but he was taking me to the spa room. He gently let my feet down to the floor. Scented candles were lit all around the room. I faced Jamie as he removed his jewelry. He unbuttoned his shirt. He removed it, then pulled me closer to him by the drawstring of my pajama pants. My entire body trembled against his as he slid his hands around my waist.

"Strip." His voice serenaded my heart.

I looked up at him, "What?"

"*Strip*," he repeated.

I shook my head, trying to back away. "Jamie, now, if you think—"

He laughed a little. "I'm not trying to fuck you, shorty. I just wanna make you feel good. Your doctor says you need to ease your mind. I'm about to help you do that. Besides, you owe me a date."

I hesitated.

Jamie laughed to himself, standing there in his wife beater. Chest, muscles, chocolaty skin exposed. He was driving me crazy when I was trying my best to hate his guts. "C'mon, shorty. Take off them clothes and get up on the bed. It ain't like I haven't seen you naked before. You remember it was *me* who showed you how to use a tampon. I even helped you find the muthafucka the day you 'lost the string.' There's nothing on your body that I haven't seen already—I have seen your *everything*, shorty."

I blushed a little as I pulled the drawstring to my pants and dropped them to the floor, stepping out of them. I slipped my tank top over my head, then stood there in my panties, arms across my chest. I was embarrassed and nervous as hell.

Jamie couldn't help but burst out laughing.

"What? Oh my goodness, this situation is awkward enough, Jamie! Why the hell are you laughing at me?" I exclaimed.

"I mean, c'mon. You standing there covering up your titties like I never seen them. I mean, I *have* seen a naked girl before, shorty. You are fine as hell, I'm not gonna lie. But I'm not here for that tonight. C'mon, take your panties off and get on the table."

I slipped my panties off and climbed onto the bed, lying on my stomach. I braced myself as Jamie stood alongside the table. He placed his warm hands on my toes. He worked his way from my toes to my calves. It took everything I had not to scream out in pleasure that night. His fingertips dug into my skin as if he was kneading dough. I mean, there wasn't a part of my body that Jamie didn't touch that night. My whole body was paralyzed as he stroked the insides of my thighs. His thumbs grazed against my pussy lips as he kneaded my butt cheeks. My whole body was in heat. I was coated in sweat by the time he started massaging my lower back. As he massaged the middle of my back, his hands slid under each breast. Purposely, he grazed his fingers across my nipples. I was on fire. I couldn't take anymore.

"Jamie, stop!" I squealed, sitting up from the bed. I had to have had at least two or three mental orgasms from his touch. My thighs, toes, pussy, and nipples were tingling and throbbing.

Jamie looked at me. He was breathing rapidly as he watched me get up from the bed, barely able to stand on my own two feet. He watched me grab my clothes from the floor and struggle to slide into my panties.

"Shorty." He grabbed my hands.

I looked up into his eyes, chest heaving in and out. "Jamie, this is too much. I can't handle shit like this! You *know* I can't handle shit like this!" I exclaimed, sliding my hands from his. I put on my tank top, which was sticking to my skin. I was sweaty as hell and needed a shower, but I knew I was too weak to stand. I braced my body up against the massage bed.

Jamie grinned, bending over to pick my pants off the floor. "Felt good, huh?"

I looked up at him, snatching the pants from him. "You said you weren't trying to fuck. Well, *that* sure as hell *felt* like fuckin' to me, Jamie!"

He laughed. "I still got it, huh?"

I shook my head. "Jamie, please. Stop, okay? Why are you doing this?"

His eyes searched mine.

"You know I'm not this kind of girl. I made some pretty irrational choices these past few weeks, I'll admit to that. But I'm not about to make any more. Don't try to change your lifestyle just because you *think* you got me back in your life again. I'm not about to have a NSA relationship with you, and you damn sure know I'm not about to be your girl again after all of these years." I struggled to get back into my pants. "I have heart failure, Jamie. I need someone who will help heal my heart, not break the muthafucka!"

"Ne'Vaeh, you're the only girl I wanna be with. You know I love sex. You know I love pussy. I love *your* pussy. You know I never cheated on you when we were together. I'd *never* cheat on you. I *can* take care of your heart, Ne'Vaeh. You remember how it felt when we were together. I can bring that feeling back—and then some. I can make you forget that I ever left. When you want me, shorty, just let me know." Jamie backed away a little.

I wasn't sure what to say.

"You need help back to your room?" He hesitated.

I shook my head, "No, Jamie. I'll just walk slowly. Please, just leave me alone."

He nodded. "All right. Well, I'm gonna go meet Rodney. Welcome home, shorty." Jamie grabbed his shirt and jewelry and walked out of the room.

Chapter 12

The Funeral

Ne'Vaeh

I don't think I slept that entire night. Helen came into my room at least every hour, checking my vitals, which hadn't improved. Once Jamie's father arrived with the other live-in nurse, the house was buzzing again. Paramedics wheeled Mr. James Green to his room. I stood in the doorway of my room watching as they wheeled him down the hallway early that morning, around 2:45. Jamie hadn't arrived back at home yet. Mr. James looked at me as they wheeled him down the hallway to his room. He didn't wave or say hello, but he winked his eye at me.

I sat in my bed that night and found myself waiting up for Jamie, and it seemed that Helen was waiting for him as well. She paced the floor for about two hours. When she checked my blood pressure around 3:30 that morning, I had to find out a little more about her.

"You're kinda sexy for a nurse. How did you even meet Jamie?" I asked after she swept the thermometer across my forehead.

"Girl, you are burning up! Here, take these ibuprofens." She handed me two pills.

I looked at her as she handed me a glass of water.

She watched as I swallowed the pills, then chased them down with cold water.

I handed her the glass, wiping the water from my lips.

Helen looked at me. "My girlfriend and I had a three-some with Jamie about three years ago at a frat party while I was in nursing school."

My mouth dropped open a little. I don't think I was prepared for that answer. "Seriously?"

Helen laughed. "Seriously. Whenever Jamie wants a threesome, I hook him up. I go after the girls *with* him."

"Wow. You really *are* the head nurse." I shook my head.

Helen laughed aloud. "Whatever Jamie wants, he gets. He's payin', so I'll provide the service. We have fun, honey. No strings attached. Yeah, I have sucked on his dick with a few chicks, but I don't let him penetrate me. I'm more into women, to be honest. They'll do anything to be with him, even if that includes being with me too. He fucks the pussy. I eat the pussy, but not before they have a full physical."

Jamie was living the life, that's for damn sure.

Helen looked at me. "You're not upset?"

I looked at her. "Why should I be? Did you *expect* me to be? Jamie is *not* my man."

Helen grinned. "Then why are you waiting up for him?"

I looked at her, rolling my eyes. "Why are *you* waiting up for him?"

She laughed to herself. "I'm just hoping he has a surprise for me when he gets back, that's all. It's been a few weeks since I had some pussy. My girlfriend is back in Tennessee. She doesn't come up for another few weeks. And Jamie tells me you're off-limits, so—"

I laughed aloud. "Oh my goodness! Girl, I needed that laugh! If I wanted to play with some pussy, I can play with my own, thank you very much!"

Helen laughed too. "You don't have to worry about me and Jamie, sweetie. I'm expendable, just like the rest of 'em."

My eyes sparkled. It was going to be a long two weeks.

For nearly a whole week, Jamie had pool parties. I stayed in my room the entire time, only coming out to go to the masseuse. I had a full-sized bathroom in my room. Breakfast, lunch, and dinner were brought to me in bed. I can't tell you how many nights I heard females giggling, tiptoeing past my room and down the hallway, at all times of the night. I'm pretty sure Helen was happy. She was glowing all weeklong. I don't think there was a day that she wasn't smiling from ear to ear.

Jamie hadn't spoken to me all week. In fact, he didn't step within five feet of my bedroom door. He didn't care that I knew that there were at least three or four female voices coming past my room every night. He didn't care that I could see the pool from my bedroom window. At least twice that week, I saw him having sex with someone in his pool. I tried not to let it bother me because *I* was the one who told him to do him. He was mad at me. He was upset with me for being in love with Aaron. He knew that was part of the reason why I didn't want to fall back in love with him again.

It had only been two weeks since I'd had sex with Aaron. Aaron had messaged me about fourteen times on Facebook. I guess he didn't get it. He was engaged. It was bad enough that Charlie was pregnant. It was even worse that they were getting married. He had me fucked up if he thought that after all of the drama that had happened over the course of two weeks, I would even want to message him on social media. I was detoxing off him. I was clearing every trace of Aaron from my system, and I wasn't about to replace one addiction with another.

The following week, on day ten, I decided to leave my room and pay Mr. James a visit. I tiptoed down the hallway to his room. It was about 10:15 at night. When I arrived at his room, Helen and the other nurse, Kristen, were changing his IVs.

Helen looked up at me as I entered the room. Her eyes sparkled, and she shook her head at me.

"He . . . He's not doing well."

I hesitated to ask, already having a gut feeling of what the answer would be.

Helen shook her head. "He has a fever that refuses to go down. We're taking him to the hospital tonight."

Mr. James looked at me, his eyes watering. "Hello, young lady," he whispered, his voice shaking. He couldn't have been over fifty-five. He looked like death, literally.

"Mr. James, what happened to you?" I had to know.

Mr. James looked away from me. "Life," he struggled to say. "Whatever you do, don't let it get to you." He looked back up at me. "He didn't mean to leave you. Don't think it was easy for my son, because it wasn't."

I looked at him.

"I needed my son. I never got the chance to know him because his mother and aunts kept him from me. When I finally found out where he was, I just showed up at his doorstep. I told him I was dying of kidney failure. I drank and smoked my life away, sweetheart. Turns out, I had lung cancer too. And six months ago, I was diagnosed with liver cancer." His chest heaved in and out. You could hear the guttural sounds from within his chest. "I-I guess it's my time."

My eyes watered. I looked up at Helen and Kristen. "Has anyone called Jamie?"

Helen nodded. "Yes. He's on his way. But we can't wait for him."

Sirens wailed outside of the bedroom window.

Kristen's light eyes focused on me. She was a petite, white girl with tan skin, blond hair, and blue eyes. She was Helen's roommate in college. "That's the paramedics," she spoke with a country twang. She left Mr. James's side and hurried off to meet them.

Mr. James reached for my hand. "If I'm not here when Jamie gets to the hospital, you tell him that I love him and—" Mr. James coughed violently.

"Stop talking, Mr. Green!" Helen exclaimed.

Mr. James shook his head. "Marry my son," he begged me.

I looked at him, shaking my head at him. "Mr. James, Jamie isn't ready for me."

He smiled. "*Make* him ready."

Paramedics rushed into the room, pushing their way past me. Helen held my arm, gently pulling me out of the way and out of the room.

Tears slid down my face as we watched the paramedics wheel Mr. James out of the room.

"He's not going to make it, is he?" I whispered.

Helen shook her head. "No, he's not, and I don't think Jamie is going to make it back in time to say good-bye either. He's coming from Virginia Beach, and he's about an hour away." Helen looked at me. "Your vitals are pretty good today. Your blood pressure has gone down to normal. You only have to be here about two more days to be monitored. But I don't want you at the hospital with us. You're still pretty fragile, sweetie."

I looked at her.

"I really wanna be there with Mr. James tonight. But if you need me here—" Helen burst out crying.

I shook my head, rubbing her shoulder. "I'll be okay. You should go with them."

Helen threw her arms around me, hugging me tightly, before hurrying down the hallway after the paramedics.

I stayed up all night, until around 4:00, waiting on a phone call or someone to come home. I sat up, wide awake, when there was a knock at my bedroom door. I looked up to see Jamie entering my room. I stood from the bed, my heart pounding in my chest as he walked toward me.

Jamie's face was flushed. His eyes were puffy. He shook his head before throwing his arms around me. I surrounded him in my arms, running my hands across his head, and he cried like a baby in my arms. "He's gone!" He wailed, his face buried in my neck.

He cried himself to sleep in my arms that night. I didn't get any more than maybe fifteen or twenty minutes of sleep that night. I lay on my bed, arms around Jamie, his face buried in between my breasts. My shirt was soaked in tears. I wasn't ready for Mr. James's death any more than Jamie was. I knew in my heart that Jamie wanted me to go with him to his father's funeral. My heart was still recovering from the nightmares of going to my little brother's funeral. There was no way I could handle going with Jamie to see his father being buried.

Jamie awoke that morning, looking into my face.

I looked down at him, eyes moist.

"Was it a dream?" he whispered.

I shook my head. "No, Jamie."

Jamie lifted his head from my chest, sitting up in bed.

I looked at him, then took his hand in mine.

Jamie looked at me. "I knew this was coming, but I guess I wasn't prepared."

"You can't prepare yourself for your father's death, sweetie. I can only imagine what you're going through. I still see my brother's blue face, lying lifeless in his bed." Tears trickled down my face.

Jamie's eyes were coated in tears. "I don't know how you do it, shorty. I don't even know how I'm gonna get through this. I was just gettin' to know Pops. I gotta take him back to Memphis this week to bury him. I gotta get my agent or my manager to let everyone know about Pop's funeral. Everybody loved him, man. You would have loved him too."

I hesitated to tell him what his father told me before he died. "I talked to him last night before the paramedics arrived."

Jamie looked at me, tears sliding down his face. "Yeah? What did he say to you?"

"That . . . that he loves you very much," I whispered.

His eyes searched my face. "Did he say anything else, shorty?"

I hesitated before I shook my head. "No."

Jamie exhaled deeply before getting up from the bed.

I knew it wasn't the time to confront him about the women, but before he asked me to go with him to Memphis, I had to let him know that I saw him in the pool. "I saw you with those girls in the pool, Jamie," I blurted out before I lost my nerve to confront him.

He looked at me.

"Jamie, it *hurt* to see those girls with you in the pool," I admitted.

His eyes dampened.

"You have a live-in freak who is down for whatever! You have girls tiptoeing past my room every night! I can hear the headboard knocking against the damn wall for fuckin' *hours!* You fucked the *shit* out of that little Puerto Rican girl in the pool the other night! You had hoes lined up around the pool, waiting on you as you fucked the person in front of them! I *watched* this shit, Jamie!" I pushed him in his chest.

Jamie laughed a little to himself to hide his pain. "Are they still here?"

"Is who still here, Jamie?" I asked.

"The hoes," he replied. "Are they still here? I only see one female standing here, sleeping in my house, getting waited on hand and foot by people who work for me. This is *my* world that you're in, Ne'Vaeh. There is nobody here with me but *you.*"

I shook my head at him, not really feeling like hearing his twisted reasoning for why he did the things that he did.

"Helen is a down-ass chick. Yeah, she'd do whatever for me. She takes care of me mentally and sexually. Nah, we haven't had actual intercourse, but she's done some things with me to other women. She's my friend, but if you said you wanted her gone, she'd be dismissed. Ne'Vaeh, you pissed me the fuck off when I found out you were fuckin' Charlie's man, yo!" Jamie exclaimed.

"So, you didn't wait for me, yet you thought I was supposed to wait for *you?*" I questioned.

He nodded. "Yeah, I know I'm an asshole for saying that, but, yes, I expected you to wait for me! I'm not gonna lie. I have cravings, but none of it compares to my feelings for you. When I'm with the other girls, I'm always thinking about you, shorty. My father died, and you steppin' to me about hoes and shit, Ne'Vaeh? If you want me, then I'll leave it all alone. But until then, shorty, you can really stay the fuck out of my business."

Damn, that hurt like hell.

I laughed to myself, trying my damnedest not to cry. "Well, Helen said that I was gonna be okay to leave in a few days since my blood pressure has improved. She says I can go back to my regularly scheduled program, so I called Renée and she's coming to get me on Friday morning. So, sweetie, I'd be *glad* to 'stay the fuck out of your business.'"

Jamie's eyes just searched my face. He looked at me as if he was expecting me to stay with him permanently.

I shook my head, looking up at him. "Jamie, I can't live with you. I love it out here in the country, in your beautiful home, but I can't stay here and watch groupies fuck you in your outdoor pool. I'm sorry if I'm being inconsiderate of your feelings, I'm sorry if your father just passed away, but I've held this in for nearly a week and a half. I can't be your friend, Jamie. We're not friends anymore. I can't trust you to be here for me when I need you. All I can trust you to do is hurt me. I know you just lost your father and you need some comfort right now, but I can't do it. Why don't you ask Helen? I'm sure she wouldn't mind going with you." I walked past him, but Jamie caught my arm, pulling me back.

I looked up at him as he let go of my arm.

"I need you in Tennessee with me, shorty. You *know* I need you." Tears slid down his face. I hated seeing him upset. Seeing Jamie cry was breaking my heart. He was always so carefree and nonchalant about everything. Seeing that he still had a heart gave mine a little boost.

My eyes moistened. "Jamie, no, I can't. I'm sorry, but I can't."

"Ne'Vaeh, I know I wasn't here for you when you needed me, but, shorty, I *need* you to be here with me. Please. I'll do anything just to have you there. Don't leave me."

How could I look him in that face and walk away from him? He needed me. I was so angry with him, but I had to let go of my own selfish feelings and be there to hold his hand.

I had never been to Memphis, Tennessee. Up until that point, the only people I had met in Jamie's family were his oldest sister and his aunt Bethany. The family church was crowded beyond capacity. I had no idea Jamie's family was so huge. His father's side of the family was on one side of the church. His mother and her side of the family were on the other side of the church. I'm sure there were some of Jamie's groupies scattered in there somewhere. Helen and her family were there. Kristen and her family were there. Jamie's entire college football team was there to support him. A few of his new Ravens teammates were there to support him. His agent and old and new coaches were there. Friends from our high school in Maryland were there, including Alisha and the entire cheerleading squad from our high school. Renée showed up with a few of her friends. I shouldn't have been shocked to see Charlie there with a few of her family members. She grew up with Jamie, just as I did, but what did shock me was when she showed up with Aaron. It was too much for my heart to handle at the moment. Jamie needed me, and I had no time to get wrapped up in my confused feelings for Aaron.

I sat with Jamie on the first row, on the side of the church where his father's family sat. His father's family was the only side of the family that supported him outside of his oldest sister Angelina and his Aunt Bethany. His mother barely looked at him while we were there, though she couldn't keep her evil glare off me. Jamie gave his father a great homecoming with the best Gospel choir in Memphis. I had to hold my composure as the ceremony closed and we walked past his open casket upon leaving the church. I held Jamie's hand tightly as we left the church, and Jamie broke down right there in front of his father. I never let go of his hand.

I can't see how people can eat after funerals. I lose my appetite as soon as I see the dead body in the casket. Jamie would not let my hand go the entire time that we were at the reception afterward. I had to basically pry his hand from mine when his agent called him over to talk with a few of his colleagues.

Renée made her way over to me, throwing her arms around me. "Cuz, are you okay?"

I was still shook from the entire event. "No, Renée, I'm not, but it's not about me, it's about Jamie."

She grinned a little. "C'mon, let's go sit with the girls. I thought Jamie would *never* let your hand go. I think a part of that has to do with Aaron being here, but I'll keep my thoughts to myself."

I rolled my eyes at her as she pulled me off to the table with her friends and my schoolmates.

It didn't take Charlie five minutes to make her way over to our table. I looked up at her as she approached, dressed in a peach Versace dress. "Ne'Vaeh, can we talk?" she asked.

Alisha rolled her eyes. "C'mon, Charlie, we're at a funeral. Are you serious?"

Charlie ignored her. "I didn't mean it when I called you a groupie."

I looked at her. "You know what, Charlie? I'm over that, I really am. You were upset, and you said the first thing to me that you knew would really hurt."

Her eyes sparkled. "Well, it's nice to see you and Jamie back together again."

I looked at her. The only reason she even spoke to me was that she thought that Jamie and I were a couple. She just knew that since Jamie was back in the picture; that meant Aaron wasn't. I shook my head at her, but before I could clarify, she walked away.

"Oh my goodness!" I put my hand on my head in frustration. "Who is saying this shit? Who the hell started the rumor that me and Jamie are back together?"

"It wasn't me!" Kelissa assured me, in her shaggy voice.

Alisha looked at me. "It's nice what you are doing for Jamie, but I heard about him and the parties at his place this week. You stayed with that nigga in the midst of all of that shit?"

I rolled my eyes. "Okay, now *who's* acting inappropriate at a funeral?"

Alisha shook her head, "I'm just saying. Shiddd, if I saw my boyfriend in the pool fuckin' a bitch, I'd be ready to cut a muthafucka's dick off in that bitch. I'd be like, 'You wanna fuck, nigga? With *what* dick, nigga?'"

Everyone burst out laughing.

Alisha had no fuckin' chill whatsoever.

I rolled my eyes. "Look, let me clear the air for *all* of you—Jamie and me are *not* back together. He just lost his father, and as you could see, his entire family on his mother's side, *including* his own damn mama, hasn't said a word to him all day. I know what it's like not to have your mother or father around. Jamie needs someone who cares, so it might as well be me." My heart beat rapidly in my chest. "The man's father just died, and y'all bitches are *still* with this drama shit? This is *exactly* why I don't hang with y'all anymore!"

Renée looked at me, watching the tears sliding down my cheeks. "Sweetie, you know Alisha is your girl. Her timing is whack as fuck, but you know she didn't mean any harm."

Alisha looked at me. "Girl, you know I got love for you. I just don't trust him. A nigga like that will murder your heart, girl, I'm tellin' you. I'm just looking out for you, Cutie. Stay the fuck away from him!"

Renée touched my hand. "You gonna be okay, cuz?"

I shook my head. "I'm . . . I'm gonna go outside to get some air." I got up from the table, hurrying outside, gasping for air.

I exhaled as soon as I reached the outside of the church—only to run dead into Aaron. His eyes lit up a little when he saw me. I started to turn around and go back into the church.

"Heaven," he called out to my heart.

I sighed, turning back around, facing him as he approached me.

He smiled a little. "Well, look at you in your Christian Dior."

I rolled my eyes. "Hi, Aaron."

"'Hi, Aaron'? That's *all* I get?"

I shrugged. "What more do you expect? Your *fiancée* already threatened to kill me if she saw me *'so much as look at you in the wrong way.'* I really ain't in the mood for her shit today. I don't wanna have to fight a pregnant chick, but I will if I have to."

Aaron laughed a little. "How are you? How have you been?"

I looked at him. I knew he'd heard where I had been the last two weeks. "Well taken care of, thank you for asking. What about you?"

He replied, "You call fuckin' bitches in your face being well-taken care of? Shorty, what are you doin' with him?"

I folded my arms. "Aaron, we're at a funeral. He was my best friend since I was in fuckin' day care. Do you actually think I *wouldn't* come to his father's funeral with him?"

Aaron looked at me, eyes tracing my face. "You held his hand for the past three hours. Dude cried in your arms, on your shoulder, in your hair. Took dude until his agent called him over to let you out of his sight. I saw the way that he looked at you. I saw the way that he held you. Dude still has feelings for you. And after the way that he did you, the fact that you found it in your heart to come with the dude proves that you still love him too."

It took everything in me to fight away the tears. "Aaron, you need to mind your own damn business because you don't know what you're talking about."

He laughed a little. "I don't? So you're not living with dude?"

I looked at him. "First of all, Aaron, I'm not *with* Jamie. Second, if I *was* with Jamie, it would really be none of your fuckin' business. And third, *stop* sending me messages on Facebook telling me how much you miss me! *Stop* fuckin' with my heart, Aaron! We both agreed that things between us were over, so *stop* trying to reach out to me! What are you even doing here? You don't even know Jamie. You just came here to fuck with me!"

Aaron looked at me. "You didn't answer me—are you living with him?"

I rolled my eyes. "Since you heard so much shit, Aaron, did you hear that I have fuckin' heart failure? He has the money and the nurses to provide home care for me so that I don't have to sit alone in a fuckin' hospital. You need to be worrying about your pregnant fiancée, instead of being overly concerned with shit that *shouldn't* even concern you."

Aaron said, "I heard about your heart condition, and I've been worried about you."

I scoffed, rolling my eyes. "Aaron, *please*."

His eyes traced my lips for a few seconds. "My feelings for you haven't changed, Heaven."

I looked up into his face. "Your 'feelings' for me? Let's get something straight—there is *no* us. There never has been, and there never will be! I can't help that as soon as you decided to build up the nerve to finally talk to me, Charlie decides to tell you that you're gonna be a daddy. You need to concentrate on being a father to that baby and a support system for her. We did our wrong, Aaron. It's *over*, Aaron."

His eyes searched my face. "You really feeling this dude? How much could he really care about you if he's fuckin' other females in your face, shorty?"

I pushed him in his chest. "Isn't that what *you* were doing to me for two years, Aaron?"

He shook his head in disagreement. "I didn't know how you felt about me until a few weeks ago, Heaven. Do you think I would actually be with Charlie if I knew how you felt about me? You can't compare what Jamie's doing to that, and you know it. You feeling him, Heaven? *That's* the type of nigga you wanna be with? *That's* the shit that you think you deserve?"

"If I recall correctly, wasn't it *you* who told me that I couldn't give up on love? I thought *you* were the one who told me that I needed to give it a shot with him, that I needed someone to take care of me, that I needed love, that I couldn't push everyone away who tries to love me," I exclaimed.

Aaron looked at me. "That was before I knew exactly what type of dude he is. Jamie doesn't love you, shorty, at least not the way that he should. And you can't love yourself all that much either if you can watch the dude fuck females in a pool outside of your window. One minute, you love me; then the next, you love him. Yeah, my niggas was right in high school when they told me that I was just gonna be a rebound if I ended up fuckin' around with you, Heaven. I didn't believe it, but turns out, they were right. One night, you're suckin' my dick, then the next, you're suckin' his."

"Go to hell, do you hear me!" I cried, as I turned from him to walk away. Aaron caught my hand, pulling me back to him.

I pulled away. "Don't touch me!" I cried. "Don't you *ever* touch me!"

"Yo." I heard Jamie's voice over my shoulder.

I turned around to see Jamie and his crew walking toward us.

I sighed, backing away from Aaron. "Jamie, please, don't start—everything is fine."

"Yo," Jamie approached my side, face-to-face with Aaron. "Charlie's not out here, dawg. Maybe you should go find her."

"Bruh, I didn't come here for any drama. I came to give my condolences for your loss." Aaron looked Jamie dead in his face.

Jamie shook his head. "Nah, you came here to fuck with Ne'Vaeh. Your chances with her have come and gone, muthafucka, so you need to go find your girl and stay the fuck away from mine."

My mouth dropped open. I can't believe the asshole was claiming me. I looked up at Jamie, then looked back up at Aaron.

Aaron grinned a little, shaking his head at me. He backed up and walked away. He would respect Jamie at his father's funeral. I wasn't so sure he was going to respect him after that point, especially after he had heard about the events at Jamie's house that past week.

Jamie grabbed my hand, pulling me along with him away from the church.

***

"Why did you tell Aaron that I was your girl? You basically implied that we had gotten back together, Jamie!" I exclaimed that afternoon at his hotel room. "Are *you* the one spreading these fuckin' rumors?"

Jamie stood in the mirror removing his tie. He was heading out with his family members to some sort of football event at his college. "Shorty, you comin' with me to Memphis State or what?"

"Jamie! I know you heard my question! Why would you do that? Everybody at that funeral heard about your fuckin' orgy in your fuckin' pool! Do you think that if we were together I would put up with that type of shit?" I yelled.

He turned around, facing me. "Why the fuck do you even care what he thinks, shorty?"

I was trying to hold back the tears so hard that my lips were trembling. "What?"

"No matter if he thinks you're my girl, why does it matter to you?" He hesitated before saying, "You still wanna be with that nigga, is that it?"

I pushed him in his chest. "Jamie, I don't want people thinking that me and you are together and you're fuckin' around on me! I've looked stupid enough as it is! Just three weeks ago, I was sleeping with my best friend's boyfriend and now, I'm—" I broke down and cried, "I'm with my ex-boyfriend at his father's funeral. I'm staying in the house with my ex-boyfriend who thinks it's cool to fuck females right in front of my face!"

His eyes sparkled. "Shorty, I wasn't trying to make you look stupid." He hesitated. "It hurt seeing you talking to Aaron, shorty. I didn't know what else to say."

I just looked at him. "I'm coming back to my senses, Jamie. I'm flushing Aaron out of my system. You never have to worry about anything *ever* happening with him again. I came here with *you*, Jamie, nobody else."

"I couldn't let your hand go today at the funeral. I thought my heart was gonna stop when I saw my dad lying there in the casket. I needed your support. You saw my mama didn't give a fuck about me. She probably only came to the funeral to actually make sure Pops was really dead." Jamie tossed his tie on the bed.

I shook my head. "Jamie, I'm so sorry about all of this." I approached him, looking up into his face. "I wasn't entirely truthful the other night when you asked me what your father said to me."

He looked at me. "What do you mean?"

"He—" I laughed to myself nervously, "he told me to marry you."

Jamie's eyes glistened. "He did? He told us to get married?"

I nodded, wiping my tears, "Yeah," I grabbed my purse off of the bed, "but *I* told him that you weren't ready. He seems to think that I can *make* you ready."

"Ne'Vaeh . . ." He reached for me because he knew I was seconds away from leaving the room.

I pulled away from him. "What, Jamie? What do you have to say about that?"

"Baby, you *know* you can make me ready." He looked at me earnestly. "Shit, I'm already ready."

I shook my head. "No, you're not ready for me. The only thing you're ready for is a different freak every night. I don't think you had sex with the same girl twice these past few days, Jamie! That's the lifestyle you're used to! One girl could *never* satisfy you!"

Jamie shook his head, "Nah, you have it all wrong. It takes *all* those girls just to satisfy my craving for *you*, shorty." He held my hands in his. "Ne'Vaeh, you know I don't care about any of them girls."

"Jamie, you're not thinking clearly. You just lost your dad. That feeling has you ready to settle down. This isn't how you really feel, Jamie!" I cried.

"Baby, I wanna be with you." His eyes watered.

I shook my head. "No, Jamie! We're not doing this again! We need to move forward, not backward! It's too late to start over!"

"Why is it too late? Don't you still love me?" He paused a moment. "You used to love me."

I cried aloud as he pulled me closer. I couldn't escape his kiss, or maybe I didn't even resist. His lips embraced mine for a few seconds before I pulled away, backing away from him. "Jamie, no! Not again!" I cried. "Please don't do this to my heart!"

Tears slid down his face. He pulled my body up against his again and gently kissed my lips again. "I miss you. I need you. I still love you. I never stopped loving you, Ne'Vaeh. Please, give me you. *Please*," he whispered.

I sighed as he kissed me repeatedly. The next thing I knew, he was unbuttoning his shirt and I was unzipping my dress. In seconds, it seems, we were completely naked on top of the bed, kissing, touching, rubbing, and sucking.

"*Fuck*, I missed this!" he cried out, sucking on my neck, yanking on my hair. He held my body oh so tight against his. "I just wanna hold you for a few minutes, *please*." He tried to calm himself.

I held on to him, crying on his shoulder. His dick was throbbing between my legs, rubbing against my clit. He felt so good, he smelled so good, and to my surprise, I missed him too.

"Jamie, I missed you too. I missed you *so* much," I whispered.

He looked into my face, tears sliding down his cheeks.

I nodded. "I did." I cried. "You just—you just hurt me, so I wanted to forget you."

Jamie ran his fingers through my hair. "I'm here, Ne'Vaeh. I won't leave you again, I promise." He gently kissed my lips.

I took in a deep breath between kisses as Jamie held my thighs and dug his way inside of me. I cried out as he began to stroke, biting down on my neck. My pussy was a little tense. She tightened around his dick, and he dug into it.

"This is *my* pussy, Ne'Vaeh," Jamie moaned with a fistful of my hair. "*Say* it's mine, shorty."

I cried, shaking my head.

He dug deeper, pulling my hair tighter. "Say it, shorty. Tell me this is *my* pussy."

I cried out, digging my nails into his back.

He dug his nails into my thighs. He stroked my pussy until she started to fart, squirt, and whistle. Even though my mouth wasn't telling him the pussy was his, my *pussy* was telling him, "I'm all yours."

"Oh!" I cried out, as my pussy tightened.

Jamie looked down into my face, and he stopped pumping.

I looked into his face, chest heaving in and out. I wanted to come, and he wouldn't let me until I gave myself to him. "Jamie, please," I cried, "Don't stop. Keep going."

He shook his head. "Is it mine?" He pulled out of me. "Baby, tell me it's mine. What do I gotta do to make you mine?" He got up from the bed, pulling me up with him. He held my face in his hands, gently kissing my lips.

My body was on fire. He wasn't playing fair. I shook my head. "*Please.* I gotta release this tension that you just built up inside of me, Jamie!" I cried.

He turned my body around, pressing my back down so that my chest rested on the bed and my ass was in the air. Again, he grabbed a handful of hair and gripped my ass with the other hand. He thrust his way inside of me as he pulled my hair. "Are you gonna tell me it's mine?" he said as he started to stroke.

My lips trembled. I couldn't even talk. Tears slid down my face as Jamie worked my soul from the inside out. He worked my body until my legs gave out. My knees buckled, and my body fell to the bed. He still didn't stop. He sucked on my neck, running his fingers through my hair, gripping my hips as he dug through me.

I couldn't take it anymore. He owned it. I squealed out his name as he sucked on my ear. "Jamie, it's yours!" I cried, biting the pillow.

"It's mine?" He pumped a little deeper, stronger, and faster. "It's really mine? You sure about that? Then throw it back, ma."

"Just take it," I cried, propping up on my elbows a little as I worked my hips and ass, throwing it back on him a little, matching my thrusts with his.

"I'm taking it." He bit down on my neck, gripping my hips.

I gripped the sheets in my hands as Jamie hit all types the spots. He gripped my pussy in his hand, pumping in and out, causing her to make all types of sounds. He growled in my ear and after about a good ten or fifteen minutes, his body trembled as he exploded inside of me. Then, all of his weight rested on top of me as I fell back down on the bed. It was a quickie, but it felt *so* fuckin' good, so good that I burst out crying.

I buried my face in the pillow. "Oh my goodness. What am I thinking?"

Jamie pulled his body from mine, lying beside me on the bed. "Shorty, look at me."

I shook my head, tears saturating the pillow. "No."

He slid his hand over my waist, pulling my body closer to his.

I felt so good in his arms. I turned to him, drying my face. "What did we just do? What does this mean?"

He just looked at me.

"Does this mean we're back together?" I whispered.

"It's your call," Jamie whispered back.

I shook my head. "I hate answers like that."

He laughed a little. "Shorty, I already told you that if you wanted me, I was all yours."

"Jamie, you got too many hoes." My eyes searched his face.

Jamie nodded. "True."

Tears slid down my face. "I swear, I never intended on sleeping with Aaron. Charlie has been my best friend since I was six years old, and over some guy, our friendship is over! I never meant to hurt her. I just needed love. I haven't felt love in so long. I thought I'd never see you again. When Aaron told me he loved me, I believed it. I made a horrible mistake that cost me the best friend that I ever had."

Jamie said, "Shorty, when I left Maryland, I was on a mission. I was gonna do something great. I was gonna have something to show for leaving the best friend that *I* ever had. You know the shit I've been through in my family. I was the only one out of twelve kids who was given up at birth. I was tossed around from house to house all my life. I was forced to do all types of shit when I stayed with my mom during the summer. No food to eat, nothing to drink, abused, misused . . . Nobody understood. I worked my ass off to make a career out of football. When my father found me, he invested so much money in my career to make sure that I achieved greatness. He did a lot for me to make sure that I never had to ask my mother for anything again." Jamie's eyes glistened. "I tried talking to her today, and she wouldn't even look at me. She always told me that I wasn't gonna be shit. And now that I *am* something, she won't even allow herself to be proud of me."

Tears slid down my face. I felt his pain.

Jamie's eyes searched mine. "Because of her, I have trust issues. I have relationship issues. I have a hard time trusting a woman. I haven't showed *any* woman any love for some years. I swear. I have had sex with at least ten girls a week for the past four years. I'm not gonna lie, Ne'Vaeh, I have done some wild shit. I have lived my life to the fullest. I may have overcompensated for the love I didn't have from my mom and for the pain of leaving you behind. I will admit, I have done wrong. Trust me. I don't mind giving up the hoes. I'm not gonna say that they will never confront you, because you know how bitches are these days. But I will say that I told each and every one how it was from jump—I told them before we had sex that if they were looking for love, they could leave."

I shook my head, pushing my hair from my face. "I have been through *so* much shit, Jamie. I'm sick and tired of being sick and tired. I need love, and I'm not even sure that you know how to give it to me anymore. You say you can give up all that pussy, but I'm not too sure that you can, and I'm not gonna force you either, Jamie. You have to show me that I'm the only one, and maybe, *then*, I can give this a shot. I can't go through any more pain, Jamie. And I already know that fuckin' around with you is gonna have me *insane*."

Jamie's eyes traced my lips. "I'm not here to hurt you. Hopefully, I can heal some of those wounds that I caused."

"I'm not sure if I'm ready to be your one and only, Jamie. I'm not even sure that I wanna feel weak again. You make my heart weak. You always had me wide open, ready to do whatever for you. I don't wanna be sprung, doing shit that I would never do. I'm not over the pain yet, Jamie. I haven't healed well enough to forgive you, and I can't forgive myself for allowing my emotions to get the best of me. I was drunk the entire time that I was sleeping with that boy! I knew what I was doing was wrong! I should have never let him touch me! What was I thinking?" I cried.

Jamie gently kissed my lips. "We all have made mistakes. I've done shit that I'm not proud of too, Ne'Vaeh, so don't think you're the only one who has some cleaning up to do." He held my face in his hands, pressing his lips against my forehead. "I know you have been through a lot, shorty. I'm here. The storm is over."

I shook my head. "It's not over—it just started, Jamie."

He shook his head back at me. "I got my baby back. I swear, I'm never letting go. It's you and me forever, baby. It may be raining a little, but the worst is over. I'll dance in the rain with you, shorty. A little rain never hurt anybody."